MODELS FOR WRITING

James Burl Hogins

Robert Earl Yarber

San Diego Mesa College

SCIENCE RESEARCH ASSOCIATES, INC.
Chicago, Palo Alto, Toronto, Henley-on-Thames, Sydney, Paris
A Subsidiary of IBM

This revision is a rhetorical edition of *Phase Blue, Revised.*

Printed in the United States of America.

Library of Congress Cataloging in Publication Data

Hogins, James Burl, Comp.
  Models for writing.

  Published in 1970 and in 1974 under title: Phase
blue.
  Includes index.
  1. English language—Rhetoric.   2. College readers.
I. Yarber, Robert E., joint comp.   II. Title.
PE1417.H6 1975   808'.04275   74–18853
ISBN 0-574-18010-9

PREFACE

When given several models for discussion and writing, most students are soon able to identify and use the principle of rhetoric that is being discussed. The result of such practice should be a more confident and better writer.

The essays in *Models for Writing* are arranged according to rhetorical concept—nine major principles and a tenth heading that includes six less-detailed ones. Clearly an entire essay will not be a pure example of *Narration* or *Argumentation*, but if it exhibits primarily one approach to writing, it is included in the appropriate group. In the table of contents, the selection may also appear in the "See also" addition to certain categories, if it includes a particularly good example of that rhetorical principle in addition to its major characteristics. For example, "California 2001" is listed as an exercise in *Description*, but it appears under *Narration* and *Sentence Variety* as well and can profitably be studied when these subjects are being discussed.

Each unit is introduced by a brief discussion of the rhetorical principle involved, and we have also indicated specific paragraphs in other essays as further illustrations. In this way the student learns that rhetorical principles can govern individual paragraphs as well as entire essays.

We wish to express our gratitude to the many instructors who offered suggestions in the development of this book. To Jim Budd, our editor, goes our appreciation for his untiring help.

J. B. Hogins
R. E. Yarber

CONTENTS

EXPLANATION OF THE ANNOTATIONS

The annotations for the first selection in each unit highlight and emphasize what we consider to be strong examples or good uses of rhetorical devices. Our selection is by no means meant to be final or complete—no doubt you will find many other striking examples.

The abbreviations in the margins identify various rhetorical means. Shorter examples are underlined, with the identification adjacent to the first underline. Longer examples are indicated by vertical rules in the margin. The entry at the top of the vertical rule (or entries separated by a slash if more than one principle is involved) refers to the entire ruled passage.

Some rhetorical terms are spelled out, but because of space restrictions the following abbreviations are used:

Allit	alliteration	Hyper	hyperbole
Allus	allusion	Imag	imagery
Anec	anecdote	Induc	induction
Angy	analogy	Irny	irony
Anly	analysis		
Arg	argumentation	Lit	litotes
		Meta	metaphor
Bal S	balanced sentence	Meton	metonymy
Beg	good beginning		
		Narr	narration
C & C	comparison and contrast	Non Seq	non sequitur
C & E	cause and effect		
Class	classification	Oxy	oxymoron
Comp	comparison		
Conc	conclusion	Paral	parallelism
Conn	connotation	Pdx	paradox
		Person	personification
		Prem	premise
Deduc	deduction		
Def	definition	Rep	repetition for emphasis
Desc	description	Emph	
Dial	dialog	Rhet Q	rhetorical question
Dict	diction		
		Sarc	sarcasm
End	good ending	Sim	simile
Exemp	exemplification	S Var	sentence variety
Expo	exposition	Symb	symbolism
Ext	extended (metaphor)	Syne	synecdoche
Fig	figurative language	Thes	thesis
		Top S	topic sentence
Gen	generalization	Tran	transition

Argumentation

ARGUMENTATION

All writing must have direction; it must have a purpose—some specific objective to attain. The four traditional kinds of writing are argumentation, exposition, description, and narration.

The purpose of argumentation is to convince the reader of the truth or relevance of your position, to persuade him to adopt your point of view, or to take the action you recommend. (It doesn't necessarily mean that you are having an argument or quarrelling with someone.) Argumentation in writing means the presentation of evidence leading to a particular conclusion—and that evidence should be convincing (based on facts).

Although argumentation does not necessarily imply conflict—two opposing sides entering into battle in order to determine a winner and a loser—it does, however, imply some degree of uncertainty or doubt. Without the element of uncertainty, there is no argument. In other words, argument implies the possibility of alternate decisions, choices, options, or opinions. Evidence is presented and weighed, and conclusions are then reached.

Ideally argument should appeal to *reason* (be logical) rather than to emotion. There are several ways to support your ideas or attitudes and persuade the reader to your point of view.

- You can present an unarguable statement: "You must attend eight of the ten classes or you will receive an F for the course."

- You may cite factual evidence: "The Oakland A's were the best team in the American League in 1972. They won the pennant that year hands down."

- You may set up a cause and effect situation: "If you handle the ceramic jars before they are dry, they will crack when they are fired in the kiln."

- Or you may cite a recognized authority: "According to Abraham Maslow, who conducted extensive research on this subject, exceptionally productive individuals share certain common traits."

However, much of the argumentative writing you encounter does *not* appeal to reason. Anyone can produce an "authority" on any given subject. Whether or not it's a reliable one is another question. Citing a questionable authority or appealing to emotion without regard for truth are easy and common forms of argument. They are persuasive, unfortunately, for the wrong reasons. People resort to such an appeal when their prime motivation is to convince or sway the reader at any cost, and they think logic and reason won't work, or they know how flimsy their evidence actually is, or they are simply too lazy or rushed to get at the truth. You realize this kind of argument isn't exactly rare: politicians, columnists, militants, and the military often use slanted (unsubstantiated) argument. (So do teachers, parents, students, friends, lovers, and others.) The mature reader learns to sort out the two forms and recognize an appeal to emotion for what it is.

Most writing involves some argumentation. It may be subtle or explicit, logical or emotional, objective or slanted. But its purpose is always to influence the reader in some way. If you state a claim, a proposition, or a thesis, you must then supply evidence. If your readers are to be persuaded or convinced by your argument, you must present your terms clearly. In other words, state your proposition, mention the supporting points and issues, and then begin to compile evidence for a logical presentation. Evidence may be a qualified authority, examples, logical deductions, or support of any rational kind (observable facts that can be verified or those based on the testimony of an established authority).

What errors should be avoided in supporting your argument? You can go astray when you make statements that you think are true or clear if you don't provide enough valid claims or supporting evidence for the reader. Fallacious reasoning, whenever it appears, is bad. Most errors are common fallacies—they are either irrelevant, or they are circular. Statements are irrelevant when they are provided for support but in reality have nothing to do with the argument.

1. A *non sequitur* is a conclusion that does not follow from previous statements: Healthy children are better students than children who eat poorly. Many healthy children eat Superspace bread. Superspace bread assures your child's success.

2. An *argument ad hominem* ignores the issue and deals with the personality of the subject instead: "What does Senator Seed know about this urban-aid legislation he's sponsoring? Why, he's a self-interested hick from Kansas."

3. In *genetic fallacy*, the truth of a proposition is attacked by referring to its source or background in a derogatory way. "Socialized medicine can't work—it's based on left-wing ideas."

4. The *you-too fallacy* is to validate one thing or action simply because someone else did the same thing or something similar: "So what if I took the change from your purse to go to the movie? Last night Dad didn't tell the waitress she undercharged us, and he spent that money on cigarettes."

5. *Appeal to unqualified authority* is fallacious. Just because a man is an athlete of renown doesn't mean he's an authority on automobiles.

6. *Appeal to ignorance* means maintaining that a claim is true simply because contrary evidence is not available: "The end of the world is upon us."

7. *Appeal to emotion* is a common fallacy that involves playing on someone's love, pity, prejudices, or greed to get sympathy for your point of view: "If one hippy family moves into your neighborhood, the value of all the homes in that block will drop drastically."

8. *Hasty generalization* results when there is unrepresentative, irrelevant (even when valid), or insufficient evidence: "All people living near the beach are lazy."

9. *Circular reasoning*, also a common error in argument, tries to support an original claim simply by restating it in other words. This type of argument is particularly seductive when the first and last statements of the unsupported claim are separated by what is supposed to be evidence for the argument.

There are many complicated and involved errors that occur with faulty logic. These are called *fallacies of proposition*. Most of them are somewhat esoteric, but you should watch out for two in particular:

Black and white fallacy is limiting a situation to two possibilities when there are really more. You ignore many subtle possibilities if you say: "Either he will become manager of that store or he will be fired for insubordination."

Verbal fallacy uses the same word in two ways so that the conclusion is invalidated: "A druggist and a junkie both sell drugs —one is no more criminal than the other."

PRACTICE

1. Write an essay in which you support your argument with reason and evidence. Consider nuclear or solar power, abolishing term-paper requirements in all subjects but the student's major field, or legalizing marijuana.

2. Analyze an essay in your anthology (or in a special interest magazine or newspaper) in which the author vigorously supports a particular claim. Point out both the accurate use of evidence and the errors in logic.

Sexuality in a Zero-Growth Society

In this essay the author deals with a subject that is controversial and therefore creates strong emotional responses in the reader. Write an essay in which you analyze the logical and emotional appeals used in this selection, considering the following points:

How does the author deal with the emotional aspect of his topic? Does he exploit it in any way?

How does he use logic to balance or counteract the inherent emotionalism of his subject?

The American Indian: A Portrait in Limbo

Write an essay taking a position on some racial problem in America. In arguing *his* issue, Farb presents certain evidence and shows the reader how and why he has taken his particular position. Follow his example in writing your own essay and avoid bias, prejudice, and nonrational appeals. Research both sides of the argument and present them fairly. Be sure to cite the sources of your evidence and state clearly any assumptions you may have to make, as well as why you are making them.

The Dangers of Exploiting Nuclear Energy

The thesis of Inglis's argument is clearly stated in the introductory paragraphs. From these two paragraphs the reader has a general idea of the argument that will be developed in the essay. Write one or two introductory paragraphs on a subject (of your choice) that is to be developed through argumentation. Concentrate on the predictive content of these paragraphs by clearly stating the thesis of your argument and the opposing points of view.

When Aristotle Fails, Try Science Fiction

In writing argumentation, the purpose is to convince the reader of the validity of your position—to cause him to change his opinion on an issue or to encourage him to do something. In this essay, Asimov appeals to the reader to read science fiction for "real ideas." Write a short essay encouraging the reader to take some sort of action. Your purpose is to persuade and influence him; therefore you must present the problem clearly, outline the type of action needed, and stimulate the reader to act.

Grammar for Today

Analyze Evans's essay and identify the characteristics that qualify it as argumentation. Then write a sketch in dialogue form, in which you present the author's thesis argument as well as all of the opposing views he considers.

- Read a newspaper and choose an article (in which the author is identified) on which to base an essay on "The Reliability of a News Story." In writing, your essay, consider the following:

    Was the information presented in the news story verified by reliable sources such as other newspapers, news magazines, news services, TV and radio broadcasts, and so on?

    Research the authorities cited (as well as the background of the writer) to determine possible bias and prejudice and whether they are qualified authorities.

    Do additional reading and research on the issue to familiarize yourself with opposing points of view and to determine whether these views were fairly considered in the story.

    Analyze the appeals used in the article. Was the argument based on logic or emotion? Did you detect any fallacious thinking? Was the writer objective, or was his argument slanted to add strength to his position?

For examples of individual paragraphs using *argumentation*, see p.16, ¶3, p.54, ¶18, p.196, ¶39–43, p.202, ¶19–21, p.227, ¶13, p.286, ¶41–47.

Sexuality in a Zero-Growth Society

ALEXANDER COMFORT

1   We are on the verge, in developed countries, of a society in which *Beg*
zero population growth will be an overriding social objective. Few
people will have more than two children, and many will have none. *Anly/*
By the mid 2000's people will probably live and remain vigorous *Induc*
longer through the control of natural aging. It will be a new game
with different rules. The concept of the family which will alter—
and is already altering—is that which folklore still maintains as our
ideal expectation—the exclusive, totally self-sufficient couple-rela-
tionship, involving the ideal surrender of identity and of personal
selfhood, which excluded kin and only grudgingly included children.
The expectation, implied in so many novels and films, was in fact
only rarely fulfilled. Unlike the older pattern, where there were
other and supporting satisfactions beside each other's company, it
was often a neurotic expectation. Young people today see this, and
without diminishing their capacity for love, shy away from the idea
of total self-surrender: "I am I and you are you, and neither of us is
in this world to live up to the other's expectations . . . I love you,
but in forty years we may be different people." This view, if not
romantic, is at least realistic in terms of human experience.

2   Yet another change is that contraception has for the first time
wholly separated the three human uses of sex—sex as parenthood, *Class/*
sex as total intimacy between two people ("relational" sex), and sex *Def*
as physical play ("recreational" sex). "Morals," in their usual and

Reprinted with permission from the December, 1972, issue of the *Center Report*, a publication
of the Center for the Study of Democratic Institutions, Santa Barbara, California.

sexual meaning, reflect in rules the culture's image of what the family should be. Religion, which in our culture traditionally rejects pleasure as a motive, has tried hard to fence in the use of recreational sex. Until lately it did this by asserting that reproduction was the only legitimate use of sexuality. With the growth of the image of the ideal couple, it changed its ground, rather behind the event, so that today, together with many of its later successors in psychiatry and counselling, it asserts that worthy sex can only be relational.   *Anly*

3   There has been no time in human history when either of these valuations was wholly true, though they have served in their time to reinforce the uses which that time made of the family. Even in the most strongly kin-based cultures, gaps were left for sexual activity which was not an expression either of a wish for children or of an all-embracing personal relationship. Such gaps concerned chiefly the male, who was often the legislator, and who claimed the right to experience sexual relations in a non-relational way, while excluding women from doing so, either by moral codes, or by the indoctrination of girls with the idea that relational sex is the sole kind of which women, as opposed to men, are capable.

The Effect of the Pill

4   The Pill has altered that. Secure from unwanted pregnancy, an increasing number of women have discovered that their capacity to experience sex at all three levels, either together or on different occasions and in different contexts, is as great as a man's, if not greater. The adult of today has all three options—sex as parenthood, sex as total relationship, and sex as physical pleasure accompanied by no more than affection. Older people looking at the young today realize increasingly how much the confusion between these modes, which they could not foresee, or even choose voluntarily between, has often complicated their lives; when play between boy and girl resulted in pregnancy and a forced marriage between mere acquaintances, when one partner misread the other's degree of involvement, or falsified his own selfishly to overcome reluctance.   *Class*

5 ·   Greater choice can bring greater problems and greater opportunities. It will bring problems in any event, and these can only be reduced by recognizing how great is the range of situations in which sex relations now take place, and learning to handle them to meet our own and our partner's needs. If we can do this, then the new freedom, though it now seems to be generating confusion, could   *Tran*

reshape our living to meet the needs which were once met by the traditional human family pattern. We have dispensed with kin—to support us in life and look after us in old age. Consequently we are lonely, and we go to "sensitivity groups" to relearn how to treat people as people. The fantasy-concept of total one-to-one suffi- ciency has let us down. Since sex is now divorced from parenthood, there are many more relationships into which it can enter if we choose.

C & E

Varied Relations

6 All that can be certainly predicted for the future is that the variety of patterns will increase as individuals find the norm that suits them. For some, parenthood will still be the central satisfaction, carrying with it the obligation of giving the children the stability they re- quire. For others sexuality will express total involvement with one person. For others, one or more primary relationships will be cen- tral, but will not exclude others, in which the recreational role of sex acts as a source of bonding to supply the range of relationships formerly met by kin—an old human pattern in which sexual con- tacts were permitted between a woman and all her husband's clan brothers, or a man and all his wife's titular sisters.

Top S

Class

7   In the zero population growth world we are all "clan brothers" and will have to find ways of expressing the hippy ideal of universal kinship. For many of the young today, a wider range of permitted sexual relationships seems to express this ideal, and even the rather compulsive wife-swapping of middle-aged couples in urban America seems to be reaching towards the same solution. What is clear is that we cannot reimpose the old rigidities. In going forward to new- er and more varied patterns, our sense of responsibility and our awareness of others is going to be severely tested if we are not to become still more confused and unhappy. If we pass the test, we may evolve into a universal human family in which all three types of sex have their place, in which we are all genuinely kin, and in which all but the most unrealistic inner needs can be met in one form or another.

Dict

Exemp

Tran

Relational Sex

8 Conventional morals are probably correct in asserting that all satis- factory sex is in some degree inherently relational—if it is satisfac- tory, and mutually so, a relation subsists. Only the wholly insensi-

Def

tive mate mechanically, even under the conditions of permitted non-discrimination which characterize a ritualized orgy. A society like ours, which has traditionally feared and rejected close personal contact, has also generated a mythology of all-or-none involvement which profoundly influences us to our hurt. Unable to exclude the recreational and the partly relational modes of sex, it has set about rejecting or falsifying them. Once rid of this ideology, it might find that the relation present in purely recreational or social sex is a uniquely effective tool in breaking down personal separateness—of which the proprietary notion of love is an offshoot—so that, for us as for many primitives, social sex comes to express and cement the equivalent of kinship through a general intimacy and nondefensiveness, reinforced by the very strong reward of realizing suppressed needs for variety and for acceptance.

Arg/ Anly

9   Our society has moved illogically in this direction by virtually institutionalizing adultery: a growing number of spouses permit each other complete sexual liberty on the conditions that there shall be no "involvement" and that the extracurricular relations are not brought to their attention. It is beginning to institutionalize ritual spouse exchange. This is more honest, and a better bet anthropologically; non-involvement is, as it were, written in, the exchange is non-secret, and the partners, instead of excluding each other, share in the arrangement. How far conventional middle-class "swingers" profit emotionally in openness from their swinging is arguable—most studies suggest that they keep it in a watertight compartment and ritualize it as a sort of charismatic hobby or secret society, which embodies all current prejudices and does little to create any universal openness. At least, however, it marks the end, or the beginning of the end, of proprietary sexual attitudes. In part it has spread to the middle-aged from the young; older couples want to imitate their freedom without abandoning present attitudes. Unless the result disturbs children and leads to a backlash generation, the genuine insight present in "swinging" by the bored and the unrealized could expand into something far more like institutionalized sociosexual openness.

S Var

Expressing Bisexuality

10   This process, so far as it has gone, would have been impossible without a gradual change in attitudes toward, and anxiety about, bisexuality. Mate-sharing, both psychoanalytically, and in primate ethology, reveals a surrogate sexual relation between males—ex-

Tran

pressed covertly so far in the gang night out and the attraction of the prostitute or "shared" woman, acceptable substitutes for overt male-male contacts because they are covert. The potential for more open bisexual contacts is greatly increased by two-couple activity. Men tend still to be disturbed by this, but women, who are in general less anxious about their bisexual potential, often embrace the opportunity with male encouragement. In fact, judging from primates, the state of sharing with another male, which reinforces individual dominance, could well help rather than hinder the heterosexuality of anxious people—dominance anxiety plays a large part in the suppression of heterosexual drives in most persons who regard themselves as constitutionally homosexual. Beside reinstating the kinship of men and women, a wider and opener use of sexuality is quite likely to reinstate, and reinforce, the kinship between men and men, which we now studiously avoid erotizing or expressing. In a fully erotized society, bisexuality, expressed or not, could cease to be a problem simply because social attitudes have changed.

Declining Jealousy

11   Another important casualty of this process is likely to be sexual jealousy. Much argument has been devoted to discussing how far jealousy is a normal emotion, the counterpart of love, and how far it is a product of indoctrination. It would probably be true to say that in the traditional family jealousy was based on reproduction (knowing that my children are mine) and ideas of property, while in the romantic couple situation it is a product of the fear of rejection implicit in a surrender so alarmingly total. Modern attempts to transcend jealousy through wife-exchange or greater tolerance of affairs are often uncertain and anxious, but they have positive features—acceptance of a more realistic view of the needs of couples and individuals for variety, and recognition that the meeting of needs rather than their frustration is a gift which expresses love rather than devalues it, and strengthens the primary bond. (One need not be like the mischievous lovers of Les Liaisons Dangereuses to recognize this.) Such a recognition is important as marking the end of the mutual proprietorship, physical or emotional, which has so often characterized human sexual relationships in the past, and which modern woman, as well as modern man, rightly rejects as neurotic and immature. To our grandchildren, nineteenth century opera may be emotionally unintelligible.

12   Some will feel that the use of wider sex as a substitute for   C ∉ C
kinship devalues love and will leave us emotionally shallow. Others
will see it as the defusing of a dangerous fantasy concerning the
total nature of human love, which no society has enacted in fact or
found satisfactory in the enactment, but which the folklore of the
postkinship family has wished on us to our hurt. The relationships   Def/
of the zero growth society will have to be relationships between   Arg
whole, adult people, dependent on their own resources, not using
kin, family and children as a bolthole or one another as climbing-
posts, but if this kind of adulthood can be attained at all widely (it
will never be practicable for all) it could lead to relations far more
supportive in a truly human sense than any we have so far known.
Certainly none of the past fictions embodied in our stereotypes of
male and female sex roles, of totally exclusive love, or even of central parenthood can readily persist unaltered.

13   We are not here talking about change which we can further or
prevent, simply about changes which are now taking place. If we
approach them on the basis of anxiety, past expectation and folklore they will only generate more of the anomie which we have now.
The alternative is to see whether we can approach them with insight
and compassion for one another.

Toward Two Lifespans

14   Extension of survival into old age has already led to the concept of   C ∉ E
"two lifespans," with a second, adolescence-like identity crisis
around the age of 40, when realized and unrealized goals are reas-
sessed: the crisis may end in a resumption of established relationships, illness or depression, or a total recasting of relationships. The
crisis is more prominent in men—their societal opportunity for a
"new start," occupationally and sexually, is the greater—and it often leads to the starting of a second family with a younger partner.
Women's opportunities are more cruelly circumscribed at this
age—they tend to find themselves deserted, having "run out of"
family and an established role. Any further extension of vigorous
life through interference with aging might put them on a more
equal footing with men; it will certainly increase the tendency for
life-styles, and families, to be serial, so that each individual has the
option of continuing in one pattern, or of entering a wholly different one, at the age when in the traditional family one was preparing
for dependent senescence. The decline of the kinship family has
born excessively hard on the old—dependency is rejected, and they

become increasingly isolated in a forced "independence" which is worsened by the shortage of kin. Perhaps more than anyone they would benefit from a "spreading" of the couple-preoccupied family into something more like a tribe of friends.

15   I would expect accordingly to see a society in which pair relationships are still central, but initially less permanent, in which childbearing is seen as a special responsibility involving a special life style, and in which settled couples engage openly in a wide range of sexual relations with friends, with other couples, and with third parties as an expression of social intimacy, without prejudice to the primacy of their own relationship, and with no more, and probably less, permanent interchange than we see in the society of serial polygamy with adultery that now exists. Such a pattern is coming into existence in America, and is beginning to become explicit. Whether it will devalue relationships or only deprive them of neurotic compulsion will depend on the persons involved, the amount of support they receive from the social ethic, and the accuracy of the expectations with which they enter maturity. If these expectations become realistic, it will be the first time that a modern generation has been reared with confidence but without illusions.

Induc

What Political Implications?

16   The political implications of universalized kinship are interesting. Marcuse, in discussing the "erotization of relationships" as a political force was once challenged to "go erotize the state of Kansas." My suggestion is that this may in fact be happening. The family is in fact the microcosm of politics with a one to two generation timelag. Institutional politics today reflect combative paternalism, which had its family counterpart in the 1850s, and liberal politics the social expression of the ideal of individualist romantic love.

Tran

Angy

17   It is possible to overstate the inherently revolutionary potential of "universal kinship," but if, as I suggest, it is explicitly erotized, it will find a counterpart socially in anarchic community action. How far it produces such action, and how far the non-possessive individual and the anti-authoritarian society are products of the same change in social requirement it is hard to say. The acceptance of sensuality, and the widening of its focus to include not one but many others, would seem in itself to be an emotional technology capable of fitting well into the less compulsive and more gentle world view of the twenty-first as against the nineteenth and twentieth centuries. Marcuse is probably right in seeing justice, non-pos-

Anly

session, non-exploitation, ecology and the wider erotization of relationships as possible correlates. We may have a rough few years ahead before this pattern emerges, but when and if it does, one could wish to live in those times.

CONSIDERATIONS

Do you accept the three-part definition of sex as defined in the second paragraph? Are relational and recreational uses of sex legitimate interpretations of the actual sexual practices of people? What changes are "conventional morals" (paragraph 8) now undergoing, if any? Are "proprietary sexual attitudes" (paragraph 9) likely to be replaced within the next generation or two? Are the potential political implications of "universalized kinship" as awesome as Comfort suggests? (paragraphs 16 and 17) Has the author ignored possible negative results in a sexually open society?

What are the main thematic divisions in this article? Does the author offer adequate analyses of his main points—for example, the concept of the changing family (paragraph 1), contraception as a determining factor in reevaluating traditional sexual relationships (paragraphs 2–4), and future patterns of sexual roles? (paragraph 9) What are his methods of analysis? Is his inductive reasoning well developed in his argument? Do the projections or predictions follow logically from the basic evidence the author sets forth?

Dr. Comfort suggests that changing sexual relations can result in a wide range of choices for life patterns: "Greater choice can bring greater problems and greater opportunities." (paragraph 5) Discuss his thesis that the new freedom "could reshape our living to meet the needs which were once met by the traditional human family pattern." (paragraphs 5, 12 and 14) What sorts of inter-people relationships might be established to replace the old roles of kinship? Do you agree or disagree with his premise that supportive kinship roles, once very important, are now far less so? Give examples to support your positions.

VOCABULARY

(6) **titular**   in title only; nominal
(7) **compulsive**   governed by an obsessive need to achieve some desired ideal of behavior

The American Indian:
A Portrait in Limbo

PETER FARB

1   The Indian can probably survive the bad housing, lack of jobs, dismal health conditions, and poor education—but not the implication that he is irrelevant to American culture. For once the Indians are deprived of the last bit of the culture that has sustained them, they will disappear into the faceless American poor. Yet, the U.S. Bureau of Indian Affairs was founded a century ago with the stated aim to alienate Indian children "from their native culture and language so they could take their place in modern society"—and that has remained an implied aim to this day. A white policy has stripped the Indian of his identity and made him embarrassed about his rich oral literature, his customs and traditions, his native foods and dress. A white education system has turned out imitation whites who succumb to the bleakness of reservation life and the prejudice around them.

2   "The American Indian today is about to go over the brink—not only of poverty and prejudice, but of moral collapse," says William Byler, executive director of the Association on American Indian Affairs. The Indian has learned that no one wants to listen or to understand when he speaks his thoughts about his own future. He is bewildered by the capricious policies handed down in Washington—first telling him to leave the reservation and get jobs in the cities, next telling him to stay on the reservation and bring industry

From the book, MAN'S RISE TO CIVILIZATION AS SHOWN BY THE INDIANS OF NORTH AMERICA FROM PRIMEVAL TIMES TO THE COMING OF THE INDUSTRIAL STATE, by Peter Farb. Copyright ©1968 by Peter Farb. Published by E. P. Dutton & Co., Inc. and used with their permission. This essay appeared originally in the SATURDAY REVIEW in a somewhat different form. Also reprinted by permission of Martin Secker & Warburg Limited.

to it. Some politicians tell him that he is a child who must be protected by the kindly White Father—and other politicians tell him that he is man enough to be cast adrift to sink or swim in the capitalist tide. The result of such confusion is widespread apathy among Indians. They find it difficult to act in concert with other Indians because whites deliberately ripped apart the intricate web of their social and political relationships.

3   The present plight of the red man is an indication of exactly how far he has fallen from his state of Noble Savage in little more than 450 years. At first, the newly discovered Indians were greatly respected and admired. Columbus brought home six Indians to show Queen Isabella and, dressed in full regalia, they quickly became the curiosities of Spain. Sir Walter Raleigh brought back Indians also and a craze swept Elizabethan England. Shakespeare complained about it in *The Tempest:* "They will not give a doit [a small coin equal to about half a farthing] to relieve a lame beggar, they will lay out ten to see a dead Indian." The French philosopher Michel de Montaigne talked with Indians who had been brought to the French Court and concluded that the Noble Savage had been found, for the Indian "hath no kind of traffic, no knowledge of letters, no intelligence of numbers, no name of magistrate, nor of politics, no use of services, of riches, or of poverty. . . . The very words that import a lie, falsehood, treason, covetousness, envy, detraction, were not heard among them."

4   The Noble Savage captivated Europe, but the colonists felt differently about living with red men. When Columbus discovered the Arawak Indians, who inhabited the Caribbean Islands, he described them as "a loving people, without covetousness. . . . Their speech is the sweetest and gentlest in the world." But in their haste to exploit the abundance of the Americas, the Spaniards set the loving and gentle Arawak to labor in mines and on plantations. Whole Arawak villages disappeared due to slavery, disease, warfare, and flight to escape the Spaniards. As a result, the native population of Haiti, for example, declined from an estimated 200,000 in 1492 to 29,000 only twenty-two years later.

5   The Puritans in New England were not immediately presented with an Indian problem, for diseases introduced by trading ships along the Atlantic Coast had badly decimated the red populations. Yet, the Puritans failed miserably in their dealings with even the remnant Indians. They insisted upon a high standard of religious devotion that the Indians were unable or unwilling to give. The Puritans lacked any way to integrate the Indians into their theoc-

racy, for they did not indulge in wholesale baptisms (as they charged the French did), nor were any Puritans specifically assigned to missionary tasks.

6   In 1637, a party of Puritans surrounded the Pequot Indian village and set fire to it after these Indians had resisted settlement of whites in the Connecticut Valley. About 500 Indians were burned to death or shot while trying to escape; the woods were then combed for any Pequots who had managed to survive, and these were sold into slavery. The whites devoutly offered up thanks to God that they had lost only two men; when the Puritan divine Cotton Mather heard about the raid, he was grateful to the Lord that "on this day we have sent six hundred heathen souls to hell."

7   The Indian came to be regarded as a stubborn animal that refused to acknowledge the obvious blessings of white civilization. Hugh Henry Brackenridge, a modest literary figure of the young nation, expressed the changed attitude when he wrote in 1782 of ". . . the animals, vulgarly called Indians." Rousseau's Noble Savage was laid to rest officially in 1790 when John Adams stated: "I am not of Rousseau's Opinions. His Notions of the purity of Morals in savage nations and the earliest Ages of civilized Nations are mere Chimeras." Even that man of enlightened homilies, Benjamin Franklin, observed that rum should be regarded as an agent of Providence "to extirpate these savages in order to make room for the cultivators of the earth."

8   After the War of 1812, the young United States had no further need for Indian allies against the British, and, as a result, the fortunes of the Indians declined rapidly. Pressures increased to get the Indians off the lands the whites had appropriated from them and, in 1830, Congress passed the Removal Act, which gave the President the right to extirpate all Indians who had managed to survive east of the Mississippi River. It was estimated that the whole job might be done economically at no more than $500,000—the cost to be kept low by persuasion, promises, threats, and the bribery of Indian leaders. When U.S. Supreme Court Justice John Marshall ruled in favor of the Cherokee Indians in a case with wide implications for preventing removal, President Andrew Jackson is said to have remarked: "John Marshall has made his decision, now let him enforce it."

9   During the next ten years, almost all the Indians were cleared from the East. Some, such as the Chickasaw and Choctaw and Cherokee, went resignedly. The Seminole actively resisted and retreated into the Florida swamps, where they stubbornly held off the

United States Army. The Seminole Wars lasted from 1835 to 1842 and cost the United States some 1,500 soldiers and an estimated $20,000,000 (about forty times what Jackson had estimated it would cost to remove all Indians). Many of the Iroquois found sanctuary in Canada. The Sac and Fox made a desperate stand in Illinois against overwhelming numbers of whites, but ultimately their survivors were forced to move, as were the Ottawa, Potawatomi, Wyandot, Shawnee, Kickapoo, Winnebago, Delaware, Peoria, Miami, and many others who are remembered now only in the name of some town, lake, county, or state.

10   Alexis de Tocqueville, who examined the young United States with a perceptive eye and wrote it all down in his *Democracy in America*, was in Memphis on an unusually cold day when he saw a ragged party of Choctaw, part of the docile thousands who had reluctantly agreed to be transported to the new lands in the West. He wrote:

> The Indians had their families with them, and they brought in their train the wounded and the sick, with children newly born and old men upon the verge of death. . . . I saw them embark to pass the mighty river, and never will that solemn spectacle fade from my remembrance. No cry, no sob, was heard among the assembled crowd; all was silent. Their calamities were of ancient date, and they knew them to be irremediable.

11   De Tocqueville described with restrained outrage how the Indians were sent westward by government agents: ". . . half-convinced and half-compelled, they go to inhabit new deserts, where the importunate whites will not let them remain ten years in peace. In this manner do the Americans obtain, at a very low price, whole provinces, which the richest sovereigns of Europe could not purchase." He reported that a scant 6,273 Indians still survived in the thirteen original states.

12   The experience of the Indians west of the Mississippi River was only a sad, monotonous duplication of what had happened east of it—warfare, broken treaties, expropriation of land, rebellion, and ultimately defeat. No sooner were the Eastern Indians dropped down on the plains and prairies than the United States discovered the resources in the West, and miners and settlers were on the move. Emigrant trains rumbled westward, and once again the aim of the frontiersman was to get the Indian out of the way.

13   The "final extermination" was hastened by epidemics that swept the West and sapped the Indians' power to resist. A mere hundred Mandan out of a population of 1,600 survived a smallpox epidemic (they are extinct today); the same epidemic, spreading

westward, reduced the total number of Blackfoot Indians by about half. The majority of Kiowa and Comanche Indians were victims of cholera. The Indians undoubtedly would have been crushed by whites in any event, but the spread of diseases made the job easier.

14   Up to 1868, nearly 400 treaties had been signed by the U.S. Government with various Indian groups, and scarcely a one had remained unbroken. The Indians were promised new lands, then moved off them to some other place. They were shifted about again and again, as many as five or six times. All of which led the Sioux chief Spotted Tail to ask wearily: "Why does not the Great White Father put his red children on wheels, so he can move them as he will?"

15   In the last decades of the last century the Indians finally realized that these treaties were real estate deals designed to separate them from their lands. Indians and whites skirmished and then fought openly with ferocity and barbarity on both sides. Group by group, the Indians rose in rebellion only to be crushed—the southern Plains tribes in 1874, the Sioux in 1876, the Nez Percé in 1877, the Ute in 1879, and the Apache throughout much of the 1880s, until Geronimo finally surrendered with his remnant band of thirty-six survivors. The massacre of more than 300 Sioux, mostly women and children and old people, at Wounded Knee, South Dakota, in 1890 marked the end of Indian resistance to white authority.

16   Humanitarians who attempted to ease the defeat of the Indians felt that the remnant populations should be given the dignity of private property. As a result, Senator Henry L. Dawes of Massachusetts sponsored the Allotment Act of 1887 to salvage some land for the Indians who otherwise might lose everything to voracious whites. When President Grover Cleveland signed the act, he stated that the "hunger and thirst of the white man for the Indian's land is almost equal to his hunger and thirst after righteousness."

17   The act provided that after every Indian had been allotted land, the remainder would be put up for sale to the public. But the loopholes with which the act was punctured made it an efficient instrument for separating the Indians from this land. The plunder was carried on with remarkable order. The first lands to go to whites were the richest—bottomlands in river valleys or fertile grasslands. Next went the slightly less desirable lands, such as those that had to be cleared before they could produce a crop. Then the marginal lands were taken, and so on, until the Indian had left to him only desert that no white considered worth the trouble to take. Between the passage of the Allotment Act in 1887 and a New Deal investiga-

tion in 1934, the Indians had been reduced to only 56,000,000 acres out of the meager 138,000,000 acres that had been allotted them—and every single acre of the 56,000,000 was adjudged by soil conservationists to be eroded. At the same time that the Indians were being systematically relieved of their lands, their birth rate rose higher than the mortality rate, and so there were more and more Indians on less and less land. The Indians did what they had always done: They shared the little they had and went hungry together.

18   The victory over the Noble Savage—reduced in numbers, deprived of land, broken in spirit, isolated on wasteland reservations—was complete except for one final indignity. That was to Americanize the Indian, to eliminate his last faint recollection of his ancient traditions—in short, to exterminate the cultures along with the Indians. There was not much culture left to eradicate, but at last zealous whites found something. Orders went out from Washington that all male Indians must cut their hair short, even though many Indians believed that long hair had supernatural significance. The Indians refused, and the battle was joined. Army reinforcements were sent to the reservations to carry out the order, and in some cases Indians had to be shackled before they submitted.

19   Most of the attention of the Americanizers, though, was concentrated on the Indian children, who were snatched from their families and shipped off to boarding schools far from their homes. The children usually were kept at school for eight years, during which time they were not permitted to see their parents, relatives, or friends. Anything Indian—dress, language, religious practices, even outlook on life—was uncompromisingly prohibited. Ostensibly educated, articulate in the English language, wearing store-bought clothes, and with their hair short and their emotionalism muted, the boarding-school graduates were sent out either to make their way in a white world that did not want them, or to return as strangers to their reservation. The Indian had simply failed to melt into the great American melting pot.

20   He had been remade in the white man's image and then cast adrift or else safely bottled up on reservations. Yet it is apparent to any objective observer that the Indian problem still nags at the American conscience. It seems that whites, both land-hungry settlers and humanitarians, have tried every possible variation in the treatment of the Indian. What, then, is the solution?

21   Many people concerned about the American Indian are coming to believe that we should simply stop offering the Indian pat solutions. Everything has been tried. The Indians have been herded

from reservation to reservation, switched from hunting to agriculture or from agriculture to hunting, moved to cities to work in factories or told instead to make room for factories on their reservations. Indians exist today as the most manipulated people on earth—and yet our Indian policy has produced only failure after failure.

CONSIDERATIONS

Farb presents many of the same facts that Degler treats in his article, with a slightly different emphasis. Does Farb offer any solutions, by implication, or is it simply his intention to clarify issues and illuminate the problems?

By using controlled irony, Farb has achieved a tone of "restrained outrage," the words he uses to describe de Tocqueville's attitude in paragraph 11. Cite examples of Farb's irony—in paragraphs 4, 6, 7, 8, 15, 16, and 17. Why is irony a better vehicle than sarcasm or righteous indignation?

If "everything has been tried," as Farb says in paragraph 21, what is the answer to our "Indian problem"? If you have specific ideas, incorporate them in an essay.

VOCABULARY

- (2) **capricious**   directed by whim
- (3) **detraction**   belittling of the reputation or worth of a person
- (5) **theocracy**   a form of government in which God or a deity is recognized as the supreme civil ruler
- (7) **chimeras**   vain or idle fancies
- (7) **homilies**   moralizing or religious discourses
- (7) **extirpate**   to remove utterly; exterminate; pull up by the roots
- (11) **importunate**   persistent in making demands
- (16) **voracious**   insatiable; eager to possess
- (18) **eradicate**   completely erase; destroy

The Dangers of Exploiting Nuclear Energy

DAVID R. INGLIS

1   The discovery about thirty years ago of nuclear fission and its chain reaction, along with its sister process, nuclear fusion, ushered in new prospects for the human race. While the A-bombs and the H-bombs are precariously restrained in a balance of terror called deterrence, the new prospect of great new supplies of nuclear power for industry and agriculture may stave off, for centuries, a condition of universal human misery on an overcrowded planet if population growth can be halted soon enough.

2   Malthus long ago foresaw the ultimate calamity of a clash between a population growing without limit and the limited resources of the earth. The prospect of great stores of energy from controlled fusion, if it can be brought to pass, or otherwise from fission in breeder reactors, may long forestall or completely avoid the Malthusian crunch with its raw human misery.

3   The need for development towards this noble end has been used as one of the false justifications for the great splurge of U.S. nuclear power-plant building on which we are now embarking. We have about twenty operable nuclear power plants, another fifty under construction, and the AEC expects that we will have about one thousand of them busily producing electricity and radioactive wastes by the end of the century.

4   These new plants are to be mostly water-moderated "uranium-

235 burners" of the general types now being constructed. They in-
efficiently consume only the rare isotope that constitutes less than
one percent of each pound of uranium supplied by nature. At this
rate, most of the uranium that can be mined at reasonable expense
will be exhausted in two or three decades. Towards the end of the
century more of the plants will be breeder reactors, which make
more efficient use of the uranium by transmuting the more abundant part into plutonium that may be used as a fuel for reactors—
or as an explosive for bombs. These plants will almost all be breeders of a particular variety known as Liquid-Metal Fast Breeder
Reactors—LMFBRs. This is the type with the most immediate
prospect of successful development promoted by not only our own
government but most other governments in the nuclear business,
almost to the exclusion of other types.

The Need for Fusion Research

5   If we were to take seriously the threat of a Malthusian crunch,
perhaps in the middle of the twenty-first century, we would approach the development differently. A larger share of effort would
go into nuclear fusion research. Power production by the nuclear
fusion method is still a gamble, but if it works out it will be a far
superior answer to the Malthusian threat than will the breeder reac-
tor. Its basic raw material, the heavy isotope of hydrogen in sea
water, is in almost limitless supply. It would discharge some radioactivity, but probably much less than fission reactors, and will have no
such inventory of militarily and physiologically dangerous material
as the plutonium from many LMFBRs.

6   But the gamble on fusion might not pay off, and there are
other possibilities that we should be developing. There are other
types of breeder reactors that may at least avoid the dangerous
inventory of plutonium, and might, in the long run, be superior in
other ways. For the sake of the twenty-first century, we should be
vigorously developing these. Instead, the research groups that would
like to explore them are languishing for lack of funds.

7   There are other possible sources of power that should be explored more aggressively. Foremost among these is solar power. If
the sunlight that falls on a square mile of desert could be harnessed
at 40 percent efficiency, it would be equal to the power generated
by one of the big new million-kilowatt nuclear power plants. It takes
a lot of doing to cover a square mile with light-gathering apparatus,
but it takes a lot of doing to build a nuclear power plant. It is not

obvious that the former, imaginatively engineered, is more difficult or expensive. The effort now being expended in this direction is meager indeed.

8   Our present splurge of loading the countryside and the power grid with nuclear reactors cannot be honestly motivated by concern for helping the human race to avoid the Malthusian threat. The U-235 burners already built, and being planned in much greater numbers, will be essentially obsolete by the turn of the century because of exhaustion of cheap fuel for them. The breeders of the near future—the LMFBRs—might be forerunners of a type that will be useful in the next century, and one or two of them should be built and put in operation, to be followed by one or two of the next generation. Instead, the expectation is that hundreds of them will be built later in this century.

9   The net effect of 1,000 or so reactors of both types in the next thirty years—if they materialize—will be to prolong and increase the disparity represented by the oft-quoted fact that we Americans, about six percent of the world's people, consume about 35 percent or 40 percent of its goods and power. On a worldwide basis, these reactors will make the rich richer and more extravagant while doing precious little for the poor. . . .

The "Expectation Explosion"

10   The rapidly increasing drain on resources comes not only from the population explosion but also from the "expectation explosion." We extravagant and energy-hungry Americans are leading the world in the explosion of rising expectations and thereby compounding the difficulties of the population explosion. The world looks to our standard of living as its goal. The aim of our new nuclear reactors, and the doubling of electric power each decade, is to help raise our standard of living still further and thereby the world's goal.

11   There are simply not enough natural resources, no matter how much power is used, for the world to attain the U.S. standard of living. We should leave something with which the underdeveloped can improve their lot. A continually rising economy is riding for a fall in power output. A nuclear moratorium would be an effective way to begin to decrease the rate of rise in power output, and would avoid the serious difficulties we are likely to encounter in the premature expansion of an insufficiently developed technology.

12   One of the most important of these difficulties is that we will be producing large quantities of highly radioactive waste products when we have not yet developed a satisfactory means for keeping

them out of the environment, where they will persist for centuries. Burying them in salt mines has been proposed but not proved out.

13   Another difficulty is the unassessable likelihood—probably small for any one nuclear power plant—of a radioactive catastrophe from a runaway accident. If the economy becomes completely dependent on the power from many nuclear plants, and such an accident should occur in one of them, killing many people in a nearby city, it would be difficult to decide whether or not the other plants should continue to operate. A further difficulty is the routine release of small amounts of radioactivity from power plants and particularly from nuclear fuel-processing plants. Accidents in the transportation of radioactive spent fuel are also a danger.

14   But perhaps foremost among the dangers is the possibility that the nuclear materials produced in the power plants might be diverted to the clandestine making of atomic bombs. All these nuclear power plants make plutonium. A single uranium-235-burning power plant of the type now being constructed—not even a breeder—creates about 1,000 pounds of plutonium a year, enough to make more than 100 atomic bombs. With hundreds of such plants in operation, and plutonium worth four times its weight in gold, a dangerous black market supplied by thefts is bound to develop. That will mean that the stuff to make atom bombs will be available to almost anybody, any petty dictator or underworld chief. The potentialities for criminal mischief that could trigger general nuclear war are ominous indeed. . . .

Production Versus Controls

15   The International Atomic Agency, abetted by our own AEC, is making an effort to control this situation but it is not sufficient to cope with the threat that is developing with so many new reactors. Just as we have gone ahead with the arms race before giving high priority to arms control, just as we have entered into the production of great amounts of radioactive fission products that must be safely sequestered for centuries before developing adequate means to do this, so we are embarking on producing, for commercial use, enormous amounts of the stuff that atom bombs are made of before having instituted substantial controls to prevent its diversion to dangerous and illicit uses.

CONSIDERATIONS

Author Inglis accepts the Malthusian principle (formulated about 1800) as the basis of his argument. There will be great power shortages as the population of the world continues to grow, quite obviously, but according to Inglis, what are our options in the impending energy crisis? Does he make clear the reasons why one process—nuclear-fission power plants—dominates the U.S. research and development in this field?

Is Inglis writing for the scientific or a nonscientific reader? Is this article primarily based on "scare tactics," or has the author sufficiently documented his claims? Analyze the introductory paragraphs (1 and 2); the information in these two paragraphs comprises the thesis of Inglis's argument. Has he selected two closely related, interconnected topics (Malthusian economics and the development of nuclear fission) for his springboard, or has he simply juxtaposed two unrelated phenomena— one scientific and one sociological-economical—for the purpose of creating an argument? Analyze his language and the development of his argument.

Comment in an essay on Inglis's points in paragraphs 9, 10, and 11: "Americans, who total six percent of the world population, consume nearly half of its goods and power, and we are doing the rest of the world a great disservice by our ever-increasing 'higher-standard-of-living' demands upon the resources of the earth." What should be our national policy regarding this dilemma? Is it now too late for us to change our course?

VOCABULARY

(1)	nuclear fission	splitting the nucleus of an atom into nuclei of lighter atoms, accompanied by the release of energy
(1)	nuclear fusion	a thermonuclear reaction in which the nuclei of light atoms join to form nuclei of heavier atoms, accompanied by the release of energy
(4)	isotope	a variation of atomic makeup of a chemical element having the same atomic number but different atomic weight
(4)	transmuting	changing from one form or substance to another
(4)	plutonium	a radioactive element, capable of self-maintained explosive fission; used as fuel in some nuclear reactors
(6)	languishing	undergoing neglect
(9)	disparity	lack of equality
(11)	moratorium	a temporary cessation of activity, especially of an activity considered hostile or dangerous or both
(13)	unassessable	undeterminable; inestimable
(14)	clandestine	secretly done, especially for purposes of subversion
(15)	sequestered	secluded; isolated

When Aristotle Fails, Try Science Fiction

ISAAC ASIMOV

1   It is odd to be asked whether science fiction is a literature of ideas. Far from doubting that it is, I would like to suggest that it is the *only* literature of relevant ideas, since it is the only literature that, at its best, is firmly based on scientific thought.

2   Of the products of the human intellect, the scientific method is unique. This is not because it ought to be considered the only path to Truth; it isn't. In fact, it firmly admits it isn't. It doesn't even pretend to define what Truth (with a capital T) is, or whether the word has meaning. In this it parts company with the self-assured thinkers of various religious, philosophical, and mystical persuasions who have drowned the world in sorrow and blood through the conviction that they and they alone own Truth.

3   The uniqueness of science comes in this: the scientific method offers a way of determining the False. Science is the only gateway to proven error. There have been Homeric disputes in the history of science, and while it could not be maintained that either party was wholly right or had the key to Truth, it could be shown that the views of at least one were at variance with what seemed to be the facts available to us through observation.

4   Pasteur maintained alcoholic fermentation to be the product of living cells; Liebig said no. Liebig, in the mid-nineteenth-century context of observation, was proved wrong; his views were aban-

doned. Newton advanced a brilliantly successful picture of the universe, but it failed in certain apparently minor respects. Einstein advanced another picture that did not fail in those respects. Whether Einstein's view is True is still argued and may be argued for an indefinite time to come, but Newton's view is False. There is no argument about the latter.

5   Compare this with other fields in which intellectuals amuse themselves. Who has ever proved a school of philosophy to be False? When has one religion triumphed over another by debate, experiment and observation? What rules of criticism can settle matters in such a way that all critics will agree on a particular work of art or literature?

6   A man without chemical training can speak learnedly of chemistry, making use of a large vocabulary and a stately oratorical style—and he will be caught out almost at once by any bright teenager who has studied chemistry in high school.

7   The same man, without training in art, can speak learnedly of art in the same way, and while his ignorance may be evident to some real expert in the field, no one else would venture to dispute him with any real hope of success.

8   There is an accepted consensus in science, and to be a plausible fake in science (before any audience not utterly ignorant in the field) one must learn that consensus thoroughly. Having learned it, however, one has no need to be a plausible fake.

9   In other fields of intellectual endeavor there is, however, no accepted consensus. The different schools argue endlessly, moving in circles about each other as fad succeeds fashion over the centuries. Though individuals may be unbelievably eloquent and sincere, there is, short of the rack and the stake, no decision ever. Consequently, to be a plausible fake in religion, art, politics, mysticism, or even any of the "soft" sciences such as sociology (to anyone not utterly expert in the field), one need only learn the vocabulary and develop a certain self-assurance.

10   It is not surprising, then, that so many young intellectuals avoid the study of science and so many old intellectuals are proud of their ignorance of science. Science has a bad habit of puncturing pretension for all to see. Those who value their pretension to intellect and are insecure over it are well advised to avoid science.

11   To be sure, when a scientist ventures outside his field and pontificates elsewhere, he is as likely to speak nonsense as anyone else. (And there may be those unkind enough to say I am demonstrating this fact in this very article.) However, since nonsense outside sci-

ence is difficult or impossible to demonstrate, the scientist is at least
no worse than anyone else in this respect.

12   If we consider Literature (with a capital L) as a vehicle of ideas,
we can only conclude that, by and large, the ideas with which it is
concerned are the same ideas that Homer and Aeschylus struggled
with. They are well worth discussing, I am sure; even fun. There is
enough there to keep an infinite number of minds busy for an infinite amount of time, but they weren't settled and aren't settled.

13   It is these "eternal verities" that are precisely what science
fiction doesn't deal with. Science fiction deals with change. It deals
with the possible advance in science and with the potential
changes—even in those damned eternal verities—this may bring
about in society.

14   As it happens, we are living in a society in which all the enormous changes—the *only* enormous changes—are being brought
about by science and its application to everyday life. Count up the
changes introduced by the automobile, by the television set, by the
jet plane. Ask yourself what might happen to the world of tomorrow if there is complete automation, if robots become practical, if
the disease of old age is cured, if hydrogen fusion is made a workable source of energy.

15   The fact is that no previous generation has had to face the
possibility and the potentialities of such enormous and such rapid
change. No generation has had to face the appalling certainty that
if the advance of science isn't judged accurately, if the problems of
tomorrow aren't solved before they are upon us, that advance and
those problems will overwhelm us.

16   This generation, then, is the first that can't take as its primary
concern the age-old questions that have agitated all deep thinkers
since civilization began. Those questions are still interesting, but
they are no longer of first importance, and any literature that deals
with them (that is, any literature but science fiction) is increasingly
irrelevant.

17   If this thought seems too large to swallow, consider a rather
simple analogy: the faster an automobile is moving, the less the
driver can concern himself with the eternal beauties of the scenery
and the more he must involve himself with the trivial obstacles in
the road ahead.

18   And that is where science fiction comes in.

19   Not all science fiction, of course. Theodore Sturgeon, one of
the outstanding practitioners in the field, once said to a group of
fans, "Nine-tenths of science fiction is crud." There was a startled

gasp from the audience and he went on, "But why not? Nine-tenths of everything is crud." Including mainstream literature, of course.

20   It must be understood, then, that I am talking of the one-tenth (or possibly less) of science fiction that is not crud.

21   This means you will have to take my word for what follows, if you are not yourself an experienced science-fiction fan. The nonfan or even the mild fan with occasional experience in the field is almost certain to have been exposed only to the crud, which is, alas, of high visibility. He sees the comic strips, the monster movies, the pale TV fantasies. He never sees the better magazines and paperbacks where the science-fiction writers of greatest repute are to be found.

22   So let's see—

23   In 1940 there was endless talk about Fascism, Communism, and Democracy, talk that must have varied little in actual content concerning the conflicts of freedom and authority, of race, religion, and patriotism, from analogous discussions carried on in fifth and fourth centuries B.C. Greece. In 1940, when the Nazis were everywhere victorious, such talk might well have been considered important. It might plausibly have been argued that these discussions dealt with the great issues of the century.

24   And what was science fiction talking about? Well, in the May 1941 issue of *Astounding Science Fiction*, there appeared a story called "Solution Unsatisfactory" by Anson MacDonald (real name, Robert A. Heinlein), which suggested that the United States might put together a huge scientific project designed to work out a nuclear weapon that would end World War II. It then went on, carefully and thoughtfully, to consider the nuclear stalemate into which the world would consequently be thrown. At about the same time, John W. Campbell, Jr., editor of the magazine, was saying, in print, that the apparent issues of the war were, in a sense, trivial, since nuclear energy was on the point of being tamed and that this would so change the world that what then seemed life-and-death differences in philosophy would prove unimportant.

25   Well, who were the thinkers who, in 1940, were considering the nuclear stalemate? What generals were planning for a world in which each major power had nuclear bombs? What political scientists were thinking of a situation in which no matter how hot the rhetoric between competing great powers, any war between them would have to stay cold—not through consideration of fine points of economics or morals, but over the brutal fact that a nuclear stalemate cannot be broken, short of world suicide?

26   These thoughts, which were, after all, the truly relevant ideas on 1940's horizon, were reserved to science-fiction writers.

27   Nowadays, articles on ecology are in great demand, and it is quite fashionable to talk of population and pollution and of all the vast changes they may bring about. It is easy to do so now. Rachel Carson started it, most people would say, with her *Silent Spring*. But did anyone precede her?

28   Well, in the June, July, and August 1952 issues of *Galaxy*, there appeared a three-part serial, "Gravy Planet," by Frederik Pohl and Cyril Kornbluth, which is a detailed picture of an enormously overpopulated world from almost every possible aspect. In the February 1956 issue of *Fantasy and Science Fiction*, there appeared "Census Takers" by Frederik Pohl in which it is (ironically) suggested that the time will come when one of the chief duties of census takers will be to shoot down every tenth (or fourteenth, or eighth, depending on the population increase in the past decade) person they count, as the only means of keeping the population under control.

29   What sociologist (not now, but twenty years ago) was clamoring in print over the overwhelming effect of population increase? What government functionary (not now, but twenty years ago) was getting it clearly through his head that there existed no social problem that did not depend for its cure, *first of all*, on a cessation of population growth? (Surely not President Eisenhower, who piously stated that if there was one problem in which the government must not interfere, it was the matter of birth control. He changed his mind later; I'll give him credit for that.) What psychologist or philosopher (not now, but twenty years ago) was pointing out that if population continued to increase, there was no hope for human freedom or dignity under any circumstances?

30   Such thoughts were pretty largely reserved, twenty years ago, to science-fiction writers.

31   There are many people (invariably those who know nothing about science fiction) who think that because men have reached the moon, science has caught up with science fiction and that science-fiction writers have "nothing to write about."

32   They would be surprised to know that the mere act of reaching the moon was outdated in science fiction in the 1920s and that no reputable science-fiction writer has been excited by such a little thing in nearly half a century.

33   In the July 1939 issue of *Astounding Science Fiction*, there appeared a story called "Trends," written by myself while I was still

a teenager. It did indeed deal with the first flights to the moon, which I put in the period between 1973 and 1978. (I underestimated the push that would be given rocket research by World War II.) My predictions on the details of the beginnings of space exploration were ludicrously wrong, but none of that represented the point of the story, anyway.

34   What made the story publishable was the social background I presented for the rocket flights. In my story, I pictured strong popular opposition to the notion of space travel.

35   Many years later it was pointed out to me that in all the voluminous literature about space travel, either fictional or nonfictional, no such suggestion had ever before been broached. The world was always pictured as wildly and unanimously enthusiastic.

36   Well, where in 1939 was there the engineer or the industrialist who was taking into serious account the necessity of justifying the expense and risk of space exploration? Where was the engineer or the industrialist who was soberly considering the possibility of space exploration?

37   Such thoughts were largely reserved for the science-fiction writer and for a few engineers, who in almost every case were science-fiction fans—Willy Ley and Wernher von Braun, to name a couple.

38   And where does science fiction stand today?

39   It is more popular than ever and has gained a new respectability. Dozens of courses in it are being given in dozens of colleges. Literary figures have grown interested in it as a branch of the art. And, of course, the very growth in popularity tends to dilute and weaken it.

40   It has grown sufficiently popular and respectable, since the days of Sputnik, for people to wish to enter it as a purely literary field. And once that becomes a motive, the writers don't need to know science anymore. To write purely literary science fiction, one returns to the "eternal verities" but surrounds them with some of the verbiage of science fiction, together with a bit of the new stylistic experimentation one comes across in the mainstream and with some of the explicit sex that is now in fashion.

41   And this is what some people in science fiction call the "new wave."

42   To me, it seems that the new wave merely attempts to reduce real science fiction to the tasteless pap of the mainstream.

43   New-wave science fiction can be interesting, daring, even fascinating, if it is written well enough, but if the author knows no

science, the product is no more valuable for its content of relevant ideas than is the writing outside science fiction.

44   Fortunately, the real science fiction—those stories that deal with scientific ideas and their impact on the future as written by someone knowledgeable in science—still exists and will undoubtedly continue to exist as long as mankind does (which, alas, may not be long).

45   This does not mean that every science-fiction story is good prediction or is necessarily intended to be a prediction at all, or that very good science-fiction stories might not deal with futures that cannot reasonably be expected to come to pass.

46   That does not matter. The point is that the habit of looking sensibly toward the future, the habit of assuming change and trying to penetrate beyond the fact of change to its effect and to the new problems it will introduce, the habit of accepting change as now more important to mankind than those dreary eternal verities, is to be found only in science fiction or in those serious nonfictional discussions of the future by people who, almost always, are or have been deeply interested in science fiction.

47   For instance, while ordinary literature deals merry-go-round-wise with the white-black racial dilemma in the United States, I await the science-fiction story that will seriously consider the kind of society America might be attempting to rebuild *after* the infinitely costly racial war we are facing—a war that may destroy our world influence and our internal affluence. Perhaps such a story, sufficiently well thought out and written, may force those who read it into a contemplation of the problem from a new and utterly relevant angle.

48   To see what I mean, ask yourself how many of those, north and south, who blithely talked abolition and secession in the 1850s in terms of pure rhetoric might not have utterly changed their attitudes and gotten down to sober realities if they could have foreseen the exact nature of the Civil War and of the Reconstruction that followed and could have understood that none of the torture of the 1860s and 1870s would in the least solve the problem of white-and-black after all.

49   So read this magazine and others of the sort by all means, and follow the clash of stock ideas as an amusing intellectual game. Or read Plato or Sophocles and follow the same clash in more readable prose. But if you want the real ideas, the ideas that count today and may even count tomorrow, the ideas for which Aristotle offers little real help, or Senator X or Commissar Y either, then read science fiction.

CONSIDERATIONS

Author Asimov claims that literature is a "vehicle of ideas" (paragraph 12), and that science fiction is the vehicle of explaining scientific fact that he calls "change" (paragraphs 13-14). Are there no "changes" other than those brought about by scientific discovery? Is all the rest of society basically static, unchanging? Do you agree that science fiction is in its own class, judged by standards apart from those applied to other forms of fiction writing?

Asimov supports the thesis of his argument with a series of examples, connected by repeating "These thoughts . . . were reserved to science-fiction writers." Cite the connecting paragraphs. How effective is Asimov's exemplification? Does he convince you that the eternal verities of Aristotle, Homer, and, presumably, Chaucer and Shakespeare et al. are "dreary" in contrast to the subject matter of science fiction? Why is the series of examples in paragraphs 22-37 a good method of development for Asimov?

Do you agree that if we define science fiction in the context Asimov explains ("real science fiction—those stories that deal with scientific ideas and their impact on the future as written by someone knowledgeable in science" (paragraph 47), it can penetrate beyond the factual, immediate changes of the present and give mankind a truly probable view of the future?

VOCABULARY

- (3) **Homeric**   imposing or heroic style
- (8) **plausible**   having an appearance of truth; seemingly credible, believable
- (8) **consensus**   general agreement; majority opinion
- (11) **pontificates**   speaks in a pompous or dogmatic manner
- (13) **verities**   things that are true
- (29) **clamoring**   raising an outcry
- (29) **cessation**   end of a trend or action
- (35) **voluminous**   enough material to fill many volumes
- (35) **broached**   mentioned or suggested for the first time

Grammar for Today

BERGEN EVANS

1   In 1747 Samuel Johnson issued a plan for a new dictionary of the English language. It was supported by the most distinguished printers of the day and was dedicated to the model of all correctness, Philip Dormer Stanhope, Fourth Earl of Chesterfield. Such a book, it was felt, was urgently needed to "fix" the language, to arrest its "corruption" and "decay," a degenerative process which, then as now, was attributed to the influence of "the vulgar" and which, then as now, it was a mark of superiority and elegance to decry. And Mr. Johnson seemed the man to write it. He had an enormous knowledge of Latin, deep piety, and dogmatic convictions. He was also honest and intelligent, but the effect of these lesser qualifications was not to show until later.

2   Oblig'd by hunger and request of friends, Mr. Johnson was willing to assume the role of linguistic dictator. He was prepared to "fix" the pronunciation of the language, "preserve the purity" of its idiom, brand "impure" words with a "note of infamy," and secure the whole "from being overrun by . . . low terms."

3   There were, however, a few reservations. Mr. Johnson felt it necessary to warn the oversanguine that "Language is the work of man, a being from whom permanence and stability cannot be derived." English "was not formed from heaven . . . but was produced by necessity and enlarged by accident." It had, indeed, been merely

"thrown together by negligence" and was in such a state of confusion that its very syntax could no longer "be taught by general rules, but [only] by special precedents."

4   In 1755 the *Dictionary* appeared. The noble patron had been given a great deal more immortality than he had bargained for by the vigor of the kick Johnson had applied to his backside as he booted him overboard. And the *Plan* had been replaced by the *Preface*, a sadder but very much wiser document.

5   Eight years of "sluggishly treading the track of the alphabet" had taught Johnson that the hopes of "fixing" the language and preserving its "purity" were but "the dreams of a poet doomed at last to wake a lexicographer." In "the boundless chaos of living speech," so copious and energetic in its disorder, he had found no guides except "experience and analogy." Irregularities were "inherent in the tongue" and could not be "dismissed or reformed" but must be permitted "to remain untouched." "Uniformity must be sacrificed to custom . . . in compliance with a numberless majority" and "general agreement." One of the pet projects of the age had been the establishment of an academy to regulate and improve style. "I hope," Johnson wrote in the Preface, that if "it should be established . . . the spirit of English liberty will hinder or destroy [it.]"

6   At the outset of the work he had flattered himself, he confessed, that he would reform abuses and put a stop to alterations. But he had soon discovered that "sounds are too volatile and subtle for legal restraints" and that "to enchain syllables and to lash the wind are equally undertakings of pride unwilling to measure its desires by its strength." For "the causes of change in language are as much superior to human resistance as the revolutions of the sky or the intumescence of the tide."

7   There had been an even more profound discovery: that grammarians and lexicographers "do not form, but register the language; do not teach men how they should think, but relate how they have hitherto expressed their thoughts." And with this statement Johnson ushered in the rational study of linguistics. He had entered on his task a medieval pedant. He emerged from it a modern scientist.

8   Of course his discoveries were not strikingly original. Horace had observed that use was the sole arbiter and norm of speech and Montaigne had said that he who would fight custom with grammar was a fool. Doubtless thousands of other people had at one time or another perceived and said the same thing. But Johnson introduced a new principle. Finding that he could not lay down rules, he gave

actual examples to show meaning and form. He offered as authority illustrative quotations, and in so doing established that language is what usage makes it and that custom, in the long run, is the ultimate and only court of appeal in linguistic matters.

9   This principle, axiomatic today in grammar and lexicography, seems to exasperate a great many laymen who, apparently, find two hundred and five years too short a period in which to grasp a basic idea. They insist that there are absolute standards of correctness in speech and that these standards may be set forth in a few simple rules. To a man, they believe, of course, that they speak and write "correctly" and they are loud in their insistence that others imitate them.

10   It is useless to argue with such people because they are not, really, interested in language at all. They are interested solely in demonstrating their own superiority. Point out to them—as has been done hundreds of times—that forms which they regard as "corrupt," "incorrect," and "vulgar" have been used by Shakespeare, Milton, and the Bible and are used daily by 180 million Americans and accepted by the best linguists and lexicographers, and they will coolly say, "Well, if they differ from me, they're wrong."

11   But if usage is not the final determinant of speech, what is? Do the inhabitants of Italy, for example, speak corrupt Latin or good Italian? Is Spanish superior to French? Would the Breton fisherman speak better if he spoke Parisian French? Can one be more fluent in Outer Mongolian than in Inner Mongolian? One has only to ask such questions in relation to languages other than one's own, languages within which our particular snobberies and struggles for prestige have no stake, to see the absurdity of them.

12   The language that we do speak, if we are to accept the idea of "corruption" and "decay" in language, is a horribly decayed Anglo-Saxon, grotesquely corrupted by Norman French. Furthermore, since Standard English is a development of the London dialect of the fourteenth century, our speech, by true aristocratic standards, is woefully middle-class, commercial, and vulgar. And American speech is lower middle-class, reeking of counter and till. Where else on earth, for instance, would one find crime condemned because it didn't *pay*!

13   In more innocent days a great deal of time was spent in wondering what was the "original" language of mankind, the one spoken in Eden, the language of which all modern tongues were merely degenerate remnants. Hector Boethius tells us that James I of Scot-

land was so interested in this problem that he had two children reared with a deaf and dumb nurse on an island in order to see what language they would "naturally" speak. James thought it would be Hebrew, and in time, to his great satisfaction, it was reported that the children were speaking Hebrew!

14   Despite this experiment, however, few people today regard English as a corruption of Hebrew. But many seem to think it is a corruption of Latin and labor mightily to make it conform to this illusion. It is they and their confused followers who tell us that we can't say "I am mistaken" because translated into Latin this would mean "I am misunderstood," and we can't say "I have enjoyed myself" unless we are egotistical or worse.

15   It is largely to this group—most of whom couldn't read a line of Latin at sight if their lives depended on it—that we owe our widespread bewilderment concerning *who* and *whom*. In Latin the accusative or dative form would always be used, regardless of the word's position in the sentence, when the pronoun was the object of a verb or a preposition. But in English, for at least four hundred years, this simply hasn't been so. When the pronoun occurs at the beginning of a question, people who speak natural, fluent, literary English use the nominative, regardless. They say "Who did you give it to?" not "Whom did you give it to?" But the semiliterate, intimidated and bewildered, are mouthing such ghastly utterances as a recent headline in a Chicago newspaper: WHOM'S HE KIDDING?

16   Another group seems to think that in its pure state English was a Laputan tongue, with logic as its guiding principle. Early members of this sect insisted that *unloose* could only mean "to tie up," and present members have compelled the gasoline industry to label its trucks *Flammable* under the disastrous insistence, apparently, that the old *Inflammable* could only mean "not burnable."

17   It is to them, in league with the Latinists, that we owe the bogy of the double negative. In all Teutonic languages a doubling of the negative merely emphasizes the negation. But we have been told for a century now that two negatives make a positive, though if they do and it's merely a matter of logic, then three negatives should make a negative again. So that if "It doesn't make no difference" is wrong merely because it includes two negatives, then "It doesn't never make no difference" ought to be right again. Both of these groups, in their theories at least, ignore our idiom. Yet idiom—those expressions which defy all logic but are the very essence of a tongue—plays a large part in English. We go to school and college, but we go to *the* university. We buy two dozen eggs but a couple *of* dozen.

Good and can mean *very* ("I am good and mad!") and "a hot cup of coffee" means that the coffee, not the cup, is to be hot. It makes a world of difference to a condemned man whether his reprieve is *upheld* or *held up*.

18   There are thousands of such expressions in English. They are the "irregularities" which Johnson found "inherent in the tongue" and which his wisdom perceived could not and should not be removed. Indeed, it is in the recognition and use of these idioms that skillful use of English lies.

19   Many words in the form that is now mandatory were originally just mistakes, and many of these mistakes were forced into the language by eager ignoramuses determined to make it conform to some notion of their own. The *s* was put in island, for instance, in sheer pedantic ignorance. The second *r* doesn't belong in *trousers*, nor the *g* in *arraign*, nor the *t* in deviltry, nor the *n* in *passenger* and *messenger*. Nor, so far as English is concerned, does the first *c* in *arctic* which so many people twist their mouths so strenuously to pronounce.

20   And grammar is as "corrupted" as spelling or pronunciation. "You are" is as gross a solecism as "me am." It's recent, too; you won't find it in the Authorized Version of the Bible. *Lesser, nearer,* and *more* are grammatically on a par with *gooder*. *Crowed* is the equivalent of *knowed* or *growed*, and *caught* and *dug* (for *catched* and *digged*) are as "corrupt" as *squoze* for *squeezed* or *snoze* for *sneezed*.

21   Fortunately for our peace of mind most people are quite content to let English conform to English, and they are supported in their sanity by modern grammarians and linguists.

22   Scholars agree with Puttenham (1589) that a language is simply speech "fashioned to the common understanding and accepted by consent." They believe that the only "rules" that can be stated for a language are codified observations. They hold, that is, that language is the basis of grammar, not the other way round. They do not believe that any language can become "corrupted" by the linguistic habits of those who speak it. They do not believe that anyone who is a native speaker of a standard language will get into any linguistic trouble unless he is misled by snobbishness or timidity or vanity.

23   He may, of course, if his native language is English, speak a form of English that marks him as coming from a rural or an unread group. But if he doesn't mind being so marked, there's no reason why he should change. Johnson retained a Staffordshire burr in his

speech all his life. And surely no one will deny that Robert Burns's rustic dialect was just as good as a form of speech as, and in his mouth infinitely better as a means of expression than, the "correct" English spoken by ten million of his southern contemporaries.

24   The trouble is that people are no longer willing to be rustic or provincial. They all want to speak like educated people, though they don't want to go to the trouble of becoming truly educated. They want to believe that a special form of socially acceptable and financially valuable speech can be mastered by following a few simple rules. And there is no lack of little books that offer to supply the rules and promise "correctness" if the rules are adhered to. But, of course, these offers are specious because you don't speak like an educated person unless you are an educated person, and the little books, if taken seriously, will not only leave the lack of education showing but will expose the pitiful yearning and the basic vulgarity as well, in such sentences as "Whom are you talking about?"

25   As a matter of fact, the educated man uses at least three languages. With his family and his close friends, on the ordinary, unimportant occasions of daily life, he speaks, much of the time, a monosyllabic sort of shorthand. On more important occasions and when dealing with strangers in his official or business relations, he has, a more formal speech, more complete, less allusive, politely qualified, wisely reserved. In addition he has some acquaintance with the literary speech of his language. He understands this when he reads it, and often enjoys it, but he hesitates to use it. In times of emotional stress hot fragments of it may come out of him like lava, and in times of feigned emotion, as when giving a commencement address, cold, greasy gobbets of it will ooze forth.

26   The linguist differs from the amateur grammarian in recognizing all of these variations and gradations in the language. And he differs from the snob in doubting that the speech of any one small group among the language's more than 300 million daily users constitutes a model for all the rest to imitate.

27   The methods of the modern linguist can be illustrated by the question of the grammatical number of *none*. Is it singular or plural? Should one say "None of them is ready" or "None of them are ready"?

28   The prescriptive grammarians are emphatic that it should be singular. The Latinists point out that *nemo*, the Latin equivalent, is singular. The logicians triumphantly point out that *none* can't be more than one and hence can't be plural.

29   The linguist knows that he hears "None of them are ready" every day, from people of all social positions, geographical areas,

and degrees of education. He also hears "None is." Furthermore, literature informs him that both forms were used in the past. From Malory (1450) to Milton (1650) he finds that *none* was treated as a singular three times for every once that it was treated as a plural. That is, up to three hundred years ago men usually said *None is.* From Milton to 1917, *none* was used as a plural seven times for every four times it was used as a singular. That is, in the past three hundred years men often said *None is,* but they said *None are* almost twice as often. Since 1917, however, there has been a noticeable increase in the use of the plural, so much so that today *None are* is the preferred form.

30   The descriptive grammarian, therefore, says that while *None is* may still be used, it is becoming increasingly peculiar. This, of course, will not be as useful to one who wants to be cultured in a hurry as a short, emphatic permission or prohibition. But it has the advantage of describing English as it is spoken and written here and now and not as it ought to be spoken in some Cloud-Cuckoo-Land.

31   The descriptive grammarian believes that a child should be taught English, but he would like to see the child taught the English actually used by his educated contemporaries, not some pedantic, theoretical English designed chiefly to mark the imagined superiority of the designer.

32   He believes that a child should be taught the parts of speech, for example. But the child should be told the truth—that these are functions of use, not some quality immutably inherent in this or that word. Anyone, for instance, who tells a child—or anyone else— that *like* is used in English only as a preposition has grossly misinformed him. And anyone who complains that its use as a conjunction is a corruption introduced by Winston cigarettes ought, in all fairness, to explain how Shakespeare, Keats, and the translators of the Authorized Version of the Bible came to be in the employ of the R. J. Reynolds Tobacco Company.

33   Whether formal grammar can be taught to advantage before the senior year of high school is doubtful; most studies—and many have been made—indicate that it can't. But when it is taught, it should be the grammar of today's English, not the obsolete grammar of yesterday's prescriptive grammarians. By that grammar, for instance, *please* in the sentence "Please reply" is the verb and *reply* its object. But by modern meaning *reply* is the verb, in the imperative, and *please* is merely a qualifying word meaning "no discourtesy intended," a mollifying or deimperatival adverb, or whatever you will, but not the verb.

34   This is a long way from saying "Anything goes," which is the

charge that, with all the idiot repetition of a needle stuck in a groove, the uninformed ceaselessly chant against modern grammarians. But to assert that usage is the sole determinant in grammar, pronunciation, and meaning is *not* to say that anything goes. Custom is illogical and unreasonable, but it is also tyrannical. The least deviation from its dictates is usually punished with severity. And because this is so, children should be taught what the current and local customs in English are. They should not be taught that we speak a bastard Latin or a vocalized logic. And they should certainly be disabused of the stultifying illusion that after God had given Moses the Commandments He called him back and pressed on him a copy of Woolley's *Handbook of English Grammar.*

35   The grammarian does not see it as his function to "raise the standards" set by Franklin, Lincoln, Melville, Mark Twain, and hundreds of millions of other Americans. He is content to record what they said and say.

36   Insofar as he serves as a teacher, it is his business to point out the limits of the permissible, to indicate the confines within which the writer may exercise his choice, to report that which custom and practice have made acceptable. It is certainly not the business of the grammarian to impose his personal taste as the only norm of good English, to set forth his prejudices as the ideal standard which everyone should copy. That would be fatal. No one person's standards are broad enough for that.

CONSIDERATIONS

Evans classifies himself a "modern grammarian." He refutes the charges of traditional grammarians who accuse linguists of the "modern" school of practicing an "anything goes" theory in regard to usage. What are the basic philosophies and teachings of Evans's school? What have they in common with Dr. Johnson and his eighteenth-century dictionary?

In paragraph 1 Evans subtly introduces a tone of ironic humor that runs as an undercurrent throughout the article. In the first paragraph he juxtaposes certain "qualifications" of Dr. Johnson in such a way as to produce a tongue-in-cheek verbal picture: the famous lexicographer's honesty and intelligence are said to be of lesser importance initially than his skill in Latin, "dogmatic convictions," and "piety." Find several other examples of irony, allusion, and juxtaposition that impart a unique flavor to a subject that traditionally (and regrettably) is approached with an absolute seriousness and pedantic, dry style.

What is the value of the study of grammar? Is there any lasting importance to it, or is its proper place only within the English classroom? Will you be at all affected by having learned basic facts about the function and form of the English language? Expand your opinions along these lines into an essay. Use personal experiences as examples.

VOCABULARY

(3)	oversanguine	overly pleased or confident
(5)	lexicographer	the writer or compiler of a dictionary
(5)	copious	abundant
(6)	volatile	difficult to capture or hold permanently
(6)	intumescence	swelling
(7)	pedant	a formalist (or any person) who overemphasizes rules or minor details
(9)	axiomatic	having the nature of a self-evident truth
(16)	Laputan	reference to a flying island in *Gulliver's Travels* whose inhabitants were devoted to visionary projects
(20)	solecism	an ungrammatical combination of words in a sentence
(24)	provincial	unsophisticated, countrified
(24)	specious	having a false look of truth or genuineness
(25)	allusive	containing implied or indirect references
(28)	prescriptive	going by the rules
(33)	mollifying	softening
(33)	disabused	set right, freed from error or fallacy
(34)	stultifying	stupid; foolish or absurd

Exposition

EXPOSITION

The primary function of exposition is to present information in order to explain or define. Whenever we explain anything to anyone, we are using exposition (as opposed to persuasion): exposition provides information. You may be explaining the method of operation in the shop where you work on weekends (here the stress is on understanding the world around us in a nonemotional fashion) or you may define the meaning of a word or phenomenon. Children ask us questions (as do adults) that virtually demand expository answers: What is that? What is it used for? How come this or that did or didn't happen? Where did it come from? Where are you going?

Exposition is considered one of the four types of prose writing (argumentation, narration, and description are the others). It fulfills the purpose of explaining or informing by

- stating facts
- explaining a process
- clarifying an object or an idea

Exposition comes closest to its pure form in encyclopedias and textbooks. Straightforward exposition is difficult to write. And it may be a major implement in supporting argumentation, but it can also be pretty dull by itself. Expository writing benefits greatly from illustration, description, and narration. Reports are expository; however, those that can be read and understood by the layman are enhanced by using analysis, examples, and statistics.

PRACTICE

1. In an expository essay explain one of the three: how the Watergate scandal occurred; what was involved in giving eighteen-year-olds the right to vote; or what factors were responsible for a particularly poor (or unusually high) voter turnout in a recent election.

2. Find several paragraphs that you consider to be pure exposition and show what rhetorical devices are used to develop the theme. (A well-written recipe is a fine example; see *Gourmet* magazine or a good cookbook.)

3. In an expository essay explain why you hold a particular belief or advocate a certain position on some current issue.

The Drug Explosion

In this essay the author presents information that answers certain questions about drug use and explains some of the problems related to it. Paragraph 6 is almost pure exposition; that is, it provides specific information without argumentation.

Write a paragraph in which you explain a certain drug problem. Your purpose is to state factual information *without* setting up a pro or con argument.

The Dark Heart of American History

In writing exposition one uses many of the same devices as in writing argumentation. For example, in this essay the author uses analysis, exemplification, comparison and contrast, and definition to illustrate his exposition. Write an expository essay in which you use some of these methods. The purpose of this essay is to explain or clarify some idea or point (or object). Following are some suggested topics:

How myths originate

The major factors responsible for the formation of Women's Lib

A report on ESP experiments

Problems of a college freshman

The American family's diet

Methods of predicting the weather

College slang

Something about English

After reading this essay, do further research on Old English, Middle English, or Early Modern English and write an expository essay based on your research.

A Technology of Behavior

Compare and contrast this type of exposition with that in the previous essay. Write a report in which you illustrate the differences in approach and development.

Privacy

In this essay the author explores the concept of privacy and provides historical background. Write an expository essay in which you trace the origin of an idea or opinion you hold. For example:

There is/is not a God.

Handling toads causes warts.

Men are better drivers than women.

- One of the most common forms of exposition is the explanation of a process. Write a paragraph in which you explain a particular process; for example:

How a phonograph record works

How to study for exams

How to bake bread

- Locate the paragraphs in one of the essays in this section that you consider to be pure exposition and identify the characteristics that classify it as such.

For examples of individual paragraphs using *exposition,* see p.67, ¶13, p.71, ¶30, p.316, ¶30–31, p.351, ¶13, p.353, ¶18, p.406, ¶1–5.

The Drug Explosion

JOEL FORT, M.D.

1   If you pick twenty adults at random, the odds are that fifteen of them drink moderately, two are problem drinkers and one is a desperate alcoholic. Two who use alcohol are also using marijuana, a couple are taking tranquilizers on doctors' orders and one or two have been popping barbiturates to relieve insomnia and are perilously close to addiction. Three or four have taken amphetamines to stay awake or to lose weight and nearly all of them drink caffeine, another stimulant. Ten or twelve of this group of twenty continue to smoke tobacco even after the medical hazards of that habit have been amply documented. One has probably taken acid or mescaline. The children of some have sniffed glue or carbon tet for kicks (thereby risking brain and liver damage), more smoke pot and some have had an LSD trip. The drug culture, as the newspapers call it, doesn't just belong to the kids; everyone's in it together.

2   The hard figures on drug use in America today are dramatic. Taking our society's favorite drugs in order of their popularity, alcohol heads the list—and has ever since Colonial times. Just twenty years after the Pilgrims landed, William Bradford was fretting in his diaries about the number of drunks running around Plymouth; and in the three centuries since, the problem has only grown with the population, quite in spite of religious disapproval, temperance movements and even a constitutional amendment. In 1970, in fact,

Originally appeared in PLAYBOY Magazine; copyright ©1972 by Playboy. Dr. Fort is founder, National Center for Solving Special Social and Health Problems—FORT HELP, San Francisco and author, *Alcohol: Our Biggest Drug Problem* and *The Pleasure Seekers*.

[margin annotations: Class; This; Top S Exmp]

23,400 highway fatalities were traceable to alcohol. That is sixty-four every day: almost three every hour.

3   WARNING: THE SURGEON GENERAL HAS DETERMINED THAT CIGA-   *Tran*
RETTE SMOKING IS DANGEROUS TO YOUR HEALTH. But the warnings are
recent and a cultural habit as widespread as smoking is not easily
changed. Among the 51,300,000 Americans who still smoke, 250,000
can be expected to die from it this year. And the prospects are for
more of the same—250,000 deaths every year until the end of this
century.

4   If there is one drug problem today that remains practically   *Tone*
invisible, it's pill taking. Chiefly through television, we've grown
accustomed to the notion that the only way to deal with those
hammers pounding in our heads, lightning bolts shooting into our   *Allus*
spines and gremlins bowling in our stomachs is to take a pill; and in
the past decade or so, we have extended that practice to include a
considerable variety of psychological ailments as well. Today
35,000,000 Americans use sedatives, stimulants or tranquilizers,
mostly obtained legally through their doctors. Despite this medical
supervision, between 500,000 and 1,000,000 of these people have
become abusers. Manufacturers, meanwhile, continue to produce
such pills abundantly and with apparent enthusiasm, turning out
roughly 80,000 pounds of amphetamines and 1,000,000 pounds of
barbiturates in 1970 alone. Some have bizarre distribution routes:
One respectable firm was discovered by the House Select Committee on Crime to be shipping to a golf hole in Tijuana, from which
the product returned to the United States and entered the black
market. Perhaps 100,000 young people who are introduced to am-
phetamine-based drugs in this way graduate to methamphetamine
(speed), which is injected into the veins like heroin and can cause
rapid mind deterioration, while chronic abuse produces severe
symptoms of paranoid psychosis. Some meth freaks graduate easily   *Slang*
to heroin, seemingly the quickest way to soothe a frantic speed trip.

5   Unlike alcohol, tobacco or speed, marijuana apparently has no
permanent and only a few transitory side effects—yet in many
states, the penalties for simple possession are severe. But all the
legal sanctions against it have had about the same effect that Prohi-   *Angy*
bition had on our drinking habits. When Harry Anslinger first convinced Congress in the mid-Thirties that pot was an evil killer weed,
it was being used almost exclusively by Mexican-Americans and
blacks. But it has flourished under oppression: In the past five years,
it has spread throughout the middle class, and right now some
twenty to thirty million people have tried it, with perhaps ten million being regular users.

6   Psychedelic-hallucinogenic drugs, credited for a brief genera- *Expo*
tion of star-wandering rock music and bright melting poster art, are
generally less popular now than they were a few years ago. Nonetheless, it's estimated that 1,000,000 Americans have tried LSD, mescaline or similar psychedelics. The number of regular psychedelic users is relatively small in comparison with drinkers or grass smokers,
but there are still enough of them—and they still manage to have
enough bad trips—to keep acid-rescue telephone services alive and
busy in almost every major city.

7   There are at least 200,000 (and perhaps as many as 400,000)
junkies in the nation today, making heroin addiction one of the
smallest yet most sensationalized of our drug problems. Recently,
the heroin habit has been changing its nature: Where most addicts
used to be poor and black, now a large percentage come from the
white middle class. More depressing: Younger children are becoming involved. New York City has had a rash of heroin-overdose
deaths of teenagers.

8   Some doctors are predicting a heroin epidemic. Others, such as
Dr. Helen Nowlis of the U. S. Office of Education and Professor
Samuel Pearlman of New York's Inter-University Drug Survey
Council, insist that students are very aware of the perils of heroin
and most want nothing to do with it. What is undeniable is that
many children who should know better are playing around with
heroin needles.

9   There is no consistent antidrug movement; but there is a
strong ideological conflict over which drugs are socially acceptable
and which are not. On one side is the booze-and-trank-using group;   *Class /*
on the other side is the pot-and-psychedelic-using group. Conven-   *Desc*
tional wisdom classifies the first group as mostly older and conservative, the second as primarily young and radical. But the lines, if they
really exist, are being crossed: Some pot users are past forty, some
of the young are conservative and use drugs more commonly associated with the older generation. Barbiturates and amphetamines, on
the other hand, are not characterized by any identifiable patterns.
LSD, which reached the peak of its popularity in most colleges
around 1968 and has been declining ever since, is just beginning to
be a fad at some Southern universities; while at Swarthmore a student told *The New York Times* that "the jocks are getting into
drugs and all the freaks are going to alcohol." Meanwhile, conflict
continues to flourish on all levels: When the mayor's office of the
District of Columbia released a recent report on drug abuse in the
capital, it was rumored that one member of the committee that had
drafted the report lit a joint during the press conference and

smoked it in front of the reporters to dramatize his opposition to the study's anti-marijuana bias.

10   None of this is as new as most commentators seem to think. Drug taking in America goes back to the Indians' tobacco farms, **Narr** their occasional use of deliriants such as Jimson weed and the religious use of peyote and magic mushrooms. The first Pilgrims brought in ample rum and made it an integral part of the slave trade; alcohol excesses, some historians think, were actually widespread in England by the eighteenth century. In the second half of the nineteenth century, along with the Civil War, came a wave of morphine addiction and, soon after, patent medicines consisting mainly of alcohol often spiked with opium derivatives began hooking some of their many users. There was even a Hashish Club in New York City in the 1850s where writers and artists met to turn on and recount their visions to one another, while scholarly Fitz Hugh Ludlow was quite legally (there was no anti-pot law then) gathering the experiences for his famous *The Hasheesh Eater.* Around the turn of the century, a Harvard psychologist named not Timothy Leary but William James was dosing himself with nitrous oxide and discovering religious significance in the experiences so gained.

11   Nor is this peculiarly American. The earliest brewery, found in Egypt, is dated at 3700 B.C. and there is evidence that people used alcohol as far back as the Stone Age. Some paleolithic tribes in the Near East even buried their dead with marijuana plants, evidently with religious intent. Around the world, people continue to chew, smoke and drink every plant and shrub that alters their consciousness, provides temporary escape or increases their pleasure: There are more than 200,000,000 Cannabis (marijuana) users in the world today, for instance, and we have only a fraction of them in the United States.

12   What is unique about the American drug scene are (1) the **Class** accelerated rate at which changes are occurring, (2) the controversy over the use of drugs and (3) the increasing lack of discrimination shown by many in their choice of intoxicants and the amounts used. The main factor is the accelerated rate of change, which is also true of all other areas of our life these days and is creating the phenomenon known as future shock. But this cultural mutation, even without the dizzying speed at which it is occurring, would have to create problems in a society that is still flirting heavily with puritanism and **Meta** still tends to believe that all behavior is molded by punishment. The reaction of people in power to drugs, both those that are truly dangerous and those that are merely annoying to their own prejudices, has been the same: Make the drug takers uncomfortable.

When this doesn't work, the next step is more punishment. Harsher laws. Longer sentences. More narcotics agents. And when this in turn doesn't work, the next move is further escalation, and so on. But it's a solution that has created more problems than it has solved. Moreover, it hasn't worked.

13   The fallacy of the punishment theory is best illustrated by the heroin problem, which is small in terms of the number of individuals involved. A free society of 200,000,000 could easily tolerate and nullify the negative effects of our 200,000 junkies. Instead, they have been criminalized, thereby driving the price of their fix up from a few cents to $50 or more a day. Since few can afford that price, most are forced to steal or become prostitutes—and to earn $50 per day from underworld fences, a man must steal at least $100 worth of property. One hundred dollars times 200,000 addicts is $20,000,000 per day that gets stolen from the rest of us, and that is 7.3 billion dollars per year. Anybody in a large city with an apartment window facing a fire escape has learned the individual application of that figure. Alcohol prohibition produced even more expensive by-products in terms of the black market in that drug, the creation of organized crime and the foundation of the narcotics traffic. Not only did alcohol and pot prohibition increase the use of those drugs but the pot laws have caused countless harmless citizens to spend long unproductive periods behind bars in the company of professional criminals. *C∅E*

14   As society moves toward grudging admission that indiscriminate criminalization in this area just does not work, sporadic efforts are being made toward drug-abuse prevention through education. This, obviously, is part of the answer, but efforts so far have been shoddy. When evaluators employed by the National Coordinating Council on Drug Education examined over 100 educational films about drugs, they found 36 of them inaccurate. Mrs. Sue Boe, assistant vice-president of consumer affairs for the Pharmaceutical Manufacturers Association, commented recently that children frequently know more about drugs than their teachers (although neither know as much as they should), and Dr. Gelolo McHugh, formerly of Duke University, after giving a drug-information quiz to 60,000 citizens, commented that correct answers were no more frequent than chance; the subjects could have done as well closing their eyes and choosing at random. It is no surprise, in this context, that students at San Mateo High School in California, asked what celebrity they would trust as narrator of an anti-LSD film, overwhelmingly answered, "Nobody." *Exmp*

15   Intercepting drug shipments from abroad is held out as a pana-

cea by some. This motivated President Nixon's ill-fated Operation Intercept, which clogged the crossover points from Mexico three years ago, infuriated the people and government of that nation and finally had to be abandoned, as marijuana use continued to rise. If some method is ever found to stop the heroin shipments from Southeast Asia, Turkey and Mexico, which feed most of our junkie market at present, without resolving the root causes, the already-high prices will probably escalate further, a handful of addicts will die and most of them will steal more than ever to pay for $100 or $250 fixes.

Arg

16   Something obviously is wrong in our attempts to adjust to the global drug village—to face up to the arrival of marijuana habits from Mexico, speed and acid and downers from the laboratory, hashish cultism from Arabia, opiates from the Orient, peyote from our Indians, magic mushrooms from the ancient Aztecs.

17   It is hard to affix blame on anyone in particular. Senator Frank Moss recently suggested that we should investigate whether the hypnotic repetitions in the aspirin and other drug commercials on TV are conditioning us to seek a drug whenever we have a problem. This may be true, but people were getting stoned long before TV. Bert Donaldson, director of programs for emotionally disturbed children in Michigan, commented that many students are "actually bored to death in their classes"; others point to the boredom of much of our work in this industrialized world. ("Guys are always stoned," a Dodge auto-plant worker told *Time* magazine. "Either they're taking pills to keep awake or they're zonked on a joint they had on a break.") Considering the interminable Vietnam war, increasing air and water pollution, the continuing threat of a thermonuclear holocaust and the dehumanizing effect of our bureaucracies, there is much cause for people to feel nervous and to take something to calm down or to get away from it all.

C&E

18   The sinister fact is not that most citizens are taking drugs; people have always done that, although never as many or as much. The real terror implicit in our current drug culture is that so many, incredulous about official pronouncements, are experimenting, sometimes lethally, with very dangerous ones.

19   If the attempt to stop people from using all psychoactive drugs is hopeless, society nevertheless can and should try to persuade its members to use fewer drugs and safer ones. Libertarians from Jefferson and Mill to the present have emphasized that government has no business trying to enforce its notions of morality via police power—and there is something absurd and repulsive about a martini-

guzzling bureaucrat imprisoning a pot user. Ideally, government and such powerful paragovernmental institutions as the schools, churches, labor unions and businessmen's organizations should be using their influence to provide positive alternatives and to genuinely enlighten people instead of trying to get them to march to a particular morality; but the times often seem less ideal than ever. If we were more committed to actually solving the problem than to whipping the people who have it, we could have been seriously and creatively looking for real solutions for over a generation. But instead we have tried to beat one another into submission with drug laws that have no parallel in the free world and can only be duplicated in totalitarian societies.

CONSIDERATIONS

Fort believes that there is drug *use* and drug *abuse*. Does he convey this point of view in this article? Do you think he would favor legalization of marijuana? Why are there such widespread differences of opinion among "experts" in the field of drug use? (paragraph 8) Are behaviors modified by punishment? (paragraph 12)

Is Fort being facetious when he uses the expression "fretting about . . . the drunks" in paragraph 2? What is his attitude toward his subject? Cite examples to support your conclusion. He speaks as an expert, or authority, on drugs. Is his presentation inappropriate for the serious subject of drug abuse, or does it give needed perspective to the situation? Does he remain dispassionate in this article, or does he reveal his personal prejudices?

Present your views on the drug situation in essay form, including a discussion of the following questions. Do you think pills, alcohol, and marijuana will become more and more "acceptable," while hard drugs are forced deeper and deeper into the subculture syndrome of crime? Do you think the drug problem *can* be handled effectively?

VOCABULARY

(5) transitory   short-lived; brief

(10) peyote   a cactus, one of two species of mescal, from which the hallucinogenic drug, mescaline, is obtained

(13) nullify   to deprive of effectiveness

(15) panacea   a remedy for all problems and difficulties

(19) libertarians   persons who advocate liberty, especially in regard to personal conduct

The Dark Heart of American History

ARTHUR SCHLESINGER, JR.

1   The murders within five years of John F. Kennedy, Martin Luther King, Jr., and Robert F. Kennedy raise—or ought to raise—somber questions about the character of contemporary America. One such murder might be explained away as an isolated horror, unrelated to the inner life of our society. But the successive shootings, in a short time, of three men who greatly embodied the idealism of American life suggest not so much a fortuitous set of aberrations as an emerging pattern of response and action—a spreading and ominous belief in the efficacy of violence and the politics of the deed.

2   Yet, while each of these murders produced a genuine season of national mourning, none has produced a sustained season of national questioning. In every case, remorse has seemed to end, not as an incitement to self-examination, but as an escape from it. An orgy of sorrow and shame becomes an easy way of purging a bad conscience and returning as quickly as possible to business as usual.

3   "It would be . . . self-deceptive," President Johnson said after the shooting of Robert Kennedy, "to conclude from this act that our country is sick, that it has lost its balance, that it has lost its sense of direction, even its common decency. Two hundred million Americans did not strike down Robert Kennedy last night any more than they struck down John F. Kennedy in 1963 or Dr. Martin Luther King in April of this year."

4   I do not quarrel with these words. Of course two hundred million Americans did not strike down these men. Nor, in my judgment, is this a question of a "sick society" or of "collective guilt." I
do not know what such phrases mean, but I am certain that they do
not represent useful ways of thinking about our problem. Obviously
most Americans are decent and God-fearing people. Obviously
most Americans were deeply and honestly appalled by these atroc-
ities. Obviously most Americans rightly resent being told that they
were "guilty" of crimes they neither willed nor wished.

5   Still, it is not enough to dismiss the ideas of a sick society and
of collective guilt and suppose that such dismissal closes the question. For a problem remains—the problem of a contagion of political murder in the United States in the 1960s unparalleled in our
own history and unequaled today anywhere in the world. If we
minimize this problem, if we complacently say it is all the work of
lunatics and foreigners, that nothing is wrong and that our society is
beyond criticism, if we cry like Macbeth: "Thou canst not say I did
it; never shake Thy gory locks at me," then we lose all hope of
recovering control of the destructive impulse within. Then we will
only continue the downward spiral of social decomposition and
moral degradation.

6   Self-knowledge is the indispensable prelude to self-control; and
self-knowledge, for a nation as well as for an individual, begins with
history. We like to think of ourselves as a peaceful, tolerant, benign
people who have always lived under a government of laws and not
of men. And, indeed, respect for persons and for law has been one
characteristic strain in the American tradition. Most Americans
probably pay this respect most of their lives. Yet this is by no means
the only strain in our tradition. For we also have been a violent
people. When we refuse to acknowledge the existence of this other
strain, we refuse to see our nation as it is.

7   We began, after all, as a people who killed red men and enslaved black men. No doubt we often did this with a Bible and a
prayer book. But no nation, however righteous its professions, could
act as we did without burying deep in itself—in its customs, its
institutions, and its psyche—a propensity toward violence. However
much we pretended that Indians and Negroes were subhuman, we
really knew that they were God's children too.

8   Nor did we confine our violence to red men and black men.
We gained our freedom, after all, through revolution. The first
century after independence were years of incessant violence—wars,
slave insurrections, Indian fighting, urban riots, murders, duels,
beatings. Members of Congress went armed to the Senate and

House. In his first notable speech, in January 1838, before the
Young Men's Lyceum of Springfield, Illinois, Abraham Lincoln
named internal violence as the supreme threat to American political
institutions. He spoke of "the increasing disregard for law which
pervades the country; the growing disposition to substitute the wild
and furious passions, in lieu of the sober judgment of Courts; and
the worse than savage mobs, for the executive ministers of justice."
The danger to the American republic, he said, was not from foreign
invasion:

> At what point then is the approach of danger to be expected? I answer,
> if it ever reach us, it must spring up amongst us. It cannot come from
> abroad. If destruction be our lot, we must ourselves be its author and
> finisher. As a nation of freemen, we must live through all time, or die by
> suicide.

9   So the young Lincoln named the American peril—a peril he
did not fear to locate within the American breast. Indeed, the sad-
ness of America has been that our worst qualities have so often
been the other face of our best. Our commitment to morality, our
faith in experiment: these have been sources of America's greatness,
but they have also led Americans into our error. For our moralists
have sometimes condoned murder if the cause is deemed good; so
Emerson and Thoreau applauded John Brown of Osawatomie. And
our pragmatists have sometimes ignored the means if the result is
what they want. Moralism and pragmatism have not provided infal-
lible restraints on the destructive instinct.

10   America, Martin Luther King correctly said, has been "a
schizophrenic personality, tragically divided against herself." The
impulses of violence and civility continued after Lincoln to war
within the American breast. The insensate bloodshed of the Civil
War exhausted the national capacity for violence and left the nation emotionally and psychologically spent. For nearly a century
after Appomattox, we appeared on the surface the tranquil and
friendly people we still like to imagine ourselves to be. The amiabil-
ity of that society no doubt exerted a restraining influence. There
were still crazy individuals, filled with grievance, bitterness, and a
potential for violence. But most of the people expended their sickness in fantasy; the Guiteaus and Czolgoszs were the exception.
These years of stability, a stability fitfully recaptured after the First
World War, created the older generation's image of a "normal"
America.

11   Yet even in the kindly years we did not wholly eradicate the
propensity toward violence which history had hidden in the national
unconscious. In certain moods, indeed, we prided ourselves on our

violence; we almost considered it evidence of our virility. "Above all," cried Theodore Roosevelt, "let us shrink from no strife, moral or physical, within or without the nation, provided we are certain that the strife is justified." That fatal susceptibility always lurked under the surface, breaking out in Indian wars and vigilantism in the West, lynchings in the South, in labor riots and race riots and gang wars in the cities.

12   It is important to distinguish collective from individual violence—the work of mobs from the work of murderers; for the motive and the effect can be very different. There can, of course, be murder by a mob. But not all mobs aim at murder. Collective violence—rioting against what were considered illegal British taxes in Boston in 1773, or dangerous Papist influence sixty years later, or inequitable draft laws in New York in 1863, or unfair labor practices in Chicago in 1937—is more characteristically directed at conditions than at individuals. In many cases (though by no means all), the aim has been to protest rather than protect the status quo; and the historian is obliged to concede that collective violence, including the recent riots in black ghettos, has often quickened the disposition of those in power to redress just grievances. Extralegal group action, for better or worse, has been part of the process of American democracy. Violence, for better or worse, *does* settle some questions, and for the better. Violence secured American independence, freed the slaves, and stopped Hitler.

13   But this has ordinarily been the violence of a society. The individual who plans violence is less likely to be concerned with reforming conditions than with punishing persons. On occasion the purpose is to protect the status quo by destroying men who symbolize or threaten social change (a tactic which the anarchists soon began to employ in reverse). A difference exists in psychic color and content between spontaneous mass convulsions and the premeditated killing of individuals. The first signifies an unstable society, the second, a murderous society. America has exhibited both forms of violence.

14   Now in the third quarter of the twentieth century, violence has broken out with new ferocity in our country. What has given our old propensity new life? Why does the fabric of American civility no longer exert restraint? What now incites crazy individuals to act out their murderous dreams? What is it about the climate of this decade that suddenly encourages—that for some evidently legitimatizes—the relish for hate and the resort to violence? Why, according to the Federal Bureau of Investigation, have assaults with a gun increased 77 per cent in the four years from 1964 through 1967?

15   We talk about the legacy of the frontier. No doubt, the frontier has bequeathed us a set of romantic obsessions about six-shooters and gun fighters. But why should this legacy suddenly reassert itself in the 1960s?

16   We talk about the tensions of industrial society. No doubt the ever-quickening pace of social change depletes and destroys the institutions which make for social stability. But this does not explain why Americans shoot and kill so many more Americans than Englishmen kill Englishmen or Japanese kill Japanese. England, Japan, and West Germany are, next to the United States, the most heavily industrialized countries in the world. Together they have a population of 214 million people. Among these 214 million, there are 135 gun murders a year. Among the 200 million people of the United States there are 6,500 gun murders a year—about *forty-eight times* as many.

17   We talk about the fears and antagonisms generated by racial conflict. Unquestionably this has contributed to the recent increase in violence. The murders of Dr. King and Senator Kennedy seem directly traceable to ethnic hatreds. Whites and blacks alike are laying in arms, both sides invoking the needs of self-defense. Yet this explanation still does not tell us why in America today we are tending to convert political problems into military problems—problems of adjustment into problems of force.

18   The New Left tells us that we are a violent society because we are a capitalist society—that capitalism is itself institutionalized violence; and that life under capitalism inevitably deforms relations among men. This view would be more impressive if the greatest violence of man against man in this century had not taken place in noncapitalist societies—in Nazi Germany, in Stalinist Russia, in precapitalist Indonesia. The fact is that every form of society is in some sense institutionalized violence; man in society always gives up a measure of "liberty" and accepts a measure of authority.

19   We cannot escape that easily. It is not just that we were a frontier society or have become an industrial society or are a racist or a capitalist society; it is something more specific than that. Nor can we blame the situation on our gun laws, or the lack of them; though here possibly we are getting closer. There is no question, of course, that we need adequate federal gun laws. Statistics make it evident that gun controls have some effect. Sixty per cent of all murders in the United States are by firearms; and states with adequate laws—New Jersey, New York, Massachusetts, Rhode Island—have much lower rates of gun murder than states with no

laws or weak ones—Texas, Mississippi, Louisiana, Nevada.

20   Still, however useful in making it harder for potential murderers to get guns, federal gun legislation deals with the symptoms and not with the causes of our trouble. We must go further to account for the resurgence in recent years of our historical propensity toward violence.

21   One reason surely for the enormous tolerance of violence in contemporary America is the fact that our country has now been more or less continuously at war for a generation. The experience of war over a long period devalues human life and habituates people to killing. And the war in which we are presently engaged is far more brutalizing than was the Second World War or the Korean War. It is more brutalizing because the destruction we have wrought in Vietnam is so wildly out of proportion to any demonstrated involvement of our national security or any rational assessment of our national interest. In the other wars we killed for need. In this war we are killing beyond need, and, as we do so, we corrupt our national life. When violence is legally sanctioned for a cause in which people see no moral purpose, this is an obvious stimulus to individuals to use violence for what they may maniacally consider moral purposes of their own.

22   A second reason for the climate of violence in the United States is surely the zest with which the mass media, and especially television and film, dwell on violence. One must be clear about this. The mass media do *not* create violence. But they *reinforce* aggressive and destructive impulses, and they may well *teach* the morality as well as the methods of violence.

23   In recent years the movies and television have developed a pornography of violence far more demoralizing than the pornography of sex, which still seizes the primary attention of the guardians of civic virtue. Popular films of our day like *Rosemary's Baby* and *Bonnie and Clyde* imply a whole culture of human violation, psychological in one case, physical in the other. *Bonnie and Clyde*, indeed, was greatly admired for its blithe acceptance of the world of violence—an acceptance which almost became a celebration. Thus a student in a film course in San Francisco noted:

> There is a certain spirit that belongs to us. We the American people. It is pragmatic, rebellious, violent, joyous. It can create or kill. Everything about *Bonnie and Clyde* captures this spirit.

> John Brown was motivated by this spirit and it has scared the hell out of historians ever since. The Black Panthers have it. Cab drivers, musicians, used car salesmen and bus drivers understand it, but doctors, dentists and real estate salesmen don't.

24   Television is the most pervasive influence of all. The children of the electronic age sit hypnotized by the parade of killings, beatings, gunfights, knifings, maimings, brawls which flash incessantly across the tiny screen, and now in "living" color.

25   For a time, the television industry comforted itself with the theory that children listened to children's programs and that, if by any chance they saw programs for adults, violence would serve as a safety valve, offering a harmless outlet for pent-up aggressions: the more violence on the screen, the less in life. Alas, this turns out not to be necessarily so. As Dr. Wilbur Schramm, director of the Institute of Communication Research at Stanford has reported, children, even in the early elementary school years, view more programs designed for adults than for themselves; "above all, they prefer the more violent type of adult program including the Western, the adventure program, and the crime drama." Experiments show that such programs, far from serving as safety valves for aggression, attract children with high levels of aggression and stimulate them to seek overt means of acting out their aggressions. Evidence suggests that these programs work the same incitement on adults. And tele-violence does more than condition emotion and behavior. It also may attenuate people's sense of reality. Men murdered on the television screen ordinarily spring to life after the episode is over: all death is therefore diminished. A child asked a man last June where he was headed in his car. "To Washington," he said. "Why?" he asked. "To attend the funeral of Senator Kennedy." The child said, "Oh yeah—they shot him again." And such shooting may well condition the manner in which people approach the perplexities of existence. On television the hero too glibly resolves his problems by shooting somebody. The *Gunsmoke* ethos, however, is not necessarily the best way to deal with human or social complexity. It is hardly compatible with any kind of humane or libertarian democracy.

26   The problem of electronic violence raises difficult questions of prescription as well as of analysis. It would be fatal to restrain artistic exploration and portrayal, even of the most extreme and bitter aspects of human experience. No rational person wants to re-establish a reign of censorship or mobilize new Legions of Decency. Nor is there great gain in making the electronic media scapegoats for propensities which they reflect rather than create—propensities which spring from our history and our hearts.

27   Yet society retains a certain right of self-defense. Is it inconceivable that the television industry might work out forms of self-restraint? Beyond this, it should be noted that the networks and the stations do *not* own the airwaves; the nation does; and, if the indus-

try cannot restrain itself, the Communications Act offers means, as yet unused, of democratic control.

28   We have a bad inheritance as far as violence is concerned; and in recent years war and television have given new vitality to the darkest strains in our national psyche. How can we master this horror in our souls before it rushes us on to ultimate disintegration?

29   There is not a problem of collective guilt, but there is a problem of collective responsibility. Certainly two hundred million Americans did not strike down John Kennedy or Martin Luther King or Robert Kennedy. But two hundred million Americans are plainly responsible for the character of a society that works on deranged men and incites them to depraved acts. There were Lee Harvey Oswalds and James Earl Rays and Sirhan Bishara Sirhans in America in the Thirties—angry, frustrated, alienated, resentful, marginal men in rootless, unstable cities like Dallas and Memphis and Los Angeles. But our society in the Thirties did not stimulate such men to compensate for their own failure by killing leaders the people loved.

30   Some of the young in their despair have come to feel that the answer to reason is unreason, the answer to violence, more violence; but these only hasten the plunge toward the abyss. The more intelligent disagree. They do not want America to beat its breast and go back to the golf course. *They do want America to recognize its responsibility.* They want us to tell it like it is—to confront the darkness in our past and the darkness in our present. They want us to realize that life is not solid and predictable but infinitely chancy, that violence is not the deviation but the ever-present possibility, that we can therefore never rest in the effort to prevent unreason from rending the skin of civility. They want our leaders to *talk* less about law and order and *do* more about justice.

31   Perhaps the old in American society might now learn that sanctimony is not a persuasive answer to anguish, and that we never cure ourselves if we deny the existence of a disease. If they learn this, if they face up to the schism in our national tradition, we all will have a better chance of subduing the impulse of destruction and of fulfilling the vision of Lincoln—that noble vision of a serene and decent society, united by bonds of affection and mystic chords of memory, dedicated at last to our highest ideals.

CONSIDERATIONS

In paragraph 6 Schlesinger suggests that the only way to understand political murder in America is to examine the self. How does his approach—and his following analyses—differ from the critics who say America is guilty of murder? Does Schlesinger differentiate between guilt and responsibility? Do you agree that as a nation and as individuals we are responsible for the political murders of the 1960s?

The key word in this selection is *violence*. How many types of violence does the author analyze? In which paragraphs does he define it? What methods does he use? Note key words that express the author's view toward violence; which examples and which images are particularly effective?

In a short paper, give your opinion about the influence of the mass media, particularly television, on the behavior (both individual and collective) of people. How much control over the media should be exercised by agencies outside the television, radio, and newspaper industries (for example, the federal government)? Is it reasonable or desirable to expect self-restraint from the television industry?

VOCABULARY

(1) **fortuitous**   occurring by chance; accidental

(1) **aberrations**   deviations from what is normal or correct

(1) **ominous**   threatening; portending evil or harm

(1) **efficacy**   effectiveness

(2) **purging**   cleansing

(7) **propensity**   leaning; inclination

(8) **incessant**   ceaseless

(9) **condoned**   approved

(9) **pragmatists**   those concerned with the practical aspects of life, and who look for the cause and effect relations in problems and human affairs

(10) **insensate**   senseless; brutal; inhuman

(11) **susceptibility**   the state of being especially subject or liable to a certain influence or mood

(11) **vigilantism**   militant, suspicious attitudes and conduct of *vigilante* groups—extralegal committees self-appointed to punish criminals

(12) **redress**   to set right or correct

(13) **anarchists**   persons who seek to overturn all constituted forms and institutions of the existing order by violence

(25) **attenuate**   weaken

(25) **ethos**   the fundamental spirit or character that underlies the actions of a social group

(31) **schism**   division; rift

Something about English

PAUL ROBERTS

Historical Backgrounds

1   No understanding of the English language can be very satisfactory
without a notion of the history of the language. But we shall have to
make do with just a notion. The history of English is long and
complicated, and we can only hit the high spots.

2   The history of our language begins a little after A.D. 600. Everything before that is pre-history, which means that we can guess at it
but can't prove much. For a thousand years or so before the birth of
Christ our linguistic ancestors were savages wandering through the
forests of northern Europe. Their language was a part of the Germanic branch of the Indo-European Family.

3   At the time of the Roman Empire—say, from the beginning of
the Christian Era to around A.D. 400—the speakers of what was to
become English were scattered along the northern coast of Europe.
They spoke a dialect of Low German. More exactly, they spoke
several different dialects, since they were several different tribes.
The names given to the tribes who got to England are *Angles*,
Saxons, and *Jutes*. For convenience, we can refer to them as Anglo-
Saxons.

4   Their first contact with civilization was a rather thin acquaintance with the Roman Empire on whose borders they lived. Probably some of the Anglo-Saxons wandered into the Empire occasion-

ally, and certainly Roman merchants and traders traveled among the tribes. At any rate, this period saw the first of our many borrowings from Latin. Such words as *kettle, wine, cheese, butter, cheap, plum, gem, bishop, church* were borrowed at this time. They show something of the relationship of the Anglo-Saxons with the Romans. The Anglo-Saxons were learning, getting their first taste of civilization.

5   They still had a long way to go, however, and their first step was to help smash the civilization they were learning from. In the fourth century the Roman power weakened badly. While the Goths were pounding away at the Romans in the Mediterranean countries, their relatives, the Anglo-Saxons, began to attack Britain.

6   The Romans had been the ruling power in Britain since A.D. 43. They had subjugated the Celts whom they found living there and had succeeded in setting up a Roman administration. The Roman influence did not extend to the outlying parts of the British Isles. In Scotland, Wales, and Ireland the Celts remained free and wild, and they made periodic forays against the Romans in England. Among other defense measures, the Romans built the famous Roman Wall to ward off the tribes in the north.

7   Even in England the Roman power was thin. Latin did not become the language of the country as it did in Gaul and Spain. The mass of people continued to speak Celtic, with Latin and the Roman civilization it contained in use as a top dressing.

8   In the fourth century, troubles multiplied for the Romans in Britain. Not only did the untamed tribes of Scotland and Wales grow more and more restive, but the Anglo-Saxons began to make pirate raids on the eastern coast. Furthermore, there was growing difficulty everywhere in the Empire, and the legions in Britain were siphoned off to fight elsewhere. Finally, in A.D. 410, the last Roman ruler in England, bent on becoming emperor, left the islands and took the last of the legions with him. The Celts were left in possession of Britain but almost defenseless against the impending Anglo-Saxon attack.

9   Not much is surely known about the arrival of the Anglo-Saxons in England. According to the best early source, the eighth-century historian Bede, the Jutes came in 449 in response to a plea from the Celtic king, Vortigern, who wanted their help against the Picts attacking from the north. The Jutes subdued the Picts but then quarreled and fought with Vortigern, and, with reinforcements from the Continent, settled permanently in Kent. Somewhat later the Angles established themselves in eastern England and the Sax-

ons in the south and west. Bede's account is plausible enough, and these were probably the main lines of the invasion.

10   We do know, however, that the Angles, Saxons, and Jutes were a long time securing themselves in England. Fighting went on for as long as a hundred years before the Celts in England were all killed, driven into Wales, or reduced to slavery. This is the period of King Arthur, who was not entirely mythological. He was a Romanized Celt, a general, though probably not a king. He had some success against the Anglo-Saxons, but it was only temporary. By 550 or so the Anglo-Saxons were firmly established. English was in England.

Old English

11   All this is pre-history, so far as the language is concerned. We have no record of the English language until after 600, when the Anglo-Saxons were converted to Christianity and learned the Latin alphabet. The conversion began, to be precise, in the year 597 and was accomplished within thirty or forty years. The conversion was a great advance for the Anglo-Saxons, not only because of the spiritual benefits but because it reestablished contact with what remained of Roman civilization. This civilization didn't amount to much in the year 600, but it was certainly superior to anything in England up to that time.

12   It is customary to divide the history of the English language into three periods: Old English, Middle English, and Modern English. Old English runs from the earliest records—i.e., seventh century—to about 1100; Middle English from 1100 to 1450 or 1500; Modern English from 1500 to the present day. Sometimes Modern English is further divided into Early Modern, 1500–1700, and Late Modern, 1700 to the present.

13   When England came into history, it was divided into several more or less autonomous kingdoms, some of which at times exercised a certain amount of control over the others. In the century after the conversion the most advanced kingdom was Northumbria, the area between the Humber River and the Scottish border. By A.D. 700 the Northumbrians had developed a respectable civilization, the finest in Europe. It is sometimes called the Northumbrian Renaissance, and it was the first of the several renaissances through which Europe struggled upward out of the ruins of the Roman Empire. It was in this period that the best of the Old English literature was written, including the epic poem *Beowulf*.

14   In the eighth century, Northumbrian power declined, and the

center of influence moved southward to Mercia, the kingdom of the Midlands. A century later the center shifted again, and Wessex, the country of the West Saxons, became the leading power. The most famous king of the West Saxons was Alfred the Great, who reigned in the second half of the ninth century, dying in 901. He was famous not only as a military man and administrator but also as a champion of learning. He founded and supported schools and translated or caused to be translated many books from Latin into English. At this time also much of the Northumbrian literature of two centuries earlier was copied in West Saxon. Indeed, the great bulk of Old English writing which has come down to us is in the West Saxon dialect of 900 or later.

15   In the military sphere, Alfred's great accomplishment was his successful opposition to the viking invasions. In the ninth and tenth centuries, the Norsemen emerged in their ships from their homelands in Denmark and the Scandinavian peninsula. They traveled far and attacked and plundered at will and almost with impunity. They ravaged Italy and Greece, settled in France, Russia, and Ireland, colonized Iceland and Greenland, and discovered America several centuries before Columbus. Nor did they overlook England.

16   After many years of hit-and-run raids, the Norsemen landed an army on the east coast of England in the year 866. There was nothing much to oppose them except the Wessex power led by Alfred. The long struggle ended in 877 with a treaty by which a line was drawn roughly from the northwest of England to the southeast. On the eastern side of the line Norse rule was to prevail. This was called the Danelaw. The western side was to be governed by Wessex.

17   The linguistic result of all this was a considerable injection of Norse into the English language. Norse was at this time not so different from English as Norwegian or Danish is now. Probably speakers of English could understand, more or less, the language of the newcomers who had moved into eastern England. At any rate, there was considerable interchange and word borrowing. Examples of Norse words in the English language are *sky, give, law, egg, outlaw, leg, ugly, scant, sly, crawl, scowl, take, thrust*. There are hundreds more. We have even borrowed some pronouns from Norse—*they, their,* and *them*. These words were borrowed first by the eastern and northern dialects and then in the course of hundreds of years made their way into English generally.

18   It is supposed also—indeed, it must be true—that the Norsemen influenced the sound structure and the grammar of English. But this is hard to demonstrate in detail.

A Specimen of Old English

19   We may now have an example of Old English. The favorite illustration is the Lord's Prayer, since it needs no translation. This has come to us in several different versions. Here is one:

> Fæder ure,
> þu þe eart on heofonum,
> si þin nama gehalgod.
> Tobecume þin rice.
> Gewurþe ðin willa on eorðan swa swa on heofonum.
> Urne gedæghwamlican hlaf syle us to dæg.
> And forgyf us ure gyltas, swa swa we forgyfað urum gyltendum.
> And ne gelæd þu us on costnunge,
> ac alys us of yfele. Soþlice.

20   Some of the differences between this and Modern English are merely differences in orthography. For instance, the sign æ is what Old English writers used for a vowel sound like that in modern *hat* or *and*. The *th* sounds of modern *thin* or *then* are represented in Old English by þ or ð. But of course there are many differences in sound too. *Ure* is the ancestor of modern *our*, but the first vowel was like that in *too* or *ooze*. *Hlaf* is modern *loaf*; we have dropped the *h* sound and changed the vowel, which in *hlaf* was pronounced something like the vowel in *father*. Old English had some sounds which we do not have. The sound represented by *y* does not occur in Modern English. If you pronounce the vowel in *bit* with your lips rounded, you may approach it.

21   In grammar, Old English was much more highly inflected than Modern English is. That is, there were more case endings for nouns, more person and number endings for verbs, a more complicated pronoun system, various endings for adjectives, and so on. Old English nouns had four cases—nominative, genitive, dative, accusative. Adjectives had five—all these and an instrumental case besides. Present-day English has only two cases for nouns—common case and possessive case. Adjectives now have no case system at all. On the other hand, we now use a more rigid word order and more structure words (prepositions, auxiliaries, and the like) to express relationships than Old English did.

22   Some of this grammar we can see in the Lord's Prayer. *Heofonum*, for instance, is a dative plural; the nominative singular was *heofon*. *Urne* is an accusative singular; the nominative is *ure*. In *urum glytendum* both words are dative plural. *Forgyfaþ* is the first person plural form of the verb. Word order is different: "urne gedæghwamlican hlaf syle us" in place of "Give us our daily bread." And so on.

23　　In vocabulary Old English is quite different from Modern English. Most of the Old English words are what we may call native English: that is, words which have not been borrowed from other languages but which have been a part of English ever since English was a part of Indo-European. Old English did certainly contain borrowed words. We have seen that many borrowings were coming in from Norse. Rather large numbers had been borrowed from Latin, too. Some of these were taken while the Anglo-Saxons were still on the Continent (*cheese, butter, bishop, kettle*, etc.); a larger number came into English after the conversion (*angel, candle, priest, martyr, radish, oyster, purple, school, spend*, etc.). But the great majority of Old English words were native English.

24　　Now, on the contrary, the majority of words in English are borrowed, taken mostly from Latin and French. Of the words in *The American College Dictionary* only about 14 percent are native. Most of these, to be sure, are common, high-frequency words—*the, of, I, and, because, man, mother, road*, etc.; of the thousand most common words in English, some 62 percent are native English. Even so, the modern vocabulary is very much Latinized and Frenchified. The Old English vocabulary was not.

Middle English

25　Sometime between the years 1000 and 1200 various important changes took place in the structure of English, and Old English became Middle English. The political event which facilitated these changes was the Norman Conquest. The Normans, as the name shows, came originally from Scandinavia. In the early tenth century they established themselves in northern France, adopted the French language, and developed a vigorous kingdom and a very passable civilization. In the year 1066, led by Duke William, they crossed the Channel and made themselves masters of England. For the next several hundred years, England was ruled by Kings whose first language was French.

26　　One might wonder why, after the Norman Conquest, French did not become the national language, replacing English entirely. The reason is that the Conquest was not a national migration, as the earlier Anglo-Saxon invasion had been. Great numbers of Normans came to England, but they came as rulers and landlords. French became the language of the court, the language of the nobility, the language of polite society, the language of literature. But it did not replace English as the language of the people. There must always have been hundreds of towns and villages in which French was never heard except when visitors of high station passed through.

27   But English, though it survived as the national language, was profoundly changed after the Norman Conquest. Some of the changes—in sound structure and grammar—would no doubt have taken place whether there had been a Conquest or not. Even before 1066 the case system of English nouns and adjectives was becoming simplified; people came to rely more on word order and prepositions than on inflectional endings to communicate their meanings. The process was speeded up by sound changes which caused many of the endings to sound alike. But no doubt the Conquest facilitated the change. German, which didn't experience a Norman Conquest, is today rather highly inflected compared to its cousin English.

28   But it is in vocabulary that the effects of the Conquest are most obvious. French ceased, after a hundred years or so, to be the native language of very many people in England, but it continued— and continues still—to be a zealously cultivated second language, the mirror of elegance and civilization. When one spoke English, one introduced not only French ideas and French things but also their French names. This was not only easy but socially useful. To pepper one's conversation with French expressions was to show that one was well-bred, elegant, *au courant*. The last sentence shows that the process is not yet dead. By using *au courant* instead of, say, *abreast of things*, the writer indicates that he is no dull clod who knows only English but an elegant person aware of how things are done in *le haut monde*.

29   Thus French words came into English, all sorts of them. There were words to do with government: *parliament, majesty, treaty, alliance, tax, government*; church words: *parson, sermon, baptism, incense, crucifix, religion*; words for foods: *veal, beef, mutton, bacon, jelly, peach, lemon, cream, biscuit*; colors: *blue, scarlet, vermilion*; household words: *curtain, chair, lamp, towel, blanket, parlor*; play words: *dance, chess, music, leisure, conversation*; literary words: *story, romance, poet, literary*; learned words: *study, logic, grammar, noun, surgeon, anatomy, stomach*; just ordinary words of all sorts: *nice, second, very, age, bucket, gentle, final, fault, flower, cry, count, sure, move, surprise, plain*.

30   All these and thousands more poured into the English vocabulary between 1100 and 1500 until at the end of that time many people must have had more French words than English at their command. This is not to say that English became French. English remained English in sound structure and in grammar, though these also felt the ripples of French influence. The very heart of the

vocabulary, too, remained English. Most of the high-frequency words—the pronouns, the prepositions, the conjunctions, the auxiliaries—as well as a great many ordinary nouns and verbs and adjectives—were not replaced by borrowings.

31 Middle English, then, was still a Germanic language, but it differed from Old English in many ways. The sound system and the grammar changed a good deal. Speakers made less use of case systems and other inflectional devices and relied more on word order and structure words to express their meanings. This is often said to be a simplification, but it isn't really. Languages don't become simpler; they merely exchange one kind of complexity for another. Modern English is not a simple language, as any foreign speaker who tries to learn it will hasten to tell you.

32 For us Middle English is simpler than Old English just because it is closer to Modern English. It takes three or four months at least to learn to read Old English prose and more than that for poetry. But a week of good study should put one in touch with the Middle English poet Chaucer. Indeed, you may be able to make some sense of Chaucer straight off, though you would need instruction in pronunciation to make it sound like poetry. Here is a famous passage from the *General Prologue to the Canterbury Tales*, fourteenth century:

> Ther was also a nonne, a Prioresse,
> That of hir smyling was ful symple and coy,
> Hir gretteste oath was but by Seinte Loy,
> And she was cleped Madame Eglentyne.
> Ful wel she song the service dyvyne,
> Entuned in hir nose ful semely.
> And Frenshe she spak ful faire and fetisly,
> After the scole of Stratford-atte-Bowe,
> For Frenshe of Parys was to hir unknowe.

Early Modern English

33 Sometime between 1400 and 1600 English underwent a couple of sound changes which made the language of Shakespeare quite different from that of Chaucer. Incidentally, these changes contributed much to the chaos in which English spelling now finds itself.

34 One change was the elimination of a vowel sound in certain unstressed positions at the end of words. For instance, the words *name, stone, wine, dance* were pronounced as two syllables by Chaucer but as just one by Shakespeare. The *e* in these words be-

came, as we say, "silent." But it wasn't silent for Chaucer; it represented a vowel sound. So also the words *laughed, seemed, stored* would have been pronounced by Chaucer as two-syllable words. The change was an important one because it affected thousands of words and gave a different aspect to the whole language.

35   The other change is what is called the Great Vowel Shift. This was a systematic shifting of half a dozen vowels and diphthongs in stressed syllables. For instance, the word *name* had in Middle English a vowel something like that in the modern word *father; wine* had the vowel of modern *mean; he* was pronounced something like modern *hey; mouse* sounded like *moose; moon* had the vowel of *moan.* Again the shift was thorough-going and affected all the words in which these vowel sounds occurred. Since we still keep the Middle English system of spelling these words, the differences between Modern English and Middle English are often more real than apparent.

36   The vowel shift has meant also that we have come to use an entirely different set of symbols for representing vowel sounds than is used by writers of such languages as French, Italian, or Spanish, in which no such vowel shift occurred. If you come across a strange word—say, *bine*—in an English book, you will pronounce it according to the English system, with the vowel of *wine* or *dine.* But if you read *bine* in a French, Italian, or Spanish book, you will pronounce it with the vowel of *mean* or *seen.*

37   These two changes, then, produced the basic differences between Middle English and Modern English. But there were several other developments that had an effect upon the language. One was the invention of printing, an invention introduced into England by William Caxton in the year 1475. Where before books had been rare and costly, they suddenly became cheap and common. More and more people learned to read and write. This was the first of many advances in communication which have worked to unify languages and to arrest the development of dialect differences, though of course printing affects writing principally rather than speech. Among other things it hastened the standardization of spelling.

38   The period of Early Modern English—that is, the sixteenth and seventeenth centuries—was also the period of the English Renaissance, when people developed, on the one hand, a keen interest in the past and, on the other, a more daring and imaginative view of the future. New ideas multiplied, and new ideas meant new language. Englishmen had grown accustomed to borrowing words from French as a result of the Norman Conquest; now they borrowed

from Latin and Greek. As we have seen, English had been raiding Latin from Old English times and before, but now the floodgates really opened, and thousands of words from the classical languages poured in. *Pedestrian, bonus, anatomy, contradict, climax, dictionary, benefit, multiply, exist, paragraph, initiate, scene, inspire* are random examples. Probably the average educated American today has more words from French in his vocabulary than from native English sources, and more from Latin than from French.

39   The greatest writer of the Early Modern English period is of course Shakespeare, and the best-known book is the King James Version of the Bible, published in 1611. The Bible (if not Shakespeare) has made many features of Early Modern English perfectly familiar to many people down to present time, even though we do not use these features in present-day speech and writing. For instance, the old pronouns *thou* and *thee* have dropped out of use now, together with their verb forms, but they are still familiar to us in prayer and in Biblical quotation: "Whither thou goest, I will go." Such forms as *hath* and *doth* have been replaced by *has* and *does;* "Goes he hence tonight?" would now be "Is he going away tonight?"; Shakespeare's "Fie, on't, sirrah" would be "Nuts to that, Mac." Still, all these expressions linger with us because of the power of the works in which they occur.

40   It is not always realized, however, that considerable sound changes have taken place between Early Modern English and the English of the present day. Shakespearian actors putting on a play speak the words, properly enough, in their modern pronunciation. But it is very doubtful that this pronunciation would be understood at all by Shakespeare. In Shakespeare's time, the word *reason* was pronounced like modern *raisin; face* had the sound of modern *glass;* the *l* in *would, should, palm* was pronounced. In these points and a great many others the English language has moved a long way from what it was in 1600.

Recent Developments

41   The history of English since 1700 is filled with many movements and countermovements, of which we can notice only a couple. One of these is the vigorous attempt made in the eighteenth century, and the rather half-hearted attempts made since, to regulate and control the English language. Many people of the eighteenth century, not understanding very well the forces which govern language, proposed to polish and prune and restrict English, which they felt was proliferating too wildly. There was much talk of an academy

which would rule on what people could and could not say and write. The academy never came into being, but the eighteenth century did succeed in establishing certain attitudes which, though they haven't had much effect on the development of the language itself, have certainly changed the native speaker's feeling about the language.

42   In part a product of the wish to fix and establish the language was the development of the dictionary. The first English dictionary was published in 1603; it was a list of 2500 words briefly defined. Many others were published with gradual improvements until Samuel Johnson published his *English Dictionary* in 1755. This, steadily revised, dominated the field in England for nearly a hundred years. Meanwhile in America, Noah Webster published his dictionary in 1828, and before long dictionary publishing was a big business in this country. The last century has seen the publication of one great dictionary: the twelve-volume *Oxford English Dictionary*, compiled in the course of seventy-five years through the labors of many scholars. We have also, of course, numerous commercial dictionaries which are as good as the public wants them to be if not, indeed, rather better.

43   Another product of the eighteenth century was the invention of "English grammar." As English came to replace Latin as the language of scholarship it was felt that one should also be able to control and dissect it, parse and analyze it, as one could Latin. What happened in practice was that the grammatical description that applied to Latin was removed and superimposed on English. This was silly, because English is an entirely different kind of language, with its own forms and signals and ways of producing meaning. Nevertheless, English grammars on the Latin model were worked out and taught in the schools. In many schools they are still being taught. This activity is not often popular with school children, but it is sometimes an interesting and instructive exercise in logic. The principal harm in it is that it has tended to keep people from being interested in English and has obscured the real features of English structure.

44   But probably the most important force on the development of English in the modern period has been the tremendous expansion of English-speaking peoples. In 1500 English was a minor language, spoken by a few people on a small island. Now it is perhaps the greatest language of the world, spoken natively by over a quarter of a billion people and as a second language by many millions more. When we speak of English now, we must specify whether we mean American English, British English, Australian English, Indian English, or what, since the differences are considerable. The American

cannot go to England or the Englishman to America confident that he will always understand and be understood. The Alabaman in Iowa or the Iowan in Alabama shows himself a foreigner every time he speaks. It is only because communication has become fast and easy that English in this period of its expansion has not broken into a dozen mutually unintelligible languages.

CONSIDERATIONS

What is the relation between the history of England and the historical development of the English language? If you had preconceived notions about rules of grammar, spelling, and idiom before reading this article, were they altered in any degree by Roberts's historical outline of the English language?

The author has condensed an emormous amount of data into this brief article. What method of organization does he use? Mark the divisions of the article: introduction, body, conclusion. Is the introduction disproportionately long, the conclusion too short? How are transitions made between each section? What stylistic devices serve to unify the parts of the article?

Using the *Oxford English Dictionary,* make a study of the etymology of every word in a short passage from a newspaper or magazine article. What are the results in percentages of "foreign" (Spanish, Latin, French, Danish, German, and so on) derivations or influences?

VOCABULARY

 (6) **subjugated**   conquered, brought under someone's control
 (6) **forays**   quick raids, sudden attacks
 (8) **restive**   difficult to control
(15) **impunity**   freedom from punishment
(20) **orthography**   spelling
(41) **proliferating**   rapidly spreading
(43) **parse**   describe grammatically

A Technology of Behavior

B. F. SKINNER

1   In trying to solve the terrifying problems that face us in the world today, we naturally turn to the things we do best. We play from strength, and our strength is science and technology. To contain a population explosion we look for better methods of birth control. Threatened by nuclear holocaust, we build bigger deterrent forces and anti-ballistic-missile systems. We try to stave off world famine with new foods and better ways of growing them. Improved sanitation and medicine will, we hope, control disease; better housing and transportation will solve the problems of the ghettos; and new ways of reducing or disposing of waste will stop the pollution of the environment. We can point to remarkable achievements in all these fields, and it is not surprising that we should try to extend them. But things grow steadily worse, and it is disheartening to find that technology itself is increasingly at fault. Sanitation and medicine have made the problems of population more acute, war has acquired a new horror with the invention of nuclear weapons, and the affluent pursuit of Happiness is largely responsible for pollution. As Darlington has said, "Every new source from which man has increased his power on the earth has been used to diminish the prospects of his successors. All his progress has been made at the expense of damage to his environment, which he cannot repair and could not foresee."

2   Whether or not he could have forseen the damage, man must repair it or all is lost. And he can do so if he will recognize the nature of the difficulty. The application of the physical and biologi-

cal sciences alone will not solve our problems, because the solutions lie in another field. Better contraceptives will control population only if people use them. New weapons may offset new defenses and vice versa, but a nuclear holocaust can be prevented only if the conditions under which nations make war can be changed. New methods of agriculture and medicine will not help if they are not practiced, and housing is a matter not only of buildings and cities but of how people live. Overcrowding can be corrected only by inducing people not to crowd, and the environment will continue to deteriorate until polluting practices are abandoned.

3   In short, we need to make vast changes in human behavior, and we cannot make them with the help of nothing more than physics or biology, no matter how hard we try. (And there are other problems, such as the breakdown of our educational system and the disaffection and revolt of the young, to which physical and biological technologies are so obviously irrelevant that they have never been applied.) It is not enough to "use technology with a deeper understanding of human issues," or to "dedicate technology to man's spiritual needs," or to "encourage technologists to look at human problems." Such expressions imply that where human behavior begins, technology stops, and that we must carry on, as we have in the past, with what we have learned from personal experience or from those collections of personal experiences called history, or with the distillations of experience to be found in folk wisdom and practical rules of thumb. These have been available for centuries, and all we have to show for them is the state of the world today.

4   What we need is a technology of behavior. We could solve our problems quickly enough if we could adjust the growth of the world's population as precisely as we adjust the course of a spaceship, or improve agriculture and industry with some of the confidence with which we accelerate high-energy particles, or move toward a peaceful world with something like the steady progress with which physics has approached absolute zero (even though both remain presumably out of reach). But a behavioral technology comparable in power and precision to physical and biological technology is lacking, and those who do not find the very possibility ridiculous are more likely to be frightened by it than reassured. That is how far we are from "understanding human issues" in the sense in which physics and biology understand their fields, and how far we are from preventing the catastrophe toward which the world seems to be inexorably moving.

5   Twenty-five hundred years ago it might have been said that

man understood himself as well as any other part of his world. Today he is the thing he understands least. Physics and biology have come a long way, but there has been no comparable development of anything like a science of human behavior. Greek physics and biology are now of historical interest only (no modern physicist or biologist would turn to Aristotle for help), but the dialogues of Plato are still assigned to students and cited as if they threw light on human behavior. Aristotle could not have understood a page of modern physics or biology, but Socrates and his friends would have little trouble in following most current discussions of human affairs. And as to technology, we have made immense strides in controlling the physical and biological worlds, but our practices in government, education, and much of economics, though adapted to very different conditions, have not greatly improved.

6   We can scarcely explain this by saying that the Greeks knew all there was to know about human behavior. Certainly they knew more than they knew about the physical world, but it was still not much. Moreover, their way of thinking about human behavior must have had some fatal flaw. Whereas Greek physics and biology, no matter how crude, led eventually to modern science, Greek theories of human behavior led nowhere. If they are with us today, it is not because they possessed some kind of eternal verity, but because they did not contain the seeds of anything better.

7   It can always be argued that human behavior is a particularly difficult field. It is, and we are especially likely to think so just because we are so inept in dealing with it. But modern physics and biology successfully treat subjects that are certainly no simpler than many aspects of human behavior. The difference is that the instruments and methods they use are of commensurate complexity. The fact that equally powerful instruments and methods are not available in the field of human behavior is not an explanation; it is only part of the puzzle. Was putting a man on the moon actually easier than improving education in our public schools? Or than constructing better kinds of living space for everyone? Or than making it possible for everyone to be gainfully employed and, as a result, to enjoy a higher standard of living? The choice was not a matter of priorities, for no one could have said that it was more important to get to the moon. The exciting thing about getting to the moon was its feasibility. Science and technology had reached the point at which, with one great push, the thing could be done. There is no comparable excitement about the problems posed by human behavior. We are not close to solutions.

8   It is easy to conclude that there must be something about

human behavior which makes a scientific analysis, and hence an effective technology, impossible, but we have not by any means exhausted the possibilities. There is a sense in which it can be said that the methods of science have scarcely yet been applied to human behavior. We have used the instruments of science; we have counted and measured and compared; but something essential to scientific practice is missing in almost all current discussions of human behavior. It has to do with our treatment of the causes of behavior. (The term "cause" is no longer common in sophisticated scientific writing, but it will serve well enough here.)

9   Man's first experience with causes probably came from his own behavior: things moved because he moved them. If other things moved, it was because someone else was moving them, and if the mover could not be seen, it was because he was invisible. The Greek gods served in this way as the causes of physical phenomena. They were usually outside the things they moved, but they might enter into and "possess" them. Physics and biology soon abandoned explanations of this sort and turned to more useful kinds of causes, but the step has not been decisively taken in the field of human behavior. Intelligent people no longer believe that men are possessed by demons (although the exorcism of devils is occasionally practiced, and the daimonic has reappeared in the writings of psychotherapists), but human behavior is still commonly attributed to indwelling agents. A juvenile delinquent is said, for example, to be suffering from a disturbed personality. There would be no point in saying it if the personality were not somehow distinct from the body which has got itself into trouble. The distinction is clear when one body is said to contain several personalities which control it in different ways at different times. Psychoanalysts have identified three of these personalities—the ego, superego, and id—and interactions among them are said to be responsible for the behavior of the man in whom they dwell.

10   Although physics soon stopped personifying things in this way, it continued for a long time to speak as if they had wills, impulses, feelings, purposes, and other fragmentary attributes of an indwelling agent. According to Butterfield, Aristotle argued that a falling body accelerated because it grew more jubilant as it found itself nearer home, and later authorities supposed that a projectile was carried forward by an impetus, sometimes called an "impetuosity." All this was eventually abandoned, and to good effect, but the behavioral sciences still appeal to comparable internal states. No one is surprised to hear it said that a person carrying good news walks

more rapidly because he feels jubilant, or acts carelessly because of his impetuosity, or holds stubbornly to a course of action through sheer force of will. Careless references to purpose are still to be found in both physics and biology, but good practice has no place for them; yet almost everyone attributes human behavior to intentions, purposes, aims, and goals. If it is still possible to ask whether a machine can show purpose, the question implies, significantly, that if it can it will more closely resemble a man.

11   Physics and biology moved farther away from personified causes when they began to attribute the behavior of things to essences, qualities, or natures. To the medieval alchemist, for example, some of the properties of a substance might be due to the mercurial essence, and substances were compared in what might have been called a "chemistry of individual differences." Newton complained of the practice in his contemporaries: "To tell us that every species of thing is endowed with an occult specific quality by which it acts and produces manifest effects is to tell us nothing." (Occult qualities were examples of the hypotheses Newton rejected when he said "Hypotheses non fingo," though he was not quite as good as his word.) Biology continued for a long time to appeal to the *nature* of living things, and it did not wholly abandon vital forces until the twentieth century. Behavior, however, is still attributed to human nature, and there is an extensive "psychology of individual differences" in which people are compared and described in terms of traits of character, capacities, and abilities.

12   Almost everyone who is concerned with human affairs—as political scientist, philosopher, man of letters, economist, psychologist, linguist, sociologist, theologian, anthropologist, educator, or psychotherapist—continues to talk about human behavior in this prescientific way. Every issue of a daily paper, every magazine, every professional journal, every book with any bearing whatsoever on human behavior will supply examples. We are told that to control the number of people in the world we need to change *attitudes* toward children, overcome *pride* in size of family or in sexual potency, build some *sense of responsibility* toward offspring, and reduce the role played by a large family in allaying *concern* for old age. To work for peace we must deal with the *will to power* or the *paranoid delusions* of leaders; we must remember that wars begin in the *minds* of men, that there is something suicidal in man—a *death instinct* perhaps—which leads to war, and that man is aggressive by *nature*. To solve the problems of the poor we must inspire *self-respect*, encourage *initiative*, and reduce *frustration*. To allay

the disaffection of the young we must provide a *sense of purpose* and reduce feelings of *alienation* or *hopelessness*. Realizing that we have no effective means of doing any of this, we ourselves may experience *a crisis of belief* or a *loss of confidence*, which can be corrected only by returning to a *faith in man's inner capacities*. This is staple fare. Almost no one questions it. Yet there is nothing like it in modern physics or most of biology, and that fact may well explain why a science and a technology of behavior have been so long delayed.

13   It is usually supposed that the "behavioristic" objection to ideas, feelings, traits of character, will, and so on concerns the stuff of which they are said to be made. Certain stubborn questions about the nature of mind have, of course, been debated for more than twenty-five hundred years and still go unanswered. How, for example, can the mind move the body? As late as 1965 Karl Popper could put the question this way: "What we want is to understand how such nonphysical things as *purposes, deliberations, plans, decisions, theories, tensions,* and *values* can play a part in bringing about physical changes in the physical world." And, of course, we also want to know where these nonphysical things come from. To that question the Greeks had a simple answer: from the gods. As Dodds has pointed out, the Greeks believed that if a man behaved foolishly, it was because a hostile god had planted ἶτη (infatuation) in his breast. A friendly god might give a warrior an extra amount of μένος with the help of which he would fight brilliantly. Aristotle thought there was something divine in thought, and Zeno held that the intellect was God.

14   We cannot take that line today, and the commonest alternative is to appeal to antecedent physical events. A person's genetic endowment, a product of the evolution of the species, is said to explain part of the workings of his mind and his personal history the rest. For example, because of (physical) competition during the course of evolution people now have (nonphysical) feelings of aggression which lead to (physical) acts of hostility. Or, the (physical) punishment a small child receives when he engages in sex play produces (nonphysical) feelings of anxiety which interfere with his (physical) sexual behavior as an adult. The nonphysical stage obviously bridges long periods of time: aggression reaches back into millions of years of evolutionary history, and anxiety acquired when one is a child survives into old age.

15   The problem of getting from one kind of stuff to another could be avoided if everything were either mental or physical, and both these possibilities have been considered. Some philosophers

have tried to stay within the world of the mind, arguing that only immediate experience is real, and experimental psychology began as an attempt to discover the mental laws which governed interactions among mental elements. Contemporary "intrapsychic" theories of psychotherapy tell us how one feeling leads to another (how frustration breeds aggression, for example), how feelings interact, and how feelings which have been put out of mind fight their way back in. The complementary line that the mental stage is really physical was taken, curiously enough, by Freud, who believed that physiology would eventually explain the workings of the mental apparatus. In a similar vein, many physiological psychologists continue to talk freely about states of mind, feelings, and so on, in the belief that it is only a matter of time before we shall understand their physical nature.

16   The dimensions of the world of mind and the transition from one world to another do raise embarrassing problems, but it is usually possible to ignore them, and this may be good strategy, for the important objection to mentalism is of a very different sort. The world of the mind steals the show. Behavior is not recognized as a subject in its own right. In psychotherapy, for example, the disturbing things a person does or says are almost always regarded merely as symptoms, and compared with the fascinating dramas which are staged in the depths of the mind, behavior itself seems superficial indeed. In linguistics and literary criticism what a man says is almost always treated as the expression of ideas or feelings. In political science, theology, and economics, behavior is usually regarded as the material from which one infers attitudes, intentions, needs, and so on. For more than twenty-five hundred years close attention has been paid to mental life, but only recently has any effort been made to study human behavior as something more than a mere by-product.

17   The conditions of which behavior is a function are also neglected. The mental explanation brings curiosity to an end. We see the effect in casual discourse. If we ask someone, "Why did you go to the theater?" and he says, "Because I felt like going," we are apt to take his reply as a kind of explanation. It would be much more to the point to know what has happened when he has gone to the theater in the past, what he heard or read about the play he went to see, and what other things in his past or present environments might have induced him to go (as opposed to doing something else), but we accept "I felt like going" as a sort of summary of all this and are not likely to ask for details.

18   The professional psychologist often stops at the same point.

A long time ago William James corrected a prevailing view of the relation between feelings and action by asserting, for example, that we do not run away because we are afraid but are afraid because we run away. In other words, what we feel when we feel afraid is our behavior—the very behavior which in the traditional view expresses the feeling and is explained by it. But how many of those who have considered James's argument have noted that no antecedent event has in fact been pointed out? Neither "because" should be taken seriously. No explanation has been given as to why we run away *and* feel afraid.

19   Whether we regard ourselves as explaining feelings or the behavior said to be caused by feelings, we give very little attention to antecedent circumstances. The psychotherapist learns about the early life of his patient almost exclusively from the patient's memories, which are known to be unreliable, and he may even argue that what is important is not what actually happened but what the patient remembers. In the psychoanalytic literature there must be at least a hundred references to felt anxiety for every reference to a punishing episode to which anxiety might be traced. We even seem to prefer antecedent histories which are clearly out of reach. There is a good deal of current interest, for example, in what must have happened during the evolution of the species to explain human behavior, and we seem to speak with special confidence just because what actually happened can only be inferred.

20   Unable to understand how or why the person we see behaves as he does, we attribute his behavior to a person we cannot see, whose behavior we cannot explain either but about whom we are not inclined to ask questions. We probably adopt this strategy not so much because of any lack of interest or power but because of a longstanding conviction that for much of human behavior there *are* no relevant antecedents. The function of the inner man is to provide an explanation which will not be explained in turn. Explanation stops with him. He is not a mediator between past history and current behavior, he is a *center* from which behavior emanates. He initiates, originates, and creates, and in doing so he remains, as he was for the Greeks, divine. We say that he is autonomous—and, so far as a science of behavior is concerned, that means miraculous.

21   The position is, of course, vulnerable. Autonomous man serves to explain only the things we are not yet able to explain in other ways. His existence depends upon our ignorance, and he naturally loses status as we come to know more about behavior. The task

of a scientific analysis is to explain how the behavior of a person as a physical system is related to the conditions under which the human species evolved and the conditions under which the individual lives. Unless there is indeed some capricious or creative intervention, these events must be related, and no intervention is in fact needed. The contingencies of survival responsible for man's genetic endowment would produce tendencies to *act* aggressively, not feelings of aggression. The punishment of sexual behavior changes sexual *behavior*, and any feelings which may arise are at best by-products. Our age is not suffering from anxiety but from the accidents, crimes, wars, and other dangerous and painful things to which people are so often exposed. Young people drop out of school, refuse to get jobs, and associate only with others of their own age not because they feel alienated but because of defective social environments in homes, schools, factories, and elsewhere.

22   We can follow the path taken by physics and biology by turning directly to the relation between behavior and the environment and neglecting supposed mediating states of mind. Physics did not advance by looking more closely at the jubilance of a falling body, or biology by looking at the nature of vital spirits, and we do not need to try to discover what personalities, states of mind, feelings, traits of character, plans, purposes, intentions, or the other perquisites of autonomous man really are in order to get on with a scientific analysis of behavior.

CONSIDERATIONS

What does Skinner mean by a "scientific analysis of behavior"? Do you believe it possible to change human behavior to such a degree as to create a stable, nondestructive society? What might Skinner recommend to facilitate this change? According to the author, why hasn't there been a development of a science of human behavior comparable to that of physics and biology?

Note the repeated use of the words *physical* and *nonphysical* in paragraph 14. What is the intent of this? How do the rhetorical questions posed in paragraph 7 strengthen Skinner's argument? Where does Skinner state his solution to the problem stated?

Discuss the following statement made by Skinner: "Twenty-five hundred years ago it might have been said that man understood himself as well as any other part of his world. Today he is the thing he understands least." Do you agree that it is not enough to "use technology with a deeper understanding of human issues"?

VOCABULARY

(4) **inexorably**   unyieldingly; inflexible; incapable of being stopped

(6) **verity**   truth

(7) **inept**   clumsy; incompetent; not apt or fitting

(7) **commensurate**   proportionate; of same size or extent

(9) **daimonic**   variant of demonic; fiendish

(11) **mercurial**   changeable in character

(12) **allay**   to lessen or relieve pain or grief; to pacify

(20) **mediator**   an intermediary to reconcile differences

Privacy

ALAN F. WESTIN

1   Are Americans worried today about invasion of their privacy? If so, just what intrusions do they fear, by whom, and are these worries real or imaginary? In August 1970, Louis Harris and Associates, Inc., a leading public opinion survey organization, published the results of a national poll of American attitudes toward invasion of privacy. The survey asked each respondent whether he felt that people are trying to find out things about him that "are not any of their business." Sixty-two percent of those queried said they did not feel that their privacy was being invaded in this way, thirty-four percent said that they felt it was, and four percent said they were "not sure."

2   One can interpret these findings in two opposite ways. On the one hand, almost two-thirds of those polled reported that they did not feel that they were being subjected to intrusive and prying practices. On the other hand, one in every three persons felt that his privacy was being invaded, and that represents a lot of people in the United States.

3   What kinds of intrusions are one in three Americans worried about? When the Harris poll asked respondents to check off specific violations of privacy that concerned them, part of the list reflected issues of neighborhood and personal life, such as "people looking in your windows"; "people overhearing your conversations with other people"; "neighbors who gossip about your family"; "hotel and motel phone operators"; and even "public opinion poll-takers."

4   But the main fears—those which 10 to 19 percent of the respon-

dents identified as their particular worries—were intrusions with a more political and institutional basis, issues that have been primary topics of public debate during the past decade. Specifically, one in every five respondents listed "computers which collect a lot of information about you" and "business which sells you things on credit" as intrusive practices. Other "violations" respondents checked off were "the government when it collects tax returns"; "people listening in to your telephone conversations"; "the government when it takes a census"; and, finally, "employment interviewing."

5   The Harris poll tends to confirm what much other evidence also suggests: concern over intrusive practices by government agencies and private organizations represents a growing issue in contemporary American political and cultural life. This concern has been heightened by the development of advanced surveillance technology, from micro-miniaturized listening and watching devices and new eye-blink emotion-reading sensors to giant computerized data banks. For many Americans, George Orwell's *1984* seems to be rushing in ahead of schedule with its portrait of the ultimate loss of privacy.

6   To sort out facts from nightmare fiction in this area, some basic definitions, concepts, history, and social analysis must be sketched in as background. First, the norms of privacy in any society will be set at three basic levels—political, sociocultural, and personal.

7   At the political level, every society sets a distinctive balance between the private sphere and the public order, based on the political philosophy of the state. In authoritarian societies, where public life is celebrated as the highest good and the fulfillment of man's purpose on earth, the concept of legally or socially protected privacy for the individual, family, social group, and private association is rejected as hedonistic and immoral. It is also politically dangerous to the regime. Such governments keep extensive records on people to watch for "deviationist" behavior and use a wide range of physical surveillance techniques to watch and listen secretly to elite groups. In contrast, constitutional democracies, with a strong commitment to individualism and freedom of association, regard the private sector as a major force for social progress and morality. The public order, government, is seen as a useful and necessary mechanism for providing services and protection, but one that is expressly barred by bills of rights and other guarantees of civil liberty from interfering with the citizen's private beliefs, associations, and acts, except in extraordinary situations and then only through tightly controlled procedures.

8   This political balance is the framework for a second level of privacy—the sociocultural level. Environmental factors, such as crowded cities, and class factors of wealth and race shape the real opportunities people have to claim freedom from the observation of others. In this sense, privacy is frequently determined by the individual's power and status. The rich can withdraw from society when they wish; the lower classes cannot.

9   Finally, within the political and sociocultural limits just described, there are levels of privacy set by each individual as he seeks an "intrapsychic balance" between his needs for privacy and his needs for disclosure and communication. This balance is generally a function of one's family life, education, and psychological makeup and reflects each individual's particular needs and desires.

10   The extent of personal privacy varies, but there are four degrees that can be identified. Sometimes the individual wants to be completely out of the sight and hearing of anyone else, in solitude; alone, he is in the most relaxed state of privacy. In a second situation the individual seeks the intimacy of his confidants—his family, friends, or trusted associates with whom he chooses to share his ideas and emotions. But there are still some things that he does not want to disclose, whether he is with intimates or in public. Either by personal explanation or by social convention, the individual may indicate that he does not wish certain aspects of himself discussed or noticed, at least at that particular moment. When his claim is respected by those around him, he achieves a third degree of privacy, the state of reserve. Finally, an individual sometimes goes out in public to seek privacy, for by joining groups of people who do not recognize him, he achieves anonymity, being seen but not known. Such relaxation on the street, in bars or movies or in the park constitutes still another dimension of the individual's quest for privacy.

11   In all these states of privacy the individual's needs usually change from time to time. At one moment, he may desperately want to be alone. At another, aloneness can be so frightening that he desperately seeks the companionship either of an intimate friend or of a complete stranger, a one-time acquaintance who will listen to his problems but who will not be encountered again.

12   The fundamental element of choice involved in personal privacy is embodied in every definition of privacy used today in law, social science, or common understanding. With some variation in terminology, these definitions all agree that privacy is the claim of an individual to determine for himself whether and how he will communicate with others—what he will reveal, when, and to whom.

13   The importance of the right to choose, both to the individual's self-development and to the exercise of responsible citizenship, makes the claim to privacy a fundamental part of civil liberty in a constitutional society. Without the power to decide when to remain private, we cannot exercise many other basic freedoms. If we are switched "on" without our knowledge or consent, we have lost our constitutional rights to decide when and with whom we speak, publish, worship, and associate. We have been made glass men.

14   So far, we have stressed the importance of privacy to the individual in a democracy. But every society must also provide for the disclosure of information necessary to the rational conduct of public affairs and must engage in some surveillance of individual and group activity in order to control illegal or antisocial acts. From the earliest periods of Western society, these disclosure-surveillance functions have been vested in five authorities: the employer-landlord, the church, the heads of other associations to which the individual belongs, local governmental officials, and the national regime. In every historical era, as conflicts for primacy raged between church and state, town and guild, or king and baron, the individual's immunity from unwanted surveillance or disclosure has been a part of these basic power struggles.

15   In fact, looking back over 2,000 years of Western political history, we can identify two basic patterns of privacy and disclosure-surveillance. In the authoritarian tradition—exemplified by Sparta, the Roman Empire, early France, and modern totalitarian regimes —unlimited or very extensive powers to compel disclosure and carry on surveillance have been an essential part of the system. In the libertarian tradition—typified by Periclean Athens, the Roman Republic, the English constitutional state, the American republic, and modern democratic nations—basic limits have been placed on the powers of the authorities to put individuals or groups under surveillance or to compel their disclosure of information considered private or privileged. While the issue of privacy is complicated historically—it has often been enmeshed in rival claims to power by the contesting authorities—it is fair to say that no political system with a reputation for liberty in its time failed to provide important legal and social limits on surveillance by authorities.

16   This is the broad background for the issue of privacy in the 1970's. Until the post-World War II era, American law and social norms provided an effective libertarian balance of privacy. Because the presence of walls and doors provided people with a shelter

within which to speak and act in private, American society forbade physical entry into the "constitutional castle" by uninvited private persons or by government officials unless the latter met the requirements of probable cause and specificity in warrants provided for in state and federal constitutions. Because torture and compulsory test oaths were the only ways to penetrate the thoughts and mind of an individual, such practices were forbidden. And because daily life in a mobile, frontier society was beyond the monitoring capacity of record-keepers, the federal government concentrated on forbidding or minimizing the practice of spying, the maintenance of dossiers by police, and the use of internal passport systems that marked the autocratic regimes of royal Europe, to all of which the American republic was fundamentally opposed.

17   In the past two decades, however, a combination of new technology and sociopolitical changes has overturned the classic balance of privacy in the United States. On the technological front, microminiaturized bugs, television monitors, and devices capable of penetrating solid surfaces to listen or photograph have dissolved the physical barriers of walls and doors. Polygraph devices to measure emotional states have been improved as a result of space research, and increased use has been made of personality tests for personnel selection. The development of electronic computers and long-distance communication networks has made it possible to collect, store, and process far more information about an individual's life and transactions than was practical in the era of typewriter and file cabinet.

18   These dramatic advances in technology—revolutionizing the means of conducting physical, psychological, and data surveillance over the citizenry—were accompanied by equally critical changes in American society. As the industrial economy became more complex and interconnected; as government took on giant programs in social welfare; as the social sciences moved toward behavioral, data-dependent theories of social explanation; and as both criminal and revolutionary groups made use of modern technology, a whole new framework for data collection and use by authorities had to be defined, and a new balance of privacy had to be worked into American law and social practice.

19   Just how this new balance should be set for the 1970's is the heart of the privacy issue today. Whether the specific concern is government power to eavesdrop on conversations, compulsory questions on the decennial census, or computerized data banks, what is really at issue is how to have both effective government and

organizational life *and* protected zones of individual and group privacy. If the United States must choose between these equally compelling aspects of civilized social life, the nation will have failed in the art of democracy.

20   With this perspective, we can identify three important suggestions that have been made for setting a new balance of privacy in the electronic age. The first suggestion, a total ban approach, calls for the use of legislation, judicial decisions, and organizational rules to forbid the use of new technological measures which intrude too deeply into personal privacy. A second approach, administrative discretion, favors letting the authorities use new methods under their own regulations and safeguards until a clear case is made that the intervention of law is needed to set standards and control abuses. The third approach calls for a variety of policy responses— bans, regulations, and nonintervention—according to the particular state of the technological art, the need for information collection, the impact on the individuals concerned, and the effect on society as a whole.

21   In my view, neither a total ban or administrative discretion is the answer, since each misunderstands both the nature of socio-technological development and the essence of constitutional government. Let me illustrate with some current controversies. Why shouldn't we simply outlaw intrusive public opinion polling, electronic eavesdropping, and computerized data banks? The answer lies in a careful assessment of what is really at stake in each situation.

22   As long as the individual is free to refuse to answer private and government opinion surveys, to close the door with a firm "I do not want to reply," it is the height of legalized puritanism to forbid Americans to speak out voluntarily and make their individual wishes, needs, and fears known to leaders of government and private institutions. Indeed, some critical changes in mores and laws have come about as a result of facts learned by such opinion surveys as the Kinsey reports, in which people willingly revealed their intimate sexual behavior. Because what is told to a legitimate opinion surveyor is kept confidential—identities are not revealed and the respondent's disclosure does not result in his being regulated—total bans on such polling are unwarranted and dangerous. On the other hand, some regulation may well be needed to forbid salesmen from posing as pollsters to push their wares, voluntary government questionnaires from being presented as though responses were legally required, or governmental agencies from violating the confidential nature of survey research data for investigative

or regulatory purposes or from selling lists or information to private business firms.

23   The issue of electronic eavesdropping is harder to resolve, since the specter of federal or local law enforcement agents overhearing conversations and building transcript files is not one to reassure citizens of a democratic nation. But the bedrock facts brought out by many legislative hearing and legal studies reveal that there are criminal and revolutionary conspiracies which do engage in violence, theft, and murder and that these groups are shrewd enough so that traditional methods of investigation are inadequate. In an era of rapid communication and mobility, no government in the world refrains from all use of electronic eavesdropping. And if any nation were to enact a total ban, it is almost certain that police working on kidnapping, bombing, and similar cases would use such techniques covertly and that the public would approve.

24   But if total bans are unrealistic, so are counsels for administrative discretion. Law enforcement agencies cannot be left to decide within executive department ranks when to eavesdrop, for how long, and what uses to make of the material they obtain. For this, a constitutional system requires legislative definition of a highly limited set of crimes for which this intrusive technique is to be permitted, judicial procedures to assess the need for eavesdropping in each case, and extensive controls over the process and products of eavesdropping. While this was the basic policy adopted by the federal Omnibus Crime Control and Safe Streets Act of 1968 and by many state legislatures under the guidelines of that act, there are still serious issues arising from that legislation. Broad powers are given the attorney general to eavesdrop without court authorization on organizations that he decides pose a threat to internal security. It was under this provision that wiretaps and bugs were used to get information on new left groups involved in the 1968 demonstrations in Chicago and on such organizations as the Black Panthers. Similarly, under the 1968 federal law, state police powers were broadened to allow electronic eavesdropping in any crime punishable under state law by more than a year's imprisonment; in some states this would allow eavesdropping for such offenses as defacing a cemetery. Either judicial interpretation or legislative amendment of such provisions seems necessary to prevent abuse.

25   A final example involves computerized data banks, one of the two issues with which the Harris poll found one-third of the population to be most concerned. At every level of government today—in city, county, state, and federal agencies—written records are gradually

being converted into computer-stored material. The same is true in business, universities, hospitals, churches, and voluntary associations. As such organizations consolidate their records about each client, patient, parishioner, customer, or member and as it becomes possible to exchange data files among organizations by machine-to-machine communication, the possibility of a complete record on every citizen arises. His educational, medical, military, employment, governmental, and civic activities could be so assembled and circulated that he would confront an "official" portrait of himself everywhere he turned, at critical stages of his life. Not only would this close off escapes from past mistakes or failures and give unprecedented powers to the authorities who compiled and used such dossiers, but it also would raise fundamental issues as to what information should be collected at all, how errors could be caught and subjective evaluations challenged, and how such files could be prevented from suffocating free expression and political dissent.

26   Confronted with these technological possibilities for the future, some critics have called for a total ban, urging that the creation of all such data banks be outlawed. Others say that no public intervention is needed at this time; aware that any total consolidation of information within agencies is unrealistic today and aware that the assembling of life dossiers using data from many organizations is even more remote, they believe that existing regulations about the confidential nature of information are enough to protect rights to privacy or to individual review of file contents.

27   Again, I believe it is the variety of responses that are most effective in dealing with the real social dilemmas. We need extensive information to manage a rational and humane society—to make judgments about individuals, programs, and policies. The computer cannot be stuffed back in the bottle of undiscovered technology, nor should we have to do so to preserve civil liberties. What is needed is a ban by law on any computerized data banks that are so dangerous per se that they should not be allowed (such as a proposal that the California national guard compile a data bank on political protesters). Among other possible responses, we might convene hearings before legislatures and regulatory commissions so that government agencies and interstate organizations may present their plans for computerized systems and demonstrate necessary safeguards before they are allowed to computerize sensitive files containing personal information. Within the computerized systems, we can reexamine existing rules, such as those which pertain to the confidential nature of data, and then formulate rules that are fully responsible to norms of privacy and due process.

28   As these examples of policy choices suggest, what confronts us is the age-old problem of how man uses the tools that nature or science make available to him. If we mean to preserve and update the right of privacy in the electronic age, there are ways to do so intelligently.

29   What may well be the underlying question for the 1970's is whether American society as a whole is able to provide the racial and economic justice and able to provide the paths to world peace which will allow the nation to become unified again, pursuing the goals of a humane democracy. If we move along those paths, we can work out the problems of balancing privacy, disclosure, and surveillance. If we do not, if the internal struggles of American society deepen, then those who oppose the structure of the society will challenge any measures that would make elected government or private institutions more effective; the claim to privacy will then become open defiance and a withdrawal from organized society. At the same time, authorities facing such challenges are likely to seek greater surveillance powers to cope with the sharpening conflict. What this tells us is that privacy is not an end in itself, for either the individual or society. It is a means for helping to achieve a healthy personality in a healthy social system. As in the time of Athens, Rome, and the early European nation-states, the enjoyment of privacy will, in the United States, depend for its vitality on the state of the nation.

CONSIDERATIONS

What evidence does Westin cite to show that Americans are concerned about the increasing invasion of their privacy? Do you agree with his interpretation of the findings? What technological developments have contributed to the loss of privacy? Should wiretapping be banned completely? Should it ever be allowed? How much surveillance and investigation are necessary for the government to function properly? Is the collection of information by the government an activity that should be halted?

Note the use of questions in the opening paragraph. What is their purpose? How do they help the reader? Why does the author repeat one of the questions? Locate several instances of the use of comparison and contrast in this selection. From time to time Westin summarizes the preceding paragraph in a single sentence. Locate several instances of this. Why is this a good device? What statistical (or other) evidence does Westin cite to support his thesis? Where is the central idea stated?

In a theme, present your reactions to one of the following statements:
If a person doesn't have anything to hide, he shouldn't object to being
investigated or having a file kept on him. Our national security requires that the government invade its citizens' privacy from time to
time.

VOCABULARY

(7)   **hedonistic**   devoted to pleasure

(7)   **deviationist**   in Communist ideology, one who departs
                          from accepted ideas

(16) **dossiers**   files

Description

DESCRIPTION

Description is one of the four classifications of prose writing. The purpose of description—as its name implies—is, simply, to describe; to directly present things. You have an image of something or someone in your mind and you attempt to create that image in the mind of your reader. Obviously pure description, like pure exposition or narration, is almost impossible in an extended essay. Description works with other techniques of development in writing. Although description can be technical—simply providing information about something, as in exposition—but more often, we consider description to be the kind of writing that gives the reader an impression of something.

You can describe something physical and concrete, but you can also describe a feeling or thought. You may use connotative, figurative, or emotional language. You may describe by using examples, comparison and contrast, or analysis.

Careful selection of detail is the key to successful description. You want to be specific, associative, fresh, vivid, and you must provide sufficient detail to produce the right degree of sensory impression. Don't overdo it, but don't be satisfied with only a bare framework either. Good description makes all types of prose writing better.

PRACTICE

1. Choose a familiar object—your car, an electric guitar, your favorite beach or mountain haunt—and describe it in two or three paragraphs. Or choose a feeling or action (your first traumatic love loss) and describe it in detail. Remember: by using written words you want to create in someone else's mind a feeling as close as possible to your own feeling.

2. Write a descriptive theme that conveys several different moods.

3. Choose a passage from Aldous Huxley or Theodore Dreiser or some other early twentieth-century writer and analyze the differences between their type of description and the kind you find in Tom Wolfe, Richard Brautigan, or Hunter Thompson.

Farewell, My Nation! Farewell, Black Hawk!

Through the use of description, the author has created both a physical and emotional environment for his essay; that is, the essay evokes images of scenes and situations as well as emotional responses. Write a descriptive essay in which you re-create in the mind of the reader the feelings you experienced when you viewed or were part of a certain scene.

California 2001

In order to create a sense of reality, this author provides certain details in his description. Write a descriptive fantasy in which you use detail to convey an image of imaginative reality. The implications of the details should create a subtle emotional atmosphere as well. For example, in *California 2001*, the description of the "people movers" (paragraph 10) sets up a mental environment of calm efficiency and a sense of security in the complex transport system. (In other words, your details should convey more than themselves.)

Middle America Has Its Woodstock, Too

Description is an essential element in writing characterizations. For example, in paragraph 10, Greenfield writes:

> At the edge of the field, on a flat-bed truck, a pleasant balding man in his sixties, who could be the principal of a small-town junior high school, is trying to spread the good word of the Gospel.

If the author had written merely "a pleasant, balding man in his sixties," we would have a more limited image of the man. But the addition of "who could be the principal of a small-town junior high school" sets up a more specific type of mental image for the reader. Write a character sketch describing someone you don't know personally (such as someone who works in the library, cafeteria, or so on). Extend the description to suggest a particular type or personality

The Sculptor Speaks

In this essay Moore describes how a sculptor must study a natural form, like a block of stone or wood, in order to determine what form the finished piece of art is to take. Write a paragraph describing some natural object which suggests other images. Then, choose a photograph, painting, or piece of sculpture that you find particularly meaningful. Describe the details of the piece in a paragraph and explain how and why those particular details cause a certain response in you.

Where I Live

Thoreau uses a number of rhetorical devices to make his essay vivid and real. For example, look at paragraph 3, in which he uses a simile. Write a descriptive essay, borrowing Thoreau's theme, "Where I Live." It can be a description of your country, state, city, neighborhood, home, or even your own room. Be sure to make your details associative and use various types of figurative language to create a strong mental picture.

• Your senses play an important part in descriptive writing. A tree, for example, excites all of the senses: you can feel the texture, the smoothness of the leaves and the roughness of the bark; you can smell the fragrance of the blossoms or the pungent odor of sap; you can hear the sound of the leaves rustling in the wind and the raspy sound of dry branches rubbing together (and you can even taste the bitterness of a crushed leaf).

   As an exercise in sensual description, listen to some music and write a description of the effect on all of the senses. Obviously you will describe the sound, but also bring your other senses into play: What visual images does the music create? What smells, tastes, or textures are suggested by the music? What particular detail of the music (individual instruments, rhythm, and so on) causes these sensations and associations?

For examples of individual paragraphs using *description*, see p.7, ¶1, p.19, ¶10, p.109, ¶10–13, p.110, ¶21–29, p.155, ¶4, p.216, ¶37, p.280, ¶4.

Farewell, My Nation! Farewell, Black Hawk!

Dictated by BLACK HAWK to ANTOINE LeCLAIR

1   Soon after our return home, news reached us that a war was going *Narr* to take place between the British and the Americans.

2   Runners continued to arrive from different tribes, all confirming the reports of the expected war. The British agent, Colonel Dixon, was holding talks with, and making presents to, the different tribes. I had not made up my mind whether to join the British or remain neutral. I had not discovered yet one good trait in the character of the Americans who had come to the country. They made *C & C* fair promises but never fulfilled them, while the British made but few, and we could always rely implicitly on their word.

3   One of our people having killed a Frenchman at Prairie du Chien, the British took him prisoner and said they would shoot him next day. His family were encamped a short distance below the mouth of the Wisconsin. He begged for permission to go and see them that night as he was to die the next day. They permitted him to go after he had promised them to return by sunrise the next morning.

4   He visited his family, which consisted of his wife and six children. I cannot describe their meeting and parting so as to be understood by the whites, as it appears that their feelings are acted upon by certain rules laid down by their preachers, while ours are governed by the monitor within us. He bade his loved ones the last sad farewell and hurried across the prairie to the fort and arrived in

time. The soldiers were ready and immediately marched out and shot him down.

5   [Interrupting the straight course of his account he says in melancholy:]

6   Why did the Great Spirit ever send the whites to this island to drive us from our homes and introduce among us poisonous liquors, disease, and death? They should have remained in the land the Great Spirit allotted to them. But I will proceed with my story. My memory, however, is not very good since my late visit to the white people. I have still a buzzing noise in my ears. . . . I may give some parts of my story out of place, but will make my best endeavor to be correct.   *Tone*

7   [Some chiefs were called upon to go to Washington to see the Great Father, who wanted them in case of war to remain neutral, promising them to let the traders sell to them in the fall goods on credit, that they might hunt and repay with furs in the spring, as the British had arranged it up to then. Everything depended for the Sac upon this institution. But—the trader refused bluntly to sell on credit.]

8   The war chief said the trader could not furnish us on credit, and that he had received no instructions from our Great Father at Washington. We left the fort dissatisfied and went to camp. What was now to be done we knew not. . . . Few of us slept that night. All was gloom and discontent.

9   [As a result of this treatment they joined the British.]

10   Our lodges were soon taken down, and we all started for Rock Island. <u>Here ended all hopes of our remaining at peace, having been forced into war by being deceived.</u> . . .   *C & E*

11   We continued our march, joining the British below Detroit, soon after which we had a battle. The Americans fought well and drove us back with considerable loss. I was greatly surprised at this, as I had been told that the Americans would not fight. . . .

12   On my arrival at the village I was met by the chiefs and braves and conducted to the lodge which was prepared for me. After eating, I gave a full account of all that I had seen and done. I explained   *C & C*
to my people the manner in which the British and Americans fought. Instead of stealing upon each other and taking every advantage to kill the enemy and save their own people as we do, which with us is considered good policy in a war chief, they march out in open daylight and fight regardless of the number of warriors they may lose. After the battle is over they retire to feast and drink wine

as if nothing had happened. After which they make a statement in writing of what they have done, each party claiming the victory and neither giving an account of half the number that have been killed on their own side. | *C & C*

13   [The British lose constantly. After a long time of consideration and many councils Black Hawk decides to make a treaty of peace with the "chief at St. Louis."] | *Narr*

14   The great chief at St. Louis having sent word for us to come down and confirm the treaty, we did not hesitate but started immediately that we might smoke the peace pipe with him. On our arrival we met the great chiefs in council. They explained to us the words of our Great Father in Washington, accusing us of heinous crimes and many misdemeanors, particularly in not coming down when first invited. We knew very well that our Great Father had deceived us and thereby forced us to join the British, and could not believe that he had put this speech into the mouths of those chiefs to deliver to us. I was not a civil chief and consequently made no reply, but our civil chiefs told the commissioners: "What you say is a lie. Our Great Father sent us no such speech, he knew that the situation in which we had been placed was caused by him." The white chiefs appeared very angry at this reply and said, "We will break off the treaty and make war against you, as you have grossly insulted us."

15   Our chiefs had no intention of insulting them and told them so, saying, "We merely wish to explain that you have told us a lie, without any desire to make you angry, in the same manner that you whites do when you do not believe what is told you." The council then proceeded and the pipe of peace was smoked.

16   Here for the first time I touched the goose quill to sign the treaty, not knowing, however, that by the act I consented to give away my village. Had that been explained to me I should have opposed it and never would have signed their treaty, as my recent conduct will clearly prove. What do we know of the manners, the laws, and customs of the white people? They might buy our bodies for dissection, and we would touch the goose quill to confirm it and not know what we were doing. This was the case with me and my people in touching the goose quill the first time.

17   We can only judge of what is proper and right by our standard of what is right and wrong, which differs widely from the whites', if I have been correctly informed. The whites may do wrong all their lives and then if they are sorry for it when about to die, all is well, but with us it is different. We must continue to do good throughout | *C & C*

our lives. If we have corn and meat, and know of a family that have none, we divide with them. If we have more blankets than we absolutely need, and others have not enough, we must give to those who are in want.

18   [As Black Hawk could not yield to the demand of the "white chiefs" and leave his village and his graveyard, a war ensued, the so-called Black Hawk War, lasting from 1831-2. Chief Keokuk, his great antagonist, who was willing to negotiate with the whites and persuaded part of the tribe to abandon the village, caused thus a rift among the Sac.]

19   I looked upon Keokuk as a coward and no brave. . . . What right had these people [the whites] to our village and our fields, which the Great Spirit had given us to live upon? My reason teaches me that land cannot be sold. The Great Spirit gave it to his children to live upon and cultivate as far as necessary for their subsistence, and so long as they occupy and cultivate it they have the right to the soil, but if they voluntarily leave it, then any other people have a right to settle on it. Nothing can be sold but such things as can be carried away.

Anly

20   [It was at Fort Crawford that Black Hawk, in the despair of defeat, said: "Farewell, my nation! Farewell, Black Hawk!"]

21   The massacre which terminated the war lasted about two hours. Our loss in killed was about sixty, besides a number that was drowned. . . .

22   I was now given up by the agent to the commanding officer at Fort Crawford, the White Beaver [General Atkinson] having gone down the river.

23   On our way down I surveyed the country that had cost us so much trouble, anxiety, and blood, and that now caused me to be a prisoner of war. I reflected upon the ingratitude of the whites when I saw their fine houses, rich harvests, and everything desirable around them; and recollected that all this land had been ours, for which I and my people had never received a dollar, and that the whites were not satisfied until they took our village and our graveyards from us and removed us across the Mississippi.

Tone

24   On our arrival at Jefferson Barracks we met the great war chief, White Beaver, who had commanded the American army against my little band. I felt the humiliation of my situation; a little while before I had been leader of my braves, now I was a prisoner of war. He received us kindly and treated us well.

25   We were now confined to the barracks and forced to wear the ball and chain. This was extremely mortifying and altogether use-

less. Was the White Beaver afraid I would break out of his barracks and run away? Or was he ordered to inflict this punishment upon me? If I had taken him prisoner on the field of battle I would not have wounded his feelings so much by such treatment, knowing that a brave war chief would prefer death to dishonor. But I do not blame the White Beaver for the course he pursued, as it is the custom among white soldiers, and I suppose was a part of his duty.

Black Hawk's Dedication to General Atkinson

26 Sir—The changes of fortune and vicissitudes of war made you my conqueror. When my last resources were exhausted, my warriors, worn down with long and toilsome marches, yielded, and I became your prisoner. The story of my life is told in the following pages: it is intimately connected, and in some measure identified with a part of the history of your own: I have, therefore, dedicated it to you.

27 The changes of many summers have brought old age upon me, and I cannot expect to survive many moons. Before I set out on my journey to the land of my fathers, I have determined to give my motives and reasons for my former hostilities to the whites, and to vindicate my character from misrepresentations. The kindness I received from you whilst a prisoner of war assures me that you will vouch for the facts contained in my narrative, so far as they came under your observation.

28 I am now an obscure member of a nation that formerly honored and respected my opinions. The pathway to glory is rough, and many gloomy hours obscure it. May the Great Spirit shed light on yours, and that you may never experience the humiliation that the power of the American government has reduced me to, is the wish of him who, in his native forests, was once as proud as you.

Dict

Tone

10th Moon 1833.   Black Hawk

A Sequence of Songs of the Ghost Dance Religion

1.

My children,
When at first I liked the whites,
I gave them fruits,
I gave them fruits.

2.

Father have pity on me,
I am crying for thirst,
All is gone,
I have nothing to eat.

3.

The father will descend,
The earth will tremble,
Everybody will arise,
Stretch out your hands.

4.

The Crow—*Ehe'eye!*
I saw him when he flew down,
To the earth, to the earth.
He has renewed our life,
He has taken pity on us.

5.

I circle around
The boundaries of the earth,
Wearing the long wing feathers,
As I fly.

6.

I'yehé! my children—
My children,
We have rendered them desolate.
The whites are crazy—Ahe'yuhe'yu!

7.

We shall live again,
We shall live again.

CONSIDERATIONS

In this brief selection Black Hawk clearly delineates the basic differences in philosophy and life style between white men and Indians.
What is the red man's attitude toward land-property for instance? Ana-

lyze the other marked polarities between whites and Indians of the eighteenth and nineteenth centuries to which Black Hawk and his biographer, LeClair, refer. Are such differences so basic to human behavior that they make coexistence virtually impossible? Will the technologically stronger men always tend to exploit the weaker?

Does the tone of this selection reinforce or negate your stereotype of Indian thought, style, and culture? For instance, when Black Hawk tells of the Indian man voluntarily showing up at his own death by firing squad, the irony of the situation is reinforced or emphasized by the tone in which the speaker tells of the incident. In what way is this so?

VOCABULARY

(14) **heinous**   odious; totally reprehensible
(27) **vindicate**   clear of suspicion

California 2001

AL MARTINEZ

1   Morning comes to California, gleaming off the amber dome of a transpoliner that streaks south out of San Francisco on a cushion of air.

The linear induction motors accelerate smoothly, pressing the multiunit commuter to its cruising speed of 300 m.p.h. just clear of the sprawling San Jose megalopolis.

The six-forty-fiver is nonstop to Los Angeles. The trip will take an hour and 20 minutes.

The day is Tuesday, Sept. 25, 2001.

5   Overhead, on its regular 18-day orbit, the manned station Skylab glides through space, its sensitive scanning equipment geared now to monitor the life of the Golden State in the golden autumn: the rush of rivers and traffic, the purity of air and ocean, the sum of resources and population, the health of crops and forests, the subtle movement of mountains and the barely perceptible erosion of granite.

All of this, translated in a flicker to analog-video-digital telemetry, is flashed to Sacramento as Skylab, its passover done, moves out of range, and as the transpoliner slips by Joaquin-1 on the western edge of the great Central Valley near Polonia Pass.

Joaquin-1 is the first of the cities conceived by a coalition of planners from government and the private sector to relieve the pressure of urbanization from California's overpopulated metropolitan centers, and it is aborning now at the confluence of a network of water and power and transportation, where need and nature destined it should be.

Here business and industry will flourish in a population complex designed to overcome the enigma of wasted space and congestion that still threatens the survival of the big cities. Here new knowledge uses land for capacity and privacy and creates an architecture at peace with nature.

The transpoliner, its computerized acceleration system ignorant of the dream coming true, is past Joaquin-1 in a twinkling and flies through the morning toward its final destination—by towns that appear with disturbing unplanned frequency in the distance, near low hills that mask the nuclear power plants of an energy-hungry state, through the far-flung outskirts of the L.A. suburbs that sprawl into Ventura County.

10   Finally, Los Angeles.

The transpoliner dips through an underground opening to the mammoth subsurface downtown DOT (Department of Transportation) terminal and glides to a stop, settling gently through the cushion of air to its base.

The doors slide open automatically and the passengers leave their cars. They board electrically operated feeder pods, the so-called people movers, that transport them to key points throughout the big city.

The pods glide with a soft whir on fixed guideways twenty feet aboveground, over the elevated pedestrian walkways and the protected malls and the small clean cars that dart through a shimmery day in a world that has discovered the value of clear air after a choking haze.

The city comes to life. The business of the day is beginning.

15   Thirteen miles northwest of the downtown section, in a multi-use high-rise building near the intersection of Mulholland Drive and the San Diego Freeway, morning has come with the clicking awake of an automated household.

A medium-impact Homemaster, the miniaturized and simplified version of a business computer, has been pre-programmed to bring the essentials of a new day to the six-room apartment.

Indirect lighting spreads automatically through each room, a microwave oven heats up, music plays, a coffee maker turns on and a video screen flashes a reminder of the day's commitments.

A family of three yawns and stretches into the routine of the morning in a scene that is repeated again and again in other high-activity centers and in the suburbs, the New Towns and the desert developments.

The Mulholland high-rise is a relatively new application in urbanized cluster living, part of the movement to utilize space and distance that evolved into multi-use structures.

20   That family of three, out of the steamy showers now and around their instant breakfast, is but one segment of the building they occupy.

Not only are there other apartments in the same building—varying as much in price, style and size as homes in a suburban neighborhood—but the unit contains services as well.

School is three levels up, and the bread-winner in the family works in a spacious sub-surface center that assembles instrumentations for the space shuttlecraft at the Vandenberg launching facility.

Other buildings in the Mulholland Cluster are devoted to specific purposes. There is a health-care center that houses a hospital, an out-patient clinic, doctors' offices, laboratories, a rehabilitation unit, a nursing home and an ambulance company.

Another structure combines police and fire headquarters and government offices, and another a wide variety of entertainment facilities from an opera hall to a sports arena. Most of the rooftops are utilized for parks and swimming.

25   School is without grades and grading, and the six-million public school children of California have emerged as individuals in a system drastically regeared to provide for individual need.

Sophisticated learning machines are utilized in open classrooms, and teachers have become managers of education.

But the human component has not been abandoned in the age of electronic gadgetry.

Senior citizens, a previously untapped reservoir of knowledge and experience, are volunteer teaching assistants. So are housewives and college students.

In the higher grades, the youngsters take a portion of their classes in the centers of communication, government, industry, law and commerce, taught by those involved in the function of society.

30   It has been a long-evolving dream to integrate learning with society, to realistically equate education with improvement of the culture, to utilize competitive technology for knowledge as well as profit.

The dream comes true not only in the skyscraper world of the high activity centers of Los Angeles, but in the far-flung suburbs as well, drenched now by the mid-morning sun on a blue-sky Tuesday of tomorrow.

The suburbs of California endure around the giant urban centers despite growing efforts to disperse and redistribute the population into the more sparsely inhabited sections of the state.

Growth Regulated

An air-cushion rapid transit system, which also ties the high-activity centers together, makes living in the suburbs and working in the cities easier, but suburban growth is regulated by law.

Building permits are frozen or only reluctantly granted in "down-zoning" programs around Los Angeles, San Francisco, Sacramento and San Diego.

35   For some areas it came too late; the residential clutter is the result along the high-speed transportation corridors of exurbia.

But in other suburban regions, streets have been closed off to provide for the kinds of parks and open spaces only grudgingly granted in the past.

Light industry and warehouse facilities which still exist beyond their specified areas are underground, and the land above them is utilized for public services.

Among the services are transportation terminals. Planners began to realize in the 1960s how instrumental the efficient movement of people would be to the survival of the cities.

They rejected as intolerable expedients the mass construction of additional freeways to meet travel demands.

40   Instead, state and federal money went into the study, design and creation of air-cushion and electric transit projects, and construction lead-time dissolved in the acid of necessity.

Rapid Transport

They had to be built, and therefore they were built.

The long-distance transpoliners, flashing between the cities, evolved along with the interurban systems, the people movers, and the smogless jitneys.

These same ground transportation systems have favored today's continued heavy reliance on jet travel by drastically lessening the time it takes to get from one's home to an airport.

A new generation of jet engines are pollution free and quiet,

and their short takeoff and landing capabilities have also minimized
the environmental impact of airports by limiting their size.

45   It was the environmental movement generally, a revolution
full-blown in the ecology-minded sixties that has resulted in today's
smogless cities.

The air snaps with a brilliance predating that era of pollution
when the sun shone orange through a deadly haze, when the stars
were blurred, when the outlines of the buildings were vague in the
brownish density that settled over them.

Now the works of men stand sharply defined against the irides-
cent sky, and nowhere—not piled against the mountainsides nor
stagnant in the land basins—is there even a hint of smog.

Water pollution is also only a distant battle—won in the war
to preserve the environment.

The victory is evident as the sun at noon shimmers off the
revitalized streams and the once dying lakes of California, the level
of their purity monitored by instruments 1,000 times more sensitive
than they once were.

50   Pollution is measured in parts per trillion, where yesterday such
minutiae was not even detectable.

Natural Coastline

But environment involves some abstracts too, and one of them is
beauty. Toward esthetic considerations, mansions along with shan-
ties have been removed by law as shoreline barriers to the blue
Pacific.

And private vehicular traffic has been permanently barred from
the mountain recreation areas in favor of public monorails to help
preserve California's forest lands in perpetuity.

All these are triumphs of the environmental wars, a conglomer-
ate name for the crusade to survive that finally unlocked the ecolo-
gists and the economists from what had become a private struggle
and got them working together for the good of the future.

Their union spawned creation in the early 1980s of the California Committee, an independent, privately financed, quasi-official
forum with Sacramento representation and approval.

55   Initially a coalescence of environmental organizations, the
California Committee assumed special status as an advisory body to
the Legislature upon successful submission of a master plan for
California.

The plan, until then only a long-standing dream, lays out state responsibility for orderly growth and assumes the function of an outline for the more substantive progress of today.

Today.

It begins to fade now as afternoon comes sliding down the western slope of the Cascade Range and flattens out over Mountain Country, the state's newest tourist mecca.

The mecca rises from the brushland southeast of Redding in the shadow of Mt. Lassen, a Disneylandish recreation center half-history and half-carnival.

To Draw Population

60 Essentially concerned with re-creating and animating early California, Mountain Country embodies at least one element of a philosophy of population dispersion.

A private undertaking encouraged by tax incentives and a state transportation system, it will hopefully be the nucleus of a whole new population center in a wide-open region.

Until it becomes that nucleus, Mountain Country at least serves to shift a portion of the yearly tourist trade away from those areas barely able to handle the influx of visitors.

Masses of people have long been a critical consideration in California's concept of the future.

Demographers were warning three decades ago that unchecked growth could result in one giant megalopolis covering 50,000 square miles from San Francisco to San Diego and jammed with 40 million people.

65 Those who feared its inevitability were already calling it San-San and were saying that a total state population as high as 50 million-plus by the year 2000 was not unrealistic.

The population of California today is 33 million.

Even at that, power needs have quadrupled over the last 30 years, urban water needs have doubled, solid waste has increased at five times the population growth, demands on the state park system have doubled.

The needs have so far been met, even to the closed-loop recycling of solid waste into new uses.

But they didn't know then, in the edgy days of the fading twentieth century, that they would, or even could, be met.

70 They called for strict migration control into California, for laws to remove all legal barriers to abortion, for tough marriage requirements among minors, for mandatory birth-control classes.

But as the population boom ended (the birthrate dropped, in-migration eased), the emphasis shifted from control to guidance.

Today, to assure that growth remains at a moderate level, revised income tax deductions discourage large families, a national employment policy has opened new job opportunities in other states and the creation of a uniform welfare system throughout the nation has ended California's reign as one of the places to go for public assistance.

Efforts at Dispersion

New energy is being concentrated now in dispersing the population within the state.

One of the results is Joaquin-1 along the route of the San Francisco-Los Angeles transpoliner and in close proximity to Interstate 5, the San Luis Reservoir, the California Aqueduct and a major power tie-in.

75   Joaquin-1 remains largely experimental to determine whether a so-called New Town, a prepackaged community of homes, services and industries, can survive—and to test how successful it might be in redirecting the state's population away from the cities.

Another effort at population redistribution is also being made in the Mojave east of Barstow where the Desert Campus of the University of California is in fall session.

College in Desert

Desert Campus contributes to the birth of a new university town, its creation enhanced by piped-in water, a direct major highway connection out of Barstow, a new jet field for STOL aircraft and the promise of air-cushion feeder service out of the Pasadena substation.

Here, around the tenth campus of the 150,000-student statewide UC system, tax incentives are again being offered to induce controlled residential and industrial development.

The state hopes that the new campus will have impact beyond education, and that simply by existing it will encourage the establishment of other desert cities—their outdoor activities domed, their transportation underground, their life geared to a blazing sun that hangs low even now over the Calico Mountains this Tuesday in September.

80   The day is fading over a California in transition.

Much has been done at this moment in time to make the Golden State a better place to live. Much remains to be done through the twenty-first century.

The sins of the past are the problems of the present. Economic ghettos exist even though low-cost housing in any residential development is a fact of law.

Inequities Persist

Some forms of animal life continue to face extinction even though hunting has been all but regulated out of existence and game reserves are widespread in the strenuous effort to preserve our wildlife.

There are inequities based on the historic divisions of race and religion and political commitment. Crime plagues the New Towns as well as the old cities. Taxes are high. Prices continue to rise. There is never enough money.

85   But there is hope. The California Committee will convene tomorrow in Sacramento to consider one more quality of life and to materialize that abstract into manageable substance.

There is talk that the committee itself has become unmanageable, that perhaps there ought to be a North Committee and a South Committee, and the irony of these internal problems is not lost on the members.

But there will be time enough for that tomorrow and the day after tomorrow and all the days after that.

For now the evening has come and the families have gathered and the business of the day has ended.

The night is Tuesday, September 25, 2001.

90   California sleeps.

CONSIDERATIONS

The author describes a family living in a multi-use structure, a high-rise apartment in the heart of the city. Why doesn't he provide more details about the community life of these living complexes? Do you get a sense of community—of real human beings actively living? Or is the atmosphere one of sterility? What advantages would there be to these urban living centers?

You might classify this article as a sketch; it touches briefly on dozens of subjects but does not probe any single subject in depth. Do you find this format a satisfactory way to treat the topic of California in 2001? Would you prefer more detail on any particular subject? What rhetorical devices unify the article? If you think it lacks cohesion, explain why it does.

If you are of a more pessimistic mind than this article reflects, present your own version of the year 2001. Emphasize the same points this writer does: population-growth trends, transportation, pollution, education, and labor situations.

VOCABULARY

(2)	megalopolis	huge, sprawling metropolis
(6)	telemetry	in electronics, the electrical transmitting of information over long distances
(7)	aborning	coming into realization or fruition
(7)	confluence	the point of junction of various parts
(8)	enigma	a puzzling or inexplicable occurrence or situation
(35)	exurbia	the generalized area composed of exurbs—small, fashionable communities beyond the suburbs of a city
(39)	expedients	means to an end, not always in the best interest of people in the long run
(42)	jitneys	small passenger buses following regular routes at regular intervals
(47)	iridescent	displaying a play of lustrous colors like those of the rainbow
(52)	perpetuity	the state or character of being perpetual, endless
(58)	mecca	a place that many people hope to visit
(64)	demographers	scientists who study and record vital statistics—births, deaths, marriages, and population trends

Middle America Has Its Woodstock, Too

JEFF GREENFIELD

1   It is a warm night, and the sky overhead is lit up by searchlights. Cars, campers, trucks, buses, station wagons—thousands of vehicles with thousands of people in and milling around them—are parked in ragged rows that stretch back and forth across the huge field at 30th Street off Georgetown Road in the All-American city of Indianapolis, Indiana.

2   A cacophony of jazz, pop, rock and roll blasts into the night from speakers hooked to radios, tape decks, and stereos. Hundreds of barbecue grills broil steaks, hamburgers, hot dogs. Oceans of beer, surely more than 100,000 bottles and cans of it, are popped and twist-snapped open. The whine of motorcycles, their single lights cutting through the dark, speed up and down the fire lanes between the rows of cars. Grown men with wives and children shout their *macho* yearnings at young women.

3   "Hey, sister, I'd sure like to get my dipstick into you!"

4   "Hey! Any of you girls wanna be liberated, you just come on over to this here camper, you hear? Sleeps six and lays twelve! Ha-ha-ha."

5   Almost as often, the men invoke another common denominator as well:
"Hey! Whattya drinkin'?"
"Coors! Great beer!"

"Aw, that's crap!"

"Goddamn, you don't know your beer!"

10   At the edge of the field, on a flat-bed truck, a pleasant, balding man in his sixties, who could be the principal of a small-town junior high school, is trying to spread the good word of the Gospel.

11   "You boys and girls, you've got to please God by faith. How about you, young lady? Would you like to be called a child of God tonight? How 'bout you, young fella? Will you overcome the world?"

12   "Somebody get the preacher a beer!" shouts a crew-cut boy of fifteen, who well might be singing in the preacher's choir on another weekend. But not this weekend. This is the Friday midnight of Memorial Day weekend, and for these thousands, it is a time for furious revelry, release, and a strange blend of fellowship and indulgence, all part of one of the most extraordinary conglomerations I have ever attended anywhere: The Indianapolis 500 Mile International Sweepstakes.

13   Every year more than 300,000 people pack the fields and stands around the track of the Indianapolis Speedway, ostensibly to witness the running of the 500 Mile Race, with its million dollars in prize money, record-breaking speeds, and a constant promise of fiery death. It is the single biggest event held in America; in any given year more Americans meet in one place at one time here at the speedway than anywhere else in the country.

14   From May 1, when the speedway opens for practice runs, through the time trials to determine who qualifies for entry into the race, up through the neosacred Race Day, a fever begins to build all through Indianapolis. Indiana newspapers fill page upon page with history, legend, predictions, and interviews with everyone from the hot-dog concessionaires to John MacKenzie, the man who carries into Victory Lane the ponderous Borg-Warner trophy with which to honor the winner. More than 100,000 people attend the time trials on the weekends before Memorial Day. By the Friday night before the race, fans who drive here from as far away as California and Oregon are settled in their beer-swilling camping areas, ready for the gates to swing open at 5:00 a.m. on Race Day, so they can guide their cars into the enormous infield area of the track. From this vantage point, where not more than a tenth of the track can be seen, the fans set up platforms and chairs on the tops of vehicles. The resulting cluster of humanity is something like a tract of suburbia writ small, each family or group carving out a few square feet of land. And there, under an increasingly hot sky, inhaling the stench

of gasoline, burning rubber and charcoal, the fans eat and drink away the dawn and the morning and finally the climactic afternoon during which thirty-three drivers in exotic-looking automobiles flash by them.

15   Why do the people come? Certainly, the city of Indianapolis is no part of the attraction. This is perhaps the worst metropolis in the entire United States—a city with endless miles of indifferent gray structures, Burger Chefs, and Kentucky Fried Chicken stands and a political climate that welcomed such spasms of paranoia as the Klan during the Twenties and the Birchers in the Sixties. Even if the Indy fans were drawn to such a city, none of them would leave their valued places at the speedway to journey downtown.

16   Still, it is not simply, or even primarily, the race that attracts the fans. It is the awesome, terrifying, hilarious spectacle surrounding the race, a spectacle that holds within itself a welter of contradictory yearnings tearing at what is left of our national spirit: glory, speed, wealth, fellowship, and death. After witnessing the Indy for a weekend, I came away with an overriding sense of sorrow at what we have done to each other and to ourselves.

17   The 500 itself is, in part, a celebration of technology, the continuation of an old American tradition, rooted in another age, when people traveled great distances from their isolated communities to hear Chautauqua speakers or witness the new marvels of the machine age: horseless carriages, dirigibles, airplanes, and the wonders of science that promised, at the turn of the twentieth century, to turn the United States into a streamlined technological paradise.

18   The first 500 Mile Race at Indianapolis was run in 1911. It was dreamed up by Carl Fisher, a local promoter-businessman and speed demon, who had originally built the track on which the races were run in order to test improvements for automobiles. Within a few years the race was attracting thousands of spectators from around the country, and it proved a powerful magnet as well for manufacturers, who saw a chance for free publicity by underwriting the cost of machines built with their parts. During the gasoline-scarce days of World War II, the speedway was abandoned. After the war it was brought back to life by Tony Hulman, its present owner and president, and since then the ties between the race and big business have become thoroughly entwined. Piston-ring makers, tire manufacturers, spark-plug producers, and the like help finance the machines, which cost up to $200,000, counting the maintenance costs. And the businessmen of Indianapolis have for fifteen years or so whipped up a promotional effort of Babbitt-sized proportions.

Checkered flags, like those used to wave autos across the finish line, decorate the city. Throughout the month of May a series of events progressively builds up excitement: Festival queens are chosen, there are gin rummy and golf tournaments, a mayor's breakfast, and finally an eve-of-race parade down streets painted with the checkered flag pattern. So ingrained is the race that even the soul-saving evangelists working the camping area pass out tracts bearing the checkered-flag emblem and titled, "Souvenir Victory Edition."

19   Boosterism, however, cannot by itself attract tens of thousands of people to Indianapolis for a week of sleeping in open fields or in the back of campers. The race itself, of course, is a powerful magnet. Each year the cars are lower, sleeker, and more ingeniously designed. This year, for example, their surprisingly fragile fiber-glass bodies are equipped with a small wing in front and a wider wing in the rear; the air pressure against these wings pushes the car down, holding it to the road at speeds that, on the straightaways, approach 200 miles per hour.

20   The sheer power of thirty-three cars roaring around the speedway is unbelievable. From the turn, you hear a high-pitched, angry whine, like a brigade of enraged, giant hornets. Suddenly, the cars appear, hurtling around the banked track and seeming to fly straight at you. Then in a flash of energy, light, sound, dirt, and with an assault of rubber and gasoline smells, they zoom by. It seems odd, given supersonic airplanes and rockets to the moon, that automobiles can be so awesome in their speed. The reason they are, of course, is that the high-speed auto fits into a fantasy that is grafted onto everyday experience. Watching the race at Indy is like attending a Walter Mitty Memorial Convention. Every fan imagines himself behind the wheel of an Olsonite-Eagle or a Ford-McLaren thundering and skidding around the track.

21   "Boy," says Jennings, head of a family of a half-dozen that journeys here every year from eastern Pennsylvania. "I'd love to get in my Chevy and drive around that track just once. They got a little bus that'll give you a tour of the track for fifty cents, but, aw, I'd love to drive around it, just once. Or even get in one of those cars. I don't see why they don't have an old car they'd let you sit in and take a picture. You'd think they'd set it up for the fans."

22   Along with the specter of glory, fame, and speed, of course, is the specter of death. Driving a car at three times the maximum speed permissible on a superhighway is, to say the least, unsafe; running over a piece of metal on the track, making a slight miscalculation in braking or steering in a turn, can send the car smashing

into a wall. And while no visitor will admit openly that it is the prospect of witnessing death that draws him to the race, the anticipation of danger is clearly present in many minds.

23   "Yeah," says Paul, a shipping clerk from Iowa. "I was here in '39 when Floyd Roberts got it, and I remember '64 when Eddie Sachs and MacDonald were burned up. Jeez, that was something. And in '68 I was right there when a guy got killed. Got a great picture of that wreck."

24   For Mike, a state trooper from Ohio who is half-Indian, witnessing the race in person cannot be equaled by television because "the thing that's wrong with TV, they try not to show the grisly part of it when it happens. Now you take this Jim Malloy, who got wrecked in the trials this year. Well, when it first happened, they didn't show the grisly stuff—you know, when he actually hit the wall, how bad it really was."

25   "You'd be surprised," says Cleek, a sun-reddened harvest hand in his sixties who drove in by himself from Oregon in a pickup. "Ninety-nine-and-nine-tenths of 'em come to see wrecks. You hear 'em say, 'Wasn't no good race, no wrecks.' Just like people watching a man on a ledge, most of 'em want him to jump. That's what a lot of people come here for, I believe. I dunno, I see it the other way. That just about ruins it for me. People gettin' pretty damned hard-hearted now. They don't give a damn about their fellow man."

26   The strange mixture of honor and bloodshed, sudden wealth and sudden death, courage and the mechanical skill involved in building a championship car and keeping it moving (a task assigned the "pit" crews who service the cars with the frantic speed and competence of a team of open-heart surgeons) can get a hold on a fan that lasts for a lifetime. It happened to Clyde de Botkin, who was stationed near the speedway during World War II, when it lay idle. "I said to myself, 'If they ever have a race here again, I want to see it.' I came back in '47, and that was it," he recalls.

27   Now in his late forties, Clyde is a round-faced, pleasant man who works as a handy man in Kaycee, Wyoming. For the last twenty-seven years the only vacation Clyde has taken has come between late April and early June. Every year, he has driven—most years by himself—to Indianapolis, taken a room in a boardinghouse, and stayed at the track from April 28 to June 5. He usually hangs out in Gasoline Alley, where the cars are stored and worked on; he has come to know the mechanics and pit crews by sight. The pride of his life is Special Pit Pass Number 777, which a speedway official gave Clyde a decade ago after he had noticed him at the 500 year

after year; the pass permits him to watch the mechanics and drivers at work. The Indy is the only event outside of his daily routine that Clyde de Botkin has experienced in his adult life. He has never even seen another part of America.

28   "Why should I want to?" Clyde says. "This is the most exciting place in the world." Too exciting, in fact. Clyde has an enlarged heart, and he must lie down several times a day in the air-conditioned press room to safeguard his health. "I know it's dangerous," he says; "but if I couldn't be here on Race Day, I just wouldn't . . ." He shrugs.

29   Unlike Clyde de Botkin, who is caught up in the drama of the long, grueling challenge, a remarkable number of Indy fans are almost totally uninterested in the race. "I'd guess about one hundred thousand people here never see the cars in action, don't know who won, and couldn't care less," says a race reporter. For the fans who pack the infield, in fact, the race is almost impossible to watch. Even the more affluent spectators in the upper grandstand can see barely a fourth of the track—it's just too big to see in its entirety.

30   "We'll be watching the backstretch," says Sam, a shipping clerk. "We'll only see a tenth of the race. But when they go by, we'll see this one's first, this one's second, and so on. So if their positions change, we'll know somebody passed."

31   For a sports junkie like me, this was odd to contemplate; it was as if I could watch a hockey game only from a ten-foot-wide stretch of ice, or a baseball game from an obstructed view that revealed only a six-foot chunk of base path. What kind of sports fan would watch an event where he could not see who scored, how, and what outstanding achievements won or lost the game?

32   "See, that's the thing," explains Bill, who has been here since Monday to be first on line to drive through the gate to the infield. "You could just not run the race, and most people here wouldn't give a damn. The main thing is that people get together, and there's no fighting or anything. . . . I know these guys—they been coming here for years. They all park in the same spot at the gate, they mess around for three or four days with each other before the race starts, buying each other beer . . . they take care of each other. When we get inside the track, there'll be friends on both sides of us where we park, everybody sharing everything, and they all have a ball. No, we don't see each other the rest of the year. Just here. And we talk about the times we had and party it up."

33   What Bill says is echoed by many of the hard-core Indy spectators. They come because it is a "good time" and "the world's big-

gest party." For three or four days they live away from the home, the factory, or office. ("Why do I come here?" asks a Bendix-Westinghouse worker from Elyria, Ohio. "Four days away from the kids, with my buddies.") They move outside their existence. They see friends who are friends for a weekend each year. They drink endless cases of beer, grill their steaks together, and yell at the young girls in hot pants and T-shirts with no bras underneath.

34   "You know what this is like?" asks a dark-haired, muscular auto worker. "This is just like that Woodstock. Only those hippies had their music and their dope; we got beer and racing."

35   "Yeah," a buddy interrupts. "Only nobody around here is taking off their clothes and running around bare-ass. Goddamnit." He laughs.

36   There *is* a sense of Woodstock here, a sense of camaraderie. That sense is kindled by staying up all night together on Friday, waiting for the aerial bombs to explode at 5:00 a.m. Saturday signaling the opening of the track, and then the furious, Oklahoma-land-rush sprint to the best positions in the track. ("The real race is at 5:00 a.m.," says a security guard. "The car race, that's just an anticlimax.") But there is also a fierce sense of personal, material pride: in the outfitting of the campers ("We got four bunk beds here, paneling, a can, running water, air conditioning") and the food ("Now, most folks have cold fried chicken. Hell, we got eggs any style, bacon, ham, home fries, and then steak, baked potato and sour cream, salad with blue cheese dressing"). The dull glow of television sets flickers in the late night air, that umbilical link with reality that cannot be turned off and left home.

37   I could not help thinking that we have at Indianapolis a metaphor for the way we live: Here before me are decent, hard-working people, seeking a sense of community and excitement beyond their individual lives, waiting patiently to be packed together with their small luxuries and large discontents, being told what is happening by electronic tote boards and a loudspeaker system, seeking what fun they can find from a spectacle whose drama they cannot very clearly see. Much of the pomp and majesty of the race—the start, the solemn intonation, "Gentlemen, start your engines," the pit stops, the salute to the victor—all of these important events go unwitnessed by those who have come the farthest and endured the most to be "where the action is."

38   An hour before the race ends, hundreds of spectators' cars are already streaming out of the speedway, under a cloud of gasoline fumes, dust, and heat, heading for home. They will not see the

climax of the race, the victorious driver receiving his kiss on the cheek from the queen, the victor's slow, triumphal circuit of the track, nor the winning driver acknowledging the cheers from the grandstand. They have gotten what they came for in the revelry and release and camaraderie; and most of them will be back again next year.

39   "I been goin' to my sister's place for Memorial Day since 1938," says Cookie, a factory hand in his fifties who made his first visit to the Indianapolis 500 this year. "This is the first time I missed going to my sister's. And I think she's never going to see me no more."

40   "One thing about this," observed Cookie, speaking as one of the latest initiates to Middle America's perennial Woodstock. "I guess you either love it or you hate it. And I love it."

CONSIDERATIONS

Is the Indy 500 comparable to a Woodstock festival? What seem to be the chief differences between the devotees of the Indianapolis 500 and their rock-freak counterparts? Do you agree that Americans have done something terrible to each other and to themselves (as Greenfield suggests in paragraphs 16 and 37) if Woodstock and Indy are their ultimate choices for a weekend of fun, excitement, and fellowship? In Greenfield's opinion, what has caused this state of affairs? Do you agree?

Do you think Greenfield has overstated his case, with such explosive images as: "a tract of suburbia writ small, each family or group carving out a few square feet of land"? (paragraph 14) Cite other images that are highly emotional. Do they add to or detract from the author's purpose? Is that purpose to inform, or would you classify the article as narration, description, or argumentation?

Is the intense pride of the recreational-vehicle owners in their gear a replacement of an earlier sort of pride such as the feeling of building your own home or owning your own land? What other directions, if any, can the pioneer spirit take in America today?

VOCABULARY

(2) **cacophony**   a discordant mixture of many sounds
(14) **neosacred**   recently declared sacred or sanctified
(16) **welter**   confusion or turmoil
(17) **Chautauqua**   a summer educational movement, begun in New York, which provided public concerts, lectures, and religious services, and which has served as a model for many twentieth century learning centers

The Sculptor Speaks

HENRY MOORE

1   It is a mistake for a sculptor or a painter to speak or write very often about his job. It releases tension needed for his work. By trying to express his aims with rounded-off logical exactness, he can easily become a theorist whose actual work is only a caged-in exposition of conceptions evolved in terms of logic and words.

But though the non-logical, instinctive, subconscious part of the mind must play its part in his work, he also has a conscious mind which is not inactive. The artist works with a concentration of his whole personality, and the conscious part of it resolves conflicts, organises memories, and prevents him from trying to walk in two directions at the same time.

It is likely, then, that a sculptor can give, from his own conscious experience, clues which will help others in their approach to sculpture, and this article tries to do this, and no more. It is not a general survey of sculpture, or of my own development, but a few notes on some of the problems that have concerned me from time to time.

Appreciation of sculpture depends upon the ability to respond to form in three dimensions. That is perhaps why sculpture has been described as the most difficult of all arts; certainly it is more difficult than the arts which involve appreciation of flat forms, shape in only two dimensions. Many more people are 'form-blind' than colour-blind. The child learning to see, first distinguishes only two-dimensional shape; it cannot judge distances, depths. Later, for its personal safety and practical needs, it has to develop (partly by means of touch) the ability to judge roughly three dimensional distances. But having satisfied the requirements of practical necessity, most people go no farther. Though they may attain considerable accuracy in the perception of flat form, they do not make the further intellectual and emotional effort needed to comprehend form in its full spatial existence.

5   This is what the sculptor must do. He must strive continually to think of, and use, form in its full spatial completeness. He gets the solid shape, as it were, inside his head—he thinks of it, whatever its size, as if he were holding it completely enclosed in the hollow of his hand. He mentally visualises a complex form from all round itself; he knows while he looks at one side what the other side is like; he identifies himself with its centre of gravity, its mass, its weight; he realises its volume, as the space that the shape displaces in the air.

And the sensitive observer of sculpture must also learn to feel shape simply as shape, not as description or reminiscence. He must, for example, perceive an egg as a simple single solid shape, quite apart from its significance as food, or from the literary idea that it will become a bird. And so with solids such as a shell, a nut, a plum, a pear, a tadpole, a mushroom, a mountain peak, a kidney, a carrot, a tree-trunk, a bird, a bud, a lark, a lady-bird, a bulrush, a bone. From these he can go on to appreciate more complex forms or combinations of several forms.

Since the Gothic, European sculpture had become overgrown with moss, weeds—all sorts of surface excrescences which completely concealed shape. It has been Brancusi's special mission to get rid of this overgrowth, and to make us once more shape-conscious. To do this he has had to concentrate on very simple direct shapes, to keep his sculpture, as it were, one-cylindered, to refine and polish a single shape to a degree almost too precious. Brancusi's work, apart from its individual value, has been of historical importance in the development of contemporary sculpture. But it may now be no longer necessary to close down and restrict sculpture to the single (static) form unit. We can now begin to open out. To relate and combine together several forms of varied sizes, sections and directions into one organic whole.

Although it is the human figure which interests me most deeply, I have always paid great attention to natural forms, such as bones, shells, and pebbles, etc. Sometimes for several years running

I have been to the same part of the sea-shore—but each year a new shape of pebble has caught my eye, which the year before, though it was there in hundreds, I never saw. Out of the millions of pebbles passed in walking along the shore, I choose out to see with excitement only those which fit in with my existing form-interest at the time. A different thing happens if I sit down and examine a handful one by one. I may then extend my form-experience more, by giving my mind time to become conditioned to a new shape.

There are universal shapes to which everybody is sub-consciously conditioned and to which they can respond if their conscious control does not shut them off.

10 Pebbles show nature's way of working stone. Some of the pebbles I pick up have holes right through them.

When first working direct in a hard and brittle material like stone, the lack of experience and great respect for the material, the fear of ill-treating it, too often result in relief surface carving, with no sculptural power.

But with more experience the completed work in stone can be kept within the limitations of its material, that is, not be weakened beyond its natural constructive build, and yet be turned from an inert mass into a composition which has a full form existence, with masses of varied sizes and sections working together in spatial relationship.

A piece of stone can have a hole through it and not be weakened—if the hole is of studied size, shape and direction. On the principle of the arch, it can remain just as strong.

The first hole made through a piece of stone is a revelation.

15 The hole connects one side to the other, making it immediately more three-dimensional.

A hole can itself have as much shape-meaning as a solid mass.

Sculpture in air is possible, where the stone contains only the hole, which is the intended and considered form.

The mystery of the hole—the mysterious fascination of caves in hillsides and cliffs.

There is a right physical size for every idea.

20 Pieces of good stone have stood about my studio for long periods, because though I've had ideas which would fit their proportions and materials perfectly, their size was wrong.

There is a size to scale not to do with its actual physical size, its measurement in feet and inches—but connected with vision.

A carving might be several times over life size and yet be petty and small in feeling—and a small carving only a few inches in height can give the feeling of huge size and monumental grandeur, because the vision behind it is big. Example, Michelangelo's drawings or a Masaccio madonna—and the Albert Memorial.[1]

Yet actual physical size has an emotional meaning. We relate everything to our own size, and our emotional response to size is controlled by the fact that men on the average are between five and six feet high.

An exact model to 1/10 scale of Stonehenge, where the stones would be less than us, would lose all its impressiveness.

25   Sculpture is more affected by actual size considerations than painting. A painting is isolated by a frame from its surroundings (unless it serves just a decorative purpose) and so retains more easily its own imaginary scale.

If practical considerations allowed me, cost of material, of transport, etc., I should like to work on large carvings more often than I do. The average in-between size does not disconnect an idea enough from prosaic everyday life. The very small or the very big takes on an added size emotion.

Recently I have been working in the country, where, carving in the open air, I find sculpture more natural than in a London studio, but it needs bigger dimensions. A large piece of stone or wood placed almost anywhere at random in a field, orchard or garden immediately looks right and inspiring.

My drawings are done mainly as a help towards making sculpture—as a means of generating ideas for sculpture, tapping oneself for the initial idea; and as a way of sorting out ideas and developing them.

Also, sculpture compared with drawing is a slow means of expression, and I find drawing a useful outlet for ideas which there is not time enough to realise as sculpture. And I use drawings as a method of study and observation of natural forms (drawings from life, drawings of bones, shells, etc.).

30   And I sometimes draw just for its own enjoyment.

Experience, though, has taught me that the difference there is between drawing and sculpture should not be forgotten. A sculptural idea which may be satisfactory as a drawing always needs some alteration when translated into sculpture.

At one time whenever I made drawings for sculpture I tried to give them as much the illusion of real sculpture as I could—that is, I drew by the method of illusion, of light falling on a solid subject. But I now find that carrying a drawing so far that it becomes a

---

[1] a massive, highly ornate monument in London erected under Queen Victoria's auspices to commemorate her deceased consort, Prince Albert (1819-1861).

substitute for the sculpture, either weakens the desire to do the sculpture, or is likely to make the sculpture only a dead realisation of the drawing.

I now leave a wider latitude in the interpretation of the drawings I make for sculpture, and draw often in line and flat tones without the light and shade illusion of three dimensions; but this does not mean that the vision behind the drawing is only two dimensional.

The violent quarrel between the abstractionists and the surrealists seems to me quite unnecessary. All good art has contained both abstract and surrealist elements, just as it has contained both classical and romantic elements—order and surprise, intellect and imagination, conscious and unconscious. Both sides of the artist's personality must play their part. And I think the first inception of a painting or a sculpture may begin from either end. As far as my own experience is concerned, I sometimes begin a drawing with no preconceived problem to solve, with only the desire to use pencil on paper, and make lines, tones and shapes with no conscious aim; but as my mind takes in what is so produced, a point arrives where some idea becomes conscious and crystallises, and then a control and ordering begin to take place.

35   Or sometimes I start with a set subject; or to solve, in a block of stone of known dimensions, a sculptural problem I've given myself, and then consciously attempt to build an ordered relationship of forms, which shall express my idea. But if the work is to be more than just a sculptural exercise, unexplainable jumps in the process of thought occur; and the imagination plays its part.

It might seem from what I have said of shape and form that I regard them as ends in themselves. Far from it. I am very much aware that associational, psychological factors play a large part in sculpture. The meaning and significance of form itself probably depends on the countless associations of man's history. For example, rounded forms convey an idea of fruitfulness, maturity, probably because the earth, women's breasts, and most fruits are rounded, and these shapes are important because they have this background in our habits of perception. I think the humanist organic element will always be for me of fundamental importance in sculpture, giving sculpture its vitality. Each particular carving I make takes on in my mind a human or occasionally animal, character and personality, and this personality controls its design and formal qualities, and makes me satisfied or dissatisfied with the work as it develops.

My own aim and direction seems to be consistent with these beliefs, though it does not depend upon them. My sculpture is becoming less representational, less an outward visual copy, and so what some people would call more abstract; but only because I believe that in this way I can present the human psychological content of my work with the greatest directness and intensity.

CONSIDERATIONS

Do you think being "form-blind" might be symptomatic of an emotional vacuum, as Moore seems to suggest? Are abstract ideas broken down into physical size for you? (paragraph 19) In what sense does physical size have emotional meaning? (paragraph 23) Are other art forms able to express more than two-dimensional experience, as sculpture does?

Moore describes European sculpture of the nineteenth and twentieth centuries as shapeless (paragraph 7). Examine the metaphor he uses. Is it effective? Is it congruous to his subject? What does he mean (in the same paragraph) by "refine and polish a single shape to a degree almost too precious"? Cite other examples in which his diction is precise.

What art form is most appealing to you, emotionally and intellectually? Give your reasons in a short theme.

VOCABULARY

(7) **excrescences**   an outgrowth or addition, usually abnormal or disfiguring

(26) **prosaic**   commonplace, unimaginative

(34) **abstractionists**   artists who favor the nonrepresentational style of the twentieth century which emphasizes color, line, and form

(34) **surrealists**   artists who subscribe to the twentieth century style which stresses the subconscious or nonrational significance of imagery; their works are highly symbolic

Where I Live

HENRY DAVID THOREAU

1   We must learn to reawaken and keep ourselves awake, not by mechanical aids, but by an infinite expectation of the dawn, which does not forsake us in our soundest sleep. I know of no more encouraging fact than the unquestionable ability of man to elevate his life by a conscious endeavor. It is something to be able to paint a particular picture, or to carve a statue, and so to make a few objects beautiful; but it is far more glorious to carve and paint the very atmosphere and medium through which we look, which morally we can do. To affect the quality of the day, that is the highest of arts. Every man is tasked to make his life, even in its details, worthy of the contemplation of his most elevated and critical hour. If we refused, or rather used up, such paltry information as we get, the oracles would distinctly inform us how this might be done.

2   I went to the woods because I wished to live deliberately, to front only the essential facts of life, and see if I could not learn what it had to teach, and not, when I came to die, discover that I had not lived. I did not wish to live what was not life, living is so dear; nor did I wish to practice resignation, unless it was quite necessary. I wanted to live deep and suck out all the marrow of life, to live so sturdily and Spartan-like as to put to rout all that was not life, to cut a broad swath and shave close, to drive life into a corner, and reduce it to its lowest terms, and, if it proved to be mean, why then to get the whole and genuine meanness of it, and publish its meanness to the world; or if it were sublime, to know it by experi-

ence, and be able to give a true account of it in my next excursion. For most men, it appears to me, are in a strange uncertainty about it, whether it is of the devil or of God, and some *somewhat hastily* concluded that it is the chief end of man here to "glorify God and enjoy him forever."

3   Still we live meanly, like ants; though the fable tells us that we were long ago changed into men; like pygmies we fight with cranes; it is error upon error, and clout upon clout, and our best virtue has for its occasion a superfluous and evitable wretchedness. Our life is frittered away by detail. An honest man has hardly need to count more than his ten fingers, or in extreme cases he may add his ten toes, and lump the rest. Simplicity, simplicity, simplicity! I say, let your affairs be as two or three, and not a hundred or a thousand; instead of a million count half a dozen, and keep your accounts on your thumb nail. In the midst of this chopping sea of civilized life, such are the clouds and storms and quicksands and thousand-and-one items to be allowed for, that a man has to live, if he would not founder and go to the bottom and not make his port at all, by dead reckoning, and he must be a great calculator indeed who succeeds. Simplify, simplify. Instead of three meals a day, if it be necessary eat but one; instead of a hundred dishes, five; and reduce other things in proportion. Our life is like a German Confederacy, made up of petty states, with its boundary forever fluctuating, so that even a German cannot tell you how it is bounded at any moment. The nation itself, with all its so-called internal improvements, which, by the way are all external and superficial, is just such an unwieldy and overgrown establishment, cluttered with furniture and tripped up by its own traps, ruined by luxury and heedless expense, by want of calculation and a worthy aim, as the million households in the land; and the only cure for it as for them is in a rigid economy, a stern and more than Spartan simplicity of life and elevation of purpose. It lives too fast. Men think that it is essential that the *Nation* have commerce, and export ice, and talk through a telegraph, and ride thirty miles an hour, without a doubt, whether *they* do or not; but whether we should live like baboons or like men, is a little uncertain. If we do not get out sleepers, and forge rails, and devote days and nights to the work, but go to tinkering upon our *lives* to improve *them*, who will build railroads? And if railroads are not built, how shall we get to heaven in season? But if we stay at home and mind our business, who will want railroads? We do not ride on the railroad; it rides upon us. Did you ever think what those

sleepers are that underlie the railroad? Each one is a man, an Irish-man, or a Yankee man. The rails are laid on them, and they are covered with sand, and the cars run smoothly over them. They are sound sleepers, I assure you. And every few years a new lot is laid down and run over; so that, if some have the pleasure of riding on a rail, others have the misfortune to be ridden upon. And when they run over a man that is walking in his sleep, a supernumerary sleeper in the wrong position, and wake him up, they suddenly stop the cars, and make a hue and cry about it, as if this were an exception. I am glad to know that it takes a gang of men for every five miles to keep the sleepers down and level in their beds as it is, for this is a sign that they may sometime get up again.

4   Why should we live with such hurry and waste of life? We are determined to be starved before we are hungry. Men say that a stitch in time saves nine, and so they take a thousand stitches today to save nine tomorrow. As for *work*, we haven't any of any conse-quence. We have the Saint Vitus' dance, and cannot possibly keep our heads still. If I should only give a few pulls at the parish bell-rope, as for a fire, that is, without setting the bell, there is hardly a man on his farm in the outskirts of Concord, notwithstanding that press of engagements which was his excuse so many times this morn-ing, nor a boy, nor a woman, I might almost say, but would forsake all and follow that sound, not mainly to save property from the flames, but, if we will confess the truth, much more to see it burn, since burn it must, and we, be it known, did not set it on fire—or to see it put out, and have a hand in it, if that is done as handsomely; yes, even if it were the parish church itself. Hardly a man takes a half hour's nap after dinner, but when he wakes he holds up his head and asks, "What's the news?" as if the rest of mankind had stood his sentinels. Some give directions to be waked every half hour, doubtless for no other purpose; and then, to pay for it, they tell what they have dreamed. After a night's sleep the news is as indispensable as the breakfast. "Pray tell me anything new that has happened to a man anywhere on this globe"—and he reads it over his coffee and rolls, that a man has had his eyes gouged out this morning on the Wachito River; never dreaming the while that he lives in the dark unfathomed mammoth cave of this world, and has but the rudiment of an eye himself.

5   For my part, I could easily do without the post-office. I think that there are very few important communications made through it. To speak critically, I never received more than one or two letters in

my life—I wrote this some years ago—that were worth the postage.
The penny-post is, commonly, an institution through which you
seriously offer a man that penny for his thoughts which is so often
safely offered in jest. And I am sure that I never read any memorable news in a newspaper. If we read of one man robbed, or murdered, or killed by accident, or one house burned, or one vessel
wrecked, or one steamboat blown up, or one cow run over on the
Western Railroad, or one mad dog killed, or one lot of grasshop-
pers in the winter—we never need read of another. One is enough.
If you are acquainted with the principle, what do you care for a
myriad instances and applications? To a philosopher all *news*, as it
is called, is gossip, and they who edit and read it are old women over
their tea. Yet not a few are greedy after this gossip. There was such
a rush, as I hear, the other day at one of the offices to learn the
foreign news by the last arrival, that several large squares of plate
glass belonging to the establishment were broken by the pressure—
news which I seriously think a ready wit might write a twelvemonth
or twelve years beforehand with sufficient accuracy. As for Spain,
for instance, if you know how to throw in Don Carlos and the
Infanta, and Don Pedro and Seville and Granada, from time to
time in the right proportions—they may have changed the names a
little since I saw the papers—and serve up a bull-fight when other
entertainments fail, it will be true to the letter, and give us as good
an idea of the exact state or ruin of things in Spain as the most
succinct and lucid reports under this head in the newspapers: and as
for England, almost the last significant scrap of news from that
quarter was the revolution of 1649; and if you have learned the
history of her crops for an average year, you never need attend to
that thing again, unless your speculations are of a merely pecuniary
character. If one may judge who rarely looks into the newspapers,
nothing new does ever happen in foreign parts, a French revolution
not excepted.

6   What news! how much more important to know what that is
which was never old! "Kieou-he-yu (great dignitary of the state of
Wei) sent a man to Khoung-tseu to know his news. Khoung-tseu
caused the messenger to be seated near him, and questioned him in
these terms: What is your master doing? The messenger answered
with respect: My master desires to diminish the number of his
faults, but he cannot come to the end of them. The messenger
being gone, the philosopher remarked: What a worthy messenger!
What a worthy messenger!" The preacher, instead of vexing the
ears of drowsy farmers on their day of rest at the end of the week—

for Sunday is the fit conclusion of an ill-spent week, and not the fresh and brave beginning of a new one—with this one other drag-gle-tail of a sermon, should shout with thundering voice—"Pause! Avast! Why so seeming fast, but deadly slow?"

7   Shams and delusions are esteemed for soundest truths, while reality is fabulous. If men would steadily observe realities only, and not allow themselves to be deluded, life, to compare it with such things as we know, would be like a fairy tale and the Arabian Nights' Entertainments. If we respected only what is inevitable and has a right to be, music and poetry would resound along the streets. When we are unhurried and wise, we perceive that only great and worthy things have any permanent and absolute existence—that petty fears and petty pleasures are but the shadow of the reality. This is always exhilarating and sublime. By closing the eyes and slumbering, and consenting to be deceived by shows, men establish and confirm their daily life of routine and habit everywhere, which still is built on purely illusory foundations. Children, who play life, discern its true law and relations more clearly than men, who fail to live it worthily, but who think that they are wiser by experience, that is, by failure. I have read in a Hindu book that "there was a king's son, who, being expelled in infancy from his native city, was brought up by a forester, and, growing up to maturity in that state, imagined himself to belong to the barbarous race with which he lived. One of his father's ministers, having discovered him, revealed to him what he was, and the misconception of his character was removed, and he knew himself to be a prince. So soul," continues the Hindu philosopher, "from the circumstances in which it is placed, mistakes its own character, until the truth is revealed to it by some holy teacher, and then it knows itself to be *Brahme*." I per-ceive that we inhabitants of New England live this mean life that we do because our vision does not penetrate the surface of things. We think that that *is* which *appears* to be. If a man should walk through this town and see only the reality, where, think you, would the "Milldam" go to? If he should give us an account of the realities he beheld there, we should not recognize the place in his descrip-tion. Look at a meetinghouse, or a courthouse, or a jail, or a shop, or a dwelling-house, and say what that thing really is before a true gaze, and they would all go to pieces in your account of them. Men esteem truth remote, in the outskirts of the system, behind the farthest star, before Adam and after the last man. In eternity there is indeed something true and sublime. But all these times and places and occasions are now and here. God himself culminates in the

present moment, and will never be more divine in the lapse of all
the ages. And we are enabled to apprehend at all what is sublime
and noble only by the perpetual instilling and drenching of the
reality that surrounds us. The universe constantly and obediently
answers to our conceptions; whether we travel fast or slow, the track
is laid for us. Let us spend our lives in conceiving then. The poet or
the artist never yet had so fair and noble a design but some of his
posterity at least could accomplish it.

8   Let us spend one day as deliberately as Nature, and not be
thrown off the track by every nutshell and mosquito's wing that falls
on the rails. Let us rise early and fast, or break fast, gently and
without perturbation; let company come and let company go, let
the bells ring and the children cry—determined to make a day of it.
Why should we knock under and go with the stream? Let us not be
upset and overwhelmed in that terrible rapid and whirlpool called a
dinner, situated in the meridian shallows. Weather this danger and
you are safe, for the rest of the way is down hill. With unrelaxed
nerves, with morning vigor, sail by it, looking another way, tied to
the mast like Ulysses. If the engine whistles, let it whistle till it is
hoarse for its pains. If the bell rings, why should we run? We will
consider what kind of music they are like. Let us settle ourselves,
and work and wedge our feet downward through the mud and slush
of opinion, and prejudice, and tradition, and delusion, and appearance, that alluvion which covers the globe, through Paris and London, through New York and Boston and Concord, through church
and state, through poetry and philosophy and religion, till we come
to a hard bottom and rocks in place, which we can call *reality*, and
say, This is, and no mistake; and then begin, having a *point d'ap-
pui*,[1] below freshet and frost and fire, a place where you might
found a wall or a state, or set a lamppost safely, or perhaps a gauge,
not a Nilometer,[2] but a Realometer, that future ages might know
how deep a freshet of shams and appearances had gathered from
time to time. If you stand right fronting and face to face to a fact,
you will see the sun glimmer on both its surfaces, as if it were a
cimeter, and feel its sweet edge dividing you through the heart and
marrow, and so you will happily conclude your mortal career. Be it
life or death, we crave only reality. If we are really dying, let us hear
the rattle in our throats and feel cold in the extremities; if we are
alive, let us go about our business.

---

[1] foundation.
[2] an ancient device used to record the rise and fall of the Nile River.

9   Time is but the stream I go a-fishing in. I drink at it; but while
I drink I see the sandy bottom and detect how shallow it is. Its thin
current slides away, but eternity remains. I would drink deeper; fish
in the sky, whose bottom is pebbly with stars. I cannot count one. I
know not the first letter of the alphabet. I have always been regret-
ting that I was not as wise as the day I was born. The intellect is a
cleaver; it discerns and rifts its way into the secret of things. I do not
wish to be any more busy with my hands than is necessary. My head
is hands and feet. I feel all my best faculties concentrated in it. My
instinct tells me that my head is an organ for burrowing, as some
creatures use their snout and forepaws, and with it I would mine
and burrow my way through these hills. I think that the richest vein
is somewhere hereabouts; so by the divining rod and thin rising
vapors I judge; and here I will begin to mine.

4

Narration

NARRATION

Narration is the telling of a story—the recounting of events, usually in chronological order. Like the other forms of writing—argumentation, exposition, and description—it is distinctive but rarely exclusive. (Even a novel, ballad, or narrative poem usually contains extensive description.) The purpose of narration is usually to inform or to entertain. It may also be used to illustrate a principle or an idea or to support an argument. It can be developed in different ways:

- It may be unified by subject and time; that is, it can tell about one subject or object and what happens to it over a period of time. For example, a biography traces the events of one person's life over a given period of time.
- The subject alone may be the unifying element, and the time of the various episodes or segments may vary. If you're talking about apples, you might mention famous apples and the events surrounding them—Eve and her fateful bite from the Genesis apple, William Tell and his trusting son, Snow White's problem with the poisoned apple, and so on.
- A single point in time can be the unifying device, and episodes then tell what happens to different things or people at that particular time.

Narration is found in many places—newspapers, autobiographies, travel epics, novels, stories. Wherever it occurs, narration is primarily the expression of action in time. As a student, however——unless you are writing fiction (short stories or novels)—you will use narration in conjunction with other methods of development. In an argument you could use a narrative anecdote to emphasize or illustrate your position. (The use of anecdotes, which are always a form of narration, is, by the way, one of the best means of attracting and holding the interest of your reader, whatever your subject may be.)

PRACTICE

1. Write a narrative theme in which the sequence of events is critically important. Remember, you can use various devices——

flashbacks, for instance. Consider a student demonstration, the process of enrolling in college courses, sports or cultural happening.

2. In your anthology or elsewhere, find three separate paragraphs that consist primarily of narration. In each case, briefly summarize why the author may have chosen that device and evaluate the effectiveness of the narrative parts.

The Roots of Radicalism

In order to illustrate an idea, Bettelheim writes a narrative (paragraph 23) in which he recounts a situation from his past life. After reading this essay, write a paragraph stating why you think the author chose this particular device, and then comment on its effectiveness.

• Write a paragraph in which you use a narrative anecdote to illustrate a particular point or idea.

• When relating an event or personal experience, we usually automatically organize our thoughts in some kind of temporal pattern, since we generally perceive experience in terms of past, present, and future. Write a narrative about a personal experience in which you bring the past into the present with a new insight. Everyone has had experiences that are meaningful only in retrospect. For example, the experience of driving a car for the first time is one highly charged with excitement and emotion. Only in later years can you see the real significance. It may have been a symbol of independence and maturity—or a means of power and popularity. In other words, we use present knowledge to illuminate the past. Don't forget to include description in your narrative to give it that quality of reality.

More Futures Than One

This essay is more than a narrative about an individual's life—it has a definite purpose and thesis. Write a brief biography of someone you know well or of some famous person, in which you narrate the important events of his life. Your essay should have a specific thesis that is illuminated by the narrative.

• Find a news story in a newspaper or magazine and rewrite it as a first-person narrative.

For examples of individual paragraphs using *narration*, see p.65, ¶1–4, p.151, ¶23, p.282, ¶22–24, p.292, ¶1,2–3, p.312, ¶14.

The Roots of Radicalism

BRUNO BETTELHEIM

1   To understand why authority in this country is under such vehe-
ment attack, one must look to American fathers. Just as the ineptitude, moral collapse, and failure of nerve of the French aristocracy
paved the way for the great Revolution of 1789, so the loss of a
distinct role for the fathers has much to do with today's rebellion of
the young. Freud found the roots of Victorian emotional problems
in the excesses of stern, authoritarian patriarchs. Conversely, if
some modern boys engage in rampages, I believe we can trace it to
the virtual abdication of their dads from any sort of clear-cut position in the family.

2   The present situation is the logical result of developments that
began in the 19th Century. In the past 70 years, women have
achieved biological and technological liberation. The advent of
contraception, while it did not greatly reduce the actual number of
children reared to maturity (which was formerly decreased by mis-
carriage, stillbirth, and childhood diseases), did put an end to the
incessant pregnancies that had drained women's time and energy.
And with the general economic prosperity resulting from technological progress, women in the upper classes of the Western nations
became able, as economist Thorstein Veblen saw it, to lead lives of
ceremonial futility. Thus, in the early years of the 20th Century, the
popular notion of normal life was that of man doing the productive
work, while woman was an ornamental consumer.

Angy

This

CuE/
Anly

3   This notion never quite matched reality, certainly not among the working classes, but it dominated the imagination of the well-to-do European and American *bourgeoisie* until World War Two. Eventually, though, women became dissatisfied with their empty existences. The War presented an opportunity to become more active. Many wives and mothers went to work. Others became socially concerned, vigorously involving themselves in reformist and humane activities—the P.T.A., the League of Women Voters, Planned Parenthood, local women's clubs, charities, and the like. The socially active housewife was able to be as busy as her husband, but her activity sprang from interest rather than necessity. As a result, her commitment was exciting, dramatic, but not necessarily enduring. If politics palled, she might turn to gardening.

C & E

Tone

4   As for the father, at the opening of this era he usually believed that his work was vitally important, because without him the family could not survive. "I have to take care of them," the middle-class father proudly told himself. "I am responsible. They are weak. Without me, they would perish."

Anly / S Var

5   Sometimes, after a husband died, a woman might go to work and be more of a financial success than her man had been. In fact, wealth has slowly been accumulating in the hands of women so that today, as a class, they possess more riches than ever before (though, unquestionably, economic power is still a male province). But the fiction of the indispensable father continued to be generally believed. Again, World War Two marked the watershed for this notion. The women who stayed at home had proved their self-sufficiency. The men who had gone forth to conquer fascism came back with a great longing for peace and comfort and were bemused by the increasing complexity of the American corporate economy. Novels of the Forties and Fifties such as *The Hucksters* and *The Man in the Gray Flannel Suit*, popular works of sociology such as *The Organization Man* and *The Lonely Crowd* tell the story. The American man, having lived through the Depression and the War, having to live now through the Cold War, settled with a sigh into the barrackslike suburban developments that mushroomed around the big cities. Since prosperity and personal affluence with its pension plans seemed to assure survival and security, his life was no longer ruled by necessity but by the wish for ever greater comfort. Its purpose seemed directed toward acquiring superfluous adornments, rather than essentials. It's easy to achieve self-respect—and with it the respect of others, which comes from the inner security they feel one possesses—if one's work provides his wife and children

Meta

Meta C & E / Anly

with the necessities of life. But when men were not working for survival and were not after real, intrinsic achievements (such as are inherent, for example, in scientific discovery), or at least after power, but merely after luxury, only their busyness prevented them from realizing how devoid of true meaning their lives had become. Today, the children of such fathers are in their late teens and early 20s. *C ø E / Anly*

6   In these affluent families, the father often describes his work as a rat-race. Indeed, the successful businessman scurries through a maze of corporate politics, spurred on by a yearning for such rewards as profit sharing, pension plans, stock options, bonuses, annuities. He is often a minor functionary in a bureaucracy whose purpose, other than to grow larger, tends to be ill-defined. His work often seems pointless to him, as he is shifted from one position to another with little say about his destiny. And if he listens to social critics inveighing against environmental pollution, cultivation of artificial needs, dollar imperialism, war profiteering, and related evils, he may begin to suspect the worth of his activities and, with it, his own value.

7   The effect of these changes in parental attitudes on the children has been drastic. The small child recognizes only what he sees. What he is told has much less of an impact on him. He sees his mother working around the house, for him. He is told only that his father also works for his well-being; he does not see it. In the suburban family, when the father commutes to work, he has to leave early and he comes home when the child is about to be put to bed. More often than not, he sees his father watching TV, hiding behind his paper, maybe taking what to the father is a well-deserved nap but to the boy seems like sheer idleness. Even if the middle-class father takes his son to his place of work some 20 or 30 miles away, it's such a different world from the child's life at home that he cannot bring the two together. And what he sees there of the father's work he cannot comprehend. How can talking on the telephone—which from his experience at home he knows is done mainly to order goodies or for fun—or into a machine secure the family's well-being? Thus, the boy's experience can hardly dispel the notion that his father is not up to much. The father's work remains unseen and seems unreal, while the mother's activities are very visible, hence real. Since he does not see him do important things, the child comes to doubt the legitimacy of the father's authority and may grow up to doubt the legitimacy of all authority. *S Var* *Tone*

8   For ages, the father, as a farmer, as a craftsman working in his

shop, had been very visible to his sons and, because of his physical prowess and know-how in doing real things in the real world, was an object of envious adulation. Now, the mother, who traditionally is the one who nurtures the child, becomes ever more the carrier of authority. If for no other reason than that she is with the child during the father's waking hours, the mother becomes the disciplinarian, the value giver, who tells the child all day long what goes and what does not. In short, mother knows best, and father next to nothing. As one boy put it—and there is some truth in the words of the most naive child—"What is my fat-her? Just a fat-her."

C ∅ £ /
C ∅ C

9   Even though the father doesn't think much of his work, he expects the son to follow in his dreary footsteps. The child is sent to the best grammar school, not to satisfy his intellectual curiosity, not to develop his mind, not to understand himself better but to make good marks and to pass examinations so that he can get into the best high school. There he is pushed to compete for the highest grades, so that he can go to a famous college, often not because he can get a better education there but because going to a school with a big name adds to the prestige of the parents. And college is merely a means to an end—admission to graduate school. Graduate work in turn furnishes the "union card," enabling him to get a good job with a big corporation, where he can work until he finally retires on a good pension and then waits to die. Given this distorted, purgatorial picture of the world of education and work, is it any wonder that many young people scornfully reject it?

Fig

10   The American social and economic system, despite its obvious shortcomings, is much more than a gigantic staircase that leads nowhere. American society is creative and progressive and offers unprecedented opportunities for individual fulfillment and achievement. But that's not the way it has been presented to many young Americans born in the Forties and Fifties. The people who taught these youngsters to despise American society were their own parents.

Meta

Irny

11   Psychoanalysis asserts that each child, growing up in a family, must choose a parent to emulate. But a son cannot emulate his father's great abilities as a worker if that father seems a little man at home, meekly taking out the garbage or mowing the lawn according to a schedule devised by his wife. The process of becoming a person by emulation is enormously important, because the child doesn't copy just external mannerisms; he tries—as far as his understanding will let him—to think and feel like the chosen parent. For boys in today's suburban society, many fathers offer little with which to

Anly

identify. The problem is not created by the father's absence due to commuting and the long executive workday—sailors and men at war have been good objects for identification though absent from the home for months and years. The problem arises because the image of the father, in the eyes of the mother and others, has been downgraded.

12   In order not to have to identify with a superfluous father, many boys in the more affluent reaches of our society try to solve the problem by identifying with their mothers. But, while this solves one problem, it creates another, not for the boys' self-respect as human beings but for their self-respect as males. This emulation of the mother is not, by the way, manifested only in long hair or unisex clothing, which are merely matters of fashion. Boys tend to adopt the consumer mentality, like their mothers, rather than their fathers' producer mentality. A mother's role is also more attractive—at least in England and America—because she is often the more cultured member of the household. She is apt to be more liberally educated, more aware of the arts than her practical husband. This attitude is typified by the couple portrayed in Sinclair Lewis' *Main Street*. On the Continent, culture is a male prerogative, and this at least has slowed down the attrition of the father's dominance in the European household.

13   In the reformist and revolutionary activities of middle-class American college men, I see a repetition of the behavior patterns of their socially conscious mothers. These boys work for a cause with emotional fervor, rather than with the approach that business or technical activities require. Accomplishment in business—indeed, in politics—demands devotion to logic, long-range planning, practicality, willingness to compromise, acceptance of routine and drudgery. These qualities, indispensable to productive work, are repellent to many young radicals. They engage passionately in a controversy but are ready to withdraw from it the moment it becomes boring or tedious. Ralph Nader has commented bitterly on the waning of student enthusiasm for the ecology movement after the initial hoopla of Earth Day 1970. During the student strike after the Kent State calamity, it was only *work* that stopped in many colleges, while fun—in the form of movies, rock concerts, and the like—went right on. And, of course, immediately after Cambodia and Kent State thousands of young men and women vowed that they would be out the following November to work for peace candidates. A little over six months later, however, the number of students actively working during the 1970 elections was insignificant when compared with those who had claimed they would.

14   Marx never said that revolution would be fun. The New Left speaks of "revolution for the hell of it" and its values are theatrical. The melodrama becomes tragedy when some young people begin to see themselves as romantic bomb throwers. They shirk the task of educating the people and building a mass movement, those long-established practical strategies of the left. They think they can do their teaching by breaking plate-glass windows, by setting fire to buildings that could be used to educate the people.

15   The student revolutionary's lack of realism is an important reason for which he is frequently rejected by members of the working class. Typically, he tries to get close to the workers through his dress; he wears blue jeans and a work shirt. Trying to get to people by dressing in a certain way is a feminine, consumer approach, focusing on external attire rather than on a basic function. It is the mother who tells a boy he can't go to church without a jacket and tie; he learns the lesson so well that ten years later, he still feels that there is a correct uniform for every occasion and he wouldn't be caught dead in the streets without blue jeans and a work-shirt. I remember that in the early days of the Communist Party in Austria, members were taught that you couldn't reach the workers merely by dressing like them; you had to learn from them long before you dared to try to teach them. Today, a left-wing student thinks he can walk into a factory wearing the appropriate garb and start lecturing the workers on the way our fascist-pig establishment oppresses the struggling third-world peoples. This is exactly the attitude of the Victorian Lady Bountiful, who feels herself above the men who do dirty work and who don't know about the really important things in life. American workingmen sense that they are being patronized and want to kick the snobbish young sermonizer right out the plant gate.

16   Such aberrant behavior as this feminized approach to politics does not take place when children are able to identify with the parent of the same sex and to love the parent of the opposite sex. To make such healthy identification possible, it is not important whether the father has all the authority or whether the mother and the father share it; it is important simply that there be specific male authority and specific female authority. It is the attractiveness of each role that makes the child want to identify with it and decide which parent he will want to choose for the object of his love. Hardly a culture in the world does not provide in some way for distinct male and female roles; only in the affluent sector of our own society does the blurring of distinctions make it difficult for the son to identify with his father.

Top S

Exemp

Dict

Tran

17   Psychoanalysis has derived its notions of the proper role a male parent should play in his children's lives from the observations Freud made in Vienna in the late 19th Century. His studies, of course, were limited to authoritarian, Victorian families. He learned that psychological problems stemmed from the faults of this type of family. But when the Victorian family worked well, mental health, as Freud understood it, resulted. Today, we are so used to hearing about the oppressive horrors of Victorian life that we forget that many of these families were happy and produced healthy children. The popular idea that the family in the 19th Century was a dreadful institution and the psychoanalytical idea that all families resemble it are both wrong.

18   In Freud's day, the male personality still developed as Goethe, both statesman and poet, had described his own: *"From father is my stately gait, / My sober way of conduct, / From mother is my sunny mind, / My zeal for spinning tales."* As Freud saw it, the paternal influence created the superego—that element in a person's character that laymen call the conscience. The mother, on the other hand, gave the child unconditional love and satisfied his needs, thus teaching him how to gratify those bodily drives and emotional needs that psychoanalysts describe as belonging to the id. A child carries images of his parents in his mind, or, as psychoanalysts say, he internalizes them. If all goes well, the boy acts as he thinks his father would want him to and he tries to be the kind of person his mother would love. The ego, which is the conscious self, is formed, according to Freud, to mediate between the conflicting images of the judging father and the loving mother.

Def

C & E

Def

19   For a child to form his personality out of interacting masculine and feminine images, the two must be truly different. Today, the mother is both nurturing and demanding, while the father often is neither. The child is not offered the example of one person representing the principle of pleasure and the other person the principle of duty. Out of this confusion, the child develops a conscience, which tells him, "You have a *duty* to enjoy life." Thus, there are young people who feel that work ought to be all fun and who look on nine-to-five drudgery as somehow immoral. They often try to drop out of the world of work and careers. Other people turn the fun of life into grueling labor: zealous tourists, dogged golf-swing improvers, fanatic car buffs, people who worry that they're not getting as much pleasure as they ought to out of sex. How impossible the pursuit of pleasure becomes, even in sex, when it assumes the character of a moral duty!

Conn

20   In old Vienna, the male parent unquestionably represented the | C∅E/
principle of duty, and sons felt respect, awe, even fear, toward their | Anly
fathers. And the boys had something to look forward to: the idea of
having similar authority and commanding similar respect when they
grew up. In adolescence, through revolt against paternal authority,
one gained further strength and masculine pride. But how can one
revolt against the weak fathers of today? They often do not seem
worth the trouble. Instead, the children revolt against the establishment. But this does not work out for them either. After a successful
adolescent revolt, the boy may reidentify with the best in the father.
But how can our student revolutionaries reidentify with a distant
and anonymous establishment? Either they get stuck in their adolescent revolt or the establishment defeats them. In either case, they
can't reach maturity and deep down they despise themselves for a
failure that is not of their own making.

21   Freud's teachings have generally been taken as the last word on
psychodynamics, but he made scientific observations, he did not
formulate laws. Freud would never have made the mistake of declaring that people in a different society, such as our own, could
follow the Victorian pattern for effective child rearing without appropriate modifications. Families can take many forms as long as
they serve the needs of children. A few years ago, I studied the | Exemp
Israeli *kibbutzim*, the collective communities, for a short time.
Here children do not live with their parents; they are raised in
groups. One of the most important factors in the lives of the children, though, is that they constantly visit both parents at work. And
when the children come, everybody stops working and explains to
the children what they're doing and why it is important to them and
to the community. Through that experience, the child gains respect
for the work of the parents. People have wondered how *kibbutz*
children grow up so well when their parents are distant figures. The
answer is that, while there are only a few basic needs, there are
many ways to satisfy them.

22   A child need not be raised by his biological parents. Freud | S Var
made so much of the Oedipus complex or Oedipal situation that
many people believe a male child *must* have a jealous desire for his
mother and an envious hatred for his father in order to grow up
normally. But there has been much argument among anthropologists about whether or not this Oedipal relationship really exists in
all societies. As I see it, the chief thing is to understand the basic
principle underlying the Oedipus phenomenon, which is applicable
to any family structure: The human infant for many years is entirely

dependent upon and in the power of some individual or individuals. If you're in someone's power, for better or worse you have to come to terms with that person. If the person doesn't abuse his power, you come to love him. But in whose power the child is, and with whom he has to come to terms, can vary greatly.

23   Consider my own history. Today, I teach psychoanalysis at the University of Chicago and, of course, my students read Freud on the subject of how all-important a child's mother is. After I've let them expound on the subject, I try to open their minds a bit more by telling them some of my personal story. During my early child- hood, the person who fed me, took care of me and was with me most of the time was not my mother but a wet nurse. This was a custom among the upper-middle classes in Vienna at the time. The nurse was a peasant girl in her late teens, who had just had a baby out of wedlock. She left the baby with relatives and hired herself out to suckle the child of a well-to-do family. To make sure she gave a lot of milk, she followed the folklore formula of drinking a lot of beer. So my entire care as an infant was entrusted to a girl who had little education, was by our standards a sex delinquent, was a little high on beer most of the time, and was so devoid of maternal instinct that she left her own child. I am the deplorable result. *Narr / Anec*

Dict / Tone

24   The reasons why a relationship that, according to theory, should have been unpromising worked so well were that the girl had no interest other than me; she took good physical care of me and, being a peasant, was without undue fastidiousness about diapering and toilet training; the beer kept her relaxed and happy; she didn't discipline me excessively and didn't overawe me intellectually. It was not an idyllic upbringing but it certainly was adequate. And because my nurse was awed by my father, I learned to look up to him by observing her. Thus, I acquired respect for him without his having to discipline me directly. My father was a very gentle man, very secure in himself, so convinced of his inner authority that he never needed to make a show of it. I didn't have continual fights with my parents, because the do's and don'ts came from the nurse, somebody who wasn't much of an authority. An infant learns very early what the power relations are in his family and these hold the key to his development. *C & E*

25   My father was a good model for me. As a child, I visited him at his place of work. I spent many hours there, watching him, more often just playing. The pace of life was still leisurely enough to permit my father to drop what he was doing and explain things to me. I saw other strong men work hard. Their respect for my father

and his for them, without my being aware of it, made a deep impression on me. Such experiences make identification with his father seem worthwhile for a boy.

26   Besides respecting the roles of the two sexes, people should be *Top S*
able to clearly differentiate between them. Dichotomy, duality, is
one of the most fundamental characteristics of both nature and
philosophy. As Buckminster Fuller says, "Unity is plural and at
minimum two." The oracular Chinese book, the *I Ching*, presents
64 figures made up of six lines. This large number of figures is made
of different combinations of just two kinds of lines, solid and broken. The solid lines represent the masculine yang principle and the
broken lines, the feminine yin principle. The child selects the characteristics he prefers, inventing his own individual mix. There are
many more than six characteristics in the human personality, each
of which has its feminine or masculine version; thus, the possible
kinds of human personality are infinite.

27   The trend I've described in today's middle-class family is that *Tran*
the loss of attractiveness and distinctness in the father's role impedes the satisfactory working out of this process. What can be
done about this situation? Obviously, we can't turn back the economic or technological clocks. But ideas as much as tangible necessities have caused the decline of the father. We must renew our
appreciation of the polarity of the sexes and be enriched by the
inner tensions it creates. While I do sympathize with liberated
women to a degree, I don't think they should make it their goal to
become as much like men as possible or to change the image of
men. They should concentrate on finding themselves as women.

28   We males cannot expect women to find roles for us that are
suitably masculine; we have to do this ourselves. The new mascu- *Top S*
line, heroic ideal may possibly focus on discovery. All through re- *Arg*
corded history, the discoverer has been a man, even the discoverer
of the pill, which may solve the most pressing problem of mankind:
overpopulation. The astronauts who set foot on the moon, and also
those who managed to return their crippled spaceship, fired the
imagination of the entire world. A new masculine pride can come
from discoveries of the mind, from the brain, not from brawn. Our
cities need to be rethought and rebuilt, the very pattern of our lives
will have to be reshaped so that men will again be able to derive
pride from what they are doing on this earth, maybe even beyond it.
The problems and possibilities are immense.

29   The task is not one that can be mastered in comfortable leisure. But leisure, the absence of struggle, order, harmony were the

ideals that the GIs of World War Two adopted, a natural but mistaken reaction to a horribly destructive conflict. The absence of tension is just as deadly as too much of it. This is one meaning of the Zen question "What is the sound of one hand clapping?" One hand alone strikes empty air and makes no sound at all. This is why the young crave confrontations. The college administrators who face student dissenters are too often men who are lacking in masculine security and have based their careers on the principle of harmony at all costs. So, instead of meeting questions and openly recognizing that unavoidable conflict exists, they try to evade it. One reason Dr. Hayakawa has succeeded in restoring some order at San Francisco State College is that he was not afraid of real confrontation in place of academic soothing syrup. He stood up to the demonstrators in a manly way, instead of pretending to be on their side while actually trying to undermine them. One of the most compelling testimonies to the life-giving properties of conflict is Sartre's description of how it felt to be in the French Resistance from 1940 to 1945: "We were never more free than during the German occupation. . . . Because the Nazi venom seeped even into our thoughts, every accurate thought was a conquest. Because an all-powerful police tried to force us to hold our tongues, every word took on the value of a declaration of principles. Because we were hunted down, every one of our gestures had the weight of a solemn commitment."

Exemp

30   Freud said that life results from an imbalance and the effort to re-establish balance. If a new imbalance is not created, however, there will be death. Hegel and Marx both summed up life as the conflict between thesis and antithesis, which is resolved in synthesis, which in turn generates a new antithesis for a new conflict. Without this process, life would come to a stop.

31   Next to sexual pleasure, one of the great experiences of life is climbing a mountain and growing hot and sweaty in the process, then coming upon a cold lake and jumping in. You may be shivering and have to jump out again in a minute, but what delight there is in the sudden change from hot to cool! Compare this with swimming in a tepid pool. Where there is no tension created, none is relieved. The affluent middle-class American wants life to run smoothly, doesn't want any difficulties. He wants the mountain to be level and the pool to be tepid. And then he wonders why his children reject him.

Angy

Meta

32   . Kant said that aesthetic pleasure of the highest order comes from the fact that the artist creates a unity out of a variety of elements. One of the oldest images of the human soul is this metaphor from Plato's *Phaedrus:*

> Let the figure be composite—a pair of winged horses and a chari- **Ext Net**
> oteer. Now the winged horses and the charioteers of the gods are all of **End**
> them noble and of noble descent, but those of other races are mixed;
> the human charioteer drives his in a pair; and one of them is noble and
> of noble breed, and the other is ignoble and of ignoble breed; and the
> driving of them of necessity gives a great deal of trouble to him.

33   At this point, the naïve utopian asks, "If both horses were alike,
wouldn't they pull together better?"

34   Yes, they might. But how empty, how boring!

CONSIDERATIONS

Bettelheim says that authority is under attack because of the American
father's weakening role. Would you agree with this assessment, or do
you think there are other reasons? How accurate is the author's description of the sincerity, goals, and attitudes of today's radicals? On
the whole, is he sympathetic to youth and their values? How do you
think future historians will describe today's youth?

How accurate is the title with respect to the content of this essay?
(Does the author actually write about something else?) What is the
purpose of Bettelheim's personal anecdote about growing up in Austria? What is the purpose of the quotation from Plato? (paragraph 32)
How does it relate to the author's thesis? How would you describe the
language used in this essay? The tone? Was it written for the "radical"
reader?

Bettelheim says that many live "lives of ceremonial futility." (paragraph
2) What evidence can you find to support this statement? In what ways
do your friends, parents, teachers, or others close to you exemplify the
statement? Are there alternate models that you believe will eventually
replace or supplement the traditional family? *Should* they? Give your
thoughts in a short essay.

VOCABULARY

 (1) ineptitude   lack of skill
 (1) patriarchs   male heads of families or homes
 (3) palled   became wearisome or diminished
 (5) bemused   confused
 (6) inveighing   protesting strongly
(11) emulate   to imitate in an effort to equal
(12) superfluous   unnecessary; excessive
(12) prerogative   a privilege or right
(16) aberrant   abnormal; deviating from the usual
(26) dichotomy   division into two parts
(27) tangible   real; material

More Futures Than One

POUL ANDERSON

1   He was born in 1970, to an upper-middle-class white American family that thought of itself as beleaguered.

2   Not that his parents were unenlightened or fanatical. On the contrary, both were college graduates, enjoyed foreign travel, left good impressions wherever they went and had friends in more than one circle. Political independents, they split their ballots as often as not. He, a rising young corporation lawyer, was a bit more conservative than she, who had flirted with radicalism in her student days. But their arguments only added liveliness to a loving relationship. At root they wanted the same things for themselves, their children and the world.

3   They were both afraid.

4   Their nightmares were shared, but certain ones came most sharply to each. He saw crime and hatred tearing his country apart and, waiting behind them, insurrection. He feared these things less in themselves than he feared the reaction they could provoke—the end of Jefferson's dreams in tyranny and genocide. Abroad, he saw spreading chaos, implacable enmity and weapons that could lay waste the earth. She saw barrenness: of the soil, the flesh and the spirit. Wasn't the start of the great famines predicted for about 1980? North America and Europe might survive a while longer; but at what cost? Faceless mobs packed elbow to elbow in rotting cities

and junk-yard countryside, the almighty state equipped with snooper systems and data banks to control every action, on a planet so gutted and poisoned that the very possibility of life seemed to be going down the same drain that was about to swallow the last vestiges of beauty and serenity. Was that any future to offer your children?

5   They had two, John and Jane. They said those names were a declaration of independence from the neonyms—Jax and Jeri and Lord knew what else—that had become the real mark of conformity. Maybe they meant it, though they said it with a laugh. In spite of their fears, they laughed quite a bit—though the children's first two decades were, in fact, hard. History would look back on them and shudder. But John and Jane remembered that time in much the way their grandparents remembered the Great Depression, their parents the Korean War or anyone who is not too cruelly unfortunate remembers growing up. In the background was trouble; sometimes it struck close, as when a cousin came home dead from Burma, or the streets of their suburb resounded to the boots of the National Guard, or inflation wrecked their father's business. But mostly they were busy exploring their existence.

6   And somehow existence continued. Somehow the ultimate catastrophes never quite came. Enough people never quit working for reform and public compassion on the one hand, for order and public decency on the other. No matter the scale on which madness ran loose, no matter the face it wore, they resisted it. Disagreeing among themselves, often profoundly, they nonetheless made common cause against the real enemy and worked together to achieve the traditional, sane equality of dissatisfaction.

7   It turned out that lawlessness could be curbed without extreme measures. When investments in education and opportunity began to pay off, the younger generation simply grew bored by talk of revolt. A high-level industrial economy proved to have remarkable powers of recuperation even from funny money. The first tactical nuclear weapon fired in anger did not automatically trigger the detonation of everything. A peace of exhaustion was not a hopelessly bad foundation on which to start building enforceable international agreements. Population patterns generally followed that of Japan as soon as the means were commonly available. The environment could be cleaned up and rehabilitated. Pollution-free machines were feasible to make and sell. A massive American reaction set in against bureaucratic interference in private affairs. None of this was perfect, none was clear-cut nor had any definite beginning

or cause. But once more—as after the fall of Rome or the wars of religion—man was groping his way back toward the light.

8   And the most savage of those years witnessed some of the most superb achievements the race had yet reached. They were in science and technology—the arts would not regain any important creativity for a while—but they were not on that account any less Bach fugues of theory, Parthenons of mechanism. John had been begotten on the joyful night man first spent on the moon. He was still in grade school when permanent bases were established there; and by then, visits to Earth-orbital stations were routine. Between lunar resources and free-space assembly, the construction of interplanetary craft had become almost cheap. This was good, because the demand for them waxed as knowledge led to spatial industries. John was in high school at the time of the Mars and Venus landings. Radiation screens and thermal conversion were then about to open up inner-most Mercury and really efficient nuclear engines were being developed for expeditions to the remote outer worlds. Speculation about reaching the stars became official.

9   On Earth, the changes were more obviously fundamental, and many of them were disturbing. Few denied that the controlled thermonuclear reaction—clean power, its source literally inexhaustible—was a good thing. Nor was there any serious argument against progress in fuel cells, energy storage units and other devices that, together, would push the combustion engine into well-deserved extinction. True, while alarmists predicted that such techniques as desalinization and food synthesis would merely fill the planet with more starvelings, those landmarks of engineering forestalled worldwide famine until such other techniques as the one-year contraceptive pill could show results.

10   But controversy went on over the effects of biology, medicine, psychology. The cracking of the genetic code made prostheses and organ transplants obsolete after the organs could be regrown. More importantly, DNA modification brought an end to diseases such as diabetes and, indirectly, to cancer. But would man now start tinkering with his own evolution? What ghastliness might his unwisdom bring on? The dangers in the growing variety of psycho-drugs and brain stimulators were not reduced by becoming a trite topic at cocktail parties. New methods of education helped ram enough poor people into the twentieth century that the threatened uprisings faded away. But since these methods involved conditioning, right down to the neural level, did they not invite any dictator to produce a nation of willing slaves? Man-computer linkages (tempo-

rary ones using electro-magnetic induction, not wires into anybody's skull) had vastly extended the range of human control, experience and thinking capability. But were they not potentially dehumanizing? And what of the machines themselves, the robots, the enormous automatic systems, the ubiquitous and ever more eerily gifted computers? What would they do to us?

11   Thus, as mankind staggered toward a degree of tranquillity and common sense, John and Jane's father wondered how relevant politics had been in the first place. It seemed to him that the future belonged to those blind, impersonal, unpredictable and uncontrollable forces associated with pure and applied science. He was an intelligent man and a concerned one. He was right about an ongoing revolution that was to alter the world. But he was looking in the wrong direction. The real cataclysm was happening elsewhere. His mistake was scarcely his fault. The revolutionaries didn't know either.

12   They were running secondhand-book stores that tended to specialize, and head shops of a thousand different kinds, and artists' cooperatives, and schools teaching assorted Japanese athletics, and home workshops, and small-circulation magazines, and their own movie companies, and subsistence farms with up-to-date equipment that took advantage of cheap power, and tiny laboratories that drew on public data-retrieval and computer systems, and consultation services that did likewise, and on and on. By these means they became independent.

13   They weren't beat, hippie, conservative, utopian; they weren't activists nor disciples. They weren't artsy-craftsy. They weren't do-it-yourselfers. They weren't the rich kids who followed sun and surf around the planet nor those who opted out to groove on rock and pot. They weren't the middle-class middle-aged men who, in real or fancied desperation, carried for a while those anesthetic guns that became the compromise between lethal weapons and none. They weren't those young men who, understanding the transfigured technology as their elders never would, used it to make themselves millionaires before the age of 30 and then used the money for their pet causes. They weren't the American blacks, *chicanos*, Indians, Orientals who decided—usually in a quiet fashion—that the culture of their liberal white friends wasn't for them after all. They weren't the medievalists who, a few years before John was born, brought back the tournaments, costumes, food and manners of a bygone era, raised banners and pavilions and generally spent a large part of their time playing an elaborate game. They weren't the many who discov-

ered that, in a world of machines, personal service—anything human, from gardening to carpentry to counseling—is in such demand
that those who render it can work when and where they choose.
The revolutionaries were none of these, because they were all of
them and more. They fitted into no category whatsoever.

14   Has the point been made? In an ultraproductive, largely automated economy, which has rationalized its distribution system so
that everyone can have the necessities of life, labor becomes voluntary. Some kinds of it are rewarded with a high material standard of
living; but if you prefer different activities, you can trade that standard off to whatever extent you wish. The way out of the rat-race is
to renounce cheese and go after flowers, which are free. Enough will
always want cheese to keep the wheel turning.

15   Many of the revolutionaries had at various times described
themselves as radical, hippie, Afro or what have you. Many still did
when John reached his maturity. Others had invented new labels,
were prophesying new salvations and trying out new life styles. But
none of that was important. The revolution had already taken
place. Every way of living that was not a direct threat to someone
else's had become possible. Naturally, John didn't notice the
change. So many other events were so much more conspicuous and
sudden. He took the results for granted, as his father had taken
antibiotics and atomic energy, his grandfather the automobile and
the airplane, his distant ancestors gunpowder, iron, fire—and all the
human consequences.

16   On the morning of his 30th birthday, John's bed woke him at
the hour he had set with the music he had chosen, converted itself
into a chaise longue and offered him coffee. After he got up, the
housekeeping robot tidied the bedcovers and cleaned up the dishes.
The robot, which vaguely resembled a vacuum cleaner with exten-
sions, was connected to a central computer beneath the building,
along with many others; thus, these machines could discriminate
and make logical judgments, if not precisely think.

17   John told the kitchen what he wanted for breakfast and, while
it was being prepared, did his exercises. They included a session
with a screen that flashed text and abstract symbols at him, for
speed and fullness of comprehension. The whole-organism training
that modern psychophysiology had developed gave him more assorted abilities that would once have been thought possible in any
single human being. The discipline, however, had to be maintained.

18   Afterward, he showered but didn't shave. His last application

of depilatory was good for several days yet. Rather than disposable clothes, he picked a suit in the timeless style made with top-grade synthetic fabrics that lasted for decades. Today he wanted to look completely self-motivated. An important potential client would be calling.

19   At his reading speed, he got through his newspaper, which the fax had printed for him off the public-data lines before finishing breakfast. It wasn't that he didn't appreciate marinated reindeer, it was just that he could be aware of several things at once. So he went on with *War and Peace,* in the Russian he had lately found convenient to acquire. Because he wanted a permanent copy, he had ordered a full-scan repro of a special edition in the central library of Moscow. Usually he dialed for a standard print-out—which was cheap and could be dropped down the reclamation chute when he was through with it—or for a simple screening.

20   After eating, John strolled onto the balcony of his apartment. It was high in a gigantic complex, a virtual city that you need never leave except for tourism. Other buildings reached inland farther than he could see, even in Los Angeles' crystalline air. Their variegated shapes and colors made a pattern that never appeared the same twice. He was sufficiently high up that in the other direction he could glimpse the ocean and, he thought, several floating homes whose stabilized barges were currently in port.

21   But he had business to take care of. He'd planned on taking this day off, until he was contacted about discussing a possible job. It sounded fascinating, not to mention being valuable to a cause he believed in. Those two considerations weighed a good deal more than the money. Besides, John's generation drew no clear boundary between work and play. His parents said, in their quaint old-time idiom, that he always did his thing.

22   Re-entering his living room, he activated a full-wall viewer and tuned in a scene he especially liked—Mount Rainier. But it was raining there today. Rather than settle for a canned animation, he dialed Angel Falls in Venezuela. Relaxed, he contemplated the view until his phone chimed and told him that the person he expected was on the line. The holographic image might almost have been the real man sitting opposite him. Little disturbed the illusion except the fade-out of background at the edges. But he spoke from Boston.

23   The problem he raised was vital. Fifteen years before, the pressure on nature along the Eastern Seaboard had suddenly passed a threshold. The network of life had been snapped in too many places—by pollution, pesticides, over-building, extermination of en-

tire species—and it came apart. Rivers and lakes filled with stinking sludge; trees withered; the very grass died over hundreds of square kilometers; dust made the heavens gray; the air grew foul, even outside the cities. Parts of earth had long been in trouble and restoration programs had been started. But it took the death of half of New England to make mankind understand how late the hour had grown.

24   Ecological management became the most urgent business in the world. It continued to be among the most valued professions. And, with the help of knowledge gained from research, it was succeeding. Desolation was being made to bloom again. Yet sections of the American Northeast Coast were proving intractable. Undesired forms had moved in after the collapse—microbes, algae, scrub plants, insects, rodents. Better adapted to gaunt soil and choked waters, they crowded out the types that man was trying to introduce. They could in time be overcome. But labor and resources were in limited supply, with other regions demanding a share. And there was need for haste, lest erosion do further harm. In short, the Government must rethink its program for this area and find one that optimized the future course of events. As was its habit these days, it turned to independent consultants.

25   John was among them. He had gone into cybernetics; but that word had come to include a Renaissance range of expertise and abilities. He was not a free-lance computer programmer, though they were common. He dealt with total systems. Given a large and ramified problem, what was the best approach to solving it? What priorities should be assigned to collecting what sorts of facts? Along what lines should the computers later be employed? What kinds of machinery, especially self-operating machinery, were likeliest to be needed after a course of action had been determined? Should research and development on wholly new apparatus, wholly new substances with special properties, be instigated? What was the most probable balance of the cost of innovation against the chance of success?

26   Think of John as a man who programmed the programmers.

27   He spent the rest of the morning on a guided tour. The projection was well arranged; he didn't expect he'd need to take a hypersonic flight across the continent for a physical look around. Newscasts had often shown him stony land, skeletal trees, slimy pools, insect clouds, crumbling ghost towns. Today he peered through microscopes, talked to specialists, absorbed a sketchy but coherent education in half a dozen branches of science. His training equipped him to ask the right questions, remember the answers and relate

them to the awesome background of organized knowledge that he already possessed. Of course, he didn't try to carry everything in his head; data banks did that. But he had to know what data to call for.

28   He made a point of interviewing supervisors in the field. No briefing could give him those subtle insights that we get from direct confrontation with a man; only those insights let us foresee what he can and will do. John had been aware that reclamation was more than a job to these people—the hard cadre of them, that is, the careerists. It was like a religion. They passed their working lives in the barren places or on the seas, where the effort went on to restock with plankton, fish, seal, walrus, whale. They saw themselves as the saviors of the planet. They were doubtless right.

29   John was relieved to confirm that they weren't fanatics, like those true believers who had found in a thousand different cults a refuge from the fact that they had nothing to give that society wanted. The reclaimers were generally relaxed, pragmatic, uncommonly cheerful. Though their dirigible homes had less space and luxury than his apartment, there was more intimacy and color. Also distinctive were their clothes, manners and ceremonies. Quite a few reclaimers were of gypsy descent, and something akin to the old close-knit Romany culture was developing among all of them. Their children attended public schools via projection but afterward played among themselves.

30   The cadre knew better, however, than to snub the floating laborers—if laborers can include skilled workmen and engineers—who made up the bulk of their forces. Such persons came for limited times to earn some money before returning to their own widely diverse private lives. Perhaps the picturesqueness and hospitality of the cadre bands, the merriment of their men and the sultry glamor of their women had evolved as methods of attracting help and keeping it awhile.

31   Having learned how many hands of how many different capabilities could be counted on, John told the official from Ecological Management that he felt able to undertake the assignment. A standard contract was signed, via fax, immediately. No physical document ever existed; the record was in the molecular patterns of data-storage cells, instantly retrievable as a projection onto a screen anywhere in the world. Naturally, the system would have to have thumbprint identification before releasing something that wasn't everybody's affair.

32   John's parents hadn't been able to get through to him on the phone until his conference was finished. They lived in Wisconsin, in

an exurban settlement typical of the many scattered across the nation. It wasn't like the dismal tracts of their youth. Their house, built cheaply by machines out of largely mass-produced parts, was nevertheless as adjustable to individual desires as a Meccano set. And few of their neighbors were stagnating. That was hard to do when whole planets were available to them in their homes, or in direct contact if they cared for travel, and when they could expect to live a vigorous century or so.

33   John's father ran a law practice and conciliation service. He specialized in settling conflicts that arose from differences between subcultures. An interesting case had just been given him, he said in the course of wishing his son a happy birthday. A young fellow from Milwaukee, wandering around, taking odd jobs whenever he needed a little credit, had come on an Arizona pueblo where the Indians were reviving certain ancient ways. Modern dry-farming techniques, including the genetic tailoring of plants and livestock, let them do this in reasonable comfort. They made the white lad welcome and he stayed for a while, sharing their lives. Social itinerants were not uncommon. John himself spent his spare time most years in a back-country Thai village, and had experimented with other milieus. They refreshed him; they enlarged his horizons; they were fun.

34   This lad, though, had gotten a local girl into bed with him. No state or Federal laws had been broken; she was of age. But this particular neo-Pueblo society had its own value system and was shocked when it learned of the affair. The girl, disgraced among her people yet unwilling to leave them, finding that the boy had no intention of marrying her and settling down, was claiming psychological damage. He was replying that a romp in the sack was no cause for scorn and Arizona was positively not his territory. John's father was trying to get both parties to accept reconditioning. Let the treatments put them in love with each other and they'd marry, thus reconciling her with her tribe. Let suitable habits and attitudes be modified and they'd find a place to live that was mutually satisfactory. They were hesitant—he probably because he didn't want to be tied down, she frankly because conscious regulation of emotions looked too unromantic.

35   John reminded his father that the kids could be right. A lot of people were worried about tranquilizers, stimulators, enhancers, mood machines, the whole paraphernalia that let you decide how you were going to feel at any moment. Might it lead to shallowness, weakness, dependence—at last to breakdown, when instinct rebelled against that tight a harnessing? Many people refused any

reconditioning, even when medically advised. Why not propose, John said, that the girl put aside her insularity, the boy his selfishness and that they simply travel around for a year together? They'd learn more than any planned program could teach them. They might well end by sharing their whole lives. Certain spots to visit could be suggested, such as a small Mexican town that John knew. . . . Well, maybe, maybe. No harm in laying the idea before them.

36   John's mother asked when he was coming to see them in the flesh. Projections were OK, but you couldn't hug them nor feed them a birthday cake. He explained how busy he was going to be, then agreed that he'd at least drop in soon. And, after all, a family reunion was planned for August—a week in the great Himalayan playground.

37   After his parents had broken circuit, John glanced at his watch. Damn, it was too late to call the moon today. All the bases there ran on G. M. T. and Randall of Hightower Chemicals was doubtless out on the town. He loved low-gravity dancing. Well, be sure to catch him tomorrow. Certain of those giant molecules that could only be made under lunar conditions might be useful for killing algae. Ask his opinion, query him on price and delivery date. And Astrid Hawkridge could enlighten John on some aspects of marine ecology, but she'd be asleep now, in Krishnamurti City beneath the Indian Ocean.

38   Lunchtime. John decided to eat out. The delivery tubes would oblige him with practically anything that wasn't in his kitchen lockers, but he wanted to roam around a bit and let his mind relax.

39   He seldom used his car in town. Dense high-speed traffic wasn't the reason. Autopilots were required to be in contact with and guided by the machines of Regional Control. As a rule, however, you had to park so far from your destination that you needed the excellent public lines anyway. John caught an express outside his building, transferred to a shuttle and in ten minutes had reached Afroville.

40   Stepping out of the station was like entering a foreign country. The rehabilitation of Watts in the Seventies and Eighties went deeper than rebuilding and renaming. Those were only the outward signs of a spiritual rebirth. The black man found that he, too, could create his own free society within the larger commonwealth. He needed only to reject the level of consumption associated with a civilization he felt was cold and greedy. No further penalties were attached. High production and efficient distribution guaranteed a reasonable minimum income. (No, it certainly wasn't that simple.

Many black people had wanted no part of a special black culture, only a fair share in the white one. This goal was delayed by brothers who too frequently—if understandably—spent more energy in giving the ancient oppressor a hard time than in constructing a solid base for their own liberation. Yet slowly, confusedly, by fits and starts, the thing happened.)

41   John sauntered between low, gaily tinted houses among folk whose garb and manner were just as sprightly. Most streets were reserved for pedestrians, bicycles and children's wagons. Music filled the air. He went by a people's park where a group was building an elaborate gazebo. The restaurant he sought stood in a flower garden. He dreaded the day when it would be discovered and go tourist; meanwhile, he enjoyed excellent food and live service at modest prices. (Cash remained in colorful use here: a matter of custom, not of the lack of bank-card scanners.) His favorite waitress was back from vacation. Like most employees, she worked a 30-hour week. Anything less and the proportion of time lost in getting organized was too great. But she had three months off per year and unlimited sick leave. She told John she'd spent this past holiday in Yugoslavia with a little-theater group. . . . After lunch, he browsed through a couple of the area's innumerable shops and found a handmade belt that would be a good present for his current girl.

42   On the way home, he realized how uncritically he'd accepted every cliché about the district. The die-hard Whitey haters were few and senescent; but some younger leaders were protesting Afroville's evolution into "another Chinatown." They had a point, though John didn't think it was major. The bulk of the community was doing serious things. Small businesses flourished, and so did cultural activities. The university's department of ethnology had long been famous. Lately, a team of its sociologists and economists had startled the world by its demonstration of how rich and octopuslike an industry the international-arms-control complex had become.

43   Back in his apartment, John found that his phone had recorded a message from his sister. Jane was sorry she'd missed him and wouldn't be able to call again today. The mahi-mahi were running and she must shortly take her boat out after them. She looked good in the image, her nude body tanned and full of health. Both her kids were with her to congratulate John on his birthday. In the background was a glimpse of dazzling beach and long blue combers.

44   Jane had joined a utopian colony—group living, no marriage— in Hawaii. The idea was to re-create tribalism in a natural setting

and thus satisfy the instincts that cities frustrated. The members weren't cranks or faddists. They made full use of appropriate technology, including that which gave their children a modern education. They earned the wherewithal by occasionally hiring out as workers or entertainers and by selling the produce of their lands and waters. They experimented carefully and thoughtfully, searching for improvements in their customs. In fact, John considered them a shade too earnest. But since Jane was happy, what the hell? He left her an answer at the village's single phone.

45   The greeting had given him a notion. Hawaii didn't hold the sole version of the simple life. He had a friend in Northern California. The friend was at home and John spent an hour talking with him. He was mayor of a settlement of yeomen. These were not idealists but individualists, each farming his private land or operating his private service enterprise on lonely Cape Mendocino. Their origin had had its unpleasant aspects. Breakdown of public safety in too many areas, during the difficult years, had convinced too many families that they must be ready to defend themselves. Nonlethal weapons encouraged the trend. It proved to be symbolic more often than practical; but man lives by symbols.

46   Meanwhile, the concentration of agriculture in mechanized latifundia—the competition of synthetic foods, fibers and lumber substitutes—threw a vast acreage in the remoter parts of the country onto a pitiless market. Inflation favored the shrewd buyer. Then, when inflation had run its course, mass unemployment triggered the Freeman movement. Chip-on-the-shoulder self-reliance; the wish to escape from turbulence and taxes; available land; cheap, sophisticated means of living off it, without the toil and isolation of old-fashioned husbandry: These things brought forth the modern homesteaders.

47   By now, resentments had faded. The Freemen were merely another subculture. John and the mayor talked amicably. The mayor said yes, he'd ask around and try to estimate how many younger sons might be interested in working in New England for the reward of a spread there when farming became possible again. But would the Government agree? Wasn't the intention to create a set of national parks? John told him that wasn't incompatible with limited agriculture, which actually could help conservation. He'd propose the idea to the authorities, and if study showed that it had merit, Congress would consider revising the present master plan. The mayor invited John to visit. Hunting was good these days; the

elk were coming back. John said he'd take a rain check and broke circuit.

48   He left the room for his adjoining office. He called it that from habit; it was really an information laboratory. The machines within it connected him to more than the public data-retrieval system. They gave him access to almost every memory bank and every type of computer in the world. He didn't own the facilities here; he rented them from IBM under a special license. Big business, big labor, Big Government had not vanished. The difference from the past was that no one was forced to depend on them.

49   What John did for the remainder of the afternoon can only be described in the paramathematical language of his specialty. In effect, he set the great interwoven system to retrieving and collating facts about his latest endeavor.

50   Around five, he knocked off. No matter how well trained, you grew fatigued from that intensity of concentration. Besides, scanning would proceed automatically for hours. Ironically, most of that period would be idle time. There were many programs as crucial as his. An inquiry must wait its turn in the crowded communication channels. Tomorrow he'd ride herd on the machines while they selected what was pertinent from the information they would have assembled for him. Thus, he would get a précis, not too enormous for him to study and comprehend. This would give him the basis for framing specific questions. His task would not be completed soon, nor would it be easy. But he felt pleased. A good start had been made. Because of him, forests would one day stand green again.

51   After a quick, refreshing round of tumbles, calisthenics and meditation, he called his girl. They got along wonderfully; of late, he'd considered proposing a formal one-year trial liaison. Tonight, though, he simply wanted some fun. She accepted his invitation to a smorgasbord and an evening of Chinese opera. She honestly enjoyed the luxuries he could buy, but with equal honesty wasn't interested in anything beyond basic credit for herself. Her poetry kept her too busy.

52   When he brought her home, landing his flitter in front of her prefab cabin on the cliffs above a moonlit Pacific, she suggested he spend the night. In the morning, on the cabin's deck, they watched the fading contrail of a rocket tender that had lifted from Armstrong Spacedrome out at sea and was climbing with supplies to the orbiting ship that would carry the first manned expedition to Saturn. They paid even closer attention to a troupe of wandering dancers, jugglers and minstrels strolling past on their way to a *fiesta*. And then John headed back to work.

CONSIDERATIONS

Assuming that the John of this story is a 3-year-old child today, do you agree that the 30-year-old man in the year 2000 will experience the conditions the author predicts? Which nightmares of John's parents seem most realistic to you as you view American society in the 1970s? Which future conditions projected in this story seem most probable? Least probable? In paragraph 11 the author sets the stage for the rest of the story. What does politics have to do with the future of man? Who are the revolutionaries he speaks of? What is the revolution, if, in fact, there is one going on?

Is this presentation effective? What if the author had used the first-person narrative point of view? Why did he choose the omniscient narrator point of view? Would the story have a different impact if it were told from a different point in time?

Do you foresee America as a nation of subcultures, as Anderson suggests? Have we become that already? What are the advantages and disadvantages of such an arrangement?

VOCABULARY

(1) **beleaguered**   surrounded with annoyances or troubles

(4) **genocide**   the deliberate and systematic extermination of a national or racial group

(4) **implacable**   unappeasable

(10) **prostheses**   the addition of an artificial part to supply a defect of the body

(10) **ubiquitous**   omnipresent

(18) **depilatory**   hair removal agent

(22) **holographic**   an entire reproduction

(25) **cybernetics**   the study of human control functions and of mechanical and electrical systems designed to replace them

(25) **ramified**   divided into branches or subdivisions

(28) **cadre**   a group of experienced persons

(29) **pragmatic**   subscribing to a practical point of view

(33) **milieus**   environments, conditions, surroundings

(35) **insularity**   narrowly exclusive

(41) **gazebo**   a garden structure with an enjoyable view

(42) **senescent**   growing old

(46) **latifundia**   large farms or estates

(49) **collating**   collect and arrange in proper order

(50) **précis**   an abstract or summary

(52) **contrail**   visible condensation of water droplets or ice crystals from the atmosphere occurring in the wake of a rocket or a high-flying jet.

Analysis

ANALYSIS

Analysis is the process of dividing or breaking something down into its own component parts. Anything that is thought of in terms of having parts can be analyzed. You can do this with physical things—a machine, a chemical compound, a tree—or with an abstraction like a theory or an argument. A poem, a short story, a musical composition, a painting, a play, or a novel can be analyzed in order to determine the relation of the parts to each other and to the whole.

The kind of analysis used depends on many things: who is doing the analyzing, the subject being analyzed, the audience it's being done for. A sunset would be analyzed differently by a painter, by a meteorologist, and by an astronomer. The first would probably talk about the aesthetic qualities and colors, the next about the clouds and dust in the air, and the last about the relative positions of the sun and earth. Each analysis is partly descriptive; but it is description that considers the parts of a particular structure in order to gain information—not just sense impressions—about the thing being described.

Analysis is not haphazard. It is a methodical way of examining the parts of a whole structure. You need to ask questions in analysis, and the kinds of questions you ask and the answers you get form the different types of analysis:

1. *Functional analysis:* What are the parts? How far can I break this down? For example, given an argument about the need for family planning, can I determine the main points and the subordinate considerations? Can I come up with an outline of this argument?

2. *Process analysis:* How do the parts work? What does each do? This is easier to see if you are analyzing a mechanical thing (rather than a theory in an argument or a work of art).

3. *Cause-and-effect analysis:* What makes something else happen? Analysis is often used in expository writing and in argumentation. When you want to dissect an argument or theory, to examine its propositions, a logical way of doing so is to follow the chain of events as presented in the argument or theory. (Situation A gives rise to Effect B which in turn causes Situation C, and so on.) Since no single event is absolutely isolated, there are always sets of circumstances that result in a given event. The poet may select a different set of circumstances to explain

the existence of a perfect rose than would the botanist; both points of view are probably valid in a given circumstance. Thus analysis is a valuable method of determining how or why things work, or happen, how parts of a structure—concrete or abstract —are related to each other and how they relate to and work together within the whole structure.

PRACTICE

1. Write an analysis of the complex nature of a process, object, or term (phrase) in terms of its parts and the relation of these parts to the whole. Consider a process such as running a political campaign or preparing a gourmet meal. Or analyze a word (*evolution*, for example) or a phrase (*peace with honor*).

2. Use a speech in which a problem is analyzed by a current political figure and write a critique of the completeness, appropriateness, and validity of the analysis. Or use a review of a current movie, play, art show, or musical concert.

3. Analyze the similarities and differences in approach to the same subject as reported in two newspapers, or as reported on several television news programs.

Human Nature Is Still Evolving

After reading this essay, analyze the truth and validity of the argument. Base your analysis on the logical structure of the essay and write a report on your findings. If the author has committed any fallacies in her logic, include an analysis of the nature of these fallacies in your report.

Double Jeopardy: To Be Black and Female

Find an essay in a popular magazine or newspaper that deals with the subject of being black and female. (Check articles written by Shirley Chisholm, for example.) Then write an essay in which you analyze the differences in approach to the same subject. An article written by a black man may make an even more interesting essay.

The Last Traffic Jam

Study an ecological problem (such as the Cuyahoga River in Ohio, which, because it was so terribly polluted, actually caught on fire!). Then write a cause-and-effect analysis in which you present a set of circumstances leading up to the event to set up a possible causal relationship.

How Sentences Mean

In this essay the author writes a functional analysis of the sentence. Write an essay on some kind of nonverbal communication, such as facial expressions, hand gestures, body language, or "vibes." If you choose gestures, for example, break down and analyze the individual gestures, how they function, what they communicate, and how the message differs among cultures, ethnic groups, sexes, and age groups. When you have analyzed all the different "parts," or kinds of gestures, consider them collectively as a "whole" category of nonverbal communication to complete your analysis.

- Compile a list of current slang expressions and write an essay in which you analyze their influence on your own speech.

- Write a report on an analysis of a process. (A good source of ideas is "The Way Things Work," which is a two-volume, illustrated encyclopedia of technology explaining the process of everything from push-button ball point pens to rockets.

For examples of individual paragraphs using *analysis*, see p.13, ¶17, p.24, ¶8-10, p.29, ¶14-17, p.38, ¶15-17, p.60, ¶19, p.175, ¶6, p.200, ¶10-11, p.211, ¶20-22, p.252, ¶4-5.

Human Nature Is Still Evolving

ELISABETH MANN BORGESE

1   Human nature is both stable and changeable. Biologists and phys-   *Expo*
ical anthropologists tend to emphasize the stable aspect; historians
and cultural anthropologists tend to emphasize the enormous
changes that have taken place.

2   Man's physical structure, including his brain capacity, has
changed remarkably little since he first appeared on this planet
about five million years ago. Even in his interaction with the environment there are some surprisingly stable features. For instance,
the number of people with whom a person establishes a real relationship throughout a lifetime has remained constant since the
Stone Age; and it does not matter whether the persons with whom
this relationship is established are clustered nearby or are dispersed
over the globe. Also today, with our sophisticated technologies, we
control the temperature of our environment, keeping it at a comfortable seventy degrees, which was just about the temperature on
the plains of Mesopotamia where the human odyssey began.

3   Still, great changes have occurred. Natural biological evolution   *Tran/*
in man is slow, but cultural evolution has become part of natural   *Thes*
evolution and has accelerated it at a dizzy rate. In a way it has
changed human nature radically. One might even say that whether
post-modern man is still *Homo sapiens* remains to be seen. A species that can fly is different from one that cannot. A species that can
transport itself out of earth's biosphere to other planets is different

Reprinted, with permission, from the March/April, 1973 issue of *The Center Magazine*, a publication of the Center for the Study of Democratic Institutions, Santa Barbara, California.

from an earthbound species. A species that can transplant vital organs from one member to another, blurring the boundaries between this individual and that individual and between life and death, is different from a species whose members cannot do this.

4   Curiously, the higher you go on the side of cultural evolution, *Pdx* the further back you go on the side of natural evolution. For instance, technology has given us wings so that we are birds again, and birds, of course, came earlier, much earlier in the process of natural evolution. Technology now is about to give us gills so that we may return to the depths of the seas where life began.

5   Or take the beginning of life. In the beginning, life was sexless. *Narr* When sexual reproduction came into existence, multiplying the possibilities of hereditary combinations and speeding up evolution, male and female alike expelled their sexual products into the surrounding waters. Fertilization was external and the maturation of the fertilized egg was external. Then fertilization was internalized, but the maturation of the fertilized egg was still external, the birth and growth of the young was external. Then gestation was internalized, and the mammal came into being. First the fetus was expelled at an early stage in the gestation and carried externally, as in a marsupial pouch. Then internal gestation was prolonged over ever-greater periods of development: the young animal, e.g., calf or horse, was born to the light in almost perfect shape and ready to cope with life on its own terms after only a few months.

6   Now we are at the turning point. *Homo sapiens* is the last *Tran* mammal. There won't be other mammals after him. His baby, far *Anly* from perfect, is helpless, unfinished, like the little marsupial. But the mother, to whom he is so long attached, is at the end of her mammality. Especially in the higher classes, in the cities, among intellectual and professional women—that is, among the most evolved specimens—breast milk is scarce. So lactation is being externalized.

7   And mothers go to work, and the more work there is for mother, the more hazardous becomes gestation. Premature births are common. Mother's physical build—tall and slender—does not seem particularly suitable for childbearing and childbirth labor. But premature births are no longer as dangerous as they used to be. There are incubators.

8   Thus, gestation is externalized; and the incubator-plus-formula corresponds to the egg.

9   Also there have been promising experiments in fertilizing a human ovum in a test tube and raising the embryo there. The first

of these was carried out in 1961 by an Italian doctor, Petrucci. He raised his externally fertilized embryo for twenty-nine days, at which point he discontinued the experiment, under pressure from the Church. So fertilization had been externalized; test tube replaced the primeval waters; and scientific planning superseded chance.

10   All this may seem scary, but not to me. Evolution is now in our hands. "Through billions of years of blind mutation," Herman Muller has said, "microbes finally emerged as man. We are no longer blind; at least we are beginning to be conscious of what has happened and of what may happen. From now on, evolution is what we make it."   *Tone*

11   While human nature—indeed, the nature of life—changes and yet remains always the same, our awareness of ourselves continues to change and expand as our awareness of our environment changes and expands. The explorations of outer and inner space and of external and internal oceans are simultaneous.   *Pdx*

12   To better understand human nature we must do four things. We must study animal nature. We must find out whether there is one human nature or whether there are different human natures— for instance, male and female. We must come to terms with the impact of technology on human nature. And we must study the interactions among world order, social organization, and human nature. These are four massive areas for exploration.   *Class*

13   Western man in the last few centuries has adopted and maintained a remarkably huffy attitude toward the animal kingdom. This was conditioned by his faith, which made him the king of creation, and by his ambition to subject all of nature to his domination. He believed that only he was endowed with an immortal soul (which sometimes he even denied to his companion, woman); he thought that only he could master a language, use or invent tools, engage in artistic activity, and have a religion. These convictions grew with the advance of reason, rationality, and Western civilization. In the process man forgot a lot of what he knew during his more primitive stages when he was immersed in myth, when he had a reverence for life and a sense of unity with nature—attitudes which have survived more in the Oriental cultures than in our own.   *Dict*

14   Now, however, our knowledge in the field of animal intelligence and our communication with animals are growing. The distinctions between man and the rest of the animal kingdom are breaking down. We see that capabilities, once assumed to be uniquely human, are in fact shared.

15   It is fascinating to search for the roots of language, technology,   *Tran*

art, even religion, in the animal kingdom. This is an infant science; we do not know yet where it is going.

16   What is certain is that animals have very complex systems of communication, and that they have the capacity to learn a new language, even our language, to a much higher degree than we would have given them credit for even a few years ago. Of course, it was primitive on our part to expect that they could use their vocal cords the way we do, and to make them go through all sorts of contortions to have them pronounce words like "mamma" or "daddy." Today we are more sophisticated. Some scientists have *Exemp* taught chimpanzees deaf-mute language; others work with other symbols, different colored shapes. In both cases the chimps can without difficulty make logical constructs or sentences—even complicated ones—and convey information or the expression of desire.

17   I work with dogs. I teach them to type on an electric typewriter. I also teach them numbers. After three months of work my English setter puppies can count to at least thirteen; they know odd numbers from even; they can identify the largest number and the smallest number in a set; and they can add. Evidently they are endowed with the instruments of logic, of symbol using, of abstraction. This is established now, not only for mammals high up on the ladder of evolution, but for simple animals, such as pigeons and goldfish. Even worms can learn.

18   As far as technology is concerned, there is an animal technology from the simple making and use of tools (e.g., a chopstick to dig eggs out of an ant hill, as chimps do, or a cudgel used as a weapon) to elaborate technologies (the beavers' damming of rivers for the transport of lumber; air-conditioning in termite structures; radar in bats, sonar in dolphins). This is what we know today, but we still know very little. We can see only what we already know. We had to *Tone* invent air-conditioning and radar and sonar before we could discover that they existed in nature.

19   As far as art is concerned, there are all sorts of proto-art in the *Exemp* animal kingdom, although we fail to recognize most of it. Among the things we do recognize and marvel at are the painting, sculpture, and mosaic work among the bower birds of Australia. They decorate their bowers with shells, colored glass, shining objects. Some paint their walls with fruit pulp, wet powdered charcoal, or paste of chewed-up grass mixed with saliva. One species, the satin bower bird, makes a tool from a wad of bark to apply the paint. Others garden for a hobby. Members of one species decorate their nine-foot-high bowers with living orchids. Others build huts before which

they plant lawns of moss and on these, most painstakingly, they   *Exemp*
arrange colored fruits, flowers, fungi, and other objects. When the
flowers are wilted, they throw them away and replace them with
fresh ones.

20   The roots of religion, or proto-religion, are hardest to determine. There is hardly any literature on this subject. However, that
there is ritual in animal behavior, that there is "superstition," exorcism, and some relationship to dream and to death have been documented.

21   If we knew more about animal art, we would understand hu-   *Arg*
man art better. If we knew more about the roots of religion we
would understand our own religiousness in a deeper way. Our new
awareness of the continuity of spiritual as well as physical life
changes the concept we have of man and his position on earth. The
more we know about animals, the more we will feel that we are part
of nature; we will feel a reverence for nature which we lost during
the last few centuries; we will fear to destroy our environment because we will see that we are thereby destroying ourselves.

22   So we are a part of animal nature. But technology, the world of   *Tran*
machines, is a part of us. Technology cannot be unnatural. Technology, too, is part of animal nature, not only because it exists
already in the animal world but also because of our own relationship to it. Technology is part of human nature. Heisenberg predicts,
"In the future, many of our technical apparatuses will perhaps belong as inescapably to man as the snail's shell does to the snail or   *Sim*
the spider web does to the spider. The apparatus would then be
rather a part of the human organism."

23   Technology has no moral dimension. What is good or bad is   *Top S*
the use we make of it. I cannot accept the idea of a technological
imperative, the notion that technology is something autonomous
and devilish which, in the end, will destroy mankind and probably
the whole world. The outstanding exponent of this theory is
Jacques Ellul. It sounds to me like a theology of doom rather than   *Tone*
a scientific theory, and I don't like it.

24   I see technology as both cause and effect of human evolution.
That is, there are feedback relationships among social systems, technology, and human nature.

25   Take war, for instance. War is a human institution that has
existed, more or less in its present form, for at least a few thousand
years. War has created a technology which in turn has considerably
changed the nature of war. I do not think I am unduly optimistic if

I say that we may have reached the point where the technology of | **Arg**
war is abolishing war itself and thereby transforming our social and
political systems. For war is a symptom rather than a cause; it is an
intrinsic part of the system of nation-states in which we still live.
And you cannot simply lop war off, as it were, and leave the rest of
the system intact. To abolish war means to transcend the system of
nation-states.

26   Now, of course, technology cannot abolish war if war is "part
of human nature." I claim it is not. War is rather the institutional-
ization of behavior that is symptomatic of the form of our social
and political organization. Slavery existed over a long period of
time, too, but it was abolished by the technology of the Industrial
Revolution. A machine-based, industrial society had no room for
slavery, so we could give vent to moral indignation against the injustice of slavery and credence to the Christian faith in the equality of
all men . . . and abolish slavery.

27   Today technology has disintegrated war as a social institution.
The destructiveness of what are now called "weapons" is such that
any act of war increasingly resembles an "act of God," that is, a | **Def**
natural catastrophe of the highest magnitude such as the sudden
disappearance of a continent. It is clear that the classical "laws of
war"—for instance, the distinction between military and civilians,
or the rules for the treatment of prisoners of war—no longer apply.

28   Furthermore, what constitutes a "weapon" is increasingly difficult to define. Weather control and modification can be a formidable weapon as well as a benefit to mankind.

29   Also weapons capable of exterminating a population can be
fabricated by a scientist—even an amateur scientist—in a basement
laboratory and can be delivered by a guerrilla.

30   It is obvious that under the impact of such weapons-technology | **C&E**
the traditional approach to disarmament, arms control, and inspec-
tion is ineffectual. But this need not make us pessimistic. It simply
means that war has ceased to be a usable instrument of policy-
making for nations. It means that nations that cannot resort to war
as a means of policy are not sovereign in the traditional meaning of
the word. Something fundamental is happening to the nation-state.
Technology has played a crucial role in transforming our social and
political system.

31   What about the interactions among social organizations, world | **Tran**
order, and human nature?

32   I do not conceive of world order as something in the future
toward which we are moving, starting, let us say, with the individu-

al—"natural man"—who then organizes his family, the families merging into tribes, the tribes into cities, the cities into nations, the nations into continents, and regional federations into a world federation of nations. Things just do not fall into place that way.

33   I think of mankind as a system—which it has always been—in which two forces, one centripetal and integrative, the other centrifugal and disintegrative, are working. In this system, under the impact of these forces, a continuous regrouping and reclustering take place.

34   For a few hundred years we have been living in an era of nation-states. We have been living in a hierarchical, vertical order, a closed order, one based on property, power, and sovereignty, an order dominated by Western, Judeo-Grecian-Roman values.

Anly

35   Now we are regrouping. We are going to live in a postnational or transnational era in which nations will still exist, but they will no longer be the sole actors, or even the protagonists, on the scene of world history. Other forces and other forms of organization—economic and cultural—are taking their place. We will live in a horizontal order, where men will again participate in the decisions that affect them. We will live in an open order, with everybody being part of and moving freely within a number of overlapping subsystems in which one's work, leisure, economic, cultural, and spiritual life are organized. It will be an order based no longer on property, on power, or on sovereignty, for all these concepts are eroding under our eyes. And it will be an order no longer dominated by Judeo-Grecian-Roman values. The new life-style will be infused with Oriental values, which is symbolized by the drama of China's entry into the world organizations.

36   The centrifugal and centripetal forces at work in this regrouping are not contradictory, but complementary.

Dict

37   Nation-states now tend to break up. This is a worldwide phenomenon, affecting developed as well as developing nations. I have only to mention Northern Ireland or Croatia, Katanga or Nigeria, East Bengal or Québec as illustrations. The Black Power movement in this country should be viewed in the same context, as should, for that matter, student power or even woman power.

Exmp

38   What is remarkable is that the forces of law and order, sophisticated and formidable though they may be, are less and less capable of coping with these internal-disintegrating movements, just as, externally, they are impotent in the face of even weak, undeveloped peoples, as in Vietnam.

39   Each of these forces or movements has its own physiognomy,

its own roots in its own history, and its own goals. But what they all have in common is an urge toward self-determination, self-management, participation in decision-making on a scale that is comprehensible in human terms.

40   Self-managing and self-governing communities—whether of a cultural, nationalistic, racial, economic, generational, or other character—will be much more important as the infrastructure of world order than they have been in the era of the centralized nation-state. This is an easy prediction.

41   If the centrifugal force thus undercuts the power of the nation-state, the centripetal force overcuts it. This force is engendered in all those areas of human activity which are too broad to be managed within the confines of a nation-state, however large that state may be. Such activities, in fact, must now be managed in a global perspective.   *C & C*

42   One such area is the management of the world's oceans and their resources. A new type of transnational organization will have to be created to take care of the oceans. This is not a pipe dream but a political reality. The Seabed Committee of the United Nations General Assembly is now preparing for a general conference on the law of the seas to draw up a treaty establishing an international ocean regime for the peaceful uses of ocean space and resources for the benefit of mankind as a whole, with special regard for the needs of the developing nations.   *Exemp*

43   In trying to establish an organization for the management of ocean resources, we must tackle all the problems of world government. This includes questions of constitutional structure, distribution of voting power, relations between large and small and developed and developing nations, planning and resource management, conservation, regional and global development, taxation, diversity and unity, sovereignty and property, rights and responsibilities, a new science policy, and the control of technology for the benefit of mankind.   *Class*

44   If we find solutions for these problems in the functionally limited and relatively noncontroversial area of ocean resource management, we may then apply these new formulae, with the necessary adaptations, to other transnational activities such as earth resource management, energy management, weather control, outer space, communications—all areas of activities that have become too large for the nation-state to manage.

45   At the Center in our work on the oceans we hit on something that might be a new approach to peace and disarmament. Two   *Tran*

things became clear. One, that the industrial uses and the military uses of ocean space conflict. As the industrial uses increase, the military uses are bound to recede. In our work on the oceans, therefore, we did not stress disarmament as a prerequisite for the establishment of an ocean regime. That approach would be hopeless. But if the peaceful uses of ocean space and economic cooperation in the oceans proceeds, the military uses will simply be crowded out. War among the members of the ocean regime will then be as unlikely as it has become among the members of the European Economic Community.   *Angy*

46   The second thing that became clear is that the same instruments on which the international community must rely for the monitoring of pollution and to perform scientific and industrial research, will also serve to uncover military secrets. As a result, they will render obsolete most of today's weapons systems.

47   The same applies to the new instruments to survey earth resources. Resource satellite pictures will have a resolution of about thirty-two meters on the ground, compared with about a five-kilometer resolution for weather pictures. Resource satellites are forcing a change in the whole concept of security, and so a new international understanding will have to be devised.   *C & C*

48   Therefore, it is not that nations must disarm in order to get peace. Rather, the kind of international organization we have—the European Economic Community—or will have—the ocean regime, or the International Earth Resource Management Organization— are intrinsically peace systems. As such, they will relegate one weapons system after another to museums of surrealistic art.   *Meta*

49   All these integrative and disintegrative forces, the trends to new forms of transnational organization and new forms of self-managing and self-governing entities on an intermediate level—whether of a political, economic, cultural, or other character—will interact.   *Tran*

50   "Interaction" may well become the new catchword to give a common denominator to many of our activities. These activities will continuously engender their own autonomy. Sovereignty, which is a static concept and territorially limited, will be transmuted into the idea of an autonomy continuously engendered by interaction, which is a dynamic concept resulting from the two forces of integration and disintegration.   *S Var*

51   But these forces do not stop at the intermediate level of the self-managing community. They affect each individual and help determine human nature.

52   I cannot conceive of man outside the context of his social | Arg
environment. The dichotomy between the individual and society is
no longer tenable. The individual is not the basis of the social structure, or the beginning of the process of social integration. The structure has no basis—let us think of it as spheric—and the process has
no beginning; it feeds back upon itself.

53   Although we are by no means "beyond freedom and dignity"—
nor do we expect or wish to get there—it is clear that when we say
we are free we are mostly deceiving ourselves. We are largely the
products of our environment, culture, economic status, and the
kind of stimuli we are exposed to from the time of conception
onward, not to speak of our genetic heritage.

54   Man is not really an individual but a network of interacting | Dict
forces, a shifting nodal point of influences. Statistically, we really
can whittle him down to nonexistence.

55   It is in his interaction with environmental forces and influ- | C&E
ences, however, that man gains his autonomy, develops his responsibility, and creates a freedom that did not exist and which must be
re-created continuously. His self-awareness increases with his awareness of his environment. And increasing awareness engenders increasing interaction, remaking his past, directing his future.

56   A final question: Is there anything that we can solidly and sta- | Tran
bly call female and that determines women's role in society once
and for all?

57   From my description of human nature it follows that there can
be no such thing as femaleness. Like all other aspects of human
nature femaleness results from forces and influences—natural, cultural, and technological. The nature of femaleness changes with
changes in social organization, and so does the role of women.
Theoretically, there is no limit to this changeability. With present
instruments of social and biological engineering we could, theoreti-
cally, even abolish the differences between male and female. This | Angy
point, far advanced on the scale of cultural evolution, would correspond to a point very far back on the scale of natural evolution
where life went on—neither male nor female—and perpetuated itself by simple cell division.

58   But we need not go as far as that. Descending once more into
the animal kingdom in order better to understand our own nature,
maleness and femaleness have taken various shapes and engendered
various relationships throughout the evolution of life. In some spe- | Class
cies the females are huge, the males are tiny; in others the females
are numerous, the males are scarce; in some species the females are

colorful and do the display, in others the males do; in some species the females are dominant, in others the male.

59   In all cases, however, the relationship between males and females and their respective roles are determined by the social organization of the species. And there seems to be another rule: the more social the species, the more important is the female; the looser the organization of the species, that is, the more individualistic it is, the less conspicuous is the female. The most social of all species, the social insects, are totally dominated by females.

60   Deep down we seem to be aware of this affinity between femininity and collectivity. It permeates our mythology, our psychology, even our language. In the history of language, the plural form and the feminine form were born together. Originally they were identical. In all languages there are still traces of this.

61   In our own social evolution, movements of women's liberation have coincided with trends toward more community-oriented social organization. All socialist and communist revolutions contain an element of feminine revolution. Primeval society, which was communal, was also matriarchal, although this thesis is now being contested. But at any rate, women have played a crucial role in society.

62   Our generation seems to be groping for a new equilibrium between society and the individual. We have developed a concept of human nature which does not recognize any conflict between these two aspects of human nature. If this is so, it will have a profound impact on the nature of femaleness and maleness and on the participation of women in the social and political order.

63   The world order that I have tried to sketch, and the order of self-managing, interacting entities articulating this world order on the one hand and individual interaction on the other will be an order in which "the feminine problem" will no longer exist.

Anly

End

CONSIDERATIONS

If, as the author contends, mankind is a part of animal nature, and technology is a part of mankind's human nature, what are the viable options open to mankind for a healthy, well-integrated future? Do you agree that a new world order is in the making now? Will there continue to be a regrouping of organizational forms as nation-states give way to a new order? What are the centripetal and centrifugal forces at work, in the opinion of Borgese? (paragraphs 33, 36, and 49) Do you agree with her definition of these forces and with the effect they will have on the future world (human) system?

Borgese's article is presented as a finely honed argument. Can you paraphrase her thesis? In which paragraph is it first stated? Study the use of figurative language in this article. (paragraph 48) How do these special uses affect the persuasiveness of the argument? Do you feel sympathetic—in agreement—with the positions taken by the author? In what respects has she selected particularly effective examples to support her thesis? Which examples are most impressive, most convincing?

Comment in an essay—in the form of argument—on the position set forth in paragraphs 54 and 55: "Man is not really an individual but a network of interacting forces, a shifting nodal point of influences. . . . It is in his interaction with environmental forces, however, that man gains his autonomy. . . ." Using these ideas as your thesis, project your vision of the future of mankind in a well-reasoned argument.

VOCABULARY

(1) **anthropologists** scientists who deal with the origins, physical and cultural development, racial characteristics, and social customs and beliefs of mankind

(3) **biosphere** the part of the earth's crust, waters, and atmosphere where living organisms can exist

(5) **maturation** in biology, a process that results in the production of mature eggs and sperms

(5) **gestation** the period between fertilization (conception) and delivery of the newborn

(6) **lactation** the period of milk production in female mammals; the secretion or formation of milk

(9) **superseded** replaced, supplanted

(10) **mutation** the act or process of changing; departures from parent types caused by a change in a gene or chromosome

(18) **radar** a method for locating an object by measuring the time (and direction) for the echo of a radio wave to return

(18) **sonar** a method of detecting and locating objects in water by means of the sound waves they reflect or produce

(19) **proto-art** earliest forms, "first" types

(19) **bower** a leafy shelter; arbor

(20) **exorcism** the act of expelling evil spirits by religious or other solemn ceremonies

(33) **centripetal** moved or directed inward toward a center or axis

(33) **centrifugal** moving or directed outward away from a center or axis

(34) **hierarchical** a system in which things are ranked one above the other; authority and power determined by the place held in the structure

(39) **physiognomy** face or countenance

(40) infrastructure   the basic underlying framework or features of a
                        structure
(48) intrinsically   innately; by nature
(50) engender   give rise to, produce, cause; procreate
(50) autonomy   independence, freedom
(50) transmuted   transformed, changed from one form to another
(52) dichotomy   division into two parts
(52) tenable   capable of being defended
(54) nodal   centering point of component parts
(60) permeates   diffused throughout; pervades

Double Jeopardy:
To Be Black and Female

FRANCES M. BEAL

1   In attempting to analyze the situation of the black woman in America, one crashes abruptly into a solid wall of grave misconceptions, outright distortions of fact and defensive attitudes on the part of many. The system of capitalism (and its afterbirth—racism) under which we all live has attempted by many devious ways and means to destroy the humanity of all people, and particularly the humanity of black people. This has meant an outrageous assault on every black man, woman and child who resides in the United States.

2   In keeping with its goal of destroying the black race's will to resist its subjugation, capitalism found it necessary to create a situation where it was impossible for the black man to find meaningful or productive employment. More often than not, he couldn't find work of any kind. The black woman likewise was manipulated by the system, economically exploited and physically assaulted. She could often find work in the white man's kitchen, however, and sometimes became the sole breadwinner of the family. This predicament has led to many psychological problems on the part of both man and woman and has contributed to the turmoil found in the black family structure.

3   Unfortunately, neither the black man nor the black woman understood the true nature of the forces working upon them. Many black women accepted the capitalist evaluation of manhood and

womanhood and believed, in fact, that black men were shiftless and lazy, that otherwise they would get a job and support their families as they ought to. Personal relationships between black men and women were torn asunder, and one result has been the separation of husband from wife, mother from child, etc.

4   America has defined the roles to which each individual should subscribe. It has defined "manhood" in terms of its own interests and "femininity" likewise. An individual who has a good job, makes a lot of money and drives a Cadillac is a real "man," and conversely, an individual who is lacking in these "qualities" is less of a man. The advertising media in this country continuously inform the American male of his need for indispensable signs of his virility— the brand of cigarettes that cowboys prefer, the whiskey that has a masculine tang or the label of the jock strap that athletes wear.

5   The ideal model that is projected for a woman is to be surrounded by hypocritical homage and estranged from all real work, spending idle hours primping and preening, obsessed with conspicuous consumption, and limited in function to simply a sex role. We unqualitatively reject these models. A woman who stays at home caring for children and the house often leads an extremely sterile existence. She must lead her entire life as a satellite to her mate. He goes out into society and brings back a little piece of the world for her. His interests and his understanding of the world become her own and she cannot develop herself as an individual, having been reduced to a biological function. This kind of woman leads a parasitic existence that can aptly be described as "legalized prostitution."

6   Furthermore, it is idle dreaming to think of black women simply caring for their homes and children like the middle-class white model. Most black women have to work to help house, feed and clothe their families. Black women make up a substantial percentage of the black working force from the poorest black family to the so-called "middle-class" family.

7   Black women were never afforded such phony luxuries. Though we have been browbeaten with this white image, the reality of the degrading and dehumanizing jobs that were relegated to us quickly dissipated this mirage of womanhood. The following excerpt from a speech that Sojourner Truth made at a Women's Rights Convention in the 19th century shows us how misleading and incomplete a life this model represents for us:

   . . . Well, chilern, whar dar is so much racket dar must be something out o'kilter. I tink dat 'twixt de niggers of de Souf and de women at de Norf all a talkin' 'bout rights, de white men will be in a fix pretty soon. But what's all dis here talkin' 'bout? Dat man ober dar say dat women needs to be helped into carriages, and lifted ober ditches, and to have de best place every whar. Nobody ever help me into carriages, or ober mud puddles, or gives me any best places, . . . and ar'nt I a woman? Look at me! Look at my arm! . . . I have plowed, and planted, and gathered into barns, and no man could head me—and ar'nt I a woman? I could work as much as a man (when I could get it), and bear de lash as well—and ar'nt I a woman? I have borne five chilern and I seen 'em mos' all sold off into slavery, and when I cried out with a mother's grief, none but Jesus heard—and ar'nt I a woman?

8   Unfortunately, there seems to be some confusion in the Movement today as to who has been oppressing whom. Since the advent of black power, the black male has exerted a more prominent leadership role in our struggle for justice in this country. He sees the system for what it really is for the most part, but where he rejects its values and mores on many issues, when it comes to women, he seems to take his guidelines from the pages of the *Ladies' Home Journal*. Certain black men are maintaining that they have been castrated by society but that black women somehow escaped this persecution and even contributed to this emasculation.

9   The black woman in America can justly be described as a "slave of a slave." Since the black man in America was reduced to such abject oppression, the black woman had no protector and was used, and is still being used in some cases, as the scapegoat for the evils that this horrendous system has perpetrated on black men. Her physical image has been maliciously maligned; she has been sexually molested and abused by the white colonizer; she has suffered the worst kind of economic exploitation, having been forced to serve as the white woman's maid and as wet nurse for white offspring while her own children were, more often than not, starving and neglected. It is the depth of degradation to be socially manipulated, physically raped, used to undermine your own household, and to be powerless to reverse this situation.

10   It is true that our husbands, fathers, brothers and sons have been emasculated, lynched and brutalized. They have suffered from the cruelest assault on mankind that the world has ever known. However, it is a gross distortion of fact to state that black women have oppressed black men. The capitalist system found it expedient to enslave and oppress them and proceeded to do so without consultation or the signing of any agreements with black women.

11   It must also be pointed out at this time that black women are not resentful of the rise to power of black men. We welcome it. We see in it the eventual liberation of all black people from this corrupt

system of capitalism. However, it is fallacious to think that in order for the black man to be strong, the black woman must be weak.

12   Those who are exerting their "manhood" by telling black women to step back into a domestic, submissive role are assuming a counterrevolutionary position. Black women, likewise, have been abused by the system, and we must begin talking about the elimination of all kinds of oppression. If we are talking about building a strong nation, capable of throwing off the yoke of capitalist oppression, then we are talking about the total involvement of every man, woman, and child, each with a highly developed political consciousness. We need our whole army out there dealing with the enemy, not half an army.

13   There are also some black women who feel that there is no more productive role in life than having and raising children. This attitude often reflects the conditioning of the society in which we live and is adopted from a bourgeois white model. Some young sisters who have never had to maintain a household or to accept the confinement which this entails, tend to romanticize (along with the help of a few brothers) the role of housewife and mother. Black women who have had to endure this function are less apt to have such utopian visions.

14   Those who portray in an intellectual manner how great and rewarding this role will be, and who feel that the most important thing that they can contribute to the black nation is children, are doing themselves a great injustice. This reasoning completely negates the contributions that black women such as Sojourner Truth, Harriet Tubman, Mary McLeod Bethune, and Fannie Lou Hamer have historically made to our struggle for liberation.

15   We live in a highly industrialized society, and every member of the black nation must be as academically and technologically developed as possible. To wage a revolution, we need competent teachers, doctors, nurses, electronics experts, chemists, biologists, physicists, political scientists, and so on. Black women sitting at home reading bedtime stories to their children are just not going to make it.

Economic Exploitation of Black Women

16   Capitalism finds it expedient to reduce women to a state of enslavement. They often serve as a scapegoat for the evils of this system. Much in the same way that the poor white cracker of the South, who is equally victimized, looks down upon blacks and contributes

to the oppression of blacks, so, by giving to men a false feeling of superiority (at least in their own homes or in their relationships with women), the oppression of women acts as an escape valve for capitalism. Men may be cruelly exploited and subjected to all sorts of dehumanizing tactics on the part of the ruling class, but at least they're not women.

17   Women also represent a surplus labor supply, the control of which is absolutely necessary to the profitable functioning of capitalism. Women are systematically exploited by the system. They are paid less for the same work that men do, and jobs that are specifically relegated to women are low-paying and without the possibility of advancement. Statistics from the Women's Bureau of the U.S. Department of Labor show that in 1967, the wage scale for nonwhite women was the lowest of all:

White Males	$6,704
Non-White Males	$4,277
White Females	$3,991
Non-White Females	2,861

18   Those industries which employ mainly black women are the most exploitative. Domestic and hospital workers are good examples of this oppression, as are the garment workers in New York City. The International Ladies Garment Workers Union (ILGWU) whose overwhelming membership consists of black and Puerto Rican women has a leadership that is nearly all lily white and male. This leadership has been working in collusion with the ruling class and has completely sold its soul to the corporate structure.

19   To add insult to injury, the ILGWU has invested heavily in business enterprises in racist, apartheid South Africa—with union funds. Not only does this bought-off leadership contribute to our continued exploitation in this country by not truly representing the best interests of its membership, but it audaciously uses funds that black and Puerto Rican women have provided to support the economy of a vicious government that is engaged in the economic rape and murder of our black brothers and sisters in our Motherland, Africa.

20   The entire labor movement in the United States has suffered as a result of the super-exploitation of black workers and women. The unions have historically been racist and chauvinist. They have upheld racism in this country and have failed to fight the white skin privileges of white workers. They have failed to fight or even make

an issue against the inequities in the hiring and pay of women work-ers. There has been virtually no struggle against either the racism of the white worker or the economic exploitation of the working woman, two factors which have consistently impeded the advance-ment of the real struggle against the ruling class.

21   This racist, chauvinist and manipulative use of black workers and women, especially black women, has been a severe cancer on the American labor scene. It therefore becomes essential for those who understand the workings of capitalism and imperialism to real-ize that the exploitation of black people and women works to every-one's disadvantage and that the liberation of these two groups is a stepping stone to the liberation of all oppressed people in this coun-try and around the world.

Bedroom Politics

22   I have briefly discussed the economic and psychological manipula-tion of black women, but perhaps the most outlandish act of op-pression in modern times is the current campaign to promote steril-ization of non-white women in an attempt to maintain the population and power imbalance between the white *haves* and the non-white *have-nots*.

23   These tactics are but another example of the many devious schemes that the ruling class elite attempts to perpetrate on the black population in order to keep itself in control. A massive cam-paign for so-called "birth control" is presently being promoted not only in the underdeveloped non-white areas of the world, but also in black communities here in the United States. However, what the authorities in charge of these programs refer to as "birth control" is in fact nothing but a method of surgical genocide.

24   The United States has been sponsoring sterilization clinics in non-white countries, especially in India, where already some 3 mil-lion young men and boys in and around New Delhi have been sterilized in makeshift operating rooms set up by American Peace Corps workers. Under these circumstances, it is understandable why certain countries view the Peace Corps not as a benevolent project, not as evidence of America's concern for underdeveloped areas, but rather as a threat to their very existence. This program could more aptly be named "The Death Corps."

25   The vasectomy, which is performed on males and takes only six or seven minutes, is a relatively simple operation. The sterilization of a woman, on the other hand, is admittedly major surgery. This

operation (salpingectomy) must be performed in a hospital under general anesthesia. This method of "birth control" is a common procedure in Puerto Rico. Puerto Rico has long been used by the colonialist exploiter, the United States, as an experimental laboratory for medical research before allowing certain practices to be imported and used here. When the birth control pill was first being perfected, it was tried out on Puerto Rican women and selected black women (poor), using them like guinea pigs to evaluate its effect and its efficiency.

26   The salpingectomy has now become the most common operation in Puerto Rico, more common than an appendectomy or a tonsillectomy. It is so widespread that it is referred to simply as "la operación." *On the Island, 20 percent of the women between the ages of 15 and 45 have already been sterilized.*

27   Now, as previously occurred with the pill, this method has been imported into the United States. Sterilization clinics are cropping up around the country in the black and Puerto Rican communities. These so-called "Maternity Clinics," specifically outfitted to purge black women and men of their reproductive possibilities, are appearing more and more in hospitals and clinics across the country.

28   A number of organizations have been formed to popularize the idea of sterilization, such as The Association for Voluntary Sterilization and The Human Betterment (!!!?) Association for Voluntary Sterilization, Inc., which has its headquarters in New York City. Front Royal, Virginia, has one such "Maternity Clinic" in Warren Memorial Hospital. The tactics used in the clinic in Fauquier County, Virginia, where poor and helpless black mothers and young girls are pressured into undergoing sterilization are certainly not confined to that clinic alone.

29   Threatened with the cut-off of relief funds, some black welfare women have been forced to accept this sterilization procedure in exchange for a continuation of welfare benefits. Mt. Sinai Hospital in New York City performs these operations on many of its ward patients whenever it can convince the women to undergo this surgery. Mississippi and some of the other Southern states are notorious for this act. Black women are often afraid to permit any kind of necessary surgery because they know from bitter experience that they are more likely than not to come out of the hospital without their insides. Both salpingectomies and hysterectomies are performed.

30   We condemn this use of the black woman as a medical testing ground for the white middle class. Reports of ill effects, including

deaths, from the use of the birth control pill only started to come to light when the white privileged class began to be affected. These outrageous Nazi-like procedures on the part of medical researchers are but another manifestation of the totally amoral and dehumanizing brutality that the capitalist system perpetrates on black women. The sterilization experiments carried on in concentration camps some twenty-five years ago have been denounced the world over, but no one seems to get upset by the repetition of these same racist tactics today in the United States of America—land of the free and home of the brave. This campaign is as nefarious a program as Germany's gas chambers and, in a long-term sense, as effective and with the same objective.

31   The rigid laws concerning abortions in this country are another vicious means of subjugation and, indirectly, of outright murder. Rich white women somehow manage to obtain these operations with little or no difficulty. It is the poor black and Puerto Rican woman who is at the mercy of the local butcher. Statistics show that the non-white death rate at the hands of unqualified abortionists is substantially higher than for white women. Nearly half of the child-bearing deaths in New York City are attributed to abortion alone, and out of these, 79 percent are among non-white and Puerto Rican women.

32   We are not saying that black women should not practice birth control. Black women have the right and the responsibility to determine when it is *in the interest of the struggle to have children or not to have them, and this right must not be relinquished to anyone.* It is also the black woman's right and responsibility to determine when it is in her own best interest to have children, how many she will have, and how far apart. Forced sterilization practices, abortion laws, and the unavailability of safe birth control methods, are all symptoms of a decadent society that jeopardizes the health of black women (and thereby the entire black race) in its attempts to control the very life processes of human beings. These are symptoms of a society that believes it has the right to bring political factors into the privacy of the bedchamber. The elimination of these horrendous conditions will free black women for full participation in the revolution and, thereafter, in the building of the new society.

Relationship to White Movement

33   Much has been written recently about the white women's liberation movement in the United States, and the question arises whether

there are any parallels between this struggle and the movement on the part of black women for total emancipation. While there are certain comparisons that one can make, simply because we both live under the same exploitative system, there are certain differences, some of which are quite basic.

34   The white women's movement is far from being monolithic. Any white group that does not have an anti-imperialist and anti-racist ideology has nothing in common with the black woman's struggle. In fact, some groups come to the incorrect conclusion that their oppression is due simply to male chauvinism. They therefore have an extremely anti-male tone. Black people are engaged in a life and death struggle and the main emphasis of black women must be to combat the capitalist, racist exploitation of black people. While it is true that male chauvinism has become institutionalized in American society, one must always look for the main enemy—the fundamental cause of the condition of females.

35   Another major differentiation is that the white women's liberation movement is basically middle class. Very few of these women suffer the extreme economic exploitation that most black women are subjected to day by day. This is the factor that is most crucial for us. It is not an intellectual persecution alone, it is not an intellectual outburst for us; it is quite real. We as black women have got to deal with the problems that the black masses deal with, for our problems in reality are one and the same.

36   If the white groups do not realize that they are in fact fighting capitalism and racism, we do not have common bonds. If they do not realize that the reasons for their condition lie in the system and not simply that men get a vicarious pleasure out of "consuming their bodies for exploitative reasons" (this reasoning seems to be quite prevalent in certain white women's groups), then we cannot unite with them around common grievances or even discuss these groups in a serious manner because they're completely irrelevant to the black struggle.

The New World

37   The black community and black women especially must begin raising questions about the kind of society we wish to see established. We must note the ways in which capitalism oppresses us and then move to create institutions that will eliminate these destructive influences.

38   The new world that we are attempting to create must destroy oppression of every type. The value of this new system will be deter-

mined by the status of the person who was lowest on the totem pole. Unless women in any enslaved nation are completely liberated, the change cannot really be called a revolution. If the black woman has to retreat to the position she occupied before the armed struggle, the whole movement and the whole struggle will have retreated in terms of truly freeing the colonized population.

39   A people's revolution that engages the participation of every member of the community, including man, woman, and child, brings about a certain transformation in the participants as a result of this participation. Once we have caught a glimpse of freedom or experienced a bit of self-determination, we can't go back to old routines that were established under a racist, capitalist regime. We must begin to understand that a revolution entails not only the willingness to lay our lives on the firing line and get killed. In some ways, this is an easy commitment to make. To die for the revolution is a one-shot deal; to live for the revolution means taking on the more difficult commitment of changing our day-to-day life patterns.

40   This will mean changing the traditional routines that we have established as a result of living in a totally corrupting society. It means changing how one relates to one's wife, husband, parents and co-workers. If we are going to liberate ourselves as a people, it must be recognized that black women have very specific problems that have to be spoken to. We must be liberated along with the rest of the population. We cannot wait to start working on those problems until that great day in the future when the revolution somehow, miraculously, is accomplished.

41   To assign women the role of housekeeper and mother while men go forth into battle is a highly questionable doctrine for a revolutionary to maintain. Each individual must develop a high political consciousness in order to understand how this system enslaves us all and what actions we must take to bring about its total destruction. Those who consider themselves to be revolutionary must begin to deal with other revolutionaries as equals. So far as I know, revolutionaries are not determined by sex.

42   Old people, young people, men and women must take part in the struggle. To relegate women to purely supportive roles or to purely cultural considerations is dangerous. Unless black men who are preparing themselves for armed struggle understand that the society which we are trying to create is one in which the oppression of *all members* of that society is eliminated, then the revolution will have failed in its avowed purpose.

43   Given the mutual commitment of black men and black women alike to the liberation of our people and other oppressed peoples

around the world, the total involvement of each individual is necessary. A revolutionary has the responsibility not only to topple those who are now in a position of power, but to create new institutions that will eliminate all forms of oppression. We must begin to rewrite our understanding of traditional personal relationships between man and woman. All the resources that the black community can muster must be channeled into the struggle. Black women must take an active part in bringing about the kind of society where our children, our loved ones, and each citizen can grow up and live as decent human beings, free from the pressures of racism and capitalist exploitation.

CONSIDERATIONS

If the enemy of women is capitalism—and not male chauvinism (paragraphs 33 and 34)—what solution does Beal propose? Do her arguments seem drastic, or eminently realistic? Why does she say in paragraph 39 that it is harder to *live* for the revolution than to *die* for it?

Is the writer's appeal primarily emotional or intellectual? Except for a few specific instances of statistical evidence, as in the Department of Labor Statistics (paragraph 17), Beal makes some general allegations against people and institutions within the present system without citing specific examples or providing detailed historical evidence to back up her claims. Do you accept her generalities as truth? What qualifies her as an expert? Does she seem to speak in anger or with objectivity?

Do you agree with the author's premise stated in the title of this article? A precondition for Beal's argument is that we are one society, one nation (restated in paragraphs 15–42). What would be the ideal new nation or society? Would there be assigned roles for females and for blacks? Give your ideas in a brief argument.

VOCABULARY

(1) **devious**   not straightforward; shifty, crooked
(2) **subjugation**   to be brought under complete control; enslavement
(5) **homage**   respect or reverence
(8) **mores**   moral values of a given group
(8) **emasculation**   deprivation of manhood; castration
(18) **collusion**   secret agreement; conspiracy
(19) **apartheid**   racial segregation and discrimination
(19) **audaciously**   shamelessly, defiantly, brazenly
(30) **nefarious**   extremely wicked
(34) **monolithic**   characterized by total uniformity of goals and purposes

The Last Traffic Jam

STEWART UDALL

1   At the moment there are more than 112 million motor vehicles on the American road. Henry Ford II recently predicted that auto buyers in this country will purchase nearly eleven million new cars this year. And other Detroit executives look forward to 178 million registered vehicles in the United States by 1985.

2   Detroit's short-run forecasts may indeed prove accurate. But how long can this growth continue?

3   The environmental effects of the automobile are well known: motor vehicles cause, for example, as much as 75 percent of the noise and 80 percent of the air pollution in our cities, and the industry must face mounting pressure from environmentalists. There is another, even more compelling constraint on the proliferation of cars. Surprising as it may seem, American oil companies, which during the 1960s increased their production of gasoline by 64 percent, will not be able to provide enough petroleum to fill the gas tanks of some 65 million additional autos expected by 1985.

4   This prediction is based on data prepared by the oil industry itself. Reports by the prestigious National Petroleum Council reveal that U.S. oil production is at, or near, its peak. And the prospects for the discovery of huge new oil fields are so poor that Interior Secretary Rogers C. B. Morton has warned of a "frightening energy scarcity" in a few years if present U.S. production and consumption trends continue.

5   If there will in fact be 178 million motor vehicles on American highways by 1985, the NPC estimates that our oil needs will increase by about 85 percent. During the next decade total U.S. oil production, however, will continue to hover near the current level of eleven million barrels per day—even if the Alaska pipeline is put into operation. (It would contribute an extra two million barrels per day, thus helping make up for a falloff elsewhere.) Unless action is taken to slacken domestic demands, this huge petroleum gap will force the United States by 1985 to import roughly 60 percent of its oil, largely from the nations of the Middle East.

6   These projections, however, tell only part of the story. At the moment, global oil supplies appear plentiful. But the oil needs of the other industrialized countries are growing faster than ours: *annual increases in world consumption are now so enormous that in the 1970s all of the world's oil-using nations will consume as much oil as was used in the hundred years from 1870 to 1970* (and these projected demands will redouble in the 1980s).

7   This surge of demand will soon begin to send shock waves through the American economy and transportation system. The impact of these tremors can already be anticipated: to the consumer they signal the end of a long love affair with the car, and to Detroit they offer an early warning that its 1985 growth aims are dangerously unrealistic. Unless we exercise foresight and devise growth-limits policies for the auto industry, events will thrust us into a crisis that will lead to a substantial erosion of our domestic oil supply as well as the independence it provides us with, and a level of petroleum imports that could cost as much as $20 to $30 billion per year. (This in turn would produce a staggering balance-of-payments problem for the United States, and give the Middle Eastern suppliers a dangerous leverage over our transportation system as well.) Moreover, we would still be depleting our remaining oil reserves at an unacceptable rate, and scrambling for petroleum substitutes, with enormous potential damage to the environment.

8   Given the fact that we are already at the edge of an energy crisis of this magnitude, why are our government and industry leaders not discussing appropriate growth-limits policies?

9   Plainly, any effort to limit economic growth violates our historic belief in progress. The President and his advisers have largely ignored this great and difficult issue, although, in his 1971 message to Congress, the President rightly called for the formation of a single agency to oversee the nation's energy policies. The stress of his message, however, fell not on limiting demand for energy but on

developing new technology to meet growing energy "needs." Despite his expressed concern over energy shortage and air pollution, the President has chosen to shore up the economy by stimulating the production of automobiles. Too often the voice of government is the voice of industry. Hollis M. Dole, Assistant Secretary of the Department of the Interior, recently outlined the alarming facts of oil scarcity—only to urge that we avert the crisis by freshly aggressive efforts to discover and extract our remaining oil. Dole has predicted that there are, in the United States, "172 billion barrels of oil remaining to be discovered," and has pointed out that that figure is more than thirty times what the nation consumed in 1970, a fact that would seem to argue the case for restraint, not development, assuming we care about the oil needs of future generations.

10   For its part, the private sector has been dominated by oil and auto industries whose executives have been unable even to contemplate production plateaus and low horsepower engines. When James Roche retired last December as chief executive of General Motors, he expressed the belief and the faith of Detroit by predicting the inevitability of the auto industry's growth. He then observed: "I think the average American today would give up about anything before he gives up his automobile."

11   When one considers recent economic history, Detroit's faith in this gospel of growth becomes understandable. The future has indeed taken care of itself. The automobile industry directly or indirectly provides roughly one-fifth of all jobs in the United States. It is one of the pacesetters of our industrial system, and its executives are convinced that U.S. prosperity cannot be maintained unless Detroit's output continually expands. Auto executives have shunned the limits-of-growth issues and concentrated nearly all their energies on the next quarter's sales and next year's models.

12   The oil industry is a somewhat different case—or ought to be. As the managers of irreplaceable resources, its executives have a plain responsibility to think and plan generations ahead. But the oilmen, too, have been beguiled by their own success. For over thirty years, their industry has been the world's number-one can-do capitalist enterprise. Ever since a consortium of U.S. companies struck oil in the Arabian sands in the late 1930s, oilmen have accomplished supposedly "impossible" feats of exploration and development on all the continents and in such seemingly unpromising places as Arctic Alaska and the backcountry of Australia. With each new oil strike, the prospect of unlimited oil supplies "for our time" seemed assured.

13   Oilmen have heard cries of scarcity before—and the very oil discoveries which discredited the "doomsayers" of the past now blind these executives to their own end-game statistics.

14   Nevertheless, the energy crisis poses specific questions which leaders of the oil industry can no longer avoid. At what point will rising U.S. oil consumption endanger our whole economy? When does a national policy that accelerates oil depletion become a threat to the long-term future of the American people? When must we adopt and enforce a remedial policy of conservation?

15   The unwillingness of the oilmen to discuss such issues is illustrated paradoxically by last year's report of the National Petroleum Council. In one breath, this document describes a grave oil shortage; in the next, it says the shortage can be overcome. This report simply urges "new oil policies" which would enhance the short-run economic position of the major oil companies and hasten the depletion of the nation's petroleum resources. Give us the tools (in the form of new tax incentives and exploration advantages), the oilmen argue, and we'll produce twice as much oil.

16   How are we to meet the nation's galloping demands for more oil? The current "game plan" of the oil industry, as reflected in the National Petroleum Council reports, proposes these stratagems to make possible "dramatic increases in domestic production":

> An increase of the oil depletion allowance.
> Liberal new tax incentives for oil drilling and exploration.
> Federal deregulation of controls over the price consumers pay for natural gas (to encourage new exploration).
> Quick access—through expansive new Interior Department leasing programs—to the oil deposits below the Atlantic coastal shelf.
> Aggressive development of Alaska's oil resources.

17   In my opinion, it is unrealistic to assume that any of these proposals could be put into effect in time to avert the energy crunch. Political signs point to a further reduction of the oil depletion allowance, and the tax incentive and gas deregulation proposals would certainly arouse a vigorous debate in Congress. When Secretary Morton proposed oil leasing on the Atlantic shelf last summer, every governor from Maine to Maryland (with a supporting chorus of sixty congressmen) stated opposition to such a move. As for Alaska, anyone familiar with the raging dispute over the Alaska pipeline knows that full-throttle oil exploitation in that state faces formidable environmental arguments. And Governor William Egan has warned that construction of oil rigs in the Gulf of Alaska will face physical obstacles more severe than those of any other continental shelf in the world.

18   To be sure, new oil provinces await discovery. But the days of

cheap wildcatting are over (as all the oilmen already know), and the environmental risks and economic costs of tapping increasingly hard-to-reach deposits will be great.

19   It is disturbing to find that the oilmen have consistently ignored the one U.S. petroleum expert who has unerringly forecast the curve of our domestic production. M. King Hubbert, a former petroleum geologist for Shell Oil Company, is now a senior professional with the U.S. Geological Survey. More than a decade ago, his scientific calculations led him to forecast that our domestic production (excluding, admittedly, then unknown Alaskan deposits) would reach its ultimate peak in the early 1970s. This estimate has now been validated by events. Hubbert estimates that the oil fields already identified in the contiguous forty-eight states—including the continental shelves—probably represent 68 to 85 percent of the total U.S. reserves that will ever be discovered, and he is convinced that, at best, Alaskan production will not come on stream in sufficient quantities to increase the total annual output of U.S. oil fields.

20   Hubbert's projections over the past sixteen years have been remarkably accurate. His method of evaluating drilling statistics make him neither an optimist nor a pessimist. Today, however, other geologists have come up with estimates far more expansive than those of Hubbert (and of the conservative analysts who share his approach to petroleum forecasting). For example, while Hubbert doubts that the unexplored Atlantic shelf will ultimately yield as much as ten billion barrels of oil, a few "boomer geologists" have glibly predicted that it will provide us with 169 billion barrels.

21   This dispute raises a crucial policy issue: should we base our national planning on expansive assumptions, or on conservative estimates of our resource potentials? In Hubbert's opinion, caution obliges us to base our plans on the bedrock of proven data.

22   In my view, it is unfortunate that most oilmen are willing to take a final ride with the boomer geologists. They apparently believe that the country should base its energy policies on the bet that another round of big oil strikes is in the offing, that an acceptable oil shale technology can be developed overnight, or that last-resort foreign imports can bail us out.

23   Extracting enormous quantities of oil from Colorado oil shale may someday be possible, but I have not spoken with a single expert who believes that this process can be developed in time to fill the petroleum gap of the next fifteen years. Oil shale development is already the subject of intense controversy. There is no known tech-

nique for extracting the oil economically, and neither the federal government nor the oil industry is pursuing the kind of crash research that might produce a big breakthrough in oil shale technology. Moreover, it is abundantly clear that environmentalists will strenuously oppose any oil shale development plans that would turn huge sections of the Rocky Mountains into a conservation disaster area.

24   Many East Coast congressmen and governors advocate big increases in imports of "cheap" Middle Eastern oil as a solution to the current energy crisis. Such a policy might make sense for a few years. However, it ignores events that are changing the whole character of the international oil business. The newly militant organization of oil-producing and exporting countries (OPEC) is determined to end the era of cheap oil. Looking ahead, those countries know that oil in the ground is better than gold in the bank, and they are already contemplating extraction slowdowns which will lengthen the life-span of their oil fields. It is doubtful that these countries will be willing to increase their output to keep pace with our voracious appetite for foreign oil. Indeed, I am convinced that reliance on "cheap imports" is the riskiest course for the United States to follow. In all likelihood, such a policy would produce chronic fuel shortages that would lead to gas rationing and/or strict control of gasoline prices.

25   A few months ago, with candor rare for his industry, Wayne E. Glenn, president of the Western Hemisphere Petroleum Division of the Continental Oil Company, issued a somber warning to his fellow oilmen. Asserting that "the days of cheap foreign oil are a thing of the past," Glenn cautioned that it would be extremely unwise for the United States to count on filling any substantial part of its future needs from Middle Eastern sources. And more recently, Commerce Secretary Peter G. Peterson cautioned that importing twelve million barrels of oil per day in 1980 would not only saddle the United States with a $26-billion-a-year burden on its balance of payments, but would also cause "indigestion, both economic and political."

26   In short, common sense dictates that we begin a transition to policies designed to avoid an energy impasse that could cripple our transportation system and imperil our economy. We must set growth limits that will allow the automobile and oil industries to maintain economic stability while conserving our resources and preserving our environment. Of course, such a reorientation will re-

quire statesmanship as well as public pressure. It will not happen unless corporate self-interest yields to a responsible outlook that serves the broader interests of the nation as a whole. Above all, this shift requires a thorough redirection of the aims of these two industries.

27   *The oil industry*, in my view, must acknowledge that conservatism (not depletion) should be the keystone of our national energy policies. They themselves must now adopt specific growth limits on imports and domestic production, and a policy of substantial energy self-sufficiency.

28   *The auto industry* must acknowledge that a rational transportation policy should seek a balance between individual convenience, the efficient use of limited resources, and urban-living values that protect spaciousness, natural beauty, and human-scale mobility. Twice as many autos and freeways as we now have would be a sentence of death for our cities. A necessary shift in public policy toward effective mass transit systems (which consume relatively little energy per passenger mile) would ameliorate the problem, but Detroit still must recognize that the time has come to begin developing external combustion engines (like the steam engine), to build sturdy engines of smaller horsepower that will travel twice as far on a gallon of gas as do today's engines.

29   Some will argue that the changes advocated above are a prescription for unemployment and recession. I believe this argument is alarmist and specious. I am not proposing that we bring our oil and auto industries to a screeching halt. There is still time to begin a series of gradual steps toward new transportation and energy policies, livable cities, and more humane, efficient transit systems. These changes will require some industries to make steady adjustments, and others to set firm new limits on production and construction.

30   A leveling off of auto production would mean a return to the ideas that inspired Henry Ford a half-century ago. Autos would be built to be durable, safe, and easily maintained. Their low-horsepower packages wouldn't get us where we are going quite so fast, but they would conserve fuel and pollute the environment much less. For Detroit, such restraints need not mean economic disaster. The industry could respond to this challenge creatively by enlarging its production. It might, for example, branch out into the market for minibuses, innovative "people movers," urban mass transit cars, and air-cushion trains. The highway construction industry would also have to think creatively. Foregoing a "second" interstate high-

way system might disappoint the concrete and macadam contractors, but huge new programs to construct mass transit systems and air-cushion tracks will require many of the same construction skills.

31   A limit on the automobile population of the United States would be the best of news for our cities. The end of automania would save open spaces, encourage wiser land use, and contribute greatly to ending suburban sprawl. It would lead to the building of more compact, sensitively planned communities in the future—and it would prompt many cities to build quick, quiet, and convenient modes of transportation ranging from bicycle paths to mass transit systems. The "bad news" for Detroit would, in part, be offset by the good news for U.S. railroads. Transportation of freight and passengers by railway uses far less energy than transportation by trucks and autos. And the rebirth of the railroads—and their movement into exciting new variants of ground transportation such as the air-cushion train—would create solid economic and environmental benefits.

32   This entire exercise in restraint would teach us the most valuable lesson of all: that the quality of our lives will be enriched if we make fewer demands on our resources. "Less is more" is a paramount tenet of environmental reform, and it is time for us to recognize its specific benefits.

33   Less horsepower, smaller cars, and fewer autos mean more safety, healthier urban environments, more constraints on suburban sprawl, more efficient use of fuel. Less oil consumption for fuel means more oil to share with our children and theirs, more energy self-sufficiency, more oil for use in basic industrial processes. Less investment in highways means more money for efficient public transportation, more open space, more investment in cheap, fast intercity trains.

34   The bonuses of "less is more" are vast. The choice facing the American people is not between growth and stagnation, but between short-term growth and long-term disaster. We can continue to pursue the growth policies of the past and let urban decay, exorbitant prices, and risks to our national security dictate stringent remedial policies a few years from now. Or we can exercise restraint and learn to live comfortably, within our means.

CONSIDERATIONS

What would Udall's proposals for a saner oil policy do to the American automobile industry? Is Udall's approach the only logical one, or is he an alarmist? What evidence does he offer to support the thesis of his argument? Does he fairly present his opponent's viewpoints?

Udall relies heavily on statistical data to supply evidence for his argument. Perhaps the most telling statistic of all is mentioned in paragraph 11: "The automobile industry directly or indirectly provides roughly *one-fifth of all jobs* [italics for emphasis—ed.] in the United States." Should Udall have provided further explanation of that statistic or any others he used? Does the writer make an emotional appeal in this article, or is he purely objective and factual? What is the purpose and effectiveness of using rhetorical questions? (paragraphs 2, 8, 14) Does the writer ably explain and defend his position that "less is more"?

Is it true that Americans have engaged in a long-term love affair with their cars? What psychological reorientation would have to take place in order for America's transportation priorities to change on a vast scale during the remaining years of the 20th century? Would Americans in general be willing to give up the "love affair" for the collective good of future generations? Discuss the future of the automobile and the importance of mass transportation in the years to come. Will the railroads come back into their own as movers of people and goods, for instance? Write your theme as a general discussion of the transportation crisis of the future.

VOCABULARY

(3)	**proliferation**	an excessive, rapid spread
(12)	**consortium**	a partnership formed to affect large business operations requiring great amounts of money
(19)	**contiguous**	adjoining, connected
(22)	**oil-shale technology**	extracting oil from shale (laminated rock structures)
(26)	**impasse**	a position from which there is no escape, deadlock
(28)	**ameliorate**	to make better, improve
(29)	**specious**	apparently good or right, but lacking real merit, deceptive
(30)	**macadam**	blacktop for highways
(34)	**stringent**	severe, rigorously binding

How Sentences Mean

ROBERT L. BENJAMIN

1   "Say, did you get an eyeful of that new . . ."

"Did I ever! In the library, you mean. He was leaning against the . . ."

"Right! That's the one. Boy he sure is . . ."

"You know it! I wonder if he's . . ."

"I don't think so because when he took off his gloves I got a look at . . ."

"Yes, but that doesn't mean anything. I mean as good-looking as he is and all . . ."

"Yeah, I guess you're right. Let's forget about it. Which reminds me, what about that . . ."

"Now you're talking!"

Surely you have heard a conversation recently which resembled the above. If you had heard this one instead of reading it you might have been tempted to say, "What is so unusual about that?" But those ominous dots at the end of each line must have called your attention to the fact that, until the end, nobody completed a sentence. The remarkable fact is that *communication took place—* successful communication, if past experience is any guide.

From SEMANTICS AND LANGUAGE ANALYSIS by Robert L. Benjamin, copyright ©1970, by The Bobbs-Merrill Company, Inc., reprinted by permission of the publisher and John Hughes, The Science of Language: An Introduction to Linguistics (New York: Random House, 1972), p. 178.

10   *Exercise:* Give a large group of people copies of the above conversation and ask them to complete (on paper working independently) each unfinished sentence as they think it would have ended had the speaker been permitted to finish. After eliminating the obvious attempts to be funny, you should find a remarkable agreement among the participants. A second and even more remarkable fact is that we should expect people to talk in sentences in the first place. What is this preoccupation with the sentence that leads teachers of English to screech with red pencils at every fragment? What is a sentence in the first place?

The Nature of the Sentence

11   Somewhere way back in school you were probably told that a sentence is a unit of language that expresses a complete thought. Unless you were the kind of person who automatically accepts everything he learns in school, you probably felt a bit uncomfortable about that definition. Perhaps you even raised some verbal objection. For surely in the proper context "ouch!" expresses as complete a thought as any sentence. And yet most grammarians would reject this single ejaculation as a candidate for sentenceship. The fact is that we define "sentence" in one way and think of it in another. And no matter how we switch the definition around it never seems quite to describe the category we want to circumscribe. It seems a sentence is one of those things we all recognize but nobody can define.

12   Assuming for a moment that you and I know a sentence when we see one, why should we care? We care because we desire truth. We want to separate truth from falsity because this will help us to control our environment. And when we look to language for truth (or for falsity) we find it comes to us in sentences. A word cannot be true. A paragraph is true in a special sense only when its component sentences are true. Thus, our momentary preoccupation as semanticists with the sentence: If we can ever get one in shape so it can be understood, perhaps we (or someone else) can examine it for truth. With this in mind it will pay us to consider the various *forms* in which legitimate sentences may appear, so that we can start setting up some criteria for their meaningfulness.

13   *Traditional (Formal) Classification of Sentences* Grammarians traditionally classify sentences as follows:

Declarative:	John went home.
Interrogative:	Did John go home?
Imperative:	John, go home.
Exclamatory:	I wish John would go home!

If we examine these forms carefully we see that the exclamation is not really a special class of sentence. Exclamations are either complete sentences, as exemplified above, or fragments (e.g., "Holy smoke!"). If they are complete sentences, they will always fall into one of the three other types (declarative, interrogative, or imperative). Thus it would be possible in theory to eliminate the exclamatory sentence as a class. But further investigation shows that the *expressive function* is an important one in language, and deserves separation from other functions. This leads us to a reclassification of sentences in terms of how they work rather than what they look like.

14   *Functional Classification of Sentences*   Many different sentential functions may be observed in everyday language. It might even be asserted that every sentence we utter has a slightly different purpose. Classical trends lead us to note three general functions, as follows:

Cognitive (information):	to convey information
Directive:	to influence conduct
Expressive:	to express (or evoke) emotion

As with the sentential forms listed earlier, these functions purport to be exhaustive; that is, to cover all the functions a sentence can have. In practice of course, the three-fold classification must on occasion break down. Many sentences may function in two or three ways at the same time. To locate the precise function of a given sentence may require deep analysis, analysis which extends beyond the sentence itself into the inner motives of its producer. This kind of spotlight we would be reluctant to shine on our own discourse, let alone someone else's. One must also contend with the argument that *any* sentence aimed at an audience functions largely as a changer of actions or attitudes; that its producer would ultimately accept only such change as a sign of communication success or failure. Nevertheless, the *immediate* function of most sentences is readily discernible and, as we shall see, sometimes remarkably different than its form would suggest.

15   *Form Versus Function*   If we are going to classify sentences by their

function rather than the more familiar *form,* then our first job is to chart some kind of equivalence so we can tell what goes with what:

FORM	FUNCTION
Declarative sentence	Cognitive
Imperative sentence	Directive
Exclamatory fragment	Expressive
Interrogative sentence	?

16   What happens to the interrogative form? Declarative sentences are presumably cognitive in function. Imperatives (commands) are directive and exclamations are expressive. But what about questions?

17   One view asserts that the question functions as a kind of directive because it seeks to evoke a special (verbal) kind of conduct. Another argument calls it a kind of cognitive; one that seeks information rather than providing it. Our inability to settle this matter immediately seems to suggest that we don't know as much about questions as we need to.

18   *Questions: Theory and Types*   As a linguistic device the question seems simple enough: One asks a question because one wants information. In a moment we shall see some other reasons for asking questions. But first we must direct our attention to the astonishing fact that as a tool of the English language the question is totally and completely expendable. We don't need it. If you doubt this, invent a situation that calls for a question, and in place of the question put a command. For example:

> What time is it? (Imperative equivalent: Please tell me the time.) Are you going to church tomorrow? (Imperative equivalent: Tell me whether you are going to church tomorrow.)

19   The same substitution can be made for any question which genuinely seeks information. Granted, the listener (who may be accustomed to more customary and polite verbal forms) may respond rather coolly to your demand for information. But this is a colloquial fetish which we would soon get over. Besides, we all know questions which, no matter how prettily we ask them, won't be answered. This discovery—that any genuine question can be replaced by a command—seems to argue for the notion that questions are after all directive in function. But before committing ourselves, let's examine some *types* of questions.

20   Of the two questions exemplified above, the second seems

more difficult to replace by a command; that is, the replacement is more awkward. In fact, grammatically these questions show little resemblance one to the other. Actually they illustrate an important distinction between two types of questions: the open-end (interrogative) question and the yes-or-no (poll-type) questions. That is, questions beginning with an auxiliary (helping) verb are (with one small exception to be noted directly) answerable by yes or no. Questions beginning with interrogative pronouns or adjectives ("who," "what," "when," "where," and the like) are not.

21   With this distinction in mind, and looking at the examples above, it would seem that yes-or-no questions function more as cognitives while open-end questions seem more like directives. But the matter is too complex to settle so easily.

> Is it later than we think?
> What are we waiting for?

With great care and effort we might be able to devise a situation where the first example could actually be requesting information. That is, the asker really wants to know if it is later by the clock than we (whomever that may include) think. Much more likely is that notion that he wants, not an answer, but rather to convey information ("it is later than we think.") or perhaps to secure action ("let's do something about it!"). For the second example we would need to look at the context before we could say whether the asker wanted information; but most likely his seeming question is a call to action. A question that functions in this way is called a *rhetorical question.*

22   How are we to know whether a question is real or rhetorical? In oral communication the tone of voice usually tells us. In writing one must rely on context; if the sentences following the question seem to provide an answer then the question was rhetorical, not real. In fact it may be stated as a general rule that in written discourse which is mass communicated (via magazines, newspapers, etc.) questions are likely to be rhetorical rather than real. The reason for this assumption is obvious. A real question calls for an answer; and the writer is separated from his readers (except in the "please write in" situation) so that an actual answer is impossible. In any case the rhetorical question which hides an assertion should be carefully watched for: it will probably require translation.

23   Another question not to be answered is the *reiterative question.*

> You don't like this subject, do you.

This so-called question is really a statement, isn't it. We call it a question because of the "do you" at the end. But all it asks for is confirmation of what is said in the first place. It tries to browbeat you into the right answer. So self-assertive is the reiterative question that in most courts of law one is permitted to use it only on hostile witnesses.

24   Still another type of question requires our attention: the *alternative question.*

> Will you have soup or salad?
> Shall we turn left, right, or go straight ahead?

25   This is the exception you were warned about earlier: a question that starts with a helping verb but still is not in its intended sense answerable by yes or no. When the asker says "soup or salad?" he obviously expects you to pick one of the two. Whether you should be bound by the alternative offered is a contextual matter; that is, in the soup-or-salad case you may wish to respond "neither" or, hopefully, "both." Of course the alternative question is technically answerable by yes or no. If you said "yes" to the soup question you would presumably be satisfied with either choice.[1] When I was learning to play golf every ball I hit would curl out of sight, first to the left and then to the right. Unsure of golfing terminology I asked my patient and experienced partner, "What's my trouble, do I slice or hook?" to which he replied safely, "Yes!"

26   After probing rather deeply into the nature of the question we still don't know whether its function is cognitive or directive. We did decide that yes-or-no questions seem more cognitive while open-end questions act more like directives. The rhetorical question by its very nature is more likely to be directive than cognitive. The reiterative question is clearly a thinly disguised cognitive with a polite "do you?" curling up from the end like a pig's tail. The alternative question, being a hybrid, could go either way. It seems in the end we must allow for both functions, which means rewriting our form-function chart as follows:

FORM	FUNCTION
Declarative sentence — — — — — — — — — = =	Cognitive
Interrogative sentence = = =	
Imperative sentence — — — — — — — — = = →	Directive
Exclamatory fragment — — — — — — — — — —	Expressive

---

[1] Logicians call this process "affirming the weak disjunction"—that is, declaring either *or both* of two alternatives to be true or acceptable.

27   We have had enough trouble getting this chart in shape; but as it was with the classification of linguistic meaning—a metaphorical or tautological *form* often hiding a referential *function*—so it is with sentences. The chart assumes a *normal* correlation between sentential form and function. That is, if one utters a declarative sentence one *normally* expects it to be cognitive in function. But as we saw in our study of questions, the form of the sentence is no guarantee as to its function. Let's look as some examples:

> Trespassers will be prosecuted.

This is a declarative sentence and we would normally expect a cognitive function; that is, we would expect the author's intent to be the conveying of some kind of information. But as we examine the sentence in its anticipated context—on a gate or in front of a lawn—we become immediately suspicious of the cognitive intent. Surely the author is less interested in informing passersby of the laws of private property than in getting them to stay off a given piece of land. Schematically, form-function disparity looks like this:

> Trespassers will be prosecuted   Form: Declarative
> (Meaning)
> Keep off the grass!   Function: Directive

And to list further examples:

> Insert (your) pencil here.   Form: Imperative
> (Meaning)
> If you insert your pencil here
> you will automatically sharpen
> it.   Function: Cognitive

> (She to him during midnight stroll)
> Oh what a beautiful moon!   Form: Exclamatory
> (Meaning)   fragment
> ?   Function: ?

Translation

28   We have now looked at two ways producers of discourse may say one thing and mean another. In Chapter Two we were concerned with language that was non-referential in form but which hid a referential intent. In this chapter we uncovered a similar disparity between form and function—with particular concern for the non-declarative sentence which clothes a cognitive intent. How are we

to react to such language? Some kind of translation is clearly in order. But before undertaking such an adventure we had best know what we are about.

29   It is important at the outset that we steel ourselves against any sense of condemnation of the discourse we propose to rewrite. We have no sure way of knowing on what level the speaker or writer wants to communicate. Maybe that high-flown extended metaphor was a deliberate attempt to be literary, with little or no referential intent involved. And maybe that question was not rhetorical at all, but a genuine attempt to secure information. In short, the assumption of cognitive intent is a big one, and should not be made lightly.

30   If, however, we do assume a referential, cognitive intent, are we still not taking a lot on ourselves to rewrite somebody's communication? After all, whoever put this discourse together probably went to considerable effort to impart style and verve to his linguistic effort. By what authority do we recommit it to laborious, pedestrian, literal prose? Clearly there is no thought to correct or improve, but rather to understand. If the author's intent is indeed literal—if there is some basic attempt to make a claim about the world—then this claim deserves to be understood. And our best chance to understand it is to put it into the form in which such claims are normally made, namely, the referential statement. For example:

31   We are discussing the difficulty of identifying Communists in the United States, and someone says, "Well, all I can say is that if something looks like a duck, walks like a duck, and quacks like a duck, it's a duck!" The hasty analyst might dismiss the remark as irrelevant, since the habits of ducks are not at issue. Such dismissal could be grossly unfair to the speaker, who quite clearly is not talking about ducks but about something else. If the remark is to be taken seriously it must be translated into referential language, perhaps as follows:

> Persons exhibiting certain characteristics (to be listed later) are (probably?) Communists.
>
> OR
>
> A Communist can be identified by his general pattern of words and deeds.

32   In the above example the entire sentence comprised a metaphor. Such figures are usually quite easy to spot, though not always easy to translate. But speakers and writers are quick to pop single-word metaphors unexpectedly into otherwise literal discourse. When someone speaks of taking a hand in a game of tennis, you are

not likely to class such language as metaphorical, even though you are aware that "taking a hand" is not meant literally. In any case, it isn't very important whether we call this communication metaphorical or not, since we all understand what was intended. But when someone characterizes militant student demonstrations as "changing the entire face of the campus," we may not be quite so sure. We know that "face" is not meant literally—but how is it meant? In the final analysis we are going to have to rewrite "face" in its literal equivalent—as nearly as we can guess what it is—before we can say we really understand what is being asserted.

33   *Sentential Translation*   As we have seen throughout this chapter finding (or rendering) discourse in referential form won't always see us home. Many kinds of sentences—notably rhetorical questions—turn up in contexts which inform us that their authors are trying to tell us something. When this happens it is once again our duty to rewrite the claim in a declarative (referential) form. Let's look again at an example from a few pages back.

Is it later than we think?

As we already noted the asker really doesn't want to know anything. But *what* he is telling us is another matter. The obvious translation would be "It is later than we think"; but taken literally this assertion borders on the absurd. How does the author know how late we think it is? Clearly he means to say more than this, perhaps something like "If we fail to act now, we may find our objectives unattainable."

34   How do we know whether the asker wants a yes or a no answer? That is, why couldn't we translate the original question: "It is *not* later than we think"? Of course the context in which the question was asked will normally tell us whether an affirmative or negative equivalent is intended. As an additional guide we may follow the general rule that questions asked *affirmatively* imply a *negative* assertion and vice-versa.[2]

Are we going to put up with this?
(Translation)
We are not going (ought not) to put up with this.
Isn't it obvious what he's after?
(Translation)
It's obvious what he's after.

---

[2] John Hughes, *The Science of Language: An Introduction to Linguistics* (New York: Random House, 1962), p. 178.

It may be easier as we study a given piece of discourse to tell *when* translation is needed than to see exactly *how* to go about it. These three steps should help you to get into referential form those passages which are cognitive in intent:

1. Search the context for cognitive intent.
2. Change the language only to the degree required to achieve referential form.
3. Say no more or less than the original justifies.

Applications

35 *For the Public Speaker* For those seeking to improve their speech composition there may seem little point in rewriting everything in referential statement form. Probably some of you have gone to considerable pains to lift your discourse out of the humdrum, and are not about to drag it back to insipid literal form. And in this bent you are eminently sound. But it will still pay you to know when you are speaking figuratively and when literally. You can profit from distinguishing rhetorical questions which you may use as introductions and transitions, from those which are actually substitutes for what you had to say. How many of the latter did you have in the last speech you delivered? Can you restate each one in referential form? If not, your preparation process—that rigorous private thinking which must precede public speaking—may need careful reexamination.

36 *For the Debater* Argumentative speakers—particularly those subject to cross-examination—will want to make careful note of the kinds of questions distinguished in this chapter. As already noted one can tell at the beginning of a question whether it will be answerable by yes or no, or whether it will require for an answer some kind of statement. This is particularly important when one is subjected to unfair yes-or-no questions. (The classic example, "Have you stopped beating your wife?" is a prototype.) The fact that a question *can* be answered yes-or-no does not mean that it should be so answered. Likewise, one needs to be alert to the reiterative question, which tends to put words in one's mouth. And finally there is the alternative question, which seeks conveniently to eliminate the possibility of a third or fourth choice.

37 *For the Bi-lingual Student* The structure and function of English sentences may often serve as a clue for pronouncing them. You may on occasion have puzzled over the advice, "Always raise your voice

at the end of a question," particularly when you found that such practice was right only about half the time! In general, yes-or-no questions take a rising inflection; open-end (interrogative) questions call for a falling intonation. In alternative questions, the voice rises with every alternative except the last, on which it falls. The reiterative question is spoken like what it really is in function: a statement.

Summary

38   Sentences come to us in three forms—not in four, as traditional grammar insists. These three forms—declarative, interrogative, and imperative—correspond to the classical functions of discourse (cognitive, directive, and expressive), though not in a one-to-one correlation. The *form* in which a sentence may appear is not a necessary indication of the *function* which may be intended. Whenever the intent is obviously cognitive, even though the form may be otherwise, better understanding may be achieved through translation to referential statement form. It is these statements and only these that are capable of truth or falsity.

CONSIDERATIONS

Are you convinced by the author's argument in this selection that our traditional classifications of sentences need additional classification into the cognitive, directive, and expressive functions? Is the functional approach to sentence structure a sensible one, or does it seem inconsequential to you?

Analyze the careful construction of this article (it is a chapter from a longer work on semantics and language analysis). The author catches our attention by the dialog at the beginning, then turns to historical explanations, defines, exemplifies, uses charts, and so on. Are all the terms clearly defined by the time you reach the author's summary? Are there any loose ends left or superfluous details floating around? How successful an argument does author Benjamin present?

Write a short dialog or narration using the techniques proposed in this article: sentences that are *interrogative* in form but *expressive* in function, *imperative* in form but *cognitive* in function, nonreferential language that is referential in intent, and so on. Do these form-function disparities add to or detract from the quality of your essay?

VOCABULARY

(11) **circumscribe**   to define carefully
(12) **semanticists**   persons who study linguistics, the meanings of words
(19) **fetish**   an abnormal devotion, usually to something unworthy or even bizarre
(26) **hybrid**   drawn from two or more sources
(27) **tautological**   needlessly repetitious expression of an idea in different words (as "widow woman")
(30) **verve**   liveliness, animation
(30) **pedestrian**   lacking in vitality, imagination
(35) **insipid**   uninteresting, pointless
(35) **bent**   a leaning; partiality

6

Classification

CLASSIFICATION

Classification is a method you may use for developing a subject for a theme or essay. To classify is to sort things or ideas according to similar characteristics. It provides one way of answering the question "What (or who) is it and where does it belong?" If you wish to classify a given subject—campus organizations, perhaps—the simplest scheme of classification is to split your subject into a two-part system, represented by the following chart:

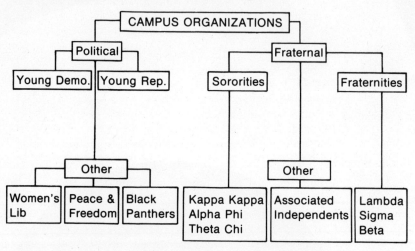

Obviously these classifications are not exhaustive. The classifications themselves may need to be explained (or analyzed) in further detail, but by using a simple system of division into categories, you can provide a working outline for yourself before you begin to write your theme.

Classification usually proceeds from the general to the specific, major to minor, or from categories that include the most of some characteristics to those that include the least. How could you classify "Campus Organizations" further? You could determine which ones are composed mostly of men and which of women; which have members predominantly in the 18–21 age group, which have most of their members in the over-25 age group; which ones are politically active, which are not; you can determine the relation between a campus chapter and its national affiliate, and so forth.

The primary caution you must remember in classifying is to take care that your subclasses are of the same rank. In the "Campus

Organization" chart, you would not equate the classes Fraternal, Young Republicans, and Theta Chi. They are different levels. However, you *can* discuss two fraternities in equal terms: you may evaluate the service projects of the two groups, for instance, or compare the financial cost of joining these two organizations, or discuss the relative effects they might have upon the student government of the whole school.

If classification is to serve as a useful tool for you in organizing your subject, you can go at it in two ways: horizontally or vertically. All of the major divisions may be discussed together and then the subcategories considered. This would be a horizontal organization. Or one major division at a time may be taken and all of its subdivisions discussed before considering the next major division. This would be vertical organization.

Classification should be simple for you as long as you remember to put like things in like classes. A factor you must keep in mind: don't classify on the basis of insufficient evidence; if you do, you will probably make a hasty generalization that will weaken your argument.

PRACTICE

1. In a theme use classification to organize a fairly complex topic, making sure that your classifications are clear and valid. For example, kinds of students, teachers, cars, dates, politicians.

Selecting Members for Your Commune

Find the paragraphs in this essay in which the author uses classification, and determine the criteria she uses to classify certain personality types and whether she adequately defines her terms. Then write an essay in which you classify kinds of teachers or students. When you label or classify them, make sure you determine the qualities common to the class and that your specific examples fit that class.

Marriage: A Little Knowledge Goes a Short Way

The opening sentence of the essay classifies Americans as "dreamers." The author deals with Americans as a class that shares certain abstract qualities—the effectiveness of the essay depends upon the agreement on the definition of the class. Break down the author's classification into three more categories of Americans, such as sex, age, religion, education, profession, or so on, and explore the different attitudes toward marriage inherent in these groups.

Americanisms That May Once Have Been Africanisms

Write an essay on the comparative speech patterns of two groups or classes of people; for instance, students and teachers, parents and grandparents, men and women. Develop and organize your essay through classification, remembering to ask yourself the following questions:

What are the particular qualities or characteristics of the class?

Do your specific examples satisfy the criteria of the class? If so, how?

Are your classifications based on sufficient evidence, or might you be guilty of hasty generalization?

Sport: If You Want to Build Character, Try Something Else

In paragraph 4 of this essay the authors isolate major elements that characterize the "problem athlete." Analyze the following ideas to determine how you might develop them through classification. Write a beginning paragraph for each, clearly stating and justifying your classifications:

Sports and the arts

The football fan

Little League parents

Logic and Illogic

Collect a number of editorials and letters to the editor and identify and classify the logical fallacies. (Refer to *Logic and Illogic* if necessary.) Then write an essay on the comparative fallacious thinking found in the two types of writing.

For examples of individual paragraphs using *classification*, see p.8, ¶4, p.38, ¶15–17, p.49, ¶1, p.52, ¶12, p.67, ¶12, p.75, ¶44, p.264, ¶1, p.331, ¶10–11, p.443, ¶5.

Selecting Members for Your Commune

KAT GRIEBE

Let's Be Realistic

1 It would be an interesting conjectural exercise to decide how to select the perfect members of the perfect commune. You can get quite intrigued with delicate questions about whether intellectual skills are as important as technical skills, whether you should try for homogeneity or variety, whether differences in religion can be tolerated in a single group, etc. Sometimes people who think of starting communes do get wound up in just such questions—quite needlessly. For it is very unlikely that you will be able to have full control over the membership of your commune, let alone selecting for ideal members. You do not have as much choice as you may think! *Beg/ Thes*

2 After all, what do you have to offer? At best you may have a nice farm or a sizeable bank account, a forceful but pleasant personality, and a store of convictions that will carry you through the hard places. Even if you have all that (and few people do), you are still bucking a credibility problem. Who believes that you can start a successful commune? You do, maybe, but who else? People are not likely to flock to you by the hundreds until your commune has established its viability. It is indeed frustrating to know that, given the cooperation of a dozen people of outstanding ability, you could get a successful commune on its feet, but not be able to attract those same able people until you have succeeded without them! But *Dict/ Tone*

Reprinted from Communities magazine: December 1972, Volume 1, issue 1. Written by Kathleen Griebe.

that is what you are up against. So don't be too fussy. You cannot have exactly the people you want, and you will have to take the people you can get, especially at first.

3   I cannot emphasize that point too strongly. It is important that you have a group of people who are prepared to do the commune venture with you, people who can be counted upon to move with you to the land, people whom outsiders or prospective members can identify as the commune people. Sympathetic professionals and well-wishers are very nice, but you need *members*. There is no substitute for a real member. So if the talented people you know won't commit themselves, settle for somebody less talented.   **Arg**

4   You may be surprised how much talent there is in very ordinary people, anyway, once they are called upon to take responsibility. This is particularly obvious in the young, but it is true of people of all ages.

5   It is particularly unwise to try to select for people who can make a monetary contribution. <u>Once you have a viable group living together and providing each other with a social environment that is attractive, people with money, as well as without it, will want to join you.</u> But as a beginning commune, you don't have a lot to sell for that money you are fishing for, and your group could flounder while you are waiting for capital. It is far better to accept people on the basis of their enthusiasm, all taking turns working in the city to earn money, than to turn away these people and keep hoping for someone with a bank account. Though it is obviously true that you need money, it is even more urgent that you have enthusiastic people. Don't shrug your shoulders at this quality on the assumption that it is always readily available. If you dally too long in forming a group, it may not be.   **C & E**

What Is an Undesirable?

6   Up to a point it is a good idea for a beginning commune to take whoever is available. But there are limits. There are lines you will need to draw. If you don't draw them too closely, your group will be healthier for a bit of reasonable discrimination.

7   For example, you are much better off if you have no loafers in your original group. People who won't do their fair share of the work cause a lot of hard feelings. Sometimes it's hard to know before actually getting onto the land just which people will be workers and which will discover a philosophy of leisure that they exercise at your expense. What we did at Twin Oaks was to write the equal-   **Exmp**

ity-of-work ethic into our bylaws, thus allowing ourselves legal lee-way to get rid of anyone who might not do his share.

8   A loafer is different from a handicapped person. There may be people who would be an asset to your group and well worth supporting, in spite of physical handicaps, because of some social skill or just because of his or her relationship to another member. As long as such dependents do not constitute more than about a fourth of your total population (and you must count little children among your dependents), you can probably manage to support them. They are different from deliberate parasites, because their disability is obvious to everyone and does not cause hard feelings among those who do the work.   *C & C*

9   You may ask why I set the figure at 25 percent, when ordinary married couples all over the nation are supporting four people on one income—a 75 percent dependence! My reason is simply that commune members living in the country are not likely to earn incomes like those of city families. Per capita income on the farm may be very low the first few years, and too great a number of dependents may cause you to go under.

10   At Twin Oaks we have found it wise to select for people who are not too aggressive and domineering, not too stubborn, not too loud and pushy. The word "too" is crucial, of course. Aggressiveness under control is another word for leadership, and stubbornness is also called commitment. Just the same, there are people who irritate most other people by their over-presence, and communities would do well to avoid taking such people. For instance, the person who dominates all group meetings while other members of the group find it difficult to get a word in, who, upon being told about this behavior, still makes little effort to change it. (He will probably sit in sullen silence for a meeting or two and then be back at his old habits.) Discriminate between the person who irritates one or two other people who disagree with his ideas (he may be a valuable thinker) and the person who irritates *everybody*. That's the person you don't need. Even if he owns the farm or has a lot of money, try to get by without him. He will cause far more trouble than he is worth.   *Class*   *Exmp/ Desc*

11   Another person to be avoided is the one who is apparently emotionally ill. This is a subjective evaluation. One commune's "crazy" may be another commune's "creative." I'm talking about the person that *your* group feels is crazy. Don't take him. No matter how sorry you feel for him, don't take him. You can't afford it.   *Tone*

12   Now I'm not talking about somebody's retarded son, whom

everybody knows is exceptional and is not expected to live up to group norms. He's a dependent, and you just have to consider whether you can live with his ways or not. I'm talking about the person who considers himself part of the group in every way, fully capable of decision-making, for instance—and whom the rest of the group views as extremely odd and unpleasant. It may be that he is the only creative one among you, and he is right and the rest of you wrong. It doesn't matter. If he's really, really different from the rest of the group, don't take him.

Exmp

Selecting for Agreement

13   So, don't accept sloths, boors, crazy people, or too many dependents. Other than that, selection considerations should probably be centered around one point—and that is *agreement*. Get a group that agrees on the basics, and put decision-making into their hands. No matter what kind of government you have, the people who have decision-making power should have a firm sense of going in the same general direction. If you choose consensus procedure (and everybody is doing consensus these days), then this point becomes extremely important.

Arg

14   Suppose you have in mind a modified primitive-living, back-to-the-land-with-spiritual-overtones sort of group. If you don't select for similar goals, you may end up with a little of everything, from Flying-Saucers-are-Real people to Jesus Freaks to Walden Twoers. You can't get anything done with a mixture like that. Certainly you'll never find consensus on anything except maybe giving up the whole idea. If you know what you believe, write it down, and select for people who believe pretty much the same things. Even then you will have disagreement, so don't worry about too much homogeneity!

Dict

15   People can disagree about anything, but I am going to list here some of the basic things that groups I know about have disagreed on, making basic trouble for the groups.

16   *Means of Making a Living*   Make sure all members are either willing to do outside work off premises or else all agree they will not do it. Also, test out the feelings of the members about the morality-in-industry issue. If you plan to make your money raising tobacco, be sure no one in the group believes it is immoral to do so.

Class/ Exmp

17   Schools make trouble, too. If you intend to have a school, everyone should know about it and approve.

18   *Government* Make sure nobody in your original group has unrealistic ideas about his role in government. This is a touchy ego problem. If you mean to use consensus, define consensus clearly. If you
are using any kind of board of directors, get them elected or ap-
pointed as soon as possible. Don't leave ambitious people hanging
around with the mistaken impression that they are the obvious candidates for leadership unless they are. There is more trouble in this
single question than in most things.

*Class /
Exemp*

19   *The Use of Drugs* People who prefer a community without drugs
will probably not stick to a group that uses them, so you may as well
sort out this question in the beginning, too.

20   *General Standard of Living* It is easy to fall into the trap of inviting people with impossible expectations along these lines. Talk
about standard of living with your group. Get specific. How many
people will have to share a room for how long? How much personal
cash allowance can be spared? Will the group pay for tobacco?
Liquor? Dope? How much labor is the group willing to put into
cleanliness, and what standards are expected? Unbelievable hassles
come out of this question, and it is well to have a tentative outline
of solutions before you get onto the land. Perhaps you have plans
for beautiful community buildings—cabins, domes, or whatever.
How soon will you actually be building these, and where are you
going to live in the meantime? If you're going to live in tents and
house trailers for two or three years before you can hope to build,
the group may as well face it ahead of time.

21   *Children* Child-raising theory hassles can be about anything, but
the most likely is the question of punishment. If you can agree
about whether to use punishment when dealing with behavior problems, and if so, what kinds, you will have made major progress.

22   This list is by no means comprehensive. There are a lot of
other things people can quarrel over, not least among which are sex,
religion, and politics. But there is danger also in asking for too
much agreement. Seeking total intellectual conformity is the same
as seeking a group of meek followers. No two thinkers are going to
agree on all issues. If you cannot tolerate disagreement at all, the
only way for you to build a community is to invite the young and
unformed and press them into your mold. That takes a special kind
of talent, and it usually doesn't occur in a commonsense commune.

23   A commonsense commune will need a central core of people
to see it through its first year or two. The core may be as small as

two or as large as seven or eight. After that it starts getting fuzzy around the edges. These people should certainly agree on certain basics, but each group will have to figure out what those basics are. The suggestions I have made are just suggestions. Some groups function very well with almost no intellectual agreement, because their union is not essentially an intellectual one. It may consist of a commonality of background, for instance, or dedication to a certain religious idea. The common assumptions may never even be expressed. But they must be there.

24   Beware of assumptions about other people's beliefs! A very common mistake is to assume that your ideas about community are all part of a package, and that anyone who agrees with part of the package will also agree on the rest. It is a rude shock to discover that some people believe in common property without believing in group marriage, or that some people practice yoga without ever considering vegetarianism or fasting.   *Tran*

25   It is a mistake to discriminate against the very young. You may long for permanent members, and people between the ages of 17 and 23 may not be permanent, but they can be immensely valuable, nonetheless. This is especially true if your group has high social ideals. Young people catch your vision more easily than more settled people who have visions of their own, and they pass it on to their age peers. A group of even three young people who are sold on the commune's principles will set the ideological tone of the place and transmit it to newcomers. Young people may bounce in and out of the commune a few times before settling down, and they may cost something in ruined tools that are sacrificed to their inexperience; but their power to establish fresh cultural norms is of inestimable value. If you are lucky enough to attract a couple of intelligent young people, not too spoiled and screwed up, grab them! Talk to them about your highest dreams, as well as your immediate plans. Do not worry about apparent conflicts between their stated beliefs and yours. Young people often change their beliefs radically within a period of months—a phenomenon that works for the commune or against it, depending on how well the commune's basic idea is working. Young people may leave after a few months and go on to try something else. But they generally leave without doing any damage; and in the meantime, others like them will have come to take their places.   *Arg*

Meta

Slang

Choosing for Skills

26   It is probably not possible to choose members on the basis of their

work skills; but if you should have this rare opportunity, I would | **Class/**
advise looking for the following: | **Exemp**

27   *Automobile mechanic*   Unless you are going to lose yourselves in
the Oregon forests and forget the highways entirely, mechanical
skill is sorely needed. Keeping the vehicles running may mean keeping the money coming in. It certainly means bringing in building
materials, groceries, and maybe members.

28   *Architecture or building experience*   You can put up buildings
without skilled people (we did), but they will be flawed. The more
knowledge that can be brought to bear on a building, the more
pleasure it will give in the long run. You have to live a long time
with leaky roofs or faulty heating systems.

29   *Economic management experience in farming or any other business*   Without this experience (and we have always been without
it), the commune will throw away an awful lot of money on things
that seem to pay off but actually cost more than they bring it.

30   *Selling ability for the commune's agricultural or manufactured
goods*   A lot of people imagine that they can sell, but it takes a
particular kind of personality that isn't easily discouraged and can
keep on being friendly under difficult circumstances. This skill is
very uncommon among the people who tend to join communes.

31   If you follow all this advice and still have a group, you will
probably be down to about three people who get along well with
each other and have a similar commitment to similar goals, plus a
couple of people who don't say a lot but do more than their share
of the work, plus a few whose primary contribution is their pleasant
company, plus a dependent or two. It may not look imposing, but it
will do. If this group can meet and decide whether to buy a certain
farm or whether to hold jobs in the city for a while or whether they
need a kitchen manager and a budget manager, all without undue
quarreling and ego-fencing, you have made a good start. Your next
selection problems will come after you are on the land.

Selection in a Successful Commune

32   Once your group is formed and you have been living together on   *Tran*
the land (or wherever you mean to settle) for a few months, select-

ing new members is much simpler; and you don't need to look for
so much agreement. The norms you will have established will operate to select for you, with much less conversation about it than was
necessary with the original group. Standard of living, for example,
need no longer be discussed. The newcomer comes and looks you
over. If his standards are very different, he won't apply for membership. The same goes for government, drug use, size goals, and means
of making a living. All you have to do at this point is state to the
potential members what your norms and goals on these matters are,
and they will either join you or not, depending on their degree of
agreement. You still have some selecting to do, but at this point
you need to consider very little else than personality. Does the
group enjoy this new person? Will you be a better group after he
joins? That is all you have to consider.

C & E /
Exmp

Moral Questions

33   All kinds of moral questions come up when you think about membership selection. Depending on the stated social goals of your
group, you may have to consider some of them seriously.

Anly

34   Given that you need to survive as a group, how much more
selection is really desirable? You don't have much choice your first
year, but after that, after you have begun to succeed as a group,
have been written up in *Communities* and the local paper, you can
begin to entertain a *philosophy* of selection. Are you trying to prove
that your kind of life is a desirable one for the population as a
whole? If so, you may have some obligation to leave your doors
open to all kinds of people. On the other hand, if you just want a
good life for yourself and a few friends, you won't have any philosophical obligation to accept anyone you don't enjoy.

The Trial Period

35   Sometimes the Why of selection is less important in the long run
than the How. You may have a perfectly well-thought-out plan of
provisional membership, at the end of which the prospective member is to be evaluated and either accepted or rejected. But if you
don't have the heart to kick anyone out at the end of that provisional period, your policies won't do you much good. Don't make
that trial period too long. If you do, and you ultimately decide
upon rejection, you have a very unpleasant experience to go

through. Twin Oaks uses two weeks to a month to get to know prospective members. It is true that we don't know much about them after that time, but if we wait much longer, they will be so entrenched that uprooting them will be impossible. The Bruderhof and the kibbutzim, on the other hand, use a long period—often a year or more—before they admit applicants to full membership. They can do this because they have developed the ability to get rid of people if they decide against them.

36   Twin Oaks relies heavily on self-selection. We make it very clear what kind of group we are. Prospective members stay for awhile as visitors, live our life, get to know the people, and make up their minds whether they want to live here. Even after they are members, they may discover things about the group's goals or norms that they cannot tolerate. If they do, they go away by themselves. Expulsion is rarely necessary.

Exmp/ Def

Expulsion

37   On those rare occasions when it is necessary to expel a member, it is best to be very open about the whole thing. Make sure all the members understand what the offenses were. Make sure you hear from the people who had befriended the offender; get their point of view. Keep in mind that those friends will feel threatened by the expulsion *unless* they feel they are part of the group that did the expelling. If the troublesome member is at all willing to go through a public meeting on the subject, by all means call one and clear up the whole thing. Never leave yourself open to the accusation of not letting the accused defend himself. Trying to keep the whole thing quiet is a mistake. The accused will almost certainly go around the community spreading his side of the story. If the group doesn't hear your side, the community's leadership will be under a cloud until the matter is cleared up.

Anly

38   Expulsion is a dangerous tool. Twin Oaks has used it only once in our five years of existence, but we have found that even the ousting of undesirable visitors has caused some hard feelings in the group. It is best if there are some clear rules about it. Undefined means of getting rid of troublemakers are most undesirable, because almost any member can feel threatened by them. A lot of people go through periods of paranoia, even in community. You don't want to lose perfectly good members just because one day in a dark mood they began to imagine that they might be next to be forced out!

Let's Get on with It

39 The fine points of selection are a luxury that you can afford to think | End
about after you have been operating for a few years and have people banging on your doors trying to get in. In the beginning, you
will have to concentrate on just keeping your group together, or just
having a group at all. At that point the criteria for selection are
pretty simple: Does he generally agree or at least go along with your
ideas? Does he have some talent (or skill, or money, or pleasing
personality) to contribute? Can you live peaceably with him? If the
answer to these three questions is yes, then accept him, by all
means, and let's get on with the work. We've got communities to
build!

CONSIDERATIONS

What picture of community group government is drawn by Kat Griebe
in this article? Are there any fallacies or loopholes that seem to be left
out in this account of membership selection? What are the strengths
and weaknesses of such a procedure? What principles involved in this
process of selection do you use in your daily life—in choosing your
companions and friends?

Does the writer of this article use a consistently clear method of definition? That is, does she define her terms precisely—for instance, *norms*
(paragraphs 12, 25, 32), *consensus procedure* (paragraph 13), and *the
morality-in-industry issue* (paragraph 16) or are such terms self-ex-
planatory in the context of the article? Are you satisfied with the character definitions, such as "crazy," "aggressive," and "dependent"?

The author states that "seeking total intellectual conformity is the same
as seeking a group of meek followers." (paragraph 22) Yet a certain—
fairly high—degree of homogeneity is paramount to the success of
community living. Discuss the homogeneity versus diversity issue as it
applies to building an "ideal community. That is, *your* ideal community.

VOCABULARY

(1)	conjectural	hypothetical; educated guess based on experimen-tal data
(1)	homogeneity	the state of being essentially alike
(2)	viability	ability to survive, grow, and prosper
(13)	sloths	people who are habitually lazy
(35)	provisional	tentative; conditional
(38)	ousting	expelling

Marriage: A Little Knowledge Goes a Short Way

NORMAN SHERESKY AND MARYA MANNES

1   Americans are dreamers. We marry out of hope, and we hope that our dreams will come true.

2   That is why we continue to marry even though the United States has the largest divorce rate in the world. We are a mobile and unauthoritarian people, increasingly rootless, shedding our past, evading our future. We live for today and shut out the reality of tomorrow in the same way that we shut out the reality of death.

3   People marry when there is a curious and too often temporary alignment of expectations and need between a man and a woman. We are attracted to our partners because they promise a fulfillment of ourselves, because they satisfy our sexual appetites, because they seem to enlarge our sense of living and loving—now.

4   Our vision is temporary. It is also still strongly affected by social attitudes concerned (as they have been for centuries) less with enduring love than with appearances. Ingrained in a majority of women is the belief that marriage combines the ideal poles of escape and security: escape from parents or the burden of single identity in the form of work or career; security in the arms and home of the protector-provider.

5   Nor is the man immune from the nudgings of social convenience and convention. A wife is good for business. A wife can supply comforts few bachelors care to be bothered with. And sex?

No lack of it anywhere, but he dreams of the sweetness of not having to leave the beds of others at dawn; of feasting at will.

6   These and the dream of love cloud deeper insights. We refuse to believe that wives can tire of mothering husbands, and husbands can tire of being surrogate fathers. Sooner or later the roles demanded by married people of each other change, and the woman who served as a splendid substitute-Mom may founder dismally as a wife. So may the bridegroom-stud fail, in due course, as the father-adviser his young bride craved.

7   We marry for the damndest reasons. A man may want a hostess, an accessory, a centerfold, a sister, a slave, or a tyrant. A woman may crave a tycoon, a stud, a brother, a brute, or a son.

8   Besides seeking mates who seemingly are able to satisfy our *present* sexual needs and our *present* needs for familial substitution, we also have other individual present needs for which we more or less unconsciously seek satisfaction. If we are drug addicts, alcoholics, or people with other compulsive habits, we tend to find mates who will satisfy us by punishing us for our habits or by continually trying to rescue us from them. If we are insecure self-doubters, we may seek the satisfaction of marrying mates whose frailties loom even larger, and whom we may criticize. If we are inefficient and unproductive, we may seek even worse bunglers from whose failures we derive consolation. If we are lonely and afraid, we may seek anybody who will give us the temporary relief of filling time and space. Very often we marry for the same reason that others take pills—"uppers" or "downers"—simply to change our state of being.

9   We seldom ask whether he or she will make a good lover, a good parent, or a good companion ten years from now. And very few of us, in a civilization where intellect is a minor desideratum (especially in a woman), suspect that its absence may lead in time to excruciating boredom.

10   Marriages crumble, finally, when each blames the other for failing to embody the original visions that impelled their union: "I would have made something of myself if it weren't for you!" or, "I could have married anybody I wanted. Why did I have to choose you?"

11   Why, indeed? But even if we chose wisely in the light of an apparent alignment of mutual needs, the crack in the marriage foundation that splits wide open is, simply, ignorance—an appalling ignorance of the realistic obligations of marriage itself.

12   Of these, ironically, ignorance about the true nature of love is a major marital fission. Ironically, because we now appear to know

everything we ever wanted to know about sex, and are bombarded daily with manuals on how to please everybody forever. Americans spend millions of dollars annually making the producers of smut and pornography wealthy because we can now allow ourselves to be openly titillated and triumphantly prurient.

13   It is still too early to know whether all this open sex, openly arrived at, will improve marriage or ultimately destroy its vital intimacies.

14   What we do know, beyond a doubt, is that ignorance about sex has been responsible for the wreck of an enormous number of marriages. We are the victims of a Puritan heritage, equating sex with sin, that has left Americans with a host of inhibitions crippling to the spirit as well as the senses, turning beauty into shame, and joy into guilt. This process, in the name of Morality, has been, in fact, a denial of humanity.

15   In redressing the balance, the pendulum may have swung too far in making sex not only a commodity but a substitute for love, a public performance rather than a private experience.

16   Yet serious students of sex, like Masters and Johnson, have made important and useful contributions to the knowledge of our sexual selves which have already saved some foundering marriages and could, if translated into less abstruse language, rescue many more.

17   There exists, in any case, a whole body of information about the sexual porblems of marriage that is now ready to be imparted to us if it were made available in simple terms. That it isn't may well reflect society's belief that we are not to be trusted with it. Instead—and again ironically—we are deluged with nonbooks by nonwriters (*The Sensuous Woman, The Sensuous Man*), which cater to an intelligent audience as well as pizzas appease fastidious palates.

18   This escalation of expectation is not only a major reason why marriages fail, but why they take place. Both partners persist in believing that the sexual pleasures they enjoy before or anticipate when they marry, will last forever, without further knowledge, effort, or growth on their part.

19   And what of our overwhelming ignorance about the obligations we took on by law when we marry? Any law student will tell you that a contract cannot exist unless the parties to it agree to each of its essential terms. But we all know that when we said, in a state of trembling euphoria, "I do," we weren't agreeing to any of these terms because—quite simply—no such contract ever existed.

20   If you are of sufficient age and mental capacity; if you are free of some diseases (but not all); if you are not a prisoner and not already married, you are free—according to the state—to marry anybody possessing the same negative assets, provided, however, that they are of the opposite sex.

21   If John, hating babies, doting on rock, disdaining all Republicans, and believing whole-heartedly in the overthrow of the United States Government by any means whatever, can convince Joan for a continuous period rarely in excess of seventy-two hours, to marry him, the state has no objection whatsoever to such portentous facts as that Joan loves large families, likes classical music, is a member of the Republican National Committee, is proud of the United States Marine Corps, and believes in the sanctity of J. Edgar Hoover.

22   The state will let you in the marriage game for the price of a license, and out at the price of a heart transplant.

23   Why does the state interfere in our lives anyway?

24   Why does it permit us to live alone virtually without restriction, but in New York, for example, harness us once we are married, with several hundreds of sections of the Domestic Relations Law, the Family Court Act and Rules, and other related statutes and decisions?

25   It seems that our legislators feel that marriages are not to be lightly discarded, even if they have been lightly contracted.

26   One of the reasons, then, why marriages so frequently fail is that they are usually entered into at a a time of our lives when we are least able to exercise sound judgement about our priorities.

27   Inflamed by passion, consumed by hope, giddy with love, we enter into matrimonial transactions without even the questionable objectivity we display in choosing a new car. Objectivity and love are very seldom partners at any time, in any case.

28   Consider, for instance, what would happen to the institution of marriage if the parties were required to familiarize themselves with the rules of the game. (After all, we do take drivers' tests.)

29   What if we required all married couples to show some basic familiarity with the laws that govern their relationship, and some familiarity with each other's views on the essential ingredients of the relationship?

30   For example, whether to have children and when, who should own what property, who is obliged to work; financial penalties, if any, if the wife doesn't work and takes care of the children; consequences of the insanity or incapacity of the other spouse; the consequences of inviting widower-Dad to join the household indefinitely.

Or, for example, the consequences of Change of Heart? Why does the state license a thoughtless marriage for life, but condemn one between two people who genuinely love and care for each other, who have honestly considered the essential terms of their contemplated agreement, but who want to commit themselves only for a period of two or three years?

31   Because the state is atrophied in patterns of the past inapplicable to present realities. So, if you are married, it is already too late.

32   But it is not too late for us to change our own minds about the process of choosing our mates. It is possible, if not enjoyable, to put a damper on our enthusiasm just long enough to inquire seriously about the contemplated relationship, about why we are marrying in the first place.

33   We are obliged, by law, to divulge to each other some of the most essential facts about ourselves so that we cannot, after the state has joined us, be charged with fraud. Concealing prior marriages, hereditary diseases, past imprisonments, unwillingness to become parents, affiliations with dubious organizations, may result in annulments and divorces based on fraud.

34   Having told the truth to each other, there are other obligations. The parties must at least occasionally engage in sexual relations. There is, of course, not the slightest obligation to enjoy such activities and not a single regulation involving frequency.

35   There is no statutory obligation to love, honor, or obey, except that wives may not refuse to cohabit with husbands in such reasonable places as the husband may designate. Each partner in a marriage must insulate the state, however, against the cost of supporting the other and the children of the marriage. The state, for instance, will not pay for the hospitalization of the husband if the wife can afford to foot the bill.

36   There are a host of other obligations that arise out of the marital relation, and which involve the ownership of property. Husbands and wives may now own property separate and apart from each other. They may contract with each other and sue each other. But since contracts between husbands and wives are scrutinized by courts and since each is assumed to have a duty to treat the other fairly and openly, contractual rights may be obliterated and "implied obligations" may be created where the husband or wife has acted unfairly to the other.

37   It is an extremely common occurrence for husbands and wives faced with impending divorce to claim that all of the property, real or personal, standing in the name of one spouse was always really

intended by both parties to be joint property. There are a myriad of conflicting statutes and decisions that question the status of real or personal property, whether or not it is held individually or jointly. In matters matrimonial it is not that the decisions or the statutes are unclear, but rather that judges hesitate to apply them with the rigidity accorded to routine commercial transactions. It is one thing to say that Joan is entitled to maintain her own bank account, but quite another when it turns out that Joan has been depositing John's checks and other funds which John didn't know about (such as the food budget) into her own account. It is perfectly all right for John to put the house in his name, but when the judge finds out that he got all the money from Joan and her parents and told her that he was only putting the house in his name to increase his borrowing capacity for business, and when it turns out his borrowing capacity has been used to augment his passion for ponies, the judge takes a different view.

38   But now we come—in the light of our revolutionary times and the progressive blurring of sex "roles"—to the real clincher. The state maintains that a husband has a duty of which he may not relieve himself—that of supporting his wife and children. A few states make this obligation of support mutual and in an appropriate case may require a wife to support a husband.

39   But what are the rules concerning alimony? They are incomprehensible, that's what they are. Although the laws vary widely from state to state, any knowledgeable attorney knows they also vary widely and inconsistently even within any single state. In some states alimony is considered to be, in part, a punishment or a reward.

40   Rarely, however, is it the husband who is punished for his misconduct in terms of alimony. When he has to pay it, it doesn't matter (theoretically, at least) whether he has sinned a little or a lot or not at all.

41   To a wife, the difference may be vital. In most states, fault plays a crucial aspect in how much support a wife may receive for herself. In New York, for example, under the "liberalized" reform law, a court may not award support to a wife where she is guilty of such misconduct as would entitle her husband to a decree of divorce. If, for example, a wife learned that her husband had been having an affair for seventeen years with her sister, and that the children had been denied a college education because her husband also had another mistress, set up in a Park Avenue penthouse, she would not be entitled to support if it is learned that during an

evening of anguish and indiscretion caused by such disclosures she was intimate with her psychiatrist. Even in California, which has a genuine no-fault divorce law, attorneys for husbands still attempt to let the judge know when the wife is at fault. For example, although the word "adultery" is theoretically meaningless and has no statutory signifigance, the husband's lawyer is bound to ask the wife, "Why do you need so much money for food? Isn't Mr. X staying with you and paying these bills?"

42   Like other states, New York by statute requires the courts, when fixing alimony, to take into consideration the ability of the wife to work. Yet some decisions frequently reflect the court's reluctance to punish working wives by diminishing their assets and preventing them from saving from inadequate salaries, particularly where the husband's assets amd income are substantial compared to the wife's.

43   We have rules, decisions, and statutes instructing the judge that wives should not be permitted to become "alimony drones"; that they should not be permitted to become self-indulgent, indolent parasites. These compete with other rules, statutes, and decisions directing that the court take into consideration the length of the marriage, the age of the wife, the age of the children, and a preseparation standard of living.

44   What all this means is that in matters matrimonial the issue of alimony is no more certain than a roll of the dice in Las Vegas, and the consequences to the litigants may be just as disastrous as they are to the gamblers, yet how often do engaged couples consider this crucial subject in advance? Or their feelings about child support? Or whether their assets and joint income should be divided or undivided? Why should a woman whose husband has permitted her and encouraged her to become a marital cripple with no economic potential be treated on a parity with a woman whose earning capacity has not been influenced or deterred by the marriage at all?

45   More importantly, why shouldn't the parties themselves make the rules before there is trouble? Why shouldn't the standard of support be agreed upon before it is imposed upon the parties? Why is it not just as sensible for newlyweds to agree on what standard or standards they wish imposed rather than to rely upon a judge to whom the marriage may have an entirely different meaning?

46   Why do lawyers arrogate themselves the function of dissuading women who truly do not want or do not feel entitled to alimony? Why do lawyers attempt to persuade their male clients to give less than they might wish to give voluntarily?

47   Decades of litigation, under a variety of different statutes and decisions, have shown that it is far better for people to agree to the rules themselves than to rely upon the courts to intervene. Obviously agreements would be reached far sooner if the parties to a marriage knew what the rules were as they went along. It occurs to us that a great many people might never get married at all if they were required beforehand to examine in depth their real reasons for taking this step.

48   What would happen if an engaged couple, Donald Brown and Ina Jones, decided to consider in advance of their marriage issues and questions which might emerge later concerning their physical, financial, and emotional attitudes and preferences? What if they wanted a document to resolve future disputes? What if they wanted to have available to them a historical reminder of how they once felt? Less poetically, what if they agreed to come clean in a calm and loving atmosphere that would probably not exist if they came to the end of their marital tether?

49   We set forth here such an agreement between such a couple, one which is no doubt invalid in every state, but which highlights the kinds of questions which "newlyweds" rarely come to grips with during the engagement period:

---

50   MEMORANDUM OF UNDERSTANDING AND INTENT made this twenty-eighth day of July, 1972, between *Donald Brown*, residing at 1142 Damon Avenue, City of Chicago, Cook County, and State of Illinois, herein called *Donald*, and *Ina Jones*, residing at 1602 North State Parkway, City of Chicago, Cook County, and State of Illinois, herein called *Ina*.

51   WHEREAS the parties about to marry desire to make full and fair disclosures to each other of significant facts and circumstances concerning their lives; and

52   WHEREAS the parties desire to make full and fair disclosures of their attitudes and expectations concerning their marital future and the future of any children born to them from the pending marriage; and

53   WHEREAS the parties desire to determine and fix by this antenuptial agreement the rights and claims that will accrue to each of them in the estate and property of the other by reason of the marriage,

54   IT IS MUTUALLY AGREED AS FOLLOWS:

ARTICLE I
Declaration of Marital Intention

55   (a) *Donald* and *Ina* each declares to the other the intention to marry in the City of Chicago, Cook County, State of Illinois, on or before September thirtieth, 1972.

56   (b) This marriage is freely and voluntarily being entered into out of mutual love and respect held by the parties for each other. Neither party has agreed to enter this marriage under any threats, emotional or otherwise, nor has any relative of either of the parties exercised any undue influence upon either *Donald* or *Ina*.

57   (c) Each party assures the other that he or she has had sufficient time and information to make the decision to marry in accordance with the terms of this MEMORANDUM

ARTICLE II
Historical Representation

58   *Donald* hereby warrants to *Ina* and guarantees that she may act in reliance upon the following representations:

59   (a) He is twenty-nine years old. He attended the University of Chicago from which he graduated in 1965 with a bachelor of science degree and with acceptable but unexceptional grades.

60   (b) His mother and father are living; until February 1963 he resided with them and contributed toward their support. He still occasionally contributes toward their support and intends to continue to the extent that he is able during marriage. *Donald's* parents react favorably to the contemplated marriage. *Donald's* parents have not been divorced, nor has his sister, but his older brother has been divorced twice.

61   (c) *Donald* was previously married in April 1963, and that marriage ended in a divorce in June 1970. There is one child of that marriage, *Michael*, age six. The decree of divorce was handed down by the Supreme Court, Cook County. It awarded custody of *Michael* to *Donald's* former wife, granted her alimony and child support in the sum of $140 weekly, and granted *Donald* visitation privileges every other weekend, holidays, and two weeks in summertime with *Michael*. A copy of the divorce decree has been shown to and read by *Ina*.

62   (d) There is no known history of mental illness in *Donald's* family. There are no hereditary or other diseases prevalent in *Donald's* family, and *Donald* is in excellent physical health.

63   (e) There is no history of any arrest or conviction of *Donald*

for any criminal behavior, nor is there any history of compulsive addiction to drugs, alcohol, or gambling.

64   (f) *Donald* is presently employed as an assistant sales manager for Rugby Electronics Company at a salary of $20,500 annually, including bonuses and exclusive of certain travel and entertainment expenses, which are made available to him by his employer. His salary during the three previous years was as follows: 1969—$14,500, 1970—$17,500, 1971—$18,500.

65   (g) The relationship of *Donald* with his parents, his brothers, and sister has been explained fully to *Ina*.

66   *Donald* and *Ina* have discussed at length his family's "tradition" of a two-week sojourn every year at the Brown residence in Michigan and *Donald's* desire to continue that tradition. *Ina* has expressed a reluctance to adhere to the tradition but agrees to be bound by *Donald's* wishes. *Donald* has agreed that he will make no arrangements for other familial visitations without the consent of *Ina* and that such visitations should be no more frequent than twice monthly.

67   (h) *Donald* has disclosed to *Ina* that his relationship with his past wife continues to be strained. He has disclosed to her that on at least two prior occasions he and his former wife have been involved in legal proceedings relating to the custody and amount of support of *Michael*. The nature of such proceedings, the reasons therefore, and all other questions of *Ina's* concerning them have been fully explored by the parties.

68   *Donald's* relationship with *Michael* has been fully explored by the parties. It is *Donald's* present feeling that the time may arise when he would wish to gain custody of *Michael*. *Ina* is reluctant, however, to consider *Donald* having custody during the first two years of their marriage. It has been agreed by *Donald* and *Ina* that, barring an emergency, no attempt will be made by *Donald* to obtain such custody for two years from the date of marriage.

69   *Donald* has made known to *Ina* his concern over *Michael's* hostility toward her. Both parties have agreed that, while the welfare of *Michael* should continue to be a paramount consideration of both parties, the relationship between *Donald* and *Ina* should not be affected by *Michael's* attitude nor should their marriage be delayed by it. It has been agreed that the parties will make clear to *Michael* that his hostility will not be tolerated as a wedge between *Donald* and *Ina* and that his conduct will have to be reasonably acceptable to both *Donald* and *Ina*. The parties have agreed that in the event they cannot cope successfully with this problem they will

seek professional guidance to help them overcome it.

70   (i) There has been nothing in the past sex life of *Donald* that requires further disclosure. There are no sexual acts that are important to him or an essential part of the sex life contemplated by him that are not presently practiced by the parties. *Donald* has been able to express himself sexually in all the ways important to the parties, and such issues as frequency of intercourse, desire for periods of sexual abstention, positions of intercourse, etc., have all been explored to *Donald's* satisfaction.

71   *Ina* hereby warrants to *Donald* and guarantees that he may act in reliance upon the following representations.

72   (a) She is twenty-one years old. She attended, but did not graduate from, the University of Michigan, which she left after her junior year in 1970. At that time her grades were passing but below average. The circumstances under which she left college and the reasons therefore have been fully explained to *Donald*.

73   (b) Her mother and father are divorced, and she has no brothers or sisters. Until October 1970 she lived with her mother. She rarely sees her father, with whom she has an extremely disagreeable relationship. *Ina's* relationship with her mother is unusually close, and she visits with her as often as three or four times weekly. *Ina* and *Donald* have had many conversations concerning what *Donald* has protested to be far too close a relationship between mother and daughter. He has sought, but has been refused, permission from *Ina* to discuss the matter directly with her mother. *Ina's* view that her mother has been left "out on a limb" by her father and that *Ina*, as a consequence, has an obligation to her mother to visit more frequently than is customary, has been rejected by *Donald*. Although *Ina* has agreed to limit her visits to her mother to two afternoons weekly and has agreed that joint visitations with her mother by her and *Donald* be limited to twice monthly, *Ina* feels such concessions should not have been asked of her.

74   *Donald* has expressed considerable hostility toward *Ina's* mother and has openly displayed such hostility. For his part, he has agreed to discontinue such practices.

75   Each party agrees that the "mother-in-law" issue has not been fully resolved between them, but they agree that their marital relationship should have priority over the relationship between *Ina* and her mother.

76   (c) *Ina's* physical and mental condition is excellent, and there is no history of hereditary or mental diseases in the Jones family.

77   (d) During 1969 *Ina* had an illegal abortion under circumstances that have been fully disclosed to *Donald*. During *Ina's* senior year of high school she was suspended for three weeks after she and a group of fellow students were detained by juvenile authorities for the possession of marijuana cigarettes.

78   (e) There has been nothing in the past sex life of *Ina* that requires further disclosure. There are no sexual acts that are important to her or an essential part of the sex life contemplated by her that are not presently practiced by both parties. *Ina* has been able to express herself sexually in all the ways important to the parties, and such issues as frequency of intercourse, desire for periods of abstention, positions of intercourse, etc., have been explored to *Ina's* satisfaction.

79   (f) *Ina* is presently employed as an assistant interior decorator for Bon Marche Department Store, and her salary this past year was $6300.

80   (g) There is no history of compulsive addiction to drugs, alcoholic beverages, or gambling.

ARTICLE III

Future Expectations

81 (a) *Donald* and *Ina* have discussed fully where they propose to reside during the course of their marriage. They agree that considerations relating to the location of their respective families should play no part in such determination. They agree their primary consideration shall be proximity to *Donald's* place of business. That factor should govern regardless of where *Ina* may be employed and regardless of whose earnings are greater.

82   (b) Neither party to this Memorandum holds any formal religious beliefs that should in any way interfere with the marriage. Neither insists on, or has even expressed any preference concerning, the other's adherence to any particular religious belief. Neither will, without the consent of the other, impose any religious belief upon any children of the marriage.

83   (c) It is the parties' present intention that *Ina* continue to work, health permitting, until such time as she may become pregnant. The parties have no exact intentions concerning the employment of *Ina* after the birth of any child or children, although *Ina* has expressed the feeling that simply caring for children would not be sufficiently stimulating to her. *Donald's* inclination at the present time is that he would prefer for *Ina* to discontinue any full-time employment if she had a child, but he would not insist upon it.

84   Both parties agree that any subsequent employment of *Ina* after the birth of a child should be such that it would permit her to spend reasonable periods of time with the child and that it should not entail any evening or weekend hours.

85   (d) Both *Donald* and *Ina* have expressed opposition to adultery. *Donald* has stated he would immediately divorce *Ina* if such an act occurred on her part, regardless of the circumstances. *Ina* has said that, although she does not wish to solicit such conduct on the part of *Donald,* nevertheless she is unable to determine her attitude toward adultery on *Donald's* part in advance of knowing what the circumstances might be. If the act were an isolated "meaningless" episode, *Ina's* opinion is that she would rather not know of it because she does not know how it would affect her relationship with *Donald.*

86   Both parties have agreed that in the event either engages in any serious or prolonged affair with anyone else, he or she is under an obligation to disclose that fact to the other.

87   Both *Donald* and *Ina* believe that their sex life together is sufficiently pleasurable and knowledgeable at present so that no serious adjustment need be made by either. *Ina* has expressed the belief that her sex life with *Donald* will become more pleasurable, and somewhat less tense, after marriage and after each party has had more "experience" with each other. She denied, however, having any apprehension concerning future sexual relations with *Donald.*

88   (e) The parties intend to have two or three children of their own. It is their desire to have such children sometime after the next two years, although the possibility of having a child prior to that time does not cause any particular anxiety in either of them. In the event *Ina* becomes accidentally pregnant, the parties' present inclination is to have such a child and not seek an abortion. Both parties feel, however, that any decision on abortion should be left entirely to the discretion of *Ina.*

89   (f) *Donald* and *Ina* have discussed and have rejected the following notions: marriage of limited duration, separate vacations, separate beds, divorce by reason of the physical incapacity of the other, divorce by reason of the inability of *Ina* to bear children.

90   (g) In the event *Ina* is unable to bear children, the parties are in conflict over whether or not to adopt a child. It would be *Ina's* desire under such circumstances to adopt, but it is *Donald's* strong feeling that he would not want to. Although the parties agree that this eventually would be of considerable importance to them, they

feel it is better to leave resolution of the question of adoption undetermined prior to its arising.

ARTICLE IV
Future Support

91 (a) In the event that either party desires a separation (by mutual agreement or legal decree) or a divorce during the first five years of marriage, provided there is no surviving child born of the marriage, neither party will request support from the other unless he or she is in dire need thereof, and then only for such temporary periods as may be deemed necessary in accordance with Article VIII hereof.

92   (b) If either party desires to separate after the first five years of marriage or if, at the time of a request for separation during the first five years, a child of the marriage is alive, either party may request support, which shall be granted or denied by arbitration in accordance with Article VIII hereof. In determining whether or not to grant support and, if so, in what amount, the arbitrator shall consider the following: the length of the marriage, the number of children, their ages, the ages and health of the parties; the ability of *Ina* to work, the number of years that *Ina* has been unemployed, the reasons therefore, and *Ina's* realistic chances of being productively employed; the disparity between the parties' incomes and income-earning potentials; the amount of property to be divided between them in accordance with this agreement; the question of which party desires such separation or divorce and the reasons therefore; *Donald's* legal obligations to his former wife and to his son, *Michael*; and the parties' pre-separation standard of living, provided such standard was reasonable. No factor shall be conclusive, and the award of support, if any, should be such as to do substantial justice between the parties after consideration of all factors.

ARTICLE V
Division of Property

93 (a) *Donald* presently has a checking account at the First National Bank of Chicago, One First National Plaza, the present balance of which is $1685.50. He maintains a savings account at the same bank, (Account No. 104F-003), the balance of which is $3750.

94   (b) *Ina* presently has a checking account in her own name at the Continental National Bank and Trust Company, 231 South La Salle Street, the present balance of which is $385. She maintains a

savings account at the same bank (Account No. 1A24-72), the present balance of which is $950.

95   (c) *Donald* owns four hundred shares of Great Western United Corporation, which is traded on the New York Stock Exchange, having a present value of approximately $4000; he owns no other securities. *Donald* is also the owner of a 1970 Buick Riviera, on which $650 in installment obligations is presently due.

96   (d) *Ina* owns no securities and does not own an automobile.

97   (e) Neither party presently owns any real property.

ARTICLE VI

Future Ownership of Property

98   (a) *Donald* and *Ina* have agreed that all property now standing in the name of either shall continue to be held in the individual names of the parties owning such property.

99   (b) Upon the marriage of *Donald* and *Ina*, they will create a joint-checking account and a joint-savings account to which each shall contribute in the same proportion as their earnings shall bear to each other. In the event that either party decides to seek a separation or divorce within a period of thirty-six months from the date of their marriage or at any time prior to the birth of a child, the proceeds of such checking and savings accounts shall be divided in the same proportion in which such funds were contributed by the parties. If either party seeks a separation or divorce after the birth of a child or at the end of said thirty-six-month period, whichever is earlier, such proceeds shall be divided between the parties equally.

100   (c) In the event that *Ina* is unable to find employment or is involuntarily unemployed or is unable to work during a period of maternity or illness, her contributions to the joint funds during the period of such unemployment, illness, or maternity shall be deemed to have been made in direct proportion to the contributions previously made by her during the period immediately preceding such unemployment, illness, or maternity.

101   (d) All questions concerning the investment of the joint funds of *Donald* and *Ina* in securities or real estate shall be decided jointly by the parties, and the ownership and division of such real or personal property shall be made in accordance with paragraphs (a) and (c) hereof.

102   (e) The parties do not contemplate a different division of property, real or personal, whether or not either or both may later be guilty of any marital misconduct as defined by the laws of the State of Illinois. Any property not held in accordance with the terms of

this article by either of the parties shall be deemed to be held in trust for the other party, and no additional private or oral understanding between the parties concerning the division of property between them is to be deemed valid until agreed to in writing in accordance with paragraph (f) hereof.

103   (f) In the event that either *Donald* or *Ina* subsequently wishes to change the rules by which their property shall be divided, the party desiring such change shall notify the other in writing and by registered mail at least one hundred and twenty days prior to such proposed change. If the other party does not wish to make such change, he or she may notify the other party in writing within the one hundred and twenty days. The matter shall be resolved by arbitration in accordance with the terms of Article VIII hereof. In making a determination the arbitrator shall fully inquire into the facts and circumstances surrounding the reasons for the proposed change. No modification of existing financial arrangements shall be made if it is determined that a substantial reason for such proposed change is that the party seeking modification has the imminent expectation of coming into a sudden period of prosperity from which the other party is to be excluded. The arbitrator may consider such other factors as he wishes in order to do substantial justice between the parties, but he may not order that any modification of the rules by which the parties have agreed to divide the property be made retroactive to the period preceding the written request for modification.

ARTICLE VII

Matters of Estate

104   After thirty-six months of marriage each party agrees to leave the other at least 40 per cent of his or her entire estate, and each agrees to make no attempt to assign, transfer, or otherwise dispose of, without valuable consideration, any portion of his or her estate with the intention of depriving the other of the benefits of this agreement.

ARTICLE VIII

Arbitration

105   Any dispute that arises under the terms of this Memorandum shall be resolved in accordance with the rules and regulations then obtaining of the American Arbitration Association, and such arbitration shall be held in the City of Chicago, Cook County, State of Illinois, unless at the time of dispute both parties reside in some other state, in which event arbitration shall take place in that state.

ARTICLE IX

Modification

106   This Memorandum may not be changed or modified except in writing, signed by the party against whom such change or modification is sought.

IN WITNESS WHEREOF, the Parties hereto have signed their hands and seals this 28th day of July, 1972.

Donald Brown

Ina Jones

CONSIDERATIONS

Do you agree with the writers' basic premise, that marriage is a woefully misunderstood contract between people who are ignorant of the legally contractual (as well as the purely personal or psychological) obligations that it entails? Would an agreement like the one proposed by Sheresky and Mannes strengthen the traditional institutions of marriage in this country? Are there any important factors that are left out of their proposed agreement? Have they included any that could be left out? Does the contract favor one party over the other in any respects, or is it mutually protective?

Would this article be classified as an analysis or an argument? Are all relevant factors considered in the authors' treatment of their subject? What is the tone of this selection? Why does a legalistic, clinical approach seem more appropriate to the subject than a more personal, emotional case would be?

What factors seem to be influencing young people today to take different tracks from the marriages of their parents and grandparents? Are these merely surface differences with no real intrinsic changes? Give your views in a short theme.

VOCABULARY

- (6) **surrogate**   substitute
- (9) **desideratum**   something desired as essential
- (11) **appalling**   inspiring horror or dismay
- (16) **abstruse**   hard to understand
- (24) **statutes**   formal documents drawn up by legislatures
- (43) **indolent**   lazy
- (44) **litigants**   persons engaged in a law suit
- (44) **parity**   equivalence, on an equal par

Americanisms That May Once
Have Been Africanisms

DAVID DALBY

1   There has been much speculation about the origin of such well-known Americanisms as OK, guy, jive, hippy, cat (meaning "person"), and dig (meaning "to understand"). Fanciful explanations have sometimes been proposed, like the traditional derivation of OK from a misspelling of "all correct," but generally there has been agreement in regarding these words as indigenous to America. It would seem, however, that these and certain other Americanisms may originally have been Africanisms, taken to the new world by West African slaves.

2   Although many items of American vocabulary were first used by American Negroes—or black Americans as they are now known—the historical role of black speech in the development of American English appears to have been underestimated. Just as black Americans have often been unjustly regarded as passive agents in the course of American history, so they have been regarded as largely passive agents in the shaping of the American language.

3   The traditional belief was that slaves lost all trace of their original African languages when they arrived in the new world, and that they were forced to imitate the language of their white captors as best they could. This belief was first challenged by Lorenzo D. Turner, a black American scholar, who drew attention to many African survivals in the "Gullah" language of isolated black commu-

Reproduced from The Times (London) by permission.

nities on the South Carolina coast: Gullah is a form of creolized English taken to the United States by slaves from West Africa, however, rather than a regular dialect of black American English. Only in the past few years have linguists begun to demonstrate that black American English has a complex grammatical structure of its own rather than being a mangled form of white speech, and it is scarcely a coincidence that this structure should frequently be reminiscent of West African languages. This leads one to investigate the degree to which African vocabulary also may have survived in black American English, and hence may have contributed to the American language at large.

Main Languages

4   Slaves were taken to the Americas from all over West Africa and beyond, and spoke many different languages. Some already had a knowledge of the creolized English which had come into use along the Guinea coast as a trade language. Senegambia, the nearest part of the African coast to North America, was a major source of slaves for the former English colonies, and many of these slaves were therefore conversant with the two main languages of Senegambia: Wolof and Mandingo. When a runaway slave who could speak no English was arrested in Pennsylvania in 1731, for example, his white interrogators had no difficulty in finding another Wolof-speaking slave to act as an interpreter.

5   The importance of the Wolof in linguistic contact between black people and white stems also from the fact that they are the nearest Negro African people to Europe (as well as to North America), and that they were frequently employed as interpreters and mariners during early European voyages along the African coast. As a result, the Wolof names of several African foodstuffs, including banana and yam, were taken into European languages. It therefore seems reasonable to look for a possible Wolof influence on the development of American English vocabulary, and the initial results of this investigation have been most encouraging. A number of resemblances have already been found between the two languages, and most relate to forms whose origin in American English has not yet been adequately explained.

6   The verb "dig," as used in American—especially black American—English to mean "to understand" and hence "to appreciate" occurs in such phrases as "d'ya dig black talk?" (do you understand black English?): there is thus a similarity in sound and meaning, to

the Wolof verb *dega*, pronounced close to English "digger" and meaning "to understand"—as in *dega nga olof?* (do you understand Wolof?). In the same way the American term "guy," especially as used in informal address is paralleled by Wolof *gay* (pronounced between English gay and guy), used also as a term of address meaning "fellows, guys," although restricted to the plural.

Jazz Era Terms

7   Several terms popularized during the jazz era also resemble words in Wolof. "Jive" had the original meaning in black American English of "misleading talk," which it retains, and can be compared to the Wolof *jev*, meaning "to talk disparagingly." The American forms hep, hip, and hippy have a basic sense of "aware" or "alive to what is going on" (including heightened awareness from drugs), while in Wolof the verb *hipi* means "to open one's eyes." The American use of cat to mean "person," as in hep-cat or cool-cat, can be likened to the Wolof *kat*, used as an agentive suffix after verbs: *hipi-kat* in Wolof means "a person who has opened his eyes."

8   The verb "sock," in the sense of "to strike," especially with something, has recently been popularized in the black American phrase "sock it to me" (with an obscene connotation), and is reminiscent of a similar-sounding verb in Wolof meaning "to beat with a pestle." In American slang, the suffix bug (as in jitter-bug) denotes a person with an enthusiastic desire or liking for something; in Wolof a similar sounding form means "to desire, like."

9   "Honkie" is used by black Americans as a term of abuse for "white man," and—since white men are often described as "red" in African languages—one may compare the term to the Wolof *hong*, meaning "red, pink" (the English word "pink" has also been used by black Americans as a term for a white man). A term of abuse in the reverse direction, namely Sambo, is similar in form to a common Wolof family name, Samb or Samba (existing also in the neighbouring Mandingo languages as *sambu*).

10   The term "fuzzy" is used in the United States to describe either a range horse or a sure bet at a horse race. In both cases one is reminded of the Wolof *fas* (pronounced between fass and fuss), meaning "horse," and it even becomes possible that the American term fuzz, used to describe a policeman, may have originated in the days when runaway slaves were hunted down on horseback. On a more domestic note, the word "cush" is used in the American South to describe "corn-meal soaked in water," whereas a similar word is used by the Wolof for millet meal soaked in water.

11   The most interesting American item with a parallel in Wolof is "OK," the origin of which has been much debated but never convincingly explained. In Wolof a common word for "yes" is *waw* (pronounced wow), and this is combined with an emphatic particle *kay* to convey the sense of "all right, certainly." The resulting form *waw kay* thus corresponds closely, in both sound and meaning, to OK, and would have required only a slight change of pronunciation (by analogy with the letters O and K) to have produced the modern American word.

12   African usage can also explain the frequent use by Americans of the interjections uh-huh, for "yes," and uh-uh for "no." Similar forms, especially for "yes," occur in scattered parts of the world, but nowhere as frequently and as regularly as in Africa, where not only Wolof but most other African languages make extensive use of "yes" and "no" words of the general *uh-huh/uh-uh* type. The fact that these same items are used far more frequently in American than in British English, and in Afrikaans (South African Dutch) than in Netherlands Dutch, points to an African influence in both cases.

13   The study of Wolof may also throw light on the term "jam" as used in "jam music" and "jam session," and in the American slang term "jamboree" (now made famous by the Scout movement). "Jam session" and "jam music" refer to the uninhibited playing of jazz musicians for their own entertainment, and "jamboree" had the original meaning of "noisy carousal" or "revel." Recalling that the few opportunities which slaves had for self-entertainment were normally riotous and uninhibited, one is inclined to speculate whether these terms might not go back to the old slave-plantations, and to the Wolof word *jaam*, meaning "slave."

"Code" for Slaves

14   In considering the old plantations, one should not forget that attempts were made to prevent newly arrived slaves from speaking African languages, in the fear that they might be used for secret communication. At the same time, the slaves had a legitimate interest in deceiving their white captors, and the examples we have considered indicate that a partial code may have been established among them by concealing African words, with their original African meanings, behind similar sounding words already existing in English: dig, cat, sock, bug, fuzz(y) and jam may be vestiges of such linguistic subterfuge.

15   It would of course be rash to suggest that all the American

items discussed here can be derived with certainty from Wolof. On the other hand the frequency of these resemblances is unlikely to be the result of chance and points to the contribution of at least one African language to American (and hence also British) vocabulary. There is now need for more detailed research, on both sides of the Atlantic, into the influence of African languages on the development of the English language at large.

16   There has been contact between English and West African languages for more than 400 years, and it is a sad reflection of old attitudes towards Africans and black Americans that the possible effects of this contact on the English language should have received so little attention. It should not be forgotten that black Americans represented the largest non-British ethnic group in the North American colonies during the formative years of American English, and that the last African-speaking ex-slaves in the United States were still alive at the beginning of this century.

CONSIDERATIONS

With the evidence Dalby offers to support his position (the proximity of Senegambia to Europe and the slave trade from Senegambia to the American colonies) and the "code" among black slaves in America, is it surprising that more attention has not been given to the possible African origins of much of American slang? What factors might have caused such neglect in research?

This report appeared in a newspaper, not a scholarly journal. What stylistic devices make it readable for the layman? Cite examples of sentence clarity and effective exemplification.

There is much talk today of Black English: certain linguistic scholars believe it is an autonomous language, basically unrelated to formal English. Write an essay in which you analyze the strengths and weaknesses of a large country such as the United States that fosters separate dialectic differences in different geographic areas. How do dialects and speech patterns affect your opinion of the people you meet?

VOCABULARY

(1) **indigenous**   native
(8) **pestle**   an instrument for pounding or mashing
(10) **millet**   a cereal grain
(13) **carousal**   a noisy or drunken revel

Sport: If You Want to Build Character, Try Something Else

BRUCE C. OGILVIE and THOMAS A. TUTKO

1   The cultural revolution has penetrated the last stronghold of the American myth—the locker room. Young athletes, having scaled new levels of consciousness, now challenge a long-standing article of faith—the belief that competition has intrinsic value. They enter sports in search of particular esthetic experience, essentially personal in nature. They no longer accept the authoritarian structure of sports, nor do they accept the supreme emphasis on winning. Outside critics who see in the sports world a metaphor for the moral deficiencies of American society add to the pressure in the once-sacred precincts.

2   Coaches and administrators defend organized sport with traditional claims that competition builds character and toughens the young for life in the real world. Coaches in particular don't want to listen to the requests of the young. The stereotype of the ideal athlete is fading fast. Long-haired radicals with life-styles and political beliefs unheard of a few years ago people the uncomfortable dreams of coaches.

Limits

3   In the midst of the controversy, psychologists find themselves being asked what personal, social or psychological significance can be attributed to organized sport. For the past eight years we have been

studying the effects of competition on personality. Our research began with the counseling of problem athletes, but it soon expanded to include athletes from every sport, at every level from the high-school gym to the professional arena. On the evidence gathered in this study, we can make some broad-range value judgments. We found no empirical support for the tradition that sport builds character. Indeed, there is evidence that athletic competition limits growth in some areas. It seems that the personality of the ideal athlete is not the result of any molding process, but comes out of the ruthless selection process that occurs at all levels of sport. Athletic competition has no more beneficial effects than intense endeavor in any other field. Horatio Alger success—in sport or elsewhere—comes only to those who already are mentally fit, resilient, and strong.

Types

4   The problem athletes who made up our original sample displayed such severe emotional reactions to stress that we had serious doubts about the basic value of athletic competition. The problems associated with sport covered a wide spectrum of behavior, but we were able to isolate major syndromes: the con-man athlete, the hyperanxious athlete, the athlete who resists coaching, the success-phobic athlete, the injury-prone athlete, and the depression-prone athlete.

5   When we confronted such cases, it became more and more difficult for us to make positive clinical interpretations of the effects of competition. In 1963, we established the Institute for the Study of Athletic Motivation to start research aimed at helping athletes reach their potentials. We wanted to examine normal players as well as problem athletes. To identify sport-specific personality traits, we and Lee Lyon developed the Athletic Motivation Inventory (AMI) which measures 11 traits common to most successful sports figures. We have since administered the AMI to approximately 15,000 athletes. The results of these tests indicate that general sports personalities do exist.

Traits

6   Athletes who survive the high attrition rate associated with sports competition are characterized by all or most of the following traits:

1) They have great need for achievement and tend to set high but realistic goals for themselves and others.

2) They are highly organized, orderly, respectful of authority, and dominant.

3) They have large capacity for trust, great psychological endurance, self-control, low-resting levels of anxiety, and slightly greater ability to express aggression.

7   Most athletes indicate low interest in receiving support and concern from others, low need to take care of others, and low need for affiliation. Such a personality seems necessary to achieve victory over others. There is some question whether these trends are temporary character traits—changing when the athlete gets out of sport—or permanent ones. Using men coaches and women physical educators as reference groups, we would predict that these character trends remain highly stable.

Women

8   We discovered subgroupings within the athletic personality. For example, outstanding women competitors show a greater tendency toward introversion, greater autonomy needs, and a combination of qualities suggesting that they are more creative than their male counterparts. They show less need for sensitive and understanding involvement with others. Women competitors are more reserved and cool, more experimental, more independent than male. Interestingly, we found that among women there was far less trait variation from one sport to another than there was among men. (Exceptions were women fencers, gymnasts and parachutists.) We attribute this to cultural repression of women—to succeed in *any* field, a woman has to be able to stand up and spit in the eye of those in charge.

Inner

9   In addition to sex differences, we were able to distinguish a team-sports personality from an individual-sports personality. Persons in individual competition tend more toward healthy introversion. They are less affiliative than team players, have a higher level of aggression and tend to be more creative.

10   For some sports we could even distinguish a particular personality type. For example, the data strongly distinguish a race-driver personality. More than participants in any other sport, drivers are tough-minded, hard-headed realists. They are reserved and cool. They override their feelings and are not fanciful. They do not show

anxiety or tension and are self-sufficient. They are tremendously achievement-oriented, far more than the average athlete.

Bare

11   Our original hypothesis about the ill effects of high-level competition turned out to be unfounded. When we completed tests on the original teams, we discovered no negative relation between athletic achievement and emotional maturity or control. On the contrary, the higher the achievement, the greater the probability the athlete would have emotional maturity or control. Sport is like most other activities—those who survive tend to have stronger personalities.

12   The competitive-sport experience is unique in the way it compresses the selection process into a compact time and space. There are few areas of human endeavor that can match the Olympic trials or a professional training camp for intensity of human stress. A young athlete often must face in hours or days the kind of pressure that occurs in the life of the achievement-oriented man over several years. The potential for laying bare the personality structure of the individual is considerable. When the athlete's ego is deeply invested in sports achievement, very few of the neurotic protective mechanisms provide adequate or sustaining cover. Basically, each must face his moment of truth and live with the consequences. The pro rookie usually gets only three or four chances to demonstrate ability before he is sent home. What sort of personality structure supports the person who can face this blunt reinforcement of reality?

Wife

13   And beyond brutally rapid and clear evaluation of competence is the stress from the neglect of basic human needs that may accompany athletic success. Take the case of a high draft-choice football player; after tearing up the camp the first few days, he turned morose and sullen. He was experiencing what often happens to men who excel in any area—the withdrawal of emotional support from those outside his field. Persons who were close to this gifted young man had pulled away, assuming that they were no longer important in his life, that he had outgrown his need for them. They anticipated rejection, but rather than live with this threat they retreated at the first opportunity. Quite often an athlete's wife experiences this reaction. Threatened by her husband's new acclaim, she may withhold love and support from him. When the tension between his

success on the field and his crumbling home life gets unbearable, the athlete sometimes manages to get a mild injury. Rare is the man who can make it in sport without the support of his wife.

Flaws

14   Under such intense pressure, with threats from so many different directions, personality flaws manifest themselves quickly. We found that personal reactions to the stress of competition remain fairly constant across the sports. Depression, combined with failure due to unconscious fear of success, hyperanxiety (the athlete who burns himself out before the competition begins), and exaggerated sensitivity to failure or criticism accounted for more than half of our referrals. The same telescoping of time and space that uncovers personality deficiencies with such rapidity, however, provides a splendid laboratory for experimentation with self-change. The rapidity and clarity of feedback in competitive sport provides a fine opportunity for the individual athlete who knows which traits he wants to change and who has the motivation to do so.

15   By showing the athlete that certain habitual ways of behaving or thinking keep him from reaching his potential, we open a collaborative approach between coach and athlete that may solve the problem. Obviously the motive to change depends on a number of variables, including the extent to which the ego is invested in sports. When we sit down with a young man who has just signed a contract for $250,000 and tell him that on the basis of his test scores he doesn't measure up to his fellow pros in certain traits, he makes only one comment: "How do I change that, Doc?" But the high-school athlete has a motivational conflict of another order when he has to decide whether he will work to support his car so that he can keep his girl friend or spend his time excelling in his sport.

Roots

16   Though we can identify the common traits of successful athletes and counsel a highly motivated youth on how to strengthen particular traits, we cannot tell how much these traits actually contribute to athletic success. Competition doesn't seem to build character, and it is possible that competition doesn't even *require* much more than a minimally integrated personality.

17   Innate physical ability is always a contaminating factor when we attempt to make statements about the relationship between character and success. Even using a sample of Olympic competitors

and professionals, we find that independent judges' ratings of ability in any given athlete fluctuate considerably. At best, judges can agree on the relative ability of athletes in the top and bottom six to 12 per cent.

18   We are similarly unable to determine the extent to which character contributes to coaching success. In this case the uncontrolled factor is the degree to which the coach is master of his science. We found that there is no way to compensate for lack of knowledge in one's field, but we do not know the degree to which this skill must be augmented by strong character traits.

19   We know from our work hundreds of outstanding competitors who possess strong character formation that complements high motor skill. But we found others who possessed so few strong character traits that it was difficult on the basis of personality to account for their success. There were gold-medal Olympic winners in Mexico and Japan whom we would classify as overcompensatory greats. Only magnificent physical gifts enabled them to overcome constant tension, anxiety and self-doubt. They are unhappy, and when the talent ages and fades, they become derelicts, while someone like Roosevelt Grier just goes on to bigger mountains. We often wonder how much higher some of these great performers might have gone if they had, say, the strong personality structure that characterized our women's Olympic fencing team.

20   A certain minimum personality development is essential. We once encountered a long-distance runner who was so gifted that, late one night, running in total darkness with only pacers and timers, he broke the NCAA record for his event. The mark would have survived for the next four years. But upon achieving this goal, he quit the team, never to compete again. He later explained that he did it to get even with his coach; but our data suggest a different interpretation. It seems that grave personal doubts about his worth as a person impaired his capacity to support the burden of success. He preferred to protect his fragile ego by showing bursts of superior performance then retreating to mediocrity so that others would not depend on him.

Lid

21   We have also seen some indications that there may be an *upper* limit on the character development needed for success in sport. Sometimes we find players who have good physical skills coupled with immense character strengths who don't make it in sports. They seem to be so well put together emotionally that there is no neu-

rotic tie to sport. The rewards of sport aren't enough for them any more, and they turn away voluntarily to other, more challenging fields. This is singularly frustrating to their coaches.

22   We quickly discovered that the coach was the crucial factor—whether we were trying to modify a disturbed athlete's behavior, or measure the influence of competition on the successful athlete's personality. Consequently, we made special efforts to identify the personality traits of coaches. We found that there was indeed a coach personality. It was similar to the competitor's, but the traits tended to be intensified, as with race drivers.

Blind

23   We found that our test data provided a more reliable personality model of athletes than the coaches' observations, that the tests gave better insights into individual differences and allowed for better gauging of individual limitations as well as strengths. Coaches are most reliable in their perception of personality tendencies that are a significant part of their own character structure. They prove to be most reliable in identifying the traits of dominance, psychological endurance and athletic drive, but are unable to recognize such traits as emotional control, self-confidence, trust, conscience, self-abasement, or tenderness. We also found that coaches tend to be blind to deficiencies in gifted athletes.

24   We find most coaches uncertain and anxious about the changes taking place in sport. They have shown an overwhelming positive response to our efforts to bring the tools of psychology into their careers. They're crying for new methods, new information. They know that they are not fully prepared for their tasks.

Win

25   Many of the changes run counter to values deeply rooted in the coach personality. Athletes who ask the basic question—"Is winning all that worthwhile?"—deny the coach's life's work, and his very existence. Most coaches go by the Vince Lombardi dictum that "winning isn't everything—it's the only thing."

26   Conflict over values manifests itself in struggles over discipline. Hair length comes to mind. The coach sees hair as a problem of authority; he orders the athlete to get it cut and expects his order to be obeyed. In contrast, the athlete sees discipline as a peripheral, frivolous issue compared with his own struggle to find identity in

the hair styles of his peers. Coach and hirsute athlete talk past each other. Value changes that involve drugs and politics put the coach under strain. Most coaches believe that a truly good athlete is also, by definition, a red-blooded, clean-living, truth-telling, prepared patriot. A top-notch competitor who disagrees with national policy is a heavy thing for a coach who undoubtedly believes that the wars of England were indeed won on the playing fields of Eton.

27   Many coaches won't be able to stand the strain. Eventually, the world of sport is going to take the emphasis off winning-at-any-cost. The new direction will be toward helping athletes make personally chosen modifications in behavior; toward the joyous pursuit of esthetic experience; toward wide variety of personality types and values. Inevitably these changes are going to force the least flexible coaches out of the business—perhaps as many as a third of them.

CONSIDERATIONS

According to the authors, why are women competitors in sports generally cooler and more experimental, independent, and reserved than their male counterparts? Does the competitive spirit in sports in any way reflect the basic philosophy of American society?

Do you feel the authors are making generalizations about the various athletic types, or do you find their evidence convincing? Comment on the general tone used in talking about coaches in this article. The authors frequently use long, periodic sentences along with occasional short ones. Is this effective? Why?

Respond to Lombardi's dictum that "winning isn't everything—it's the only thing." Do you feel that the sports world has been mainly male dominated because men feel threatened by competitive women?

VOCABULARY

(4) **syndromes**   signs or symptoms that characterize a disease
(4) **phobic**   having persistent, often illogical fears
(6) **attrition**   wearing away or wearing down by friction
(8) **introversion**   directing one's thoughts and interests inward
(8) **autonomy**   condition or quality of being self-governing or operative
(14) **manifest**   clearly apparent to the sight or understanding
(18) **augmented**   increased or made greater
(19) **overcompensatory**   exerting excessive effort to overcome a defect
(26) **peripheral**   pertaining to the outermost region of a boundary
(26) **frivolous**   marked by flippancy; silly; impractical

Logic and Illogic

BERNARD F. HUPPE and JACK KAMINSKY

1   Some of the basic obstacles to obtaining and communicating reliable information will be discussed. These obstacles will be arranged, for utility and ease of reference, under three main headings: Emotional Argument, Faulty Reasoning, Misuse of Language.

Emotional Argument

2   *Argument Ad Hominem*   When someone attempts to argue by attacking the personal character of his opponent, he is making what is called an argument *ad hominem*. For example, in a discussion of higher wages, if the proponent of higher wages is a union official, his opponent may be strongly tempted to resort to the argument *ad hominem* by pointing out that the union official's argument must be discounted because he is an "interested party," a member of the union. But knowledge of a man's motives and attitudes has no bearing on the correctness of his argument, except in so far as it causes us to be much more careful in evaluating the argument. The question of whether a man is "right" or "wrong" does not depend on his occupation or his personality.

3   Very often the *ad hominem* argument is very vicious. Some people characteristically argue by making personal slurs against their opponents. They will say a particular person is wrong because he is a Jew or a Catholic, a Fascist or a Communist. Because name

calling is frequently as effective as it is misleading, courts of law have strict rules to govern the attempts of lawyers to discredit witnesses in cross-examination. A lawyer may criticize the personal character of a witness only if such criticism is directly connected with the reliability of evidence. Thus the state of a man's eyesight would be highly relevant to his testimony concerning an accident he observed from a distance. But his marital status, for instance the fact that he had just married his fifth wife, would be totally irrelevant to the testimony.

4   A new dimension has been given to the *ad hominem* argument in recent years through the popularization of discoveries in psychology. Now if a man argues for social security he is told that he argues this way because he has an "inferiority complex," or if he argues too strongly for free enterprise he has a "superiority complex." But it should be apparent that one does not answer an argument merely by pointing out that an individual has a "complex" of some kind. A scientist may have neurotic tendencies and may beat his wife, but these facts do not discredit his theories.

5   *Genetic Fallacy* This fallacy involves the attempt to destroy the value of an argument by criticizing its origin. Thus, some have argued that religion is no more than a superstition because it originated out of superstition. But even if it is true that religious views resulted from superstition, this does not mean that such views are still to be equated with superstition. Even though chemistry originated in alchemy, chemistry is not therefore to be regarded as a prejudiced and superstitious study. Yet the appeal to "bad" origin is often sufficient to arouse enough emotion so that the real argument is obliterated.

6   The attempt to discredit an argument by reflecting on the proponent's background combines the *genetic fallacy* with the *ad hominem*. But because a man has grown up in a bad family and a worse environment, it does not follow that he himself is a bad human being nor does it follow that his arguments are false. Conversely a man who comes from a good family and a good environment does not always turn out to be a good human being.

7   In a more subtle way some social scientists have fallen into this fallacy by claiming that human beings are merely products of their environment. But a man may come from a very bad environment and still grow up to be a normal, healthy human being.

8   *Appeal to the People* Because the public speaker or writer must gain the confidence of his audience if he is to make his point, he

may often attempt to establish an atmosphere of friendliness. One of the ways in which he accomplishes this is by depicting himself as "one of the boys." The use of such expressions as "fellow citizens" or "friends and neighbors" is primarily an attempt to make an audience friendly and responsive. A similar purpose is served by such statements as "We're all Americans here and we all share one great ideal, etc.," or "I'm a fellow worker. You and I know how tough it is to earn a buck. My talk ain't fancy, but . . ." or "Because I am addressing a college-trained audience, I know that I can speak of difficult matters seriously." Generally, such appeals are not very dangerous. But when demagogues use them to stir up strong emotions, then the consequences can be disastrous. Lynch mobs have often been formed as a result of strong emotional appeal to group unity.

9   In its more subtle forms the appeal to the people occurs when we try to meet an argument by saying "it isn't natural" or "it isn't common sense." People once used to argue that flying machines were "not natural" and "against common sense." But such criticisms are totally irrelevant to the argument.

10   *The Appeal to Pity*   The appeal to the people relies for its effect on the feeling of group unity. But a similar effect can be obtained when pity and sympathy are aroused. Lawyers will frequently use this means to defend a client. They have him wear shabby clothes, and then try to arouse the jury's sympathy by pointing out how he has suffered. Similarly, MacArthur's use of the refrain "Old soldiers never die; they just fade away" was designed to arouse sympathy and pity. In fact, anyone who argues by describing examples of personal persecution or martyrdom is appealing to pity and sympathy, rather than logic and evidence.

11   Appeals to the people and to pity can be important rhetorical devices, for in these ways effective speakers are able to arouse desired emotions. Unfortunately, effective speakers are not always effective thinkers, and only too often people have been led by demagogues who were effective persuaders but bad reasoners. Some congressmen have succeeded in getting their audience to weep with them and for them. They arouse reactions, not thought. But the *method of persuasion* and the *method of reasoning* must always be clearly differentiated.

12   *The Appeal to Authority*   This fallacy arises when we attempt to justify an idea by appealing to authority. Thus for many years peo-

ple refused to accept the theory of evolution because it seemed to contradict the Bible and the Church Fathers. But the truth or falsity of a doctrine rests on the empirical and logical evidence that is given for it. Even the most scientifically attested hypothesis is not made acceptable merely because Einstein or some other scientist approves it; rather it is accepted because of the empirical evidence which attests to the reliability of the hypothesis. Einstein does not make the theory of relativity true, any more than a man of distinction makes a whisky good. On the contrary, Einstein would probably have been the first to claim that the theory is not based on his *word*, but rather on the evidence which anyone could obtain if he had the proper training in mathematics and the natural sciences.

13   Of course there is good reason to rely on authorities, but only when their views have been carefully examined to determine (1) whether they have based these views on verifiable fact and not merely subjective feelings, and (2) whether they are *really* authorities. The fact that a scientist is an expert in physics does not automatically make him an expert in political science. Eisenhower may be a great military general, but this does not qualify him to be an expert scientist.

14   *Appeal to Force*   The attempt to gain a point by threatening physical or other harm is an *appeal to force*. The appeal to force is resorted to more subtly when it is insinuated that a person may "lose his job" or "be reported to the authorities" because of his beliefs. It also occurs when an argument is attacked as "dangerous." In such instances we try to *destroy* rather than *resolve* the argument.

15   An infamous example of the use of the appeal to force appears in Thucydides' account of the Athenian attempt to "persuade" the small island of Melos to join them.

> "You know," says the Athenian, "as well as we do, that, in the logic of human nature, Right only comes into question where there is a balance of power, while it is Might that determines what the strong extort and the weak concede. . . . Your strongest weapons are hopes yet unrealized, while the weapons in your hand are somewhat inadequate for holding out against the forces already arrayed against you. . . . Reflect . . . that you are making a decision for your country . . . a country whose fate hangs upon a single decision right or wrong." [Toynbee's translation]

16   It is important to remember that appeals to force are rarely this obvious. Whenever there is a hidden threat to an opponent's social, economic, or political status, the appeal to force is being used.

Faulty Reasoning

17   *Faulty Generalization*   Any sweeping claim which is based on a very few selected instances is a faulty generalization. A statement such as "Foreigners just don't understand democracy" is usually based on hearsay or on one or two unfavorable encounters with foreigners. A fairly common type of faulty generalization rests on the acceptance of slogans, proverbs, or "tabloids." In the 1932 presidential election the Republicans told the nation to keep them in office because "You shouldn't change horses in the middle of the stream." The Democrats answered by saying "It's time for a new deal." In 1952 the slogans were reversed. People have often been told "never put off for tomorrow what you can do today," that is, when not told that "haste makes waste." Men who have associated with Communists are often regarded suspiciously because "birds of a feather flock together." The reply is, "You can't judge a book by its cover." Such slogans or proverbs are clever and often persuasive. But for the important purpose of deciding whether or not an argument is sound they are useless.

18   Sometimes a generalization is accepted as an unalterable truth. An argument against wartime censorship of the press on the basis of the statement, "Democracy can exist only as long as the press is free," ignores the fact that all generalizations hold only for specific circumstances and that this particular generalization might not hold under other circumstances. Even an important generalization such as "Thou shalt not kill" may have exceptions; soldiers are permitted to break this rule, and so are those who kill in self-defense.

19   *The Post Hoc Ergo Propter Hoc Fallacy*   (After this, therefore because of this.) This fallacy occurs when the cause of some occurrence is attributed to an event that immediately preceded it, as when our stomach-ache is attributed to the last meal eaten, a causal relationship which might or might not be true. Sequence of events does not necessarily imply causal relationship. Yet people constantly think that, because event X occurred immediately before event Y, therefore event X is the *cause* of event Y. "I walked under a ladder; I failed the exam I had immediately afterward; therefore walking under the ladder was the cause of my failure." Superstitions are generally based on the *post hoc* fallacy. Political success has frequently been based on the argument: "See! Since I've been in office, things have gone well."

20   Newspapers sometimes make clever use of the *post hoc* fallacy. Thus such headlines as MINERS STRIKE; REDS GAIN IN KO-

REA may refer to two completely independent events. But linking the two events in the same headline gives the impression to many readers that the Communists are gaining in Korea *because* the miners are striking.

21   If something occurred just prior to an event it is not necessarily the cause of the event. An infinite number of things all over the universe occur the second before a given event. One of these may be the cause. But much more knowledge is required than the simple fact that it occurred a second or even a split second before the happening.

22   *Begging the Question—Circular Reasoning*   Begging the question, or reasoning in circular fashion, consists in the mere reassertion of the meaning of the premises in the conclusion. In its most obvious form it can be seen in the argument: "John is a good man. Why? Because he's good, that's why." In this example the conclusion "John is a good man" does no more than repeat the premise.

23   Of course begging the question is usually not this obvious. Usually the premise is repeated but in different words: "John is a good man. Why? Because he is virtuous." But it should be apparent that "virtuous" and "good" are synonymous and therefore the argument is circular.

24   Sometimes an argument is quite complex and then it is more difficult to check for circularity: "Freud claims that we are often frustrated because our sex drives are blocked and they become blocked because we are thwarted in our desires." The circularity here may be difficult to discover until "frustrated" is seen to have the same meaning as "thwarted in our desires."

25   *Special Pleading*   This fallacy occurs when a deliberate attempt is made to "stack the cards" in favor of some given position. Politicians are notoriously adept in employing this fallacy. They very often completely ignore or refuse to look for any evidence that could invalidate their views. . . .

26   In a sense all of us are engaged in "special pleading." When we favor some position we tend to minimize any data that criticize the position. Lawyers are often concerned with *minimizing* unfavorable evidence. But only a dishonest lawyer would deliberately *ignore* such evidence.

27   *The Appeal to Ignorance*   This fallacy consists in an attempt to justify a belief even if there is no evidence for it. Thus people will sometimes be found to argue: "The occurrence of psychic phenom-

ena is indeed a fact because no one has ever disproved it." But because something has never been proved *false*, it is not therefore to be considered true. The statement "A green-eyed elf sits on the other side of the moon" may not ever be disproved. But this does not mean that an elf does sit on the other side of the moon.

28　*Irrelevance*　This fallacy is probably the most frequently used. We start out by trying to prove one statement and then end up by trying to prove a different statement. Women sometimes argue in the following way:

> Mrs. X: But she's so stupid! Every time you ask her a question she has nothing to say. Furthermore, I know her I.Q. is very low.
> Mrs. Y: But wasn't that a nice blouse she was wearing?

29　　In this example Mrs. X is trying to prove someone's stupidity. But Mrs. Y diverts the issue into another channel.

30　　Examples abound in English themes, as in the following excerpt from a theme:

> In this paper I should like to comment on Ibsen's *Ghosts*. The play was very sincere and honest. Sincerity and honesty are two qualities that are praiseworthy. All people should be sincere and honest.

31　　The student begins the theme by telling us he will discuss Ibsen's *Ghosts*. But he concludes by telling us that sincerity and honesty are good qualities.

32　*Imperfect Analogy*　Analogy is frequently a very compelling method of reasoning. For example, we might argue: "Conditions today are like conditions prior to World War II. Therefore, since war followed then, war will follow now." Similarly, Spengler argued that since conditions in modern Western civilization are just like those which were present during the decline of many ancient civilizations, Western civilization is also in the process of declining. But analogies of this kind can be satisfactory only if they compare two elements that have very few differences. We can argue that one tomato will be like all the others because one tomato is not different in any important respects from another, that is, tomatoes are generally considered to be homogeneous. But analogy is of little value in comparing civilizations. There are just as many important differences among civilizations as there are similarities. When we ignore differences and base analogy on a few similarities, we are involved in the fallacy of imperfect analogy.

33   Unfortunately, analogy has found frequent use as a dangerous political weapon. At one time it was fashionable to argue that circular motion was natural because the earth revolved around the sun. Consequently, it was also natural for society to consist of a monarch around whom the rest of the nation revolved. Marxists have frequently argued that opposition of social classes is necessary in capitalistic societies by analogy with the opposition of physical forces in the universe.

34   However, analogy can sometimes serve a useful purpose in suggesting new and fruitful approaches to problems. The study of animal behavior has led to important clues concerning the principles motivating human behavior. The analogy between the flow of electricity through a wire and the flow of water through a tube served to stimulate the search for new and more complex properties of electricity. But such advantages of analogy must be weighed against the disadvantages.

Misuse of Language

35   *Misuse of Metaphor* The argument from analogy rests on presumed resemblances between otherwise unrelated events. Similar to analogy is *metaphor,* the use of a word to express a likeness. But whereas analogy usually rests upon a number of resemblances, metaphor utilizes only a limited number of resemblances. People are called "tigers," "angels," "wolves," "monsters," and so forth on the basis of one or two characteristics. Such metaphors are sometimes picturesque, sometimes clever, but very often they are misleading and confusing. They cause us to over-simplify our judgments of people and to attribute too much or too little to them. Calling a man a "tiger," for example, causes us to attribute to him many characteristics which he may not really possess—anger, hatred, ferocity, etc. Mark Twain's novel, *Pudd'nhead Wilson,* provides a good illustration. On the basis of one remark, Wilson, a promising young lawyer, new to a small town, was called "pudd'nhead." It took years for him to establish his practice because the townspeople judged him by the name he was given.

36   Metaphor, like analogy, is faulty only when it is misused, as it is in the following:

> Tree planting and similar *soft-headed quack remedies* would be in vogue. The dollar would be dishonest. The budget would be a national *laughing stock.* A spending *orgy* would be *gaining a momentum* which could hardly be checked. Class prejudice would be *rampant.* The treasury would have been *looted.*

37   The writer had misgivings about what would happen when Roosevelt became president of the United States in 1932, but notice that by his use of the italicized metaphors his misgivings are made to appear as if they related to actual events. Or, again, an editorial (1933) presents the following highly emotional metaphorical warning:

> Whatever menace appears to these rights is a *dread specter* before the women of America of wrecked homes, wrecked lives, and a WRECKED FUTURE.

38   It is somewhat of a relief to discover that the warning was occasioned by a bill before Congress which would license interstate corporations!

39   A very glaring example of the misuse of metaphor is seen in the following:

> [Winston Churchill], the archbishop of torydom, came to tell us how we shall live. And what is the life he maps for us? An Anglo-American tyranny to ride roughshod over the globe. He said that it was against Communism that he wanted the armies and navies combined. The words are Churchill's but the plan is Hitler's. Churchill's own domain of plunder is ripping at the seams and he asks Americans to save it for him. We are to be the trigger men, we are to provide him billions of money to regain what the robber barons are losing. (*New Masses*, March 19, 1946.)

40   Notice how various pictorial phrases such as "archbishop of torydom," "domain of plunder," "ripping at the seams," "trigger men," and "robber barons" are able to convey the impression that Churchill is a criminal, trying to get us to join his "gang." The writing is colorful and vivid and serves to build up in our minds an association between Churchill and the "typical gangster." And, of course, this is precisely the association that the paragraph seeks to convey. But we are duped by metaphorical writing when we accept such writing as if it were actually true.

41   *Hypostatization*   Not only may the unscrupulous writer take advantage of the normal uncritical response to metaphor, but he may also avail himself of a tendency in people to assume that abstract words refer to concrete entities. This tendency to speak of *democracy, justice, liberty,* as if they had reference to specific entities, is called *hypostatization.* The fallacy could be defined as a failure to distinguish between abstract and concrete words. The objects referred to by *table* and *chair* can be pointed to; the ideas represented by *justice* and *truth* cannot be pointed to. Examples of hypostatiza-

tion can be found everywhere, as is suggested in the following list of slogans:

> The State can do no wrong.
> Nature decrees what is right.
> The Spirit of the Nation produces its art and literature.
> Science makes Progress.
> Democracy safeguards human liberty.

The effect of hypostatization is—like metaphor—to produce emotion. A statement, "Justice triumphs over all," has emotional appeal. But it is too abstract to convey information about any specific situation.

42   *Semantic Ambiguity or Equivocation*   Almost all words are potentially ambiguous because almost all words have more than one meaning. Actually the meaning of a word is governed chiefly by the context in which it is found, as, for example, *bad* in the following sentences:

> Susie, don't be bad.
> He feels bad.
> She's not a bad number.
> That's too bad.
> It was a bad day at Black Rock.

43   When deliberately or mistakenly we use the same word with different meanings in the same context we are said to "equivocate." Equivocation causes trouble because of the habitually uncritical use of language. We tend to forget that a word has many meanings, so that meaning A which Mr. X has in mind may be very different from meaning B which Mr. Y has in mind, although both are using the same word.

> Mr. X: Don't you agree that *progress* is very important for a nation?
> Mr. Y: Yes, I agree with you.
>   Several days later:
> Mr. X: to a friend: Mr. Y and I are in complete agreement. We both believe in *progress*, that is, that contemporary institutions should never be allowed to deteriorate. Therefore, I'm sure he will vote against a revision of the constitution.

44   This example is an instance of *apparent* agreement but *real* disagreement. The following is an instance of *real* agreement but *apparent* disagreement.

> Mr. X: I think you're wrong. Men are not *equal*. Some are stron-
>   ger than others. Some have more intelligence.
> Mr. Y: You're wrong. They are *equal*. The law states that as far
>   as the law is concerned each man is supposed to get
>   *equal* treatment.
> Mr. X: Oh, I agree. I admit that every man is supposed to re-
>   ceive *equal* treatment in law courts. I thought you
>   meant that all men have the same physical and intellec-
>   tual abilities.

45   Equivocation can be used to make a point effectively, with no attempt at dishonesty, as with Benjamin Franklin's witty equivocation, "If we don't hang together, we'll hang separately." His equivocation served simply to enforce the grave reality behind his words. But equivocation is only too frequently used dishonestly. The communist dictatorship has developed a technique of equivocation which George Orwell has satirized in *Animal Farm*, where he imagines an animal revolution led by the pigs. When the animals have triumphed, the pigs take the place of the old human masters, and the revolution which began with the slogan "All animals are *equal*" ends with the pigs proclaiming the equivocation, "All animals are *equal*. But some animals are more *equal* than others."

46   *Syntactic Ambiguity*   Not only words, but also the *structure of sentences* (syntax) may cause confusion. Ambiguity resulting from faulty sentence structure is termed *syntactic ambiguity*. Here are a few examples:

1. Horse shows increased profits.
2. State plan aids devastated area.
3. Out of gas she had to walk home.
4. With her enormous nose aimed toward the sky my mother
   rushed to the plane.

47   A subtle form of syntactic ambiguity is called the *complex question*. This question is usually so phrased that any answer to it is self-incriminating.

> Mr. Jones: Have you stopped avoiding people you owe money
>   to?

Mr. Smith: No.

Mr. Jones: Oh, so you're still avoiding them, you rascal.

Mr. Smith: I meant "yes."

Mr. Jones: Oh, so you've been avoiding them, just as I thought.

48   Some lawyers employ such techniques deliberately. A witness who is asked, "When did you buy the murder weapon?" cannot answer without admitting that he owned the weapon. Not only lawyers but politicians and editorial writers frequently employ the technique of the complex question. For example, during the Roosevelt-Truman administrations newspapers frequently made use of the complex question, "Are you going to stop this trend toward Socialism?" This was an unfair question because both the "yes" and "no" answer imply that such a trend existed. Writers of "letters to the editor" make use of the complex question, as in the following: "Are the financial resources of this government without a limit, that four billion dollars can be applied for purposes that will eventually damn the American people?" Any way this question is answered would involve damaging admissions.

49   Pause and emphasis can be used to make syntactic distinctions. The sentence "America without her security is lost" can give two different meanings, depending on punctuation or pauses in speech:

America, without her, security is lost.
America, without her security, is lost.

The meaning of almost any sentence is subject to alteration through emphasis. If after a dinner party someone said, "I enjoyed the dinner," he would not want to emphasize the I, "*I* enjoyed the dinner," because this might imply that the others had not. Emphasis on *dinner* might suggest that he *at least* found this part of the evening, *the dinner*, enjoyable. As he was leaving with his friends, he would not say, "*I* had a good time." Again the implication would be that the others had not enjoyed themselves. Mark Antony's funeral address in Shakespeare's *Julius Caesar* is a brilliant example of the way in which emphasis can be used to sway an audience.

CONSIDERATIONS

Do the obstacles to clear communication analyzed in this article seem to refer primarily to spoken language? Why would such examples of illogical reasoning be more apparent in verbal than in written communication? Might logical fallacies be more damaging in print—in newspaper coverage and political or historical writing, for instance—than in speech? Which of the obstacles discussed and analyzed in this article are used most frequently and to more vicious ends than the others? Are all these "obstacles" necessarily employed deliberately by speakers and writers?

Nearly every example used to illustrate the principles of emotional argument and misuse of language includes an analogy. (See paragraphs 4, 5, and 12.) Do the authors base their analogies on general experience or on their own personal prejudices? What, if anything, do the analogies reveal about the authors' personal philosophies and tastes? What types of effective exemplification, in addition to analogy, appear in this article?

Reread an essay you have written for this class or any other class; underline logical fallacies, misuses of language, and any specific faults outlined in this article. Then rewrite your essay or the passages that contain errors in style or logic. Analyze your finished product for clarity and impact.

VOCABULARY

(2) **proponent**   supporter, advocate

(5) **alchemy**   a medieval form of chemistry aimed chiefly at trying to transform baser metals into gold

(6) **fallacy**   a deceptive or erroneous idea

(8) **demagogues**   leaders who gain power by arousing the emotions, passions, and prejudices of the people

(12) **empirical**   based on or derived from experience

(15) **extort**   to force something from someone by violence, intimidation, or abuse

(15) **infamous**   having an extremely bad reputation

(32) **homogeneous**   alike

Exemplification

EXEMPLIFICATION

Exemplification can be defined, pure and simply, as the giving of examples, perhaps the most common way to explain or clarify an incident, theory, or philosophical position. If the reader can relate whatever you are saying to something else that he already knows (*or can easily visualize*), he can better understand you. Also, examples can show that what you are suggesting has certain validity. Suppose you are discussing the dangers of air pollution, and you want to convince people that mass transit systems could significantly relieve the problem in urban areas. You would want to provide examples of mass transit systems that are presently in operation and have alleviated smog problems in their respective areas.

Exemplification can be used as an organizational tool. A general theory or idea may be defined and then treated in various examples. If your theory is that recent American novels and short stories have reflected the disquiet prevalent in society, you would want to illustrate your position with examples from works by Philip Roth, John Hersey, Bernard Malamud, and Joyce Carol Oates to name a few. Or the examples can be discussed first and a general statement concluded from them. This is *extended exemplification*.

A special form of exemplification is the use of an anecdote for the purpose of illustration. Although an anecdote is a form of narration, when you use it to illustrate, its function is to exemplify.

PRACTICE

1. Write a short theme (four or five paragraphs) explaining why something or someone appeals to you—a particular rock group, commune living, a sport, or a hobby. Use exemplification as your main developmental tool. Try several different ways of introducing examples, including anecdote.

2. In a novel find at least four paragraphs that contain examples and explain why they are particularly effective. Do the same exercise for a magazine article treating a contemporary or controversial subject. What is the function of exemplification in the nonfiction you analyzed?

Why Johnny Can't Flunk

Identify the paragraphs in this essay that contain exemplification. Then write a paragraph using extended exemplification to develop each of the following thesis sentences:

The pressure of exams leaves students little time for writing term papers.

There are systems of evaluating a student's work other than the grading system.

Professor X is the best lecturer on campus.

There are ways to take good notes at a lecture.

Jokes Negroes Tell on Themselves

Hughes's essay is actually a series of jokes that are examples used to illustrate his thesis. Write an essay on the type of humor that makes you laugh, using exemplification as your main means of development.

America's New Superstars—They Shout "No!" to Tradition

See paragraph 14 of this essay for a good example of exemplification and explain its effectiveness. Write an essay on a superstar in any field—sports, music, or art, in which you analyze his popularity. Use striking examples to illustrate certain generalizations you make about the star's appeal.

• Write a narrative about a personal experience and use anecdotes to exemplify.

For examples of individual paragraphs using *exemplification,* see p.19, ¶15–17, p.30, ¶23–25, p.39, ¶19–20, p.147, ¶13, p.177, ¶19, p.202, ¶19–22, p.252, ¶6, p.271, ¶36, p.337, ¶31.

Why Johnny Can't Flunk

PHILIP ROSENBERG

1   "Hi," said the proprietor of Academic Marketplace, which is the | *Dial*
New York branch of a multimillion-dollar nationwide chain of
term-paper companies. "I'm Nat."

"Nat what?" I asked.

"Just Nat."

Nat's office on lower Broadway was bare except for a scarred | *Desc*
Steelcase desk and a counter with piles of mimeographed forms and
three loose-leaf binders on top of it. The wall behind the counter
held a large hand-lettered sign reading "We Understand," and,
nearby, a poster-sized picture of Albert Einstein.

5   "This is a seasonal business," Nat said. "In the spring the | *Tone*
phone is ringing all the time and there's always five or six customers
in here."

"Buying term papers?"

"Buying *research*," he corrected. Research is the industry's
code name for its product.

"You don't sell term papers, I take it?"

"No, we don't." He pulled open a desk drawer and rested his
ankles on it.

10   "What's the difference between research and term papers?" I | *Top S*
wanted to know. Only a few months before, his company had been
called Enjay Term Papers Inc., and it was still listed that way in the
phone book.

"It depends on what's done with the product. Research is to help a student or anyone else in the preparation of an assignment. Term papers are term papers."

"But couldn't a student just turn in the research you sell him as a term paper?"

"Sure."

"Well, then. . . ."

15   "Well nothing," he said with impressive finality.

It was much the same with the economics. Hard figures are not ⟨*Tran*⟩ easy to come by in this business; and most of the practitioners talk no more openly than Nat, primarily because they are in an uneasy relationship with the law. New York has passed a rather bizarre ⟨*S Var*⟩ piece of legislation stipulating that "No person shall sell or offer for sale to any person enrolled in a university, college, academy, school or other educational institution within the state of New York any assistance in the preparation, research or writing of a dissertation, thesis, term paper, essay, report or other written assignment. . . ." Massachusetts and Ohio have also outlawed the selling of term papers, and at least half a dozen other states are thinking of doing so.

17   I had caught Nat during the uneasy interval between the passage of the law just quoted and the moment, a few months in the future, when the Attorney General would force him out of business. It was just a question of getting out with as much as possible in the meanwhile. Only a month before, the state had successfully lopped off a sister branch in the corporate structure of which Nat's company was an insignificantly small limb. And the records seized from that office showed $35,000 worth of business for one particular three-month period in the middle of winter. Nat would be happy if his business lasted through one more exam season.

18   Even in states where no laws ban the selling of term papers, industry people are afraid of too much publicity about their dollar volume. Attorneys general don't much care, on the whole, about cheating in school—that, after all, is the school's lookout. But when the cheating is part of a multimillion-dollar business, the secular ⟨*Meta*⟩ arm of the law begins to twitch.

19   Not that the twitching has dampened business. These days, no ⟨*Meta*⟩ college community is complete without its term-paper company, and college newspapers regularly carry ads for their services. Their names are sometimes stuffy ("Possibilities Unlimited"), sometimes evasive ("Academic Marketplace"), and sometimes coy ("Planned Paperhood"), but in all cases they are making it as easy to buy

homework as it is to buy such other staples of academic life as tape   *Sarc*
cassettes and abortions.

20   To be sure, most of the term-paper companies are not what
could be called successful in any conventional business sense of the
term. Some, perhaps a majority, represent no more than the temporary efforts of a graduate student to capitalize his typewriter. These
resemble nothing so much as the old fraternity files that were available to brothers in the market for prefabricated scholarship.

21   But one should not be misled by the fact that the bulk of the
term-paper mills are of the hole-and-corner variety. There is nothing
amateurish about Educational Research Inc., a term-paper company in Washington that keeps an 800 number so that patrons
across the country can call in their orders toll-free, nor about the
Termpaper Arsenal of Los Angeles, which advertises as far east as
Queens College in New York. It is these giant term-paper mills that   *Tran*
do most of the business, and among them one outfit and one man
was, until quite recently, preeminent.

22   Ward Warren was still an undergraduate at Babson Institute in   *Narr*
suburban Boston when he discovered the possibilities inherent in
the professionalization of homework. Last year, at twenty-three, he
was a self-made millionaire and the prime mover behind Ward
Warren Enterprises—a string of corporations that included a computerized college-placement service, a wholesale operation that sold
term papers from Warren's files to other term-paper companies,
and a string of perhaps fifty offices located around campuses across
the country for retail sale of term papers. Now, all these operations
have closed down and Ward Warren has disappeared. I visited the
offices last fall, however, before the ax fell, and I learned something
of his operation.

23   A girl in white pants was assigned to show me around. She
explained, "All the papers we own are listed here in these loose-leaf
binders, indexed by subject and title. Last time we counted we had
over ten thousand papers. When a student special-orders a paper,
we assign it to one of our writers. When it's finished one copy goes
to the customer and one goes into the file for resale. Of course, an
original, custom-made paper costs more than one from the catalog.
Original material sells for three-eighty-five a page and up, depending on how specialized it is. Catalog papers are just two dollars a
page."

24   I examined the neat, mimeographed pages. Down the left margin ran a column of titles—the pedantic sorts of titles that could

only belong to undergraduate essays—e.g.: "A Study of the Thoughts of Kunen's *The Strawberry Statement* and Keniston's *Young Radicals.*" To the right of each title, in straight vertical columns, were numerical and alphabetical codes that told the number of text pages, the number of footnotes, and the number of bibliography pages. Bibliography pages cost extra but footnotes did not.

25   "The letters tell you the level of the paper," the girl explained.   *Class*
"If there's no letter it means it's a basic-level paper for college students. An A means advanced—for higher-level college courses and graduate work. G means strictly graduate work. And C is for corporate work. We do a lot of that, you know. An executive or a salesman may have to give a report at a meeting, so he'll come to us for it. Either he supplies the data or we do, depending on the situation."

26   Ward Warren himself told me, "All of my employees are college graduates. The writers all have at least M.A.s and most of them have Ph.D.s. Except for maybe the Rand Corporation, I probably have the most highly educated staff of any company in the country. We have a training program for the people who run the various offices, so that everything is done in a very businesslike manner."

27   So businesslike had the operation become that last November two restraining orders were issued to all Massachusetts term-paper companies—one by Boston University and one by the Attorney General's office in cooperation with the University of Massachusetts. Ward Warren was ordered to produce his records for the court. He refused and was served with a contempt complaint initiated by Boston University. There is now a bench warrant for his arrest and quite some interest in finding him.

28   Clark Kerr commented a few years ago that the knowledge   *Angy*
industry was the biggest growth industry in America and that the university would play the same role in the economic life of the end of this century that the railroad played a hundred years earlier. This being the case, the emergence of a Ward Warren is easily explicable, for it stands to reason that clever young would-be entrepreneurs would keep a keen eye out for the type of profit such a situation implies. In the nature of things it would be unrealistic to expect that the best minds of a generation would be content for long with the modest salaries available from universities and publishing houses, and they have not been. After the discovery that cheating is   *Sarc*
as inevitable a spin-off of academic education as orange drink is of

space travel, the growth of the term-paper industry was in the cards, its health dependent on one other factor of production which the knowledge explosion itself was kind enough to supply. This factor was a waste product of the knowledge industry, and it took the form of what might be called an intellectual lumpen proletariat. In the Fifties we heard a lot of talk about dropouts—mostly young people drafted into higher education by parental or peer pressure, who somehow got through maybe their sophomore year before they disappeared from the college scene to join the ranks of the unskilled and the half-educated.

Meta /
Angy

29   Berkeley, though, in the Sixties, was the first college to bring to public awareness the fact that the process of dropping out was changing. The Berkeley dropouts didn't disappear. Rather, like empty bottles waiting to be recycled, they hung around under the sinks of the academic world. Raskolnikov in his garret, living on the scraps of intellectual life, became, for the first time in American university life, a fixture on the scene.

Sim

30   Sometimes these new Raskolnikovs had only unfinished dissertations between them and what is called "satisfactory completion," sometimes they had dropped from the college's active files as juniors or seniors. Although most were at least semi-retired, they called themselves students. Perhaps a year or two of teaching, or part-time work in a campus bookstore, or editing other people's dissertations at three dollars an hour kept them alive while they shared two rooms with a friend or two of either sex. But the point is that they stayed on in Cambridge, on Morningside Heights, or on Telegraph Avenue, where they formed a potential source of cheap educated labor for entrepreneurs who realized that the margins of academic life contain potentially rich pickings.

C & E

31   Without these intellectual proletarians, the term-paper revolution would not have been possible. But as it is, they are there in large enough numbers to allow of their being hired for two dollars a page (for the original sale—there are no residuals); they are economically naïve enough to imagine that they are ripping someone off when they get twenty or thirty dollars for doing the sort of work for which they used to be paid only in aggravation; and they are cynical enough about academic life and academic values to feel scarcely a twinge of compunction about the nature of the work. On the contrary, they often take pride in it as a sort of grubby sabotage, for they are by long practice thoroughly habituated to using the clichés of educational radicalism as a handy ad hoc justification.

Anly

32   Peter is a graduate student at Columbia on an indefinite leave

of absence. Nineteen Seventy-one was a good year for him, for in addition to teaching part-time at a college in the city's mammoth university system, he also wrote term papers more or less regularly for a company in downtown Manhattan. According to the contract he signed with each job, he was required to submit to the company neatly typed copy "that is commencerate [sic] in quality with work sufficient to be accepted in a Graduate Program at an accredited University"—a level of quality he soon found he could reach while turning out pages almost as fast as he could type them. **Sarc**

33   "Did you ever assign term papers while you were teaching?" I asked. **Dial**

34   "Sure. Everyone does. It's required by the department."

35   "Do you know if any of your students bought them?"

36   "I don't think so. I tried to be kind of careful. I was teaching lower-level English courses and my kids had a lot of writing to do throughout the semester, so I knew pretty much what they wrote like. It would have been easy to spot. Besides, I worked with them on the papers—you know, they'd give me a draft, I'd give them suggestions, another draft, more suggestions, and so on. If you work like that there's no way anyone can suddenly turn in something he just bought." Then, after a pause: "Well, there are ways, but it's not likely."

37   "What would you do if you did get one?"

38   "What the hell could I do? I suppose I'm entitled to throw the kid out on his ass, but I couldn't very well do that, could I? Not if I'm writing them. You know what I used to think about? I used to think that someday a kid would turn in to me a paper I wrote. There were a couple of close calls, too. There were a few times when I wrote papers on books I was teaching in my class. But they turned out to be for someone else, I guess, because I never saw them." He laughed at the thought. "Waste of time if it happens, too, isn't it? I mean, if I knew I was going to be the one to read it, I could save myself the time of writing it. Really, though, I don't know what I'd do if it happened. It's like two respectable guys running into each other coming out of a peep show on Forty-second Street. I guess they just pretend they didn't see each other." **Tone** **Angy**

39   "I started Termpapers Unlimited," Ward Warren told me last fall, "when I had a term paper to write and ran all over Boston looking for books. Do you know how many libraries there are in Boston? I was struck by the inefficiency of the process. For six hours of reading I had to spend three days on the M.T.A. So I figured if **C&E**

a student could hire someone to do the research, he could save himself a lot of time."

40   He paused to let this sink in, but it didn't. What the hell is | Tone research anyway? A student wouldn't know what to do with a package of research if he saw one, assuming of course that such a thing could exist. I told Warren this.

41   "Let me ask you a question," he said by way of answering. | Arg "What's the most important ingredient in education?" I shrugged. "Time, right? Well, that's what I'm really selling when you get right down to it. It's a service to save students time. They have a lot to do, and they're not going to learn anything running from one library to another looking for a bunch of books, half of which will be charged out or missing anyway."

"And you do the running around for them, is that it?"

"Yes, that's it."

"So that buying term papers from you is a more efficient way to learn?"

45   "No, that isn't it. I don't know that they learn anything from the stuff they buy. I suppose they might. After all, the material *is* supposed to be research. In fact, if anyone comes right out and tells us that he's just going to turn it in for a grade, then we can't sell it to him. I've actually turned down a few people that way. Probably they were cops. But most of the time they don't say that and we don't ask. We make them sign a release that says the material is 'for research and reference purposes only and that any other use is done without the authority or consent of the seller.' I suppose a lot of them are just turning in the papers anyway. In fact, you could almost say I know it. But that's not the point. The point is that the time he saves on a paper he doesn't give a damn about he can spend on something he does give a damn about. It's that simple."

"What makes you think he's going to spend the time he saves doing something else educational?"

"Did you ever know a student who had a lot of time to kill?" Warren asked. I was about to say yes when he went on. "Not really. Sure, they kill a lot of time, but that doesn't mean they have time to kill. If I save them time, maybe they'll just spend it screwing around. I don't know and it doesn't matter. The thing is they would have done the screwing around anyway. The time they save has to come in somewhere, and wherever it comes in, it's all profit for them."

48   At Queens College in New York, the English department's

offices are in a shed at the corner of the parking lot and I went there
to meet Bill Green, a professor of English. Green was active in the
lobby that pushed New York's anti-term-paper bill.

49   "Now that the bill has passed," I asked him, "I suppose you
know that companies are still selling term papers?"

50   "Oh, of course. In fact, there are still ads for them in the
school papers. Look at this." He showed me a clipping advertising
the services of the Washington firm with the 800 number. "They're
out of state," he explained, "so there's not much we can do about
them."

I wanted to know if the school was doing anything itself about
the problem, besides the legal steps. Anything administrative or
educational?

"Yes, of course. The first thing is that we're beefing up the
section on plagiarism in the student handbook. In fact, I was working on that when you came in." He slid a paper across his desk
toward me.

"Is that going to help?"

"Well, it used to talk about the student's responsibility to himself, that sort of thing. Now it's a lot stronger."

55   "How big a problem is this?"

"Oh, it's very big. I don't have any figures, but there are dozens
of companies advertising, so they must sell a lot of them. And it's so
damned hard to detect."

"What do you do when you catch them?"

"You mean, what would I do if someone handed one in to
me?" he asked.

"Haven't you ever got one?"

60   "Not that I know of," he said and then took me around to
meet half a dozen other members of his department, all of whom
knew that store-bought term papers were a menace to American
higher education and none of whom had ever seen one.

61   This is not surprising. At the University of Wisconsin, for ex-   *Exmp*
ample, six hundred students, some of them seniors, had their records held up last June after documents subpoenaed from a local
term-paper mill revealed that they had purchased materials there.
Clearly, these arrested records represented six hundred cases of
scholarly chicanery that passed undetected through the machinery
of academic scrutiny.

62   It is this fact, more than anything else, that has the academic
community in such a tizzy. "Last year," Ward Warren explained,
"the presidents of half a dozen colleges here in the Boston area met

to discuss what to do about the term-paper problem. By which they   *Hyper*
mean me. Now these are college presidents who have had fifty thousand students on their sidewalks ready to burn down the libraries,
and they never got together before. So if they're getting together
now, they must be in a panic."

63   As Stephen Mindell, a deputy chief in New York's Bureau of   *Anly*
Consumer Frauds and Protection who handled the state's prosecu-
tion of a term-paper mill, explained, "The sad part of this whole
business is that if we close down enough of these companies and get
them to go out of business, or even underground, all we'll succeed
in doing is reducing the problem to an acceptable level. What
seems to bother the schools more than anything else is the problem's visibility. I'm no expert on teaching, but it seems to me there
has to be something wrong with what the schools are doing when
this kind of cheating is possible. The term-paper mills are a big
embarrassment to them because they make everyone see that, and
just by their presence they could force some changes."

64   Clearly, one reason why term-paper cheating has proliferated   *C & E*
to the extent it has is that most of the schools offer precious little
inducement for the students to do otherwise. In the cafeteria of   *Exmp*
New York's City College, one undergraduate agreed to talk to me
in exchange for a pledge not to use his name. "There are lots of
reasons why I buy term papers," he explained, measuring sugar into
his coffee. "But mostly it all comes down to the fact that the papers
are too much trouble."

65   "Too hard?"
66   "Hell no. I could always write an A or a B paper if I had to. In
fact, my first two years here I did; there weren't any of these companies around then. I've even written some for other people."
            "For money?"
            "Sure, for money. Not for any of the big companies, you know.
They won't hire undergraduates; only M.A.s and Ph.D.s. But this
guy I know had a little business of his own and I used to write
papers for him."
            "You buy papers for your own courses but write them for other
people? What sense does that make?"

70   "Makes a lot of sense. Say I'm taking an economics course. I'm   *Anly*
a psych major. I don't know all that much about economics—how
much do you learn in an introductory course? Not a whole helluva
lot. So anything I'd write would probably be kind of silly—you
know, read a couple of books so you can put in footnotes and then

fill up seventeen pages. And it takes a long time. Then you turn it in *Anly*
when you come to take the final, some guy'll spend twenty-five
minutes reading it, put a B-plus on the cover, and leave it on the
table outside his office so you can pick it up over the summer.
There's no percentage in that. In the time it takes me to write it, I
could write three psych papers because I know something about it,
and I get to keep the difference. If that doesn't make sense, tell me
what does."

71   "Aren't you afraid of getting caught?"

72   He shook his head no, took a tentative sip from the steaming
cup, and commenced to explain. "Who's going to catch me? The
economics prof never saw anything I wrote, so how can he know
what I could write and what I couldn't? Besides, he has to read
eighty-five of them between the final exam and when he has to turn
in grades. Even if he thinks something funny is going on, there's not
much he can do about it. He could call me into his office to talk
about the paper, but what could he prove? It's not like the paper is
copied from anywhere. Then all he would have to do is find what
it's copied from. But this stuff is made to order, so if you just read
it before you turn it in so you know what it says, you're pretty safe."

73   Indeed, it seems to be the case that a major part of the term- *Tran*
paper industry's clientele consists of just such students who could
get by perfectly well without cheating if they chose to, but who find
it more convenient, for one reason or another, to cheat.

74   And if good students see no reason to avoid patronizing the
local term-paper mills, poor students of course see even less. In their
case the risk of detection is theoretically greater, but the punish- *Irny*
ment is less inasmuch as flunking for not having done your own
work is at least a gain in efficiency over flunking for having done it.
"Sure, I'm scared whenever I do it," a sophomore at Boston University told me, scarcely disguising his reluctance to talk about the
subject. "But what choice do I have? In a lot of courses your grade
depends on two things—the final and the term paper. Well, there's
not much I can do about the final, so I bust my ass studying for it.
And by then I don't have any time for the paper. If I tried to do
both, I'd only screw them both up. Besides, I can buy a lot better
paper than I could ever write."

75   "Does it ever bother you that this is cheating?"

"Sometimes, especially when I think about what would happen
if I got caught. But it sure doesn't bother me as much as flunking
the course would."

"Do you ever write your own papers?"

78   "No," he answered, grinning thinly and looking around the Commonwealth Avenue plaza to see if the thought police were about to bust him. When he saw that they weren't, he confessed to me that he was a term-paper junkie. "I can't," he said. "Once you start using these things you're more or less hooked. You can't take C's and D's when you know you could buy A's and B's, and besides, if anyone found out what I really write like, then they'd know I didn't write the things they'd already given me good grades for. You know how sometimes in a textbook there are questions at the end of the chapters, and the teacher will tell you to write a few paragraphs on some of them for homework. I've even had to buy that."

Slang

79   It must have been a student such as this who was responsible for the order form in the files of a term-paper mill in New York. The order is for a study of John Donne's Holy Sonnets, and the client specifies by number the sonnet to be studied, the particular lines to be concentrated on, adds the suggestion that references to other sonnets will be welcome, and then writes, with an innocence so touching that one can only be thankful no one will ever have to read the paper he would have written if he had done it himself: "The paper should be well planned, well organized, and should indicate serious thought."

Conc

Irny / Sarc

CONSIDERATIONS

What point does Rosenberg make by citing that the professors he talked with did not know of *any* cases of bought research being turned in to them? How justified is the claim of Stephen Mindell, of the Bureau of Consumer Frauds in New York, that the real problem lies with the schools themselves? What part does morality and ethics play in this controversy? Is the term-paper industry an inevitable spin-off from the college and university system of today? What long-term effects might articles such as Rosenberg's have on school policies regarding term-paper requirements?

What is the overall tone of this article? What specific rhetorical devices help set that tone and maintain it consistently from beginning to end? What about the extensive use of dialog? The narrative technique? The frequent use of analogy (paragraph 28), simile (paragraph 29), metaphor (paragraphs 18, 19, and 28), and sarcasm? (paragraph 32)

The largest single indictment presented in this article is that most schools offer "precious little inducement" (paragraph 64) for their students not to take advantage of store-bought, made-to-order term-papers. To what extent do you agree or disagree that this is the case? Are term papers valuable or intrinsically worthwhile from the student's

point of view? What alternatives could replace the term-paper requirement in most courses? Support your opinions with reasoned argument
and facts.

VOCABULARY

(16) **bizarre**   markedly unusual; strange, odd, or eccentric

(21) **preeminent**   above others; supreme; peerless

(24) **pedantic**   inappropriately or overly learned or scholarly

(28) **entrepreneurs**   organizers or managers of business enterprises

(28) **lumpen**   of or pertaining to disenfranchised and uprooted individuals or groups, especially those who have lost status
in their class

(28) **proletariat**   the working class, especially those who must sell
their labor in order to survive

(31) **residuals**   additional pay given to an author for repeated sales,
or use, of his work

(31) **compunction**   any uneasiness or hesitation about the righteousness of an action; remorse for wrongdoing

(31) **ad hoc**   for this special purpose only

(61) **chicanery**   trickery or deception by the use of clever devices

Jokes Negroes Tell on Themselves

LANGSTON HUGHES

1   They say once there was a Negro in Atlanta who had made up his mind to commit suicide, so one day he went down to the main street and took the freight elevator up to the top of the highest building in town, in fact, the highest skyscraper in Georgia. Negroes could not ride the passenger elevators, but he was so anxious to commit suicide that he did not let Jim Crow stand in his way. He rode as freight. Once at the top of the building, he took off his coat, drew a deep breath, approached the ledge and jumped off. He went hurtling through the air and was just about to hit the sidewalk when he saw a white woman come around the corner. He knew he had better not fall on that white woman, so he curved and went right on back up.

2   There was another Negro who one day came to a strange town in Mississippi where he had never been before. When he got off the bus he did not see any of the race around, so he asked a white man, "Where do the colored folks hang out here?"

3   The white man pointed at a great big tree in the public square and said, "Do you see that limb?"

4   Negroes in Arkansas, when you ask them what life is like in Tennessee, will tell you the white folks are so bad in Memphis that black folks can't even drink white milk. But if you ask Negroes in Tennessee what it is like in Arkansas, they will say, "Man, in that

state you better not even put your black feet in no white shoes!"

5   There are innumerable variations on the use of the word *white* in the South. They say, for example (presumably in fun), that the reason Negroes eat so many black-eyed peas in Dixie, and in Louisiana so many red beans, is because for years after the Emancipation, colored people did not dare ask a storekeeper for white beans. Red beans or black-eyed peas, okay. But it was not until folks began using the term *navy beans*, that Negroes had the nerve to purchase white beans, too. In a Wylie Avenue hash-house one day I heard a Negro say to another one at the counter, "Here you are up North ordering white bean soup. Man, I know you are really free now." Everybody laughed.*

6   Some of these types of jokes are even laid on animals. They say there was once a black cat in Mobile who decided to head for Chicago because he had always heard that up North there was no color line. Hardly had that cat gotten to Chicago than he met a white cat. Desirous of being shown about a bit,

> The black cat said to the white cat,
> "Let's go round the town."
> But the white cat said to the black cat,
> "You better set your black self down."

7   In some places, so another pleasantry goes, white folks are so mean they will not give a Negro the time of day. A colored man said to a white man, "What time is it, sir?"

8   The white man asked the Negro, "Do you play chess?"

9   The Negro said, "Yes, sir."

10   The white man said, "Then it's your time to move."

11   These, and hundreds of other jokes of a similar nature which Negroes tell on themselves, belong in the category of:

> White is right,
> Yellow mellow,
> But black, get back!

---

*One of the most interesting Negro jokes about "white" culture concerns a young Negro girl who addresses a question to a mirror on a wall: "Mirror, mirror on the wall, who's the fairest one of all?" And the mirror answers, "Snow White, you black bitch, and don't you forget it." This text suggests the futility of Negroes attempting to use white folklore. White folklore, symbolized by the fairy tale of Snow White (Aarne-Thompson tale type 709) reflects white society, not black. The very name of the heroine demonstrates again the built-in symbolic color bias of "white" society. The moral, so-to-speak, is that Negroes should not expect to get ego support from white stories with magical mirrors which continue to reflect the same old prejudice. Negroes need to have recourse to their own folklore where, with cultural mirrors like "The blacker the berry, the sweeter the juice," they can take pride in being black: "I'm black and I'm proud." "Black is Beautiful!"

12   Their humor is the humor of frustration and the laughter with which these sallies are greeted, for all its loudness, is a desperate laughter. White people often do not understand such humor at all. Negroes do, and such jokes told at appropriate moments amuse them no end.

13   Shortly after the big Detroit race riots, a cartoon appeared in a Negro newspaper that Harlemites thought highly, if wryly, hilarious. But no white person to whom I have ever shown it even cracks a smile, let alone laughs aloud. The cartoon pictures a wall in a sportsman's den on which the heads of the game he has bagged are hung—a deer's head, an elk's head, a tiger's head. Among them, mounted like the others, is a Negro head. Two little white boys are looking at the head. One little boy, pointing at the Negro's head, tells the other youngster, "My daddy got that one in Detroit last week."

14   Most such jokes, however, are at the expense of the South. In Harlem they say a young mother-to-be, about to bear her first child, decided to go back down South to be with her mother when the great event came. Her young husband tried to keep her from going, pointing out to her that aside from having better hospital facilities, New York had no Jim Crow wards, and colored physicians could attend patients in the hospitals. In the South one often has to have a white doctor since many hospitals there will not permit Negro doctors to practice inside their walls. Still the expectant mother insisted on going home to mama.

15   The father in Harlem waited and waited for news of the birth of his child. No news came. The ninth month passed. The tenth month passed. Finally he phoned his wife and told her something must be wrong, to go to the hospital anyhow and be examined. She went. The white physician marvelled that her child had not yet come. Putting his earphones to his ears and baring her abdomen, he pressed his instrument against her flesh to listen for the pre-natal heartbeats of the unborn child. Instead, what he heard, quite clearly and distinctly inside the body of the mother, was a Sugar Chile Robinson type of voice singing the blues:

> I won't be born down here!
> I won't be born down here!
> If you want to know
> What it's all about—
> As long as South is South,
> I won't come out!
> No, I won't be born down here!

He wasn't. She had to come on back to New York to have her baby. Harlemites swear that that colored child had plenty of sense.

16   A great many jokes with which Negroes regale each other, but seldom tell white folks, are hardly complimentary to racial intelligence. Jokes relating to tardiness are among them. Some such jokes even go so far as to blame the darkness of race upon a lack of punctuality on that morning long ago in the dawning of creation when the Lord called upon mankind to wash in the River of Life. They say that everybody promptly went down to the water to wash—except the Negroes. The Negroes lingered and loitered along the way, dallied and played, and took their own good time getting down to the river. When they got there, the other folks had used up all the water and had emerged whiter than snow. In the river bed after so much washing, the Negroes found only a little mud. Into the mud they waded with their bare feet. Late, in their desperation, they bent down and put the palms of their hands in the mud, too. By that time, even the mud was used up. Therefore, to this day, nothing is light about Negroes except the palms of their hands and the soles of their feet. Late, always late.

17   Other jokes relate to behavior and how a Negro (insofar as these jokes go) will always snarl things up, even in heaven. They say the first time a Negro went to heaven, all the other angels became excited when they heard he was coming and had prepared a great welcome for him. Even Saint Peter and the Lord were moved at the prospect of greeting the first member of the darkest race into celestial glory. In honor of the occasion the Gates of Pearl were shining and the Streets of Gold had been polished until each cobblestone gleamed. But what did that Negro do?

18   That Negro was so excited when he first got his wings that he took off then and there at top speed and would not stop flying. He flew, and he flew, and he flew, and he flew. In his crown of gold and his snow white robes he lifted up his wings and flew like mad from the East to the West, from the North to the South, up and down and all throughout the universe. He whizzed by the Golden Throne at 100 miles per hour, wings spread like a Constellation. He flew around God's footstool so fast the Cherubims thought he was greased lightening. He went past Saint Peter at such speed that he started a tailwind up the Golden Streets. Finally Saint Peter said, "Whoa!" But that Negro did not stop.

19   Peter sent a band of angels out to catch him but they could not get anywhere near the Negro. Gabriel blew his horn but he paid him no mind. He was a flying soul! He made wings do what wings

had never been known to do before. He looped a loop in the sky, then he looped another loop, and tied a knot. That Negro was gone, solid gone! He scattered feathers all over heaven and stirred up such a gale that the Lord God himself stood up and cried, "Stop!"

20   When he stopped, that Negro skidded bang! into the Pearly Gates, broke one wing smack off, knocked his crown into eternity, snagged his robes wide open, and fell panting at the foot of the Throne.

21   Saint Peter just looked at him and said, "Just like a Negro!"*

22   In the category of the bawdy joke there are hundreds illustrating the prevalent folk belief in the amorous prowess of the Negro male. Many such jokes cut across the color line in boastful fashion. They say a white man came home one cold winter night to find his golden blond wife on the living room divan deep in the loving arms of a great big dark Negro. Petrified, in his astonishment the white man forgot to close the front door. The icy winds rushed in. Thinking his wife was being raped, in a frenzy he cried, "Darling, what shall I do to this Negro?"

23   She sighed from the couch, "Just shut the door so he won't catch cold."

24   Even in hell, according to the joke makers, a Negro is hell. Since for so long Negroes had had such a hard time on earth, as compensation, up until the end of the Civil War all of them automatically went to heaven when they died. But after Lincoln signed the Emancipation Proclamation and things got a little easier for Negroes on this globe, the Lord decided to send a few colored folks to hell. The first Negro consigned to the Devil was a tall strapping man of color who in his day had been a great lover from St. Louis to the Gulf. Because his boudoir skills left him so little time for grace, the Lord said, "Send that Negro to hell." So Peter threw him out of heaven.

25   No sooner did the Negro set foot in hell than he grabbed the Devil's daughter and ruined her. Ten minutes later he enticed the Devil's wife behind a hot rock and ruined her. About this time the Devil's mother came along. The Negro grabbed her and ruined her.

---

*In a version of this joke reported in William H. Grier and Price M. Cobbs, *Black Rage*, there is a different ending. After flying around heaven in reckless fashion "scaring the hell out of cherubim and seraphim," the newly arrived Negro is grounded by "the management" and his wings removed. A black brother comes along and scolds him for having abused his privileges: "and now here you sit grounded with no wings!" The protagonist's response is, "But I was a flying son of a bitch while I had 'em, wasn't I!"

The Devil suddenly became aware of this mighty despoilation. Trembling, for the first time since he had been ruler of hell, he fell to his knees and called on God for help, "Lord *please*, take this Negro out of here before he ruins me!"

26   Whether or not hell then began to draw the color line, the story does not say. But Negro jokes often draw a color line through their humor in such a fashion that only a Negro can appreciate them. Certain aspects of the humor of minority groups are often so inbred that they are not palatable for outside consumption. There are thousands of Jewish jokes that rarely reach the ears of Gentiles, and if they did they might be embarrassing to the ears of both groups. So it is with Negro humor—a part of it is intended only for Negroes. To others such jokes are seldom funny anyhow. The point is lost for often the nuances are too subtle for alien comprehension. A joke is not a joke when nobody laughs.

CONSIDERATIONS

All of the jokes quoted in this selection are miniature allegories. Analyze each one, placing it in historical and social perspective: which ones are directed at all whites? At the U.S. in general? At the South? At blacks? Hughes says some of these are jokes born of desperation (paragraph 11); even today you find few whites who can laugh with blacks at Negro jokes. Why would "liberal" whites not laugh at the "big game" joke in paragraph 13?

This selection was published in 1951. If Hughes or a contemporary author were to publish such a collection of jokes today, what differences in presentation would there be? Would there be extensive use of dialect? By using restrained language, has Hughes limited his audience to whites? How might blacks today react to this style?

Hughes points out that ethnic jokes very often derive much or part of their humor from the fact that they are intended only for insiders (paragraph 26). Discuss humor (anecdotes, jokes, and so on) in two parts—how it helps to unify diverse groups of people, and how ethnic jokes are a symptom of the desire for class or group identity. If you are a member of a particular ethnic group, what does the humor of that group mean to you? Does it keep you separate from outsiders and unify the members of the group?

VOCABULARY

(22) **prowess**   exceptional or superior ability
(26) **palatable**   acceptable or pleasing to the taste
(26) **nuances**   subtle shades of meaning

America's New Superstars—They Shout "No!" to Tradition

DAVID SHAW

1 Americans have always been a fiercely competitive and uniquely vicarious people—basking in the reflected glory of others' triumphs, sharing and paying homage to the class and spirit of a Kennedy, the wealth and power of a Hughes, the courage and daring of a Patton, the glamor and mystery of a Garbo.

2 But nowhere, on a day-to-day basis, have Americans been more worshipful of the big winner—the champion—than in the arena of athletic combat. For generations, Americans have thrilled to the exploits of Babe Ruth and Jack Dempsey, Red Grange and Joe Louis, Willie Mays and Ben Hogan and Bob Cousy and Joe Di-Maggio.

3 They competed at different times, under different conditions, in different sports, and yet, somehow, they all seemed to fit the same basic Jack Armstrong mold—heroic but self-effacing, idolized but modest—clean-cut, clean-living . . . men playing boys' games, and gleefully grateful for the opportunity to do so.

4 Come now America's newest sports champions—chess king Bobby Fischer and Olympian swimmer Mark Spitz—who have shattered stereotypes, as well as records. Both are representative of a new breed of sports hero. They are individualists, iconoclasts, mavericks—cocky to the point of arrogance—and they join Muhammad Ali, Joe Namath, Kareem Abdul-Jabbar, Dick Allen, Billie Jean

King and a host of other contemporary sports heroes who have, in effect, rejected the traditional Boy Scout-as-superstar image.

5   Dempsey didn't serve in the Army during World War I, but he spent much of his career trying to hide that, not trumpeting it throughout the world as a political cause the way Ali has done.

6   Louis and Mays are black, but neither has made blackness a crusade the way Ali and Abdul-Jabbar have done.

7   Ruth often drank himself into a stupor, and DiMaggio wooed and won (and lost) Marilyn Monroe, but neither man gave out interviews boasting of his favorite brand of liquor and his latest sexual contest the way Namath has done.

8   And who could imagine Mays or Cousy saying he didn't really enjoy his sport (as Spitz said in Munich), Hogan or Grange denouncing American imperialism (as Ali and Abdul-Jabbar have done), DiMaggio or Sandy Koufax threatening to boycott the World Series (as Fischer did the chess tourney).

9   The one characteristic, above all, that sets the new breed of sports hero apart from his predecessor is brashness—sheer, unadulterated gall. He's good and he knows it and he sees no reason to adhere to the hypocrisy of false modesty so long expected of champions. After all, Babe Ruth called his shot on that one home run in the 1932 World Series, but he didn't make a habit of predicting the defeat—and utter humiliation—of his opponents, as Fischer and Spitz and Namath and Ali have so consistently done.

10   An argument could be made, of course, that Fischer and Spitz don't fit the new mold any more than they fit the old one—that chess is not really a sport at all, an exercise more cerebral than physical, and that swimmers have never been accorded the same pedestal in the pantheon of sports heroes as boxers and baseball, football and basketball players.

11   But one glance at Fischer's long, arduous training schedule—physical and emotional, as well as mental—dispels any notion that chess, whatever else it is, is not a sport, too. And Spitz's rightful position among the new sports heroes, if not as secure as Fischer's, is at least as obvious as his Omar Sharif moustache (try picturing Babe Ruth with a moustache), his swaggering bravado in Mexico City in 1968 and his detached indifference in Munich in 1972. Nor is Spitz America's first Olympic swimming hero; remember Johnny Weissmuller?

12   Admittedly, Fischer and Spitz do have one advantage over the Namaths and Alis; they carry America's colors into international competition—against the Russians, among others—and the kind of

fan most likely to resent their departure from the stereotype of old is precisely the sort of fan whose own conservative nature and traditional impulses all but compel him to root for them anyway. He can jeer at Namath, but he's just too steeped in tradition, too much the chauvinist, to root for Boris Spassky against Bobby Fischer, however reprehensible he might otherwise find Fischer's behavior.

13   But what of the others in the new breed—the Namaths and Alis and Allens and Abdul-Jabbars, the new champions who don't have the emotional pull of patriotism to offset their often-harsh iconoclasm? They are criticized, but they are more frequently idolized, and that, most assuredly, would not have been the case thirty or twenty or even ten years ago. Then they would have been jeered as prima donnas, not cheered as heroes.

14   (Need an example? Just look at how poorly Ted Williams generally fared in the inevitable comparisons with Joe DiMaggio and Stan Musial. He may have been respected, albeit grudgingly, for his hitting ability, but they were respected—revered—as men, Jack Armstrong types, by fans and sportswriters alike. Unlike Williams, they didn't go around spitting, swearing, making obscene gestures and calling a United States senator "a gutless son of a bitch.")

15   It's not so difficult to understand what forces have created the new breed of sports heroes—the Ted Williamses of today. Their outspoken confidence is born, in part, of security and experience; they expect to win in sports because they have usually won in life. Unlike many of their predecessors, they didn't live through a Depression, and—even for blacks, as bleak as life often still is—conditions are clearly better now than they were a generation or two ago.

16   More significantly, however, most athletes are young, and young people in the 1970s—like blacks, women and other groups and institutions in contemporary society—are in revolt, changing, fragmenting, regrouping, trying desperately to right many of the ancient wrongs, to replace exploitation with equality, oppression with opportunity.

17   Ali, in that sense, is no different from any angry black in the ghetto, Namath no different from any swinging student on campus, Billie Jean King no different from any stifled housewife in suburbia.

18   They are all, these new breed, saying, shouting, "NO!" to tradition—whether it's the "NO!" Ali and Abdul-Jabbar say to racial discrimination, the "NO!" Namath says to repressively hypocritical and Puritanical mores or the "NO!" Ms. King and Dick Allen say to the practice of treating people as property.

19   And when they say "NO!" the television cameras are there to record it, to exploit it, to force-feed it to the world, and the reaction

that sets in encourages more of the same. Babe Ruth might have had a few complaints, too, but he just couldn't call a nationwide, televised press conference to voice them, so few people beyond the Yankee front office ever heard them.

20   But if the personal and political iconoclasm of the new breed is understandable, the public's general acceptance of the new breed is surprising.

21   The typical sports fan, you'll agree, is more likely to be a beer-guzzling TV addict who sneers at long hair and snarls at black militance than a free-thinking, free-loving radical or intellectual who embraces the new morality and the new politics. Why, then, with a few exceptions, does he continue to cheer for the Fischers and Namaths and Alis?

22   One possible explanation is that the sports fan looks on the athlete as ONLY an athlete, a body, and sees his on-the-field performance as an exercise, a game, a fantasy that has little relation to the problems and complexities of the real world. If the athlete wants to make speeches or predictions—or women—off the field, well, he reasons, who the hell cares?

23   A second explanation of the phenomenon is most sports fans tend to exalt excellence beyond behavior.

24   When a quarterback can throw a football with the speed and precision of a Joe Namath, the fans—most of them—will forgive his cock-sure demeanor and bacchanalian life style.

25   When a fighter can jab and dance with the speed and precision of a Muhammad Ali, the fans—most of them—will forgive his boastfulness and radicalism.

26   When any athlete can perform with the sustained brilliance and domination of a Bobby Fischer, a Kareem Abdul-Jabbar, a Billie Jean King, the fans—most of them—will forgive their stubborn independence, unyielding demands and temperamental eccentricities.

27   But there is more than this to public acceptance—even adulation—of the new breed. The explanation goes far deeper, into the very fabric of contemporary society.

28   Increasingly, over the past decade, America has become a congested, contentious society, overcrowded, aswirl with the mind-numbing conflict between bigger and bigger problems and bigger and bigger institutions.

29   We have become, in a word, depersonalized. Many people, sports fans among them, no longer feel like individual human beings, each with some measure of control over his destiny. They feel, instead, like integers, numbers, ciphers—deprived of their human-

ity, overwhelmed by the sheer size and complexity of everyday life, powerless to say or do anything of consequence.

30   Thus entrapped, they live vicariously through the off-the-field behavior, as well as the on-the-field performance, of today's superstar athletes.

31   Where once they were content to be Walter Mitty in football pads, throwing the game-winning touchdown pass, now they want to be Mitty-like off the field, too, joining Joe Namath when he drinks the best scotch, sleeps with the prettiest women and—most important of all—says precisely what he thinks and gets precisely what he wants.

32   The fan may resent Ali's refusal to go to war or Fischer's insistence on pristine playing conditions or even Abdul-Jabbar's name change, but he envies their ability to do such things and not only survive but thrive.

33   The fan has trouble getting a plumber when he needs one, can't talk to his own son and feels as impotent in his office as at the polls, and here's Ali standing off the United States Army, Spitz saying he's the best in the world and proving it, Fischer humiliating the Russians, Namath lolling in a king-size bed filled with booze and broads and bread.

34   You gotta hand it to them, he thinks.

35   And you're gonna keep on handing it to them. There will be more of the new breed, not fewer, in the foreseeable future.

36   Jack Armstrong is dead! Long live Bobby Muhammad Namath!

CONSIDERATIONS

Do you agree that the athletes mentioned in this article are all characterized by brashness and gall? (paragraph 9) Can you cite specific examples that tie these athletes together in the eyes of the general public? Billie Jean King is the only woman mentioned; with the growing feminist movements of today, do you think there will be more female antiheroes in sports?

Shaw makes a series of comparisons in this article relating the new breed of athlete to the old, the new athlete to the sports fan, and athletics to society in general. Analyze his observations. How appropriate are the comparisons? The theme of vicarious experience unifies the entire series of comparisons. Why is it an effective transitional device?

How do you react personally to the athletes described in this article? Formulate your feelings in an essay.

VOCABULARY

(3) **self-effacing**   humble; staying in the background
(4) **iconoclasts**   persons who attack cherished beliefs and traditional institutions
(10) **cerebral**   characterized by the use of intellect
(10) **pantheon**   the realm of the heroes venerated by any group
(12) **chauvinist**   a zealous, belligerent patriot
(12) **reprehensible**   deserving of reproof; blameworthy
(24) **bacchanalian**   noisily drunken; carousing
(28) **contentious**   quarrelsome; tending to argue

Definition

DEFINITION

In conversation and in comments from your English teacher you often hear or read, "What do you mean by that? Define your terms!" To define is to limit, to set bounds for the use of a word. Like classification, definition is a natural process, one we use in ordinary speech almost without thinking.

Definition is a major concern in writing. It isn't the quantity of words that determines the success of clear writing—very often the less said the better. But exact words clarify by establishing a common ground of understanding between you and your reader; they help transfer to his mind the image or idea you have in yours.

When you write the word *man*, you limit your subject; you have located your subject in terms of its larger class, species, or group. You may have a lot more defining to do, but at least you are rejecting other images—your reader is not going to see a giraffe or an automobile or a bumblebee when you say *man*. What happens if you say *black*? Does this create a more precise image? What if you say *black man*? That limits or defines the image even further.

Classification can help define a word. You can define *teacher* by classifying *teacher* according to characteristics: human, adult, worker, professional, one who instructs others.

A word can be defined by description and exemplification. Amphibia are vertebrates that live part of their lives in the water, part on land. You can also define amphibia by giving examples: frogs, newts, salamanders, and so on.

A word can be defined by analysis; that is, by describing its component parts. For example, a hot fudge sundae is made up of ice cream, chocolate sauce, chopped nuts, and a lot of other stuff on top. A word that involves a process or sequence of events may be defined operationally. Photosynthesis is a process in which light acts on chlorophyll in plant leaves to produce carbohydrates.

A word can be defined by what it is not—by contrast. A horse is *not* a mule or a zebra.

Most words can be defined by several of these methods, depending on the purpose, the speaker, and the audience. *Foot* may be defined differently by you, by a doctor, and by a mathematician.

Yard may be defined differently by a child, a fabric salesperson, or a cement manufacturer.

You should be careful in using synonyms to define words. A quick trip to Roget's Thesaurus may not always be the best means to an end. If you give *nuncupation* as a defining synonym for *orismology*, you may accomplish nothing (or *pundit* for *luminary*, *bedlamite* for *energumen*).

Whether it be a one-word synonym, a paragraph, or an essay exploring the infinite details of meaning, a definition should always aim at answering the questions: What is it and what does it mean?

PRACTICE

1. Write an extended definition—a theme of 500 words or so—of an abstract concept such as relevance, pleasure, happiness, success, progress, morality, personal responsibility, or duty. Use the methods discussed in this section as your guideline.

2. Define at least two of the important terms used in a recent political speech, such as "the easiest course," "criminals at heart," "peace with honor," or "an equitable balance of trade."

Chicano Is Beautiful

The author of this essay defines *honor* in terms of the Latin American culture (paragraph 18). Write a definition of an abstract concept such as beauty, truth, power, happiness, superiority. Try to use exact words in order to create a definite image or idea for the reader.

I Look at the Audience

The author defines *tragic and comic* as including "all forms of drama" (paragraph 12). "Tragic" and "comic" are also classifications. Write an essay in which you define a word or term through classification. (For example, you might define a play by classifying it according to certain qualities: an imitation of life, entertainment, a story told by actors, a theatrical performance, or a dramatic art.) Following are some suggested words and terms:

sign and symbol

"vibes"

war of attrition

culture

Jim Crow

- Write a definition of something by means of analysis; that is, by breaking down the thing or idea into its component parts. For example, you can define a symphony orchestra by describing the various instruments and the roles of the musicians and the conductor.

- Write an essay defining some aspect of student life in which you use the methods of classification, description, and exemplification to extend your definition.

For examples of individual paragraphs using *definition*, see p.29, ¶13, p.59, ¶12, p.108, ¶7, p.208, ¶13, p.329, ¶5, p.332, ¶16, p.353, ¶20, p.382, ¶6, p.446, ¶17–19.

Chicano Is Beautiful

CELIA S. HELLER

1   The Mexican Americans share with the Blacks in the United States   *C ∅ C*
the common situation of being a large disadvantaged minority.
Both rank way below the majority group in occupation, income,
and education. Also, Mexican Americans like American Blacks are
characterized by ghetto life, little intergenerational advancement,
and home socialization that is dissonant with the socialization received at school.

2   The above has led liberals in general, and some social scientists   *C ∅ E*
in particular, to lump Mexican Americans and Blacks together and
to assume that they would fit together because of common interests
(interests in the Marxist sense of the term). Significantly, the fact
that they are disadvantaged minorities has seldom brought them
together and—in the rare instances when they came in contact for a
common cause—has not proved sufficient to hold them together. In   *Exmp*
regard to the latter, the examples of the March on Washington or
the divisions within the Third World Liberation Front are very
much to the point. As for the first, by and large Mexican Americans
have kept apart from the Negro struggle for equality. The sharp
example is that of Mexican Americans voting heavily in California
in November of 1964 for Proposition 14, to outlaw *anti*-discrimina-
tion legislation in housing. Fernando Penalosa, a Mexican sociologist, explained this vote thus: "Mexican Americans apparently failed

to realize that the measure was directed against them as well as against the Negroes."

3   Central to the understanding of what divides these groups is the exploration of the self-identity of each. My main theme here is *This* that the basis, the manifestations and problems of identity among Mexican Americans are essentially different from those among Blacks. I am fully aware that there are today very vocal Mexican American youths who are beginning to emulate the rhetoric and the tactics of Black militants, but I want to stress that this is emulation and it is a conscious and purposive emulation.

4   The rhetoric and the tactics of Black militancy have emerged *C & E* from the Negroes' desperate search for identity to counteract long-nurtured inferiority feelings. As is recognized by Stokely Carmi- *Anly* chael, the author of the phrase, Black Power represents more than an attempt to raise the socio-economic status of the Negro: it aims at the improvement of the Negro's self-image. Martin Luther King who rejected its strategies nevertheless acknowledged that Black Power expresses "a psychological call to manhood."

5   In contrast, Mexican Americans who are adopting Black Pow- *C & C* er's tactics do so mainly in order to improve the socio-economic conditions of Mexican Americans. Their reasoning is very pragmatic: these tactics have yielded results for Blacks while the usual Mexican American responses have not brought comparable results. They point to such examples as the following: although there are about twice as many Mexican Americans as Negroes in California, in the Berkeley Opportunity Program Negroes outnumber Mexican Americans nine to one.

6   Black militancy represents a pattern hitherto not manifested by any immigrant group in the United States. But then the Negroes' status as a minority in the United States was not brought about by immigration but, in a sense, by conquest. Thus they resemble in their history and in their responses more the pattern of colonial peoples than immigrant groups in the United States. Mexican Americans, on the other hand, largely fit the pattern of immigrant groups. True, the areas in which Mexican Americans are concentrated originally belonged to Mexico. But the Mexican American population of today consists mostly of immigrants and children or grandchildren of immigrants. They, unlike the Blacks, were not brought here by force but, like other immigrants, came here to improve their lot.

7   Recent immigrants to the United States, irrespective of country of origin, are generally concentrated at the bottom of the socio-

economic ladder. Among many ethnic groups, the process of moving toward the occupational distribution of the majority population
starts with the second generation; among a few groups, such as Jews
and Japanese, it begins in the first generation, and among others
later. The findings of my empirical study on mobility-oriented
youth, as well as other studies, suggests a new trend toward upward
mobility which would indicate that Mexican Americans do not constitute an exception to the pattern of intergenerational advancement. The process of responding to the American ideology of advancement observed in all other immigrant groups is similarly
reenacted here although it took longer to initiate it. What typically
took place in immigrant groups in the second generation is now
occurring among third- and fourth-generation Mexican Americans.

8   One of the factors that slowed down Mexican American mobility and is closely tied to the question of ethnic identity is that, in a
sense, "passing" was easier for Mexican Americans than other immigrant groups. Accomplished Mexican Americans had a ready-made
road which they could follow and spare themselves many of the
hardships experienced particularly by Negroes but also the descen-
dants of foreign laborers and peasants in general. They could claim
to be "Old Spanish" and thus be acceptable in the higher strata of
American society, if only their Indian mixture did not betray them.
The presence in the Southwest of the alternate definition, "Old
Spanish," without the disparaging connotation of "Mexican" provided "a ready rationalization for the vertically mobile individuals
and the host population." Often it even spared the Mexican Americans the trouble of name-changing since the Spanish name carried a
prestige value in the higher circles of the Southwest. This is connected with the widespread "Hispano" myth.

9   But the claim to be "Old Spanish" which proved so advanta-
geous to individual Mexican Americans proved disadvantageous for
the Mexican American community. It slowed down the process of
upward mobility for Mexican Americans as a whole. This practice
deprived the younger generation of success models and success heroes. Noteworthy is the absence among Mexican Americans of a
folklore of success comparable to that which exists among other
immigrant groups in the United States: the poor Mexican from the
ghetto who made good.

10   There are indications, however, that the pattern of the successful Mexican Americans' forsaking the community is being abandoned. Actually the change is a postwar phenomenon. The ex-G.I.'s
returning from war must have remembered that they fought on

foreign battlefields, and many of their comrades died there, without having to claim to be "Old Spanish." At any rate, many of the returning G.I.'s who were determined to advance, chose not to take the road of "passing" as "Old Spanish." Thus a number of men, who have achieved prominence since World War II, have maintained and emphasized their ties with the Mexican American community.

11   As for the mobility-oriented Mexican American boys whom I interviewed in the summer of 1965, none of them thought that they would follow the road of "Old Spanish" and give up their Mexican American identity. While the choice of breaking with the community does not yet present itself as an actual alternative to the ambitious youngsters (as we said, it comes to those who have reached some prominence), the alternate definition, calling oneself "Spanish," does tempt them. It presents itself in the experience of not being recognized as being Mexican, being referred to as Spanish, being told that one is the exception among Mexicans. The thought is born that one could, if one wanted to, not be Mexican any longer.

12   As Everett Hughes put it, this is the kind of betrayal to which we are all subject in some degree. Use of the alternate designation may pave the way for an eventual break with the Mexican American community. Surely it would be a smoother transition for the person who heard himself designated as Spanish and referring to himself as Spanish to add, when the proper time came, "Old" to the designation. But it is far from easy, psychologically speaking, for a youth to begin to consider himself Spanish, especially when at home he has been taught to "be proud" of being Mexican.

13   Let me illustrate from the interview with Joe Valdez (fictitious name), a nineteen-year-old Los Angeles high school graduate working as a dental technician. He related:

14   "I work in Beverly Hills. I went to cash my check in a bank. *Anec* There was a lady there: her name was Vargas. And I don't know what got into me. Instead of asking her whether she is Mexican I asked her: 'Are you Spanish?' She got kind of annoyed. 'No,' she said, 'I'm Mexican.' It was kind of shocking. I got thinking. I asked her if she was Spanish; deep inside I didn't want to offend her; I didn't want to hurt her feelings (by asking her if she was Mexican). I thought about it and I felt like a fool. She said, 'No, I'm Mexican.' Just like that."

15   Although no exact studies exist on this subject, observers agree that "Spanish" as a self-designation is on the wane among young

Mexican Americans. As a matter of fact, the term "Chicano," formerly confined to use only when in the presence of other Mexican Americans, is now gaining prominence as a general designation.

16   We know that "passing" is only one of the ways—and an infrequent one—in which marginal people try to solve the problems of marginality. The Mexican American youths of today, often third- and fourth-generation Americans, are facing the problems of marginality and assimilation which many other immigrant groups met in the second generation. Their identity is imbedded in the Mexican culture and their concern is with being American. How different this is from the concern of the Negroes!

17   The question of being American is not problematical for Blacks: they are preoccupied with creating an identity. Through slavery, the Blacks, who were forcefully brought to America, were stripped of their native cultures. Their tribal organization, religion, family life and language were systematically destroyed. Black militants are trying to reconstruct quickly a heritage and a past. But Mexican Americans possess fairly structured images of their past. And they have retained important elements of the Mexican heritage, including the language.

18   Take the element of honor, so central in Latin American culture, which Mexican Americans have continued to adhere to. Honor, in their conception, is tied to an inner integrity which every person is supposed to have as part of his Latin-American birthright and which he is to guard jealously against all. The separate system of honor has protected Mexican Americans psychologically—as it has some other immigrant groups such as Jews and Japanese—against the effects of stigmatization by the larger society. Ethnicity and race are to a large measure considered to carry a stigma in the United States. But the separate Mexican American system of honor—like that of some other immigrant groups—has cushioned the blows that accompany stigmatization. This contrasts sharply with the situation of the Negro who neither possesses a cultural mechanism for cushioning stigmatization nor the possibility of escaping it through "passing." The recent slogans of "Black is beautiful" and its manifestations represent a conscious attempt to forge such a mechanism.

19   The commitment to the Mexican value of honor can serve to illustrate the larger proposition that Mexican culture has continued to have a hold on third- and fourth-generation Mexican Americans to a degree that the ethnic culture has not on the third- or fourth-

C&C

Def

Prem

generation of other large immigrant groups, including Jews. Thus, Mexican American youth faces the problems of cultural conflict that other groups faced in the second generation. Its solutions, however, are not typical second-generation solutions.

Tran

20   The typical second-generation solution of other immigrant groups was the rejection of the parental culture, especially the parental language. To the immigrant parents the ethnic culture was a way of life, in great measure unquestioned. The second generation viewed it as a 'dead hand of the past' and tended to perceive the parental language and customs as obstacles standing in the way of their full Americanization. However, as Nahirny and Fishman explain, "the very attempt of some of the sons to cut loose all the ties that bound them to the ethnic community reflected their manifold involvement in it." They were rooted in the ethnic culture which they consciously rejected.

Anly

21   Similar to the second generation and in contrast to the third and fourth generation of other immigrant groups, Mexican American youths are characterized by a manifold involvement in their ethnic community. And yet they do not manifest the extensive rejection of the parental culture that characterized the second generation of immigrants. Furthermore, since Mexican Americans have not gone through a stage of purposive estrangement from the traditional culture to the extent that other immigrant groups have, they are not likely to develop the kind of "rediscovery" of the traditional culture that has been peculiar in the third generation. The usual pattern in America is that the ethnic heritage and language cease to play a viable role in the third generation. The grandchildren of immigrants are largely untouched by the culture of their grandparents. But some of them find what their parents rejected interesting (in an exotic sense) and try to revive certain aspects of it. The third generation's revival lacks, however, the emotional depth that marked the rejection of the ethnic culture by the second generation.

C & C

Anly

22   The Mexican American response to marginality is not that of rejecting the traditional culture and language. Neither is it that of a rediscovery of the parental culture and language in the manner manifested in the third generation of other immigrant groups, described above. The typical Mexican American response to marginality is rather that of combining the ethnic status with the status of American in a way as to broaden and redefine the latter: to reduce "both the inner dilemma and the outward contradiction" of the two statuses.

C & E

Evolution of an Idea

23   How has this response evolved? Following World War II, an idea emerged among Mexican Americans, the idea of "the best of two worlds." Some mobile Mexican Americans were voicing this sentiment and searching for ways to combine what they considered best in the parental and the host cultures. But in the late Fifties and beginning Sixties it seemed that this response was being overshadowed by the typical second-generation response of rejecting the parental language and customs. Nevertheless, in the last few years the "best of the two worlds" response has become the dominant one. I *Prem* am convinced that the Negroes' search for identity was a strong influence in this direction. Mexican Americans gained a new appreciation for the ethnic identity to which they were heirs when they saw how hard Blacks were trying to shape an ethnic identity.

24   When I interviewed mobility-oriented boys in the summer of *Top S* 1965, I was struck by their preoccupation with the issue of how to be American and yet retain some elements of the Mexican culture. They felt American and wanted to be considered as such. However, in contrast to the sparse mobility-oriented Mexican Americans of the past generations, they did not reject their heritage but valued some of its features. This came out convincingly at various points of the interviews. Let me illustrate from the interview with Ricardo Montez, an eighteen-year-old who had just completed a year's work at a major university:

25   "They say you are culturally deprived, a stupid term. It's just *Dict* another thing that after a while you just laugh at. It shows the mentality of the people who use it. How in heaven can you be culturally deprived when you have lived in one culture and inherited another one? You are bicultural, you are bilingual, and you are 'culturally disadvantaged'. . . . The way I look at it, you're caged *Meta* within one culture and you don't necessarily have to be. . . . You are actually in a cage. . . . But if you have two cultures and you are drawing from both of them, you don't necessarily have to take one thing because it's there. You find what's more useful from one culture or the other and you take it."

26   Another eighteen-year-old, Peter Camacho, who had just graduated from an industrial course in high school and hoped to be an electrical engineer, had this to say:

27   "I think even the Irish or Jewish had at one time to prove themselves. There was a time when they had to make themselves fit into the American way of life. I think this is the stage we are going

through now. We have to prove ourselves and fit into the American way of life."

28   *I:* "Are there any difficulties in fitting into the American way of life?"

29   *He:* "For one thing we have a culture that we really don't want to let go. . . ."

30   In the past generation one of the first things mobility-oriented Mexican Americans (who were not numerous) gave up consciously was their language. They spoke English to their children and purposefully avoided exposing them to Spanish. Behind it was their strong conviction that this was the only way to overcome the handicaps of their children, to make them monolingual like the children in the majority population.   *Anly*

31   Today mobility-oriented youths tend to speak English to their parents, who often address them in Spanish. In doing so they display a pattern of language behavior which is relatively new among Mexican Americans but which manifested itself among other immigrant groups in the second generation. However, in contrast to the latter—many of whom understood but did not speak the language of their parents—all the boys I interviewed spoke some Spanish, even those whose parents spoke English to them.

32   The aim of the mobility-oriented boys is to master English as the main language of communication but at the same time to know Spanish. The fact that they attach importance to the parental language, which the second generation of other immigrant groups did not, is partly due to the new appreciation for foreign languages in America. Another factor in the retention of the language is the close contact with grandparents, for extended family ties persist strongly among Mexican Americans. Also, young people are able to make occasional visits to Mexico, a short trip from many places in the Southwest. Obviously, visits to the country of origin were not as easy for the children of other immigrants. But these visits across the border tend to have a double effect: on one hand they strengthen their consciousness of a Mexican heritage but, on the other hand, they heighten their awareness of how American they are.

33   The responses I have been discussing are those of mobility-oriented Mexican American youths. The emergence of the "ambitious" as a social type among Mexican American youth is a postwar phenomenon. They are the actual and future "college boys." The phrases often used by adults and youngsters, "He wants to go to college" or "He's a college boy," have a built-in image of a type that differs from most Mexican American boys and contrasts   *Def*

sharply with the delinquent, formerly known as *pachuco* and now as *cholo*. Actually the "ambitious" and the "delinquent" can be regarded as polar types—in terms of value orientation and behavior—and the great bulk of Mexican American youth falls somewhere between.

34   These three types of youths differ markedly but are not isolated either physically or socially from one another, for their paths often cross. It can be said that Mexican American youth society is characterized by social differentiation without much isolation. What caught my attention when talking to ambitious boys was that, despite their great devotion to success, they displayed not contempt but, on the contrary, tolerance for those who did not seek success but followed more traditional paths. Their attitude contrasted sharply with the negative images of "lazy" and "uncooperative" that the "college" boys had of the "street corner" boys in William Foote Whyte's *Street Corner Society*. The attitude of the ambitious Mexican American boys is consistent with the Mexican respect for the individual and his right to determine his own course of action.

C & C

35   This accommodating relationship that exists among the different types of Mexican American youths suggests that the "ambitious" youths of today will emerge as the effective leaders of the Mexican American community tomorrow. The answer to the question whether they will lead them along indigenous Mexican American paths or along paths borrowed from the Black militants does not lie with them alone. It lies more with the dominant group. The way it seems now is that the dominant group is not willing to yield to Mexican Americans even that which Blacks have achieved through riots and militant tactics.

Conc/ End

36   Also, the mass media of communication are focusing attention on the incipient Mexican American militancy. Unlike in the past when Mexican American life was almost completely ignored, the Mexican American spokesmen and manifestations of militancy are brought dramatically into the limelight. The mass media may thus play a role in the development of Mexican American militancy which emerged in the emulation of Blacks.

CONSIDERATIONS

What goals are Mexican Americans striving for? According to this article, why is the mobility-oriented youth a post-World War II phenomenon? By implication, what was the pre-War situation of earlier generations of Mexican Americans? Why is cultural identity a psychological advantage to a minority group?

The method of development used in this article is comparison and contrast. The author states the thesis of her argument in paragraph 3. From that point on, does she consistently follow the compare and contrast method introduced in paragraphs 1 and 2? What are the main points under discussion?

Three major minorities in the United States—Blacks, Chicanos, and Indians—have become progressively more vocal, more visible and certainly more threatening to the status quo. What are the major reasons behind the "new" tactics (militancy) and new bases (changing self-images) of these struggles for recognition and equal rights? Are there advantages for all Americans emerging from these inner conflicts in our country, or are these causes inherently destructive to the existing white power structure?

VOCABULARY

(1) **dissonant**   disagreeing; incongruous; out of harmony

(3) **emulate**   try to equal or excel through imitating

(5) **pragmatic**   pertaining to the practical point of view or practical considerations

(7) **empirical**   depending on experience; derived from experience or experiment

(8) **disparaging**   belittling; bringing reproach or discredit upon someone or something

(16) **marginal**   marked by contact with disparate cultures, and acquiring some but not all of the traits or values common to any one of them

(16) **assimilation**   the merging of cultural traits from previously distinct cultural groups

(18) **stigmatization**   mark of disgrace or infamy

(21) **viable**   workable

(35) **indigenous**   native; natural

I Look at the Audience

DAME SYBIL THORNDIKE

1   I suppose the art of the theatre is the only form of art of which the public is an integral part, the only form that is not complete without the spectator. In the fine arts of painting, sculpture or letters, the work is complete without any effort of the outside world. It is very helpful to the artist, no doubt, when good hard cash is paid down and the work is sold; but nothing that the purchaser does or feels or thinks about the particular work can alter it. It is a complete and perfect thing, materialized from the artist's imagination and soul. In music the composition is a complete thing in itself—even a performance of a work can be finished without the public participating, though here again appreciation is extremely pleasant, and helpful, both to pocket and self-esteem.

2   All forms of art seem to exist completely and separately. They may be understood or not, they may rouse sympathy or not, but the created thing is here. I believe this is why they are called the Fine Arts.

3   The popular art of the theatre, however, stands on quite another footing. (I do not include the Cinema, because that is also a finished product before it reaches the public, and the performance can never be altered however differently the audiences are feeling about it. In fact, I don't know how to place the Cinema and its canons. I do certainly feel it cannot be judged as the art of the

theatre, which depends on interplay between actors and audience. Neither is it a Fine Art. It is, I suppose, a growth from the theatre, but it must be judged separately.)

4   A play is not for all time, it is for the actual moment. (Reading plays to one's self, by one's own study fire, is a pastime of the intellectual which, with a great many people, has taken the place of visiting the theatre and joining in performance—what a great pity this is!)

5   It may be that a particular play is chosen to be played again and again through the ages, but the rite of performance is the important thing, and it is newly created with each performance. It may be, and most frequently is, that the actors choose the same outward signs and movements—vocal or otherwise—at each performance, but these must be freshly selected and born at the moment, and not just copies of those of previous performances.

6   Many actors will tell you of that curious sensation we have when entering the stage, as of one's other half-being waiting to be transformed. An expectant force is there, not just separate men and women but an entity, a personality made up of all those men and women who have sunk their separate individualities in the larger common soul of the mob, and this thing has to be shaped and used and made to move by the mind directing. Don't think this absurdly fantastic. I know many widely differing types of actor who feel this in common with me. This mob-soul is a force that is continually baffling us, it is always an unknown quantity. On our first entrance, before a word has left our mouths, we are conscious of this large thing confronting us. Sometimes one knows it is a thing to be fought and struggled with in order to move it and use it, and on these occasions the performance is a big effort, as every sensitive actor will tell you. At other times one is conscious of a something that is feeding one with life, and if the actor is well equipped technically and sensitively, and has something to express, it is on these occasions he can rise to heights greater than he thought possible. He is being given greater life, and the audience gets what is often called "a great performance."

7   I think audiences realize extraordinarily little how much they make or spoil performance in the theatre, and sometimes I wish— and especially do I wish this when the play is of large vision—that (as in Church one has, or is given, a little manual to show what one's attitude of mind should be, and hints how to behave, that the service may not be unfruitful) members of an audience should be handed a few choice words, setting down that too much eating of

chocolate, too much blowing of nose and clearing of throat, too much fidgeting of any sort, will prevent the full enjoyment of the play. And let it also be pointed out that these things and their like are a constant source of irritation to fellow members of the audience and induce in the unfortunate actor a feeling closely akin to murder. A quiet body, with few beads and chains to jangle (the dreadful days of the bangle are over, we hope), a quiet untrammeled mind and a quiet tongue—these three good things will give an atmosphere in which imagination can work. Shakespeare in his Prologues tells the hearers how to receive the play and conduct themselves.

8   "Don't forget we've come out for an evening's entertainment, will you?" my friends in the audience will say. No, I don't forget that, and I realize there are differences of approach to various entertainments. I am told that a good dinner, with good wine, is the best way to prepare for the enjoyment of a good play. A good dinner— a choice, spare dinner—maybe, but a large dinner and a full content makes the feeder a hard thing to move, and only the most obvious cast-iron humor will reach him, and only the most obvious sentiment will cause the tears to flow down his cheeks.

9   For the enjoyment of sensitive, subtle humor or sentiment—in order to appreciate the full flavor of Gracie Fields or Edith Evans— I suggest spare feeding, because through these artists, and their like, you will be filled to overflowing with a food of life which will the better spread to all parts of your body if it is not clogged with meat, poultry, suet and ice-cream. For the healthy and normal-stomached, a not-too-vigorous fasting is an excellent preparation for enjoyment. It whets the appetite for exercise, and the mind and body prepared for exercise are the sort of mind and body the actor hopes to encounter as he leaps or crawls or saunters on the stage, ready to give forth the superabundant creative energy that he can scarcely restrain.

10   Who was it that said of actors "Poor pale ghosts—shadows of Life?" I think that is what our rather hectic, over-busied, over-catered-for life asks of the theatre. "Be ascetic in your life, that in your art you may be violent," said a great French writer. That's better! Give us not pale ghosts or shadows, give us creatures with greater life than we know. Give us a larger-sized life than we actually experience, give us violences; shocks; beings that surge with vigor and electricity, that touching them in spirit we may be charged with that same energy and our grasp and scope be larger.

11   How wonderful if an audience asks this of its actors. "Give us more," is a cry we seldom hear, but the opposite we hear always and

then we wonder why the actors of great energy are all swallowed by revue and music-hall—part of the theatre certainly, the only part that does demand abundant vitality and strength, but, don't let us make any mistake, only a part.

12   In the Tragic Theatre of England we have nothing which compares with the energy and the life of the Comic Theatre in our midst. Comedy and Tragedy (the words Tragic and Comic include all forms of drama) are the whole, and until we embrace both we are one-sided cripples—one part dead—disused; delicate and ailing.

13   Whose fault is this? The actor knows it is the audience; the audience knows it is the actor; it is probably a bit of both. But how often we do hear that stupid refrain, "But we have tragedy in real life. Why should we have it in the theatre?" Every time this is said to me, with sickening, irritating regularity, it is only by the grace of God and amazing self-control that I am prevented from hurling myself on the speaker.

14   "You are the servants of the public, you actors. Give the public what it wants." We answer "We are not servants of anyone who does not demand the fullest life. We are the servants of the theatre, of which the public is only a part, and the public doesn't know what it wants till it sees it. Our business is to discover its needs—a very entertaining, intriguing and heartbreaking business. Servant of the public by all means, if by that is meant one who seeks to serve those who do not know what to ask for. The theatre serves those who say 'Show us life and that will suffice us.'"

CONSIDERATIONS

How is the audience integral to the success and "completion" of a play? When you go to see a play, do you prepare yourself to be an active participant as an audience member? Or do you believe there should be no such requirements for the audience?

In paragraph 7 Dame Sybil suggests an actor may feel hostility to the point of murder. Note how she picks up the imagery of violence again in paragraph 13. What words in this paragraph reveal the precise feelings of the writer? What is her attitude? Does impassioned speech detract from what she is saying?

Do you agree with Dame Sybil that the stage performance should reveal characters and situations with "greater life than we know" (paragraph 10) or is that a self-contradictory statement? Do you prefer live stage productions or movies? Why? How do the acting requirements differ in each medium? In your estimation, which is the more demanding type of acting?

Comparison
and
Contrast

COMPARISON AND CONTRAST

The basic operation of this rhetorical device is simple comparison. You have one thing or idea and you want to clarify it with another or others. If you do this to show how they are alike, you are comparing; to show how they are different, you are contrasting.

Comparison is a natural method of defining or describing something or someone. When you are talking with your friends and you want to describe to them a new rock music group you have heard performing, you probably will compare it with a second group with which they are familiar: "That new group sounds a lot like the old Credence Unclearwater Revival;" or "the lead singer in that new group plays the piano and sings much like so and so."

Listen to the conversations between parents and young children. Most questions from curious 4-, 5-, 6-, 7- and 8-year-olds are answered, however adequately or insufficiently, by means of comparison: "What is a drought, Mommy?" "Do you remember last August when we came home from our vacation trip and the vegetable garden had dried up because we forgot to have Grandpa water it? Well, that's what happens in a drought." The unfamiliar can be explained in terms of the familiar.

Characteristics that are compared or contrasted must be logically comparable. What are you trying to suggest or prove through your comparison? You must state your purpose or aim in unequivocable terms, or the comparison is likely to fall on its face. If you are trying to explain the flavor of a honeydew melon, you will be heading up the wrong trail by comparing it to another round green fruit, the lime.

Characteristics that are compared or contrasted are emphasized, highlighted. They are better understood and better remembered than if they were just stated.

Comparison-and-contrast arguments can be organized in two ways:

1. If there are many details and points to be brought out about both items, it is sometimes better to discuss one detail of the first and then a similar detail of the second, then a second detail of the first followed by a second detail of the second item, moving back and forth between the two until all the pertinent features are covered.

2. If the points to be brought out are fairly general, the first item can be described fully and then the second described in the same way.

PRACTICE

1. Choose some activity with which you are familiar (surfing, baking, mountain climbing, music arranging) and write a letter to a friend—or an article for a newspaper—explaining it by comparing it to a simpler activity *they* might be familiar with.

2. Try to recall an idea you had when you were younger, (say in high school), and compare or contrast it with your current views on the same subject.

3. Choose two essays on a similar topic, either from your text or from current magazines. Compare and contrast the views of both.

The Alternative to Schooling

In order to illustrate his point, Illich uses the device of comparison and contrast in paragraphs 16 and 8. He contrasts and compares our modern system of compulsory learning with its occult foundations. A student once said, "College is high school with ashtrays." Do you agree? Write an essay in which you compare and contrast college and high school.

On Civil Disobedience: Two Statements

After reading these two points of view, analyze the argumentation and write an essay contrasting the two positions. Include commentary on methods of persuasion in terms of whose is most effective and why, the differences in tone, diction, logic, and general approach. Include a comparison of any points the two authors make that you feel are similar in thought.

Indians and Other Americans

In paragraph 9 the author contrasts the attitude of blacks with that of Indians. The attitudes of each are antithetical to the other; therefore, they are logically contrasted. Write a paragraph in which you develop by constrast one of the following topics:

The relative influence of TV news broadcasts and newspapers

The esthetic qualities of a modern church and an old European cathedral

The emotional responses evoked by classical music and rock or jazz

The attitude toward alcohol of college students and the "over-30" age group

The American Nature of Football

In this essay the author compares and contrasts baseball with football (paragraph 13). He compares two things that are in the same class—sports. You can also compare and contrast two things that are not in the same class, but which have similar qualities. This type of comparison and contrast is related to the *analogy*. For example, when Shakespeare writes, "Shall I compare thee to a summer's day" he is presenting qualities that such a day might have in common with a particular person. Write a paragraph in which you contrast and compare two objects or ideas in different classes which have certain common characteristics. For example:

life . . . a game or a journey

marriage . . . a battle

sleep . . . death

books . . . food

a man . . . a machine

a university . . . a factory

- Find a love poem or sonnet written before 1900 and one modern one. Write a report in which you contrast and compare sentiment, diction, attitude, or tone.

For examples of individual paragraphs using *comparison and contrast*, see p.11, ¶11, p.12, ¶12, p.28, ¶6–9, p.40, ¶26–28, p.101, ¶1–4, p.102, ¶12, p.155, ¶2, p.332, ¶16, p.338, ¶34, p.355, ¶24.

The Alternative to Schooling

IVAN ILLICH

1   For generations we have tried to make the world a better place by providing more and more schooling, but so far the endeavor has failed. What we have learned instead is that forcing all children to *C&E* climb an open-ended education ladder cannot enhance equality but must favor the individual who starts out earlier, healthier, or better prepared; that enforced instruction deadens for most people the will for independent learning; and that knowledge treated as a com- *Angy* modity, delivered in packages, and accepted as private property once it is acquired, must always be scarce.

2   In response, critics of the educational system are now propos- ing strong and unorthodox remedies that range from the voucher plan, which would enable each person to buy the education of his choice on an open market, to shifting the responsibility for educa- tion from the school to the media and to apprenticeship on the job. Some individuals foresee that the school will have to be disestab- lished just as the church was disestablished all over the world during the last two centuries. Other reformers propose to replace the uni- versal school with various new systems that would, they claim, bet- ter prepare everybody for life in modern society. These proposals *Class* for new educational institutions fall into three broad categories: the reformation of the classroom within the school system; the dispersal of free schools throughout society; and the transformation of all

Ivan Illich is the author of DESCHOOLING SOCIETY and TOOLS FOR CONVIVIALITY, both published by Harper and Row.

society into one huge classroom. But these three approaches—the reformed classroom, the free school, and the worldwide classroom—represent three stages in a proposed escalation of education in which each step threatens more subtle and more pervasive social control than the one it replaces.

3   I believe that the disestablishment of the school has become inevitable and that this end of an illusion should fill us with hope. But I also believe that the end of the "age of schooling" could usher in the epoch of the global schoolhouse that would be distinguishable only in name from a global madhouse or global prison in which education, correction, and adjustment become synonymous. I therefore believe that the breakdown of the school forces us to look beyond its imminent demise and to face fundamental alternatives in education. Either we can work for fearsome and potent new educational devices that teach about a world which progressively becomes more opaque and forbidding for man, or we can set the conditions for a new era in which technology would be used to make society more simple and transparent, so that all men can once again know the facts and use the tools that shape their lives. In short, we can disestablish schools or we can deschool culture.   *Arg*

4   In order to see clearly the alternatives we face, we must first distinguish education from schooling, which means separating the humanistic intent of the teacher from the impact of the invariant structure of the school. This hidden structure constitutes a course of instruction that stays forever beyond the control of the teacher or of his school board. It conveys indelibly the message that only through schooling can an individual prepare himself for adulthood in society, that what is not taught in school is of little value, and that what is learned outside of school is not worth knowing. I call it the hidden curriculum of schooling, because it constitutes the unalterable framework of the system, within which all changes in the curriculum are made.

5   The hidden curriculum is always the same regardless of school or place. It requires all children of a certain age to assemble in groups of about thirty, under the authority of a certified teacher, for some 500 to 1,000 or more hours each year. It doesn't matter whether the curriculum is designed to teach the principles of fascism, liberalism, Catholicism, or socialism; or whether the purpose of the school is to produce Soviet or United States citizens, mechanics, or doctors. It makes no difference whether the teacher is authoritarian or permissive, whether he imposes his own creed or teaches students to think for themselves. What is important is that   *Def*

students learn that education is valuable when it is acquired in the school through a graded process of consumption; that the degree of success the individual will enjoy in society depends on the amount of learning he consumes; and that learning *about* the world is more valuable than learning *from* the world.

6   It must be clearly understood that the hidden curriculum translates learning from an activity into a commodity—for which the school monopolizes the market. In all countries knowledge is regarded as the first necessity for survival, but also as a form of currency more liquid than rubles or dollars. We have become accustomed, through Karl Marx's writings, to speak about the alienation of the worker from his work in a class society. We must now recognize the estrangement of man from his learning when it becomes the product of a service profession and he becomes the consumer.   *Anly*

7   The more learning an individual consumes, the more "knowledge stock" he acquires. The hidden curriculum therefore defines a new class structure for society within which the large consumers of knowledge—those who have acquired large quantities of knowledge stock—enjoy special privileges, high income, and access to the more powerful tools of production. This kind of knowledge-capitalism has been accepted in all industrialized societies and establishes a rationale for the distribution of jobs and income. (This point is especially important in the light of the lack of correspondence between schooling and occupational competence established in studies such as Ivar Berg's *Education and Jobs: The Great Training Robbery.*)

8   The endeavor to put all men through successive stages of enlightenment is rooted deeply in alchemy, the Great Art of the waning Middle Ages. John Amos Comenius, a Moravian bishop, self-styled Pansophist, and pedagogue, is rightly considered one of the founders of the modern schools. He was among the first to propose seven or twelve grades of compulsory learning. In his *Magna Didactica,* he described schools as devices to "teach everybody everything" and outlined a blueprint for the assembly-line production of knowledge, which according to his method would make education cheaper and better and make growth into full humanity possible for all. But Comenius was not only an early efficiency expert, he was an alchemist who adopted the technical language of his craft to describe the art of rearing children. The alchemist sought to refine base elements by leading their distilled spirits through twelve stages of successive enlightenment, so that for their own and all the world's benefit they might be transmuted into gold. Of course, al-   *C & C*   *Meta*

chemists failed no matter how often they tried, but each time their | C&C
"science" yielded new reasons for their failure, and they tried again.

9   Pedagogy opened a new chapter in the history of Ars Magna. Education became the search for an alchemic process that would bring forth a new type of man, who would fit into an environment created by scientific magic. But, no matter how much each generation spent on its schools, it always turned out that the majority of people were unfit for enlightenment by this process and had to be discarded as unprepared for life in a man-made world.

10   Educational reformers who accept the idea that schools have | Class / failed fall into three groups. The most respectable are certainly the | Conn great masters of alchemy who promise better schools. The most seductive are popular magicians, who promise to make every kitchen into an alchemic lab. The most sinister are the new Masons of the Universe, who want to transform the entire world into one huge temple of learning. Notable among today's masters of alchemy are certain research directors employed or sponsored by the large foundations who believe that schools, if they could somehow be improved, could also become economically more feasible than those that are now in trouble, and simultaneously could sell a larger package of services. Those who are concerned primarily with the curriculum claim that it is outdated or irrelevant. So the curriculum is filled with new packaged courses on African Culture, North American Imperialism, Women's Lib, Pollution, or the Consumer Society. Passive learning is wrong—it is indeed—so we graciously allow students to decide what and how they want to be taught. | Sarc Schools are prison houses. Therefore, principals are authorized to approve teach-outs, moving the school desks to a roped-off Harlem street. Sensitivity training becomes fashionable. So, we import group therapy into the classroom. School, which was supposed to teach everybody everything, now becomes all things to all children.

11   Other critics emphasize that schools make inefficient use of modern science. Some would administer drugs to make it easier for the instructor to change the child's behavior. Others would transform school into a stadium for educational gaming. Still others would electrify the classroom. If they are simplistic disciples of McLuhan, they replace blackboards and textbooks with multimedia happenings; if they follow Skinner, they claim to be able to modify behavior more efficiently than old-fashioned classroom practitioners can.

12   Most of these changes have, of course, some good effects. The experimental schools have fewer truants. Parents do have a greater

feeling of participation in a decentralized district. Pupils, assigned
by their teacher to an apprenticeship, do often turn out more competent than those who stay in the classroom. Some children do
improve their knowledge of Spanish in the language lab because
they prefer playing with the knobs of a tape recorder to conversations with their Puerto Rican peers. Yet all these improvements
operate within predictably narrow limits, since they leave the hidden curriculum of school intact.

Dict

13   Some reformers would like to shake loose from the hidden
curriculum, but they rarely succeed. Free schools that lead to further free schools produce a mirage of freedom, even though the
chain of attendance is frequently interrupted by long stretches of
loafing. Attendance through seduction inculcates the need for educational treatment more persuasively than the reluctant attendance
enforced by a truant officer. Permissive teachers in a padded classroom can easily render their pupils impotent to survive once they
leave.

Sarc

14   Learning in these schools often remains nothing more than the
acquisition of socially valued skills defined, in this instance, by the
consensus of a commune rather than by the decree of a school
board. New presbyter is but old priest writ large.

15   Free schools, to be truly free, must meet two conditions: First,
they must be run in a way to prevent the reintroduction of the
hidden curriculum of graded attendance and certified students
studying at the feet of certified teachers. And, more importantly,
they must provide a framework in which all participants—staff and
pupils—can free themselves from the hidden foundations of a
schooled society. The first condition is frequently incorporated in
the stated aims of a free school. The second condition is only rarely
recognized, and is difficult to state as the goal of a free school.

Class

16   It is useful to distinguish between the hidden curriculum,
which I have described, and the occult foundations of schooling.
The hidden curriculum is a ritual that can be considered the official
initiation into modern society, institutionally established through
the school. It is the purpose of this ritual to hide from its participants the contradictions between the myth of an egalitarian society
and the class-conscious reality it certifies. Once they are recognized
as such, rituals lose their power, and this is what is now beginning to
happen to schooling. But there are certain fundamental assumptions about growing up—the occult foundations—which now find
their expression in the ceremonial of schooling, and which could
easily be reinforced by what free schools do.

Def/
C&C

17   Among these assumptions is what Peter Schrag calls the "immigration syndrome," which impels us to treat all people as if they were newcomers who must go through a naturalization process. Only certified consumers of knowledge are admitted to citizenship. Men are not born equal, but are made equal through gestation by Alma Mater.

Tone

18   The rhetoric of all schools states that they form a man for the future, but they do not release him for his task before he has developed a high level of tolerance to the ways of his elders: education *for* life rather than *in* everyday life. Few free schools can avoid doing precisely this. Nevertheless they are among the most important centers from which a new life-style radiates, not because of the effect their graduates will have but, rather, because elders who choose to bring up their children without the benefit of properly ordained teachers frequently belong to a radical minority and because their preoccupation with the rearing of their children sustains them in their new style.

S Var

19   The most dangerous category of educational reformer is one who argues that knowledge can be produced and sold much more effectively on an open market than on one controlled by school. These people argue that most skills can be easily acquired from skill-models if the learner is truly interested in their acquisition; their individual entitlements can provide a more equal purchasing power for education. They demand a careful separation of the process by which knowledge is acquired from the process by which it is measured and certified. These seem to me obvious statements. But it would be a fallacy to believe that the establishment of a free market for knowledge would constitute a radical alternative in education.

Arg

20   The establishment of a free market would indeed abolish what I have previously called the hidden curriculum of present schooling—its age-specific attendance at a graded curriculum. Equally, a free market would at first give the appearance of counteracting what I have called the occult foundations of a schooled society: the "immigration syndrome," the institutional monopoly of teaching, and the ritual of linear initiation. But at the same time a free market in education would provide the alchemist with innumerable hidden hands to fit each man into the multiple, tight little niches a more complex technocracy can provide.

21   Many decades of reliance on schooling has turned knowledge into a commodity, a marketable staple of a special kind. Knowledge is now regarded simultaneously as a first necessity and also as soci-

ety's most precious currency. (The transformation of knowledge into a commodity is reflected in a corresponding transformation of language. Words that formerly functioned as verbs are becoming nouns that designate possessions. Until recently dwelling and learning and even healing designated activities. They are now usually conceived as commodities or services to be delivered. We talk about the manufacture of housing or the delivery of medical care. Men are no longer regarded fit to house or heal themselves. In such a society people come to believe that professional services are more valuable than personal care. Instead of learning how to nurse grandmother, the teenager learns to picket the hospital that does not admit her.) This attitude could easily survive the disestablishment of school, just as affiliation with a church remained a condition for office long after the adoption of the First Amendment. It is even more evident that test batteries measuring complex knowledge-packages could easily survive the disestablishment of school—and with this would go the compulsion to obligate everybody to acquire a minimum package in the knowledge stock. The scientific measurement of each man's worth and the alchemic dream of each man's "educability to his full humanity" would finally coincide. Under the appearance of a "free" market, the global village would turn into an environmental womb where pedagogic therapists control the complex navel by which each man is nourished.

Exemp

Sarc / Irny

Sync / Allus

Tran

22   At present schools limit the teacher's competence to the classroom. They prevent him from claiming man's whole life as his domain. The demise of school will remove this restriction and give a semblance of legitimacy to the life-long pedagogical invasion of everybody's privacy. It will open the way for a scramble for "knowledge" on a free market, which would lead us toward the paradox of a vulgar, albeit seemingly egalitarian, meritocracy. Unless the concept of knowledge is transformed, the disestablishment of school will lead to a wedding between a growing meritocratic system that separates learning from certification and a society committed to provide therapy for each man until he is ripe for the gilded age.

23   For those who subscribe to the technocratic ethos, whatever is technically possible must be made available at least to a few whether they want it or not. Neither the privation nor the frustration of the majority counts. If cobalt treatment is possible, then the city of Tegucigalpa needs one apparatus in each of its two major hospitals, at a cost that would free an important part of the population of Honduras from parasites. If supersonic speeds are possible, then it must speed the travel of some. If the flight to Mars can be

conceived, then a rationale must be found to make it appear a necessity. In the technocratic ethos poverty is modernized: Not only are old alternatives closed off by new monopolies, but the lack of necessities is also compounded by a growing spread between those services that are technologically feasible and those that are in fact available to the majority.

24　　A teacher turns "educator" when he adopts this technocratic ethos. He then acts as if education were a technological enterprise designed to make man fit into whatever environment the "progress" of science creates. He seems blind to the evidence that constant obsolescence of all commodities comes at a high price: the mounting cost of training people to know about them. He seems to forget that the rising cost of tools is purchased at a high price in education: They decrease the labor intensity of the economy, make learning on the job impossible, or at best, a privilege for a few. All over the world the cost of educating men for society rises faster than the productivity of the entire economy, and fewer people have a sense of intelligent participation in the commonweal. *Anly*

25　　A revolution against those forms of privilege and power, which are based on claims to professional knowledge, must start with a transformation of consciousness about the nature of learning. This means, above all, a shift of responsibility for teaching and learning. Knowledge can be defined as a commodity only as long as it is viewed as the result of institutional enterprise or as the fulfillment of institutional objectives. Only when a man recovers the sense of personal responsibility for what he learns and teaches can this spell be broken and the alienation of learning from living be overcome.

26　　The recovery of the power to learn or to teach means that the teacher who takes the risk of interfering in somebody else's affairs also assumes responsibility for the results. Similarly, the student who exposes himself to the influence of a teacher must take responsibility for his own education. For such purposes educational institutions—if they are at all needed—ideally take the form of facility centers where one can get a roof of the right size over his head, access to a piano or a kiln, and to records, books, or slides. Schools, TV stations, theaters, and the like are designed primarily for use by professionals. Deschooling society means above all the denial of professional status for the second-oldest profession, namely teaching. The certification of teachers now constitutes an undue restriction of the right to free speech; the corporate structure and professional pretensions of journalism an undue restriction on the right to free press. Compulsory attendance rules interfere with free assem- *C&E*

bly. The deschooling of society is nothing less than a cultural mutation by which a people recovers the effective use of its Constitutional freedoms: learning and teaching by men who know that they
are born free rather than treated to freedom. Most people learn
most of the time when they do whatever they enjoy; most people
are curious and want to give meaning to whatever they come in
contact with; and most people are capable of personal intimate
intercourse with others unless they are stupefied by inhuman work
or turned off by schooling.

27   The fact that people in rich countries do not learn much on
their own constitutes no proof to the contrary. Rather it is a consequence of life in an environment from which, paradoxically, they
cannot learn much, precisely because it is so highly programed.
They are constantly frustrated by the structure of contemporary
society in which the facts on which decisions can be made have
become elusive. They live in an environment in which tools that can
be used for creative purposes have become luxuries, an environment
in which channels of communication serve a few to talk to many.

28   A modern myth would make us believe that the sense of impotence with which most men live today is a consequence of technology that cannot but create huge systems. But it is not technology
that makes systems huge, tools immensely powerful, channels of
communication one-directional. Quite the contrary: Properly controlled, technology could provide each man with the ability to understand his environment better, to shape it powerfully with his own
hands, and to permit him full intercommunication to a degree
never before possible. Such an alternative use of technology constitutes the central alternative in education.

29   If a person is to grow up he needs, first of all, access to things,
to places and to processes, to events and to records. He needs to
see, to touch, to tinker with, to grasp whatever there is in a meaningful setting. This access is now largely denied. When knowledge
became a commodity, it acquired the protections of private property, and thus a principle designed to guard personal intimacy became a rationale for declaring facts off limits for people without the
proper credentials. In schools teachers keep knowledge to themselves unless it fits into the day's program. The media inform, but
exclude those things they regard as unfit to print. Information is
locked into special languages, and specialized teachers live off its
retranslation. Patents are protected by corporations, secrets are
guarded by bureaucracies, and the power to keep others out of
private preserves—be they cockpits, law offices, junkyards, or clin-

Anly

Tran
S Var

ics—is jealously guarded by professions, institutions, and nations. Neither the political nor the professional structure of our societies, East and West, could withstand the elimination of the power to keep entire classes of people from facts that could serve them. The access to facts that I advocate goes far beyond truth in labeling. Access must be built into reality, while all we ask from advertising is a guarantee that it does not mislead. Access to reality constitutes a fundamental alternative in education to a system that only purports to teach *about* it.

30   Abolishing the right to corporate secrecy—even when professional opinion holds that this secrecy serves the common good—is, as shall presently appear, a much more radical political goal than the traditional demand for public ownership or control of the tools of production. The socialization of tools without the effective socialization of know-how in their use tends to put the knowledge-capitalist into the position formerly held by the financier. The technocrat's only claim to power is the stock he holds in some class of scarce and secret knowledge, and the best means to protect its value is a large and capital-intensive organization that renders access to know-how formidable and forbidding.

Arg / Sarc

31   It does not take much time for the interested to acquire almost any skill that he wants to use. We tend to forget this in a society where professional teachers monopolize entrance into all fields, and thereby stamp teaching by uncertified individuals as quackery. There are few mechanical skills used in industry or research that are as demanding, complex, and dangerous as driving cars, a skill that most people quickly acquire from a peer. Not all people are suited for advanced logic, yet those who are make rapid progress if they are challenged to play mathematical games at an early age. One out of twenty kids in Cuernavaca can beat me at Wiff'n'Proof after a couple of weeks' training. In four months all but a small percentage of motivated adults at our CIDOC center learn Spanish well enough to conduct academic business in the new language.

Top S

Exmp

32   A first step toward opening up access to skills would be to provide various incentives for skilled individuals to share their knowledge. Inevitably, this would run counter to the interest of guilds and professions and unions. Yet, multiple apprenticeship is attractive: It provides everybody with an opportunity to learn something about almost anything. There is no reason why a person should not combine the ability to drive a car, repair telephones and toilets, act as a midwife, and function as an architectural draftsman. Special-interest groups and their disciplined consumers would, of

Anly

course, claim that the public needs the protection of a professional guarantee. But this argument is now steadily being challenged by consumer protection associations. We have to take much more seriously the objection that economists raise to the radical socialization of skills: that "progress" will be impeded if knowledge—patents, skills, and all the rest—is democratized. Their argument can be faced only if we demonstrate to them the growth rate of futile diseconomies generated by any existing educational system.

33   Access to people willing to share their skills is no guarantee of learning. Such access is restricted not only by the monopoly of educational programs over learning and of unions over licensing but also by a technology of scarcity. The skills that count today are know-how in the use of highly specialized tools that were designed to be scarce. These tools produce goods or render services that everybody wants but only a few can enjoy, and which only a limited number of people know how to use. Only a few privileged individuals out of the total number of people who have a given disease ever benefit from the results of sophisticated medical technology, and even fewer doctors develop the skill to use it.   *Tran*

34   The same results of medical research have, however, also been employed to create a basic medical tool kit that permits Army and Navy medics, with only a few months of training, to obtain results, under battlefield conditions, that would have been beyond the expectations of full-fledged doctors during World War II. On an even simpler level any peasant girl could learn how to diagnose and treat most infections if medical scientists prepared dosages and instructions specifically for a given geographic area.   *C & C*

35   All these examples illustrate the fact that educational considerations alone suffice to demand a radical reduction of the professional structure that now impedes the mutual relationship between the scientist and the majority of people who want access to science. If this demand were heeded, all men could learn to use yesterday's tools, rendered more effective and durable by modern science, to create tomorrow's world.

36   Unfortunately, precisely the contrary trend prevails at present. I know a coastal area in South America where most people support themselves by fishing from small boats. The outboard motor is certainly the tool that has changed most dramatically the lives of these coastal fishermen. But in the area I have surveyed, half of all outboard motors that were purchased between 1945 and 1950 are still kept running by constant tinkering, while half the motors purchased in 1965 no longer run because they were not built to be repaired.   *Exmp*

Technological progress provides the majority of people with gad- *Pdx*
gets they cannot afford and deprives them of the simpler tools they
need.

37   Metals, plastics, and ferro cement used in building have greatly
improved since the 1940s and ought to provide more people the
opportunity to create their own homes. But while in the United
States, in 1948, more than 30 per cent of all one-family homes were
owner-built, by the end of the 1960s the percentage of those who
acted as their own contractors had dropped to less than 20 per cent.

38   The lowering of the skill level through so-called economic de- *Exmp*
velopment becomes even more visible in Latin America. Here most
people still build their own homes from floor to roof. Often they
use mud, in the form of adobe, and thatchwork of unsurpassed
utility in the moist, hot, and windy climate. In other places they
make their dwellings out of cardboard, oildrums, and other industrial refuse. Instead of providing people with simple tools and
highly standardized, durable, and easily repaired components, all
governments have gone in for the mass production of low-cost
buildings. It is clear that not one single country can afford to provide satisfactory modern dwelling units for the majority of its people. Yet, everywhere this policy makes it progressively more difficult *Irny*
for the majority to acquire the knowledge and skills they need to
build better houses for themselves.

39   Educational considerations permit us to formulate a second
fundamental characteristic that any post-industrial society must
possess: a basic tool kit that by its very nature counteracts technocratic control. For educational reasons we must work toward a society in which scientific knowledge is incorporated in tools and components that can be used meaningfully in units small enough to be
within the reach of all. Only such tools can socialize access to skills. *S Var*
Only such tools favor temporary assocations among those who want
to use them for a specific occasion. Only such tools allow specific
goals to emerge in the process of their use, as any tinkerer knows.
Only the combination of guaranteed access to facts and of limited
power in most tools renders it possible to envisage a subsistence
economy capable of incorporating the fruits of modern science.

40   The development of such a scientific subsistence economy is
unquestionably to the advantage of the overwhelming majority of
all people in poor countries. It is also the only alternative to progressive pollution, exploitation, and opaqueness in rich countries.
But, as we have seen, the dethroning of the GNP cannot be
achieved without simultaneously subverting GNE (Gross National
Education—usually conceived as manpower capitalization). An

egalitarian economy cannot exist in a society in which the right to produce is conferred by schools.

41   The feasibility of a modern subsistence economy does not depend on new scientific inventions. It depends primarily on the ability of a society to agree on fundamental, self-chosen anti-bureaucratic and anti-technocratic restraints.

42   These restraints can take many forms, but they will not work unless they touch the basic dimensions of life. (The decision of Congress against development of the supersonic transport plane is one of the most encouraging steps in the right direction.) The substance of these voluntary social restraints would be very simple matters that can be fully understood and judged by any prudent man. The issues at stake in the SST controversy provide a good example. All such restraints would be chosen to promote stable and equal enjoyment of scientific know-how. The French say that it takes a thousand years to educate a peasant to deal with a cow. It would not take two generations to help all people in Latin America or Africa to use and repair outboard motors, simple cars, pumps, medicine kits, and ferro cement machines if their design does not change every few years. And since a joyful life is one of constant meaningful intercourse with others in a meaningful environment, equal enjoyment does translate into equal education.

Exmp

43   At present a consensus on austerity is difficult to imagine. The reason usually given for the importance of the majority is stated in terms of political or economic class. What is not usually understood is that the new class structure of a schooled society is even more powerfully controlled by vested interests. No doubt an imperialist and capitalist organization of society provides the social structure within which a minority can have disproportionate influence over the effective opinion of the majority. But in a technocratic society the power of a minority of knowledge capitalists can prevent the formation of true public opinion through control of scientific know-how and the media of communication. Constitutional guarantees of free speech, free press, and free assembly were meant to ensure government by the people. Modern electronics, photo-offset presses, time-sharing computers, and telephones have in principle provided the hardware that could give an entirely new meaning to these freedoms. Unfortunately, these things are used in modern media to increase the power of knowledge-bankers to funnel their program-packages through international chains to more people, instead of being used to increase true networks that provide equal opportunity for encounter among the members of the majority.

Anly / Arg

44   Deschooling the culture and social structure requires the use of technology to make participatory politics possible. Only on the basis of a majority coalition can limits to secrecy and growing power be determined without dictatorship. We need a new environment in which growing up can be classless, or we will get a brave new world in which Big Brother educates us all.

CONSIDERATIONS

How did the "hidden structure" (paragraph 4) become a part of the American educational system? In what ways would a "free market" abolish this structure? Do you think we will either deschool the culture or disestablish schools in this century? What basic attitude changes would have to take place within the culture before the educational system could be restructured?

Illich has written a tightly organized, unified article, held together by satiric wit and sarcasm. Cite examples of the satire and sarcasm. What tone does the author convey through these examples? Is it consistent with his theme? Is the use of satire inappropriate for a serious subject such as this?

In a brief essay discuss the following questions. Do you see any present trends that may lead to a "modern subsistence economy"? (paragraphs 35–44) If so, are they too specialized or too minimal to effect overall changes in society? Which fields presently monopolized by professionals or specialists should be managed by a "majority coalition"? (paragraph 44)

VOCABULARY

(3) **demise**   termination of existence; death
(3) **opaque**   cloudy; hard to understand
(4) **invariant**   constant throughout
(9) **pedagogy**   the function or work of a teacher; teaching
(13) **inculcates**   teaches persistently and earnestly; instills
(19) **entitlements**   particular, specialized titles
(20) **technocracy**   a controlled social-governmental system in which engineers and technologists determine values and priorities
(22) **meritocracy**   a class of persons making their way on the basis of their own ability and merits rather than class privileges
(23) **ethos**   underlying sentiment that determines the beliefs, customs, or practices of a group
(30) **formidable**   discouraging or awesome, dreadful

On Civil Disobedience: Two Statements

WILLIAM F. BUCKLEY, JR., and NOAM CHOMSKY

WILLIAM F. BUCKLEY, JR.

1   Of the two grounds for disobeying civil authorities, the first—that the United States is not legally at war because Congress hasn't gone through the drill specified by the Constitution—strikes me as particularly phony. To begin with, it is being used by gentlemen whose lives are scarcely lived in scriptural fidelity to the Constitution. If the head of the American Bar Association were to decline to support the Vietnam war on the ground of its shaky constitutional genealogy, that is one thing. But when the Constitution is suddenly discovered by Dwight Macdonald, one puts that down (or at least I put that down) to opportunism. It isn't that the question doesn't worry me, it does. A great deal of thought will have to go into the elision of general resolutions (like Tonkin) and all-out wars. But this isn't the moment for such reviews, any more than the dark days of the Civil War were appropriate for questioning Abraham Lincoln's use of his Presidential powers.

2   On the second ground, it ought to be the individual's right to refuse to go along with his community, but the community, not the individual, should specify the consequences. These, in an enlightened society, should vary according to the nature of the insubordination, and according as the insubordination is plausibly rooted in

deep philosophical attachments. For instance, it seems to me right and obvious that a pacifist should be permitted to remain far from even those battlefields at which the safety of the pacifist is secured, and right, also, that young pacifists of draft age should be required to perform some duty or other, in some way commensurate with those performed by fellow citizens who are conscripted. But those others who ask to retain a personal veto over every activity of their Government, whether it is a war in Vietnam or the social or educational policies of a municipal administration, are asking for the kind of latitude which breaks the bonds of civil society.

3 That which is anarchic within me (which is very strong) tunes in strongly on the idea of a society in which people decide for themselves what taxes to pay, what rules to obey, when to cooperate and when not to with the civil authorities. But that which is reasonable within me, which I am glad to say most often prevails, recognizes that societies so structured do not exist, and cannot exist: an insight as ancient as Socrates's, so patiently explained to Crito. The indicated consequence for studied and aggravated civil disobedience seems to me to be obvious: deportation. Ideally, of course, a citizen whose disagreements with his country are organic and apparently unreconcilable should take the initiative and seek out more compatible countries.

NOAM CHOMSKY

4 Although I feel that resistance to United States policy is justified—in fact, a moral necessity—I do not think that dissent should be abandoned. Critical analysis of American policy can extend opposition to this war and can help modify the intellectual and moral climate that made it possible. Government propaganda has shifted to a new position: American self-interest. Correspondingly, critical analysis can now be directed to such questions as these: Whose interest is served by this war? What motivates the hysterical claim that if we do not stand fast in Vietnam we shall have to fight in Hawaii and California?—"a frivolous insult to the United States Navy," as Walter Lippmann rightly comments. Would the richest and most powerful nation in the world be justified in imposing such suffering and destruction even if this were in its "self-interest?"

5 What justifies an act of civil disobedience is an intolerable evil. After the lesson of Dachau and Auschwitz, no person of conscience can believe that authority must always be obeyed. A line must be drawn somewhere. Beyond that line lies civil disobedience. It may be quite passive, a simple refusal to take part in Government-initi-

ated violence. An example is refusal to pay war taxes; refusal to serve in Vietnam is a far more meaningful, far more courageous example. It may involve symbolic confrontation with the war-making apparatus, as in the Washington demonstrations, a confrontation that becomes civil disobedience when the participant stands his ground in the face of Government force. It may go well beyond such symbolic acts.

6   Each citizen must ask himself whether he wishes to take part in the annihilation of the people of Vietnam. He has a range of actions available to him. Docility and passive acquiescence is one possible course. It is the course of full complicity in whatever the Government will do in his name.

7   The limits of civil disobedience must be determined by the extent of the evil that one confronts, and by considerations of tactical efficacy and moral principle. On grounds of principle and tactics, I think that civil disobedience should be entirely nonviolent, but space prevents a discussion of the reasons for and the consequences of this conclusion.

8   The final question posed is the crucial one. Those who defend American policy speak vaguely of Communist "aggression." Just when did this "aggression" take place? Was it in 1959, when Hanoi radio was urging that the leaders of the insurrection desist, when Diem spoke of having an Algerian war on his hands in the South while his agents were being parachuted into North Vietnam? Or was it perhaps in April, 1965, when North Vietnamese troops were first discovered in the South, two months after the bombing of North Vietnam began—400 in a guerrilla force of 140,000, at a time when more than 30,000 American troops were helping protect the Saigon Government from its own population?

9   Or is it now, when a vast American army of occupation has taken over the conduct of the war, with about as many South Korean mercenaries as there are North Vietnamese troops in the South?

10   Or does Hanoi's "aggression" consist in the sending of supplies and trained South Vietnamese cadres to the South? By these standards our aggression in the South has always been imcomparably greater in scale, and we are engaged in such aggression in half the countries of the world. It is pointless to continue. If an objective observer were to listen to American voices speaking of aggression from Hanoi or of the necessity for *America* to contain *China's* aggressive expansionism, he would not challenge our arguments but would question our sanity.

11   American Government sources freely admit that United States military force was introduced to prevent a political, organizational, agit-prop victory by the N.F.L. (see Douglas Pike, "The Vietcong"). The terrible consequences of the use of American military might are apparent to anyone with eyes and ears. I will not try to describe what everyone knows. To use inadequate words to tell what we have done is an insult to the victims of our violence and our moral cowardice. Yes, civil disobedience is entirely justified in an effort to bring to a close the most disgraceful chapter in American history.

12   I'll finish with two quotes, each very true, from opposite extremes of the moral spectrum.

> (1) "Naturally the common people don't want war . . . it is the leaders of the country who determine the policy, and it is always a simple matter to drag the people along, whether it is a democracy, or a Fascist dictatorship, or a parliament, or a Communist dictatorship. Voice or no voice, the people can always be brought to do the bidding of the leaders. That is easy. All you have to do is to tell them that they are being attacked, and denounce the pacifists for lack of patriotism and exposing the country to danger. It works the same in every country."
>
> (2) "Unjust laws and practices survive because men obey them and conform to them. This they do out of fear. There are things they dread more than the continuance of the evil."

13   The first quote is from Hermann Goering. Those who counsel civil disobedience are expressing their hope that it doesn't "work the same" in this country. The second quote is from A. J. Muste, paraphrasing Gandhi. These words have never been more appropriate than they are today.

CONSIDERATIONS

Buckley states his definition of, and position on, civil disobedience in less than 360 words; Chomsky has written an article twice as long and gives the impression that there is considerably more to be said on the subject (specifically, paragraph 7). Does Buckley's approach seem cursory, or has he presented an adequate defense of his position? Is Chomsky less reasonable, more emotional, and, therefore, more vulnerable? Are there two sides to the question of civil disobedience in all cases, or only in the instance of the American war in Vietnam?

Analyze the examples each writer uses to support his claims. What is the effect of diction in each example: of "so patiently explained to Crito" (paragraph 3), "the lesson of Dachau and Auschwitz" (paragraph 5), "the annihilation of the people" (paragraph 6), or "our moral cowardice" (paragraph 11), and so on? What is the difference between Buckley's and Chomsky's method of persuasion?

Chomsky asks, "Whose interest is served by the war in Vietnam?" Applying your knowledge of the history of American involvement in Southeast Asia, answer his question in a theme. Have American interests changed over the course of the war in Vietnam, or has American involvement been based on certain principles and reasons from the beginning? Be as unemotional—objective—as possible in your presentation.

VOCABULARY

(1) **opportunism**   the practice of exploiting opportunities without regard to ethical or moral principles

(1) **elision**   omission

(2) **commensurate**   equal in measure or extent

(2) **conscripted**   drafted for military service

(3) **organic**   of, relating to, or constituting the law by which a government exists

(6) **acquiescence**   passive or tacit acceptance

(6) **complicity**   the state of being an accomplice or partner in wrongdoing

(7) **efficacy**   effectiveness

Indians and Other Americans

CARL N. DEGLER

1   In the confrontation between the American Indian and the white man over the course of the past three centuries, no single episode is more revealing or more devastating in its moral implications than the removal of the Cherokees from their ancestral lands in the 1830s. The phrase applied to the last stage of the removal, "trail of tears," sums up the price some six thousand Cherokees paid in being forcibly evicted from their homes in Georgia and Tennessee by the United States Army in order to make the trek in the dead of winter to the new Indian Territory in what is now Oklahoma.

2   Today the policy of removal, like the historical United States policy toward the Indian in general, is widely condemned as brutal, rapacious, and wrong. And it was brutal and rapacious, even by the standards of the time, for some contemporaries condemned it in much the same terms as modern critics have. But apart from the *way* the policy was carried out, was there any alternative to it? Two possibilities suggest themselves. The first is that the Cherokees, and by extension, Indians in general, ought to have been left undisturbed. The second is that they ought to have been absorbed or assimilated into American society. Examining each of these alternatives in turn will help us appreciate the special place which Indians occupy in the social history of the United States.

3   The argument that Indian culture ought to have been left undisturbed rests, at bottom, on the principle that any culture, how-

ever "primitive" or undeveloped it may be, deserves to survive because no culture is really superior to any other. This is the argument from cultural relativism. Although I am prepared to accept the principle, it is worth noting that it cuts both ways. Both Indian and white cultures deserve to exist. The idea of leaving the Indians undisturbed implies that the white Americans ought to have stopped short of the Appalachians or at the Mississippi or at some other line not defended by power. To expect this, however, is equivalent to asking white Americans to deny *their* cultural drives for land, wealth, and power while contending that the Indians should be protected in theirs. Moreover, no expanding people in history, whether in the New World, in Australia, in Africa, or in Siberia, has ever behaved any differently when confronted by a technologically weaker people. To say this is not to condone the ruthlessness and violence that have characterized European encounters with aboriginal peoples around the world, but it does make evident that there was nothing unique about the American treatment of the Indians.

4   The danger in this kind of argument, of course, is that it can justify almost any action taken by white men against Indians—or, for that matter, by any people against any other people or culture. And indeed it has been so used. But one can at least ask that a dominant culture accept the conquered on the same basis as it accepts its own members. This principle then brings us to the second possible alternative to the policy of removal. Could not the Indians have been absorbed, assimilated, or integrated into white society, rather than being forcibly removed and eventually herded onto reservations? Unlike the idea of leaving the Indians undisturbed, this alternative was actually tried and therefore we have some historical experience to use in thinking about it.

5   Here again the best approach is through the example of the Cherokees. Certainly if any Indian people could have "fitted" into white society, the Cherokees gave promise that they were such a people. A fierce and savage tribe in the middle of the eighteenth century, the Cherokees by the early years of the nineteenth century (not unlike the Japanese nation later, and also in response to the experience of being subjected to superior military and technological power) had undertaken to transform themselves into white men with red skins. They became farmers and cattle raisers, like their white neighbors. They put on white men's clothes and their leaders sent their sons to white men's schools. They bought and used black slaves in plantation agriculture just as the white Southerners did among whom they lived. They even took white men's names:

among the Cherokee leaders of the early 19th century were John Ross, Elias Boudinot, and John Ridge. Their own genius, Sequoyah, invented an alphabet, thereby laying the basis of a literature for his people. In 1827 the Cherokees drew up a constitution for themselves, which was clearly modeled after that of the United States; it not only provided for a tripartite division of government and a bill of rights, but it also excluded blacks from voting and holding office.

6   Not all the Cherokees, to be sure, could read or write Sequoyah's new alphabet, nor did they all cultivate fields like white men or live in the manner of their leaders, some of whom were not only planters of wealth but men of high culture as well. Nevertheless, by the time white Georgians increased their pressure to enter Cherokee lands, especially after the discovery of gold there in 1829, the Cherokees were no longer a savage and unlettered people. They had demonstrated that Indians could follow the guidelines suggested to them by President Thomas Jefferson years before. "When once you have property," Jefferson had counseled, "you will want laws and magistrates to protect your property and person. . . . You will find that our laws are good for this purpose . . . You will unite yourself with us, form one people with us, and we shall all be Americans. . . ."

7   The question which Jefferson did not consider, apparently, was whether his fellow white Americans were prepared to carry out their part of his suggested policy. Where the Cherokees were concerned, as in earlier confrontations between Indians and whites, the answer was no, even though—in the Cherokee instance—the Indians had gone far in the direction Jefferson had advised. Generally speaking, at least until the nineteenth century, the whites treated the Indians as a separate people, to be pushed aside, deprived of their land, and excluded from society. Although many whites, particularly in Washington, defended the claims of the Cherokees, few were prepared to use force to protect Indians against white men—despite the fact that the white man's own laws and promises were on the side of the Indians. In short, the case of the Cherokees, with their herculean adjustment to white men's ways, is probably the most powerful evidence for contending that the blame for the failure to try assimilation as an alternative to removal should be placed primarily upon the whites.

8   But that is not the end of the story. For if the Cherokees are the best example of Indian adaptation to the culture of the white man, they also come close to being the only one; most Indian peo-

ples did not want to become like white men. In fact, even the Cherokees, for all their remarkable adoption of the ways of white men, did not want to be integrated into white society. They still intended to live separately from whites, preferring for example to remain outside the jurisdiction of the state of Georgia.

9   This separatist attitude of the Indians is in marked contrast with the attitude of blacks, whose principal goal after slavery was to become an integral part of white society, as it had been for free Negroes during the era of slavery. Indians resisted the white man's education and his religion, as the missionaries found out on the early reservations even before the Civil War. The precise opposite was true of blacks. One of the dramatic developments of the Reconstruction period in the South was the enthusiasm with which the former slaves flocked to the schools that the Freedmen's Bureau and Northern philanthropists established after the war. Moreover, it was black eagerness for white men's education that was one of the strong forces behind the founding of the first free public schools in the Southern states during Reconstruction.

10   Resistant as Indians may have been toward the culture of the whites, their own culture, or cultures—for these ran the gamut from the most primitive, like that of the Shoshone of the Great Basin, to the highly developed, like the sedentary and organized societies of the Natchez of the lower Mississippi valley and of the Iroquois confederation of western New York—were by no means unchanging or static. A number of Indian cultures absorbed and creatively used a great many traits and technics not only from other Indian societies but from white culture as well. The cultural borrowings from whites ranged from tools and guns to horses and liquor. Some of these new technics the Indians quickly adapted to their own purposes; others—like alcohol—they failed to control. The horse is perhaps the most brilliant example of Indian borrowing. Prior to the arrival of the Spanish in the New World there were no horses in North America. Yet within a mere two hundred years the Indians worked out a whole new cultural pattern that centered on the horse and the bison, a pattern which most white Americans today erroneously think of as typically Indian and, equally erroneously, as having origins lost in the dim recesses of the past.

11   Nevertheless Indian cultures did resist assimilation to the culture of the whites, and they continued to resist even when, after the Civil War, the whites began to press systematically for Indian integration. This new policy toward the Indians was undoubtedly influenced by the fact that the debate over the future of the black man

had concluded that Negroes would be citizens and would be granted the same rights and opportunities as other Americans. Indeed, among the figures in the early fight for Indian rights after the Civil War were old stalwarts of the anti-slavery crusade like Harriet Beecher Stowe, Lydia Maria Child, and Wendell Phillips. To such people it seemed evident that the proper place for the Indian—whose conquest was being completed just as slavery had also come to an end—was precisely that which had been written into the Constitution for blacks and long applied to immigrants.

12   The principle of assimilation was epitomized by a Commissioner of Indian Affairs in 1887 when speaking of the need for Indians to give up their native languages. "Instruction of Indians in the vernacular," he contended, "is not only of no use to them but is detrimental to the cause of education and civilization and will not be permitted in any Indian school over which government has any control. . . . It is believed that if any Indian vernacular is allowed to be taught by missionaries in schools on Indian reservations it will prejudice the pupil as well as his parents against the English language. . . . This language which is good enough for a white man or a black man ought to be good enough for the red man. . . . The impracticality, if not impossibility, of civilizing Indians of this country in any other tongue than our own would seem obvious."

13   Probably the most extreme example of the effort to destroy Indian culture in the name of civilizing the Indian is encountered in the person and program of Captain Richard Henry Pratt. Significantly, Pratt came to the question of Indian assimilation from a prior experience with blacks. His first assignment in the United States Army was as an officer of a Negro regiment in the West, where he also first encountered Indians. In pursuit of a growing interest in working out ways of integrating Indians into American society, Pratt visited Hampton Institute in Virginia. Founded after the Civil War by Samuel Armstrong as a school for former slaves, Hampton was opened to Indians in the 1870's as a way of doing for them what was being done for blacks. Pratt soon came to disapprove of mixing blacks and Indians in the process of assimilation because he thought their problems were different. The most important need of the Indian, Pratt insisted, was greater contact with whites and their culture—something that Negroes had experienced all their lives under slavery. Once Indians and whites could see one another on a day-to-day basis, he was convinced, they would accept one another and separation between red and white would end. Years later Pratt summed up his purpose in the revealing remark

that "it was surely only necessary to prove that Indians were like other people and could be as easily educated and developed industrially to secure the general adoption of my views. All immigrants," he went on, "were accepted and naturalized into our citizenship by that route and thus had a full fair chance to become assimilated with our people and our industries. Why not the Indian?" Pratt's concluding question defined the Indian issue for white Americans for almost a century.

14   The method that Pratt proposed became the famous Carlisle Indian School, which he set up under government auspices in southeastern Pennsylvania in 1879. Pratt cajoled Indian families to send, voluntarily, their sons and daughters to his school, with the understanding that the young people would be completely removed from contact with Indian culture. Not only would the school train them in white men's arts and language at a place far removed from the Indian reservations but the young Indians would also be boarded with white families over the summer.

15   Over the years several thousand Indians attended the Carlisle and other boarding schools subsequently established, and in demonstrating how quickly individual Indians could adopt white culture, these institutions were highly successful. Nor was there any difficulty in locating white families who would take in the young Indians as boarders; in fact, the demand for Indians always exceeded the supply. It is hard to imagine many white families volunteering to take in black children for purposes of socializing them. It is often forgotten, in this same connection, that Andrew Jackson, despite his reputation as a hater of Indians, took an Indian orphan into his home to be raised as his son. So far as is known, he never took a black child into his home, though they were all around him in the slave quarters.

16   But the Carlisle Indian school was not the most important measure of the interest in the 1880s in assimilating Indians into white America. That honor belonged to the Dawes Act of 1887. Before the passage of the Dawes Act the movement to assimilate Indians had been unsystematic and largely unofficial. Under the new law the United States government itself embarked upon a deliberate policy of requiring assimilation by breaking up the reservations. Each household of Indians would be allotted 160 acres of land, which would become the property of the head of the family, thereby making him a landowner, like most other American farmers. Indians who obtained such allotments would also become citizens, like the former slaves.

17   Soon after the policy was implemented, its disastrous effects on the Indian became apparent. Through fraud, or trickery, or out of sheer ignorance of the law and economics, the Indians lost their lands at a prodigious rate. Those who managed to hold on to their land soon found it difficult, if not impossible, to make a decent living on the poor-quality and relatively small tracts allotted them by the government. And, of course, under the new policy government annuities ceased going to Indians who lived on the allotments, for the purpose of the policy was to put the Indian on his own. Not surprisingly, the Indian population of the country declined ominously and some experts began to talk of the "vanishing American."

18   Clear failure though it was, the policy of assimilation was not officially repudiated until 1934, when John Collier, a new chief of the Bureau of Indian Affairs, prevailed upon Congress to pass the Wheeler-Howard Act, which repealed the Dawes Act and inaugurated a new Indian policy. In the intervening forty-seven years almost two-thirds of Indian lands had passed into the hands of the whites, but Collier, under the authority of the new law, sought to reconstitute Indian culture on the reservations. Indian rituals and customs long discouraged, or even forbidden, were now permitted and encouraged; some of the Indian lands once lost were bought back. The Indian population began to grow, so that today there are about as many Indians in the country as there were when Europeans arrived in the seventeenth century.

19   Collier's efforts were widely praised by anthropologists and other experts here and in other countries, where aboriginal populations faced similar threats. Yet the existence of an unassimilated group in the midst of society was an anomaly to most Americans and to their government. Always there lurked the hope or expectation that the Indian would become, as blacks and immigrants had, a part of the going society. As Pratt had said, not in hostility but in friendship, "Why not the Indian?"

20   It is this persistent expectation which helps us understand why government policy toward Indians has fluctuated so widely since the days of the Indian wars. For the shift from separation to integration (the Dawes Act) and then back to separation with the Wheeler-Howard Act in 1934 was not the end of the story. In 1953 the Eisenhower administration once again changed policy. This new approach to the Indian, ominously called "termination," was not really new at all. It provided for the federal government to conclude its special relationship with the Indians by turning the reservations

as quickly as possible over to the control of the states, which, it was anticipated, would then break them up and put the Indians on their own. As many anthropologists and Indians had warned, termination turned out to be no less disastrous than the Dawes Act before it. Where it was instituted the Indians lost their remaining lands and, when forced off the reservations, they were unprepared to compete with whites.

21   In consequence, policy was soon shifted once again 180 degrees. In July 1970 President Nixon announced the end of termination and a return to the preservation and encouragement of Indian life. He promised financial support for the development of economic enterprises that would make Indian communities truly viable; in 1971 he relinquished government control over the lands around Blue Lake, New Mexico, to the Taos Pueblo Indians, for whom the area had long been sacred; and an Indian was named as head of the Bureau of Indian Affairs.

22   These vacillations in policy over the last century have stemmed largely from the refusal of white Americans to recognize that the Indians are not like other minorities, and particularly not like the blacks with whom they have so often been misleadingly compared. Over the years, it is true, individual Indians have left the reservations and made their way into the surrounding society. Others have done so selectively, working outside the reservation for a time and then returning to their people. But the striking fact is that whenever the Indians have been able to express their preferences either in words or "with their feet," they have made it clear that they do not want to be integrated into American society. As recently as 1952 over 60 per cent of the Navajos—the largest single Indian group in the country—still did not speak English. Even among those tribes in which a much higher proportion speak English, it remains a second language. As the anthropologist Edward Spicer has pointed out in regard to the Indians of the Southwest under Spanish, American, and Mexican jurisdiction: "At the end of 430 years, it was clear that, despite intensification of communication among all the peoples of the region, through the adoption of common language and a great deal of cultural borrowing and interchange, most of the conquered people had retained their own sense of identity. Moreover, there was little or no ground for predicting that even by the end of half a millennium of contact the native peoples would have ceased to exist as identifiable ethnic groups."

23   Nor has this refusal been principally a response to hostility from white society. Although there are and always have been un-

doubted acts of discrimination against Indians, white society has, on the whole, long been willing to accept Indians socially and economically to a degree that stands in marked contrast to its attitude toward blacks. Today a white person with Indian ancestry, for example, will readily admit to that ancestry—perhaps even with a certain amount of pride. Rare, however, is the white person who will own to any African ancestry, for to do so is to assume all the social and economic burdens that blackness incurs in American society.

24   There is a perverse irony in American practice toward Indians and blacks. America has offered to Indians what blacks have long wanted but been denied, while insisting upon for blacks what Indians have wanted but which blacks reject. Or, put another way, Indians have had the choice of becoming white men with red skins or remaining Indians. Generally speaking, blacks have enjoyed no such choice, even in theory, for from the time of slavery they have been forced to be a part of white culture. (The culture of the ghetto is at most a subculture and not comparable to the distinct Indian cultures even of today.)

25   Indians, when confronted with the choice, have chosen to be red men. This is why Indians, unlike blacks, do not demand civil equality. For to do so would be to acknowledge that they are an integral part of the white man's culture. Indians have consistently shown that they want to be treated as red men only.

26   It is just that insistence upon difference that has been so difficult for white Americans to accept. Immigrants and Negroes have insisted only upon individual acceptance and economic opportunity, and in theory, if not in practice, the dominant culture has found no difficulty in agreeing to these demands. The Indian demand for separate existence simply has no antecedent or analogy in the American experience. White native Americans, it is true, have known of other colored peoples at various times in the past who were judged incapable of becoming "white men"—Negroes, Chinese, and Japanese, for example. Never before, however, have white Americans encountered people who *refused* the opportunity to become Americans.

27   Perhaps because this refusal constitutes a blow to the national pride, white Americans have stubbornly continued to believe that Indians would eventually consent to become like them. Even a modern liberal organization like the Fund for the Republic has been unable to shake off the idea that the traditional approach to minorities in the United States must also be the proper one for Indians. On the opening page of the study *The Indian: America's*

Unfinished Business, which the Fund financed and published in 1966, the goal was described as "making the Indian a self-respecting and useful American citizen. This policy involves restoring his pride of origin and faith in himself after years of crippling dependence on the federal government and arousing his desire to share in the advantages of modern civilization." Significantly, the last chapter of the study is devoted to "Policies Which Impede Indian Assimilation."

28   What are the implications for national policy of this recognition that Indians bear no real analogy to other social groups in the United States? The principal conclusion, it would seem, is to abandon the idea of making Indians over into white men with red skins. The right of *individual* Indians to leave the reservation and compete in the world outside should of course be retained. But it is time for other Americans to give up, once and for all, the expectation that somehow, in some way, at some time, the Indians in general will be absorbed into white society. The question should no longer be, "Why not the Indian?" but rather, "Why cannot the Indian remain an Indian?" Starting from where they are now, deciding their own future course of economic action, Indians ought to be helped to work out a way of life for themselves as separate communities within the larger American society.

29   If that policy can be carried out then the United States will have embarked upon an experiment in pluralism rare in the history of European expansion. Few modern governments have undertaken to protect and nurture a technologically weaker culture for the indefinite future. In America the basis of pluralism has been acceptance by the minority of the principal or central values of the society, with their differences from the majority remaining confined to relatively minor values or cultural traits. Thus Poles, or Irish Catholics, or Jews can be recognized as different in some habits and practices from the dominant culture, but at the same time the dominant culture assumes that each of the minorities will eventually learn English, participate in the standard occupations of the society, and live in a style that fits into an industrial and urban social order.

30   A special place for the Indian in American pluralism is justified by the fact that none of the forces or influences which have made assimilation an acceptable goal for other minorities are operative for him. Unlike any other minority, Indians did not come here voluntarily with a ready-made commitment to assimilation; unlike blacks, Indians have preferred to maintain a way of life distinct from the way of the whites.

31   A special place for Indians in American pluralism is justified, too, by the many treaties of recognition and support that white America so solemnly entered into with Indians over the years and then broke. For unlike any other social group in American history, Indians were promised support and encouragement in return for having given up their lands to European invaders. To accept Indianness as a social fact and as a part of American pluralism is but to acknowledge the debt that was incurred when one culture encountered another and pushed it aside. It is futile today to make a moral judgment of that epic clash of cultures; within the cultural context of the nineteenth century, let alone the seventeenth, that conflict does not seem to have been avoidable. Today, however, the Indians pose no threat, military or otherwise, to the dominant white culture. And certainly they no longer possess any large amounts of wealth that can further excite the cupidity of others.

32   In short, by recognizing what the past reveals to us about Indians and their culture, we are in a position to transcend our own history, and to recognize, in policy as well as in theory, that "the only good Indian" is a real Indian, not a white man with red skin.

CONSIDERATIONS

Degler's basic thesis is that American Indians are unlike other minority groups in this country in that they do not want to be integrated or assimilated into the dominant white culture. Do you feel he has offered sufficient evidence to support the conclusion that real Indian culture should be encouraged and nurtured, not assimilated? What role should the federal and state governments have in deciding Indian policy?

This article is in the form of an argument, and the author presents his thesis within the framework of historical perspective. Has he fairly delineated all aspects of the Indian situation? Note the author's personal detachment. Why is it effective? In which particular examples would an emotional or extremely personal attitude have weakened Degler's argument?

Is pluralism the most desirable policy for America to follow in its future "treatment of the Indians"? Should pluralism be extended to other minority, technologically weaker culture groups, or is assimilation the best course to take? Present your ideas in the form of an argument, carefully formulated, and supported with examples and facts.

VOCABULARY

(2) **rapacious**   inordinately greedy
(2) **assimilated**   absorbed; brought into conformity; adapted

(3) relativism   a theory which holds that criteria of judgment are relative, varying with individuals and their environments

(3) aboriginal   native; indigenous; original

(5) tripartite   three-part-legislative; executive; judicial

(7) herculean   in the manner of Hercules; gigantic effort to perform a difficult task

(12) vernacular   language of the people

(17) prodigious   extraordinarily high

(17) annuities   specified incomes payable at stated intervals for a fixed period, often for the recipients' life time

(19) anomaly   an incongruity or deviation from the common type or norm

(21) viable   practicable; workable

(22) vacillations   fluctuations in opinions, policies

(23) incurs   brings undesirable consequences upon oneself

(29) pluralism   philosophical theory that more than one separate and distinct basic substances can co-exist

(31) cupidity   greed or avarice

(32) transcend   exceed or surpass; go beyond former limits

The American Nature of Football

JOHN FINLAY

1 In the last two decades North America has witnessed a startling rise in the popularity of football, so that this game and not baseball is now *the* American game. An explanation has been offered by Marshall McLuhan, who writes that "the TV image . . . spells for a while, at least, the doom of baseball. For baseball is a game of one-thing-at-a-time, fixed positions and visibly delegated specialist jobs such as belonged to the now passing mechanical age. . . . In contrast, American football is nonpositional, and any or all of the players can switch to any role during play. . . . It agrees very well with the new needs of decentralized team play in the electric age."

2 In order to isolate the elements of American football that are prized, it is not sufficient to compare it with baseball. Rather, it is necessary to examine not merely the American game, but other brands of football, too. These games are not independent; until about the middle of the nineteenth century there was but an ill-defined "ur-football." It was from this that the individual varieties crystallized, and in doing so they seized upon and developed aspects of the game that appealed to the host society.

3 Ur-football was weakly structured, but any game that is to become a professional mass spectacle must impose limits upon itself. Time is an aspect of limitation. In soccer and rugby the referee is the sole judge of time. Given his other duties, his timing must be

rather hit-and-miss. The division of the games is similarly rudimentary; in order to equalize the advantage of sun, slope and so on, the game is simply divided into halves. In North America, not only is the measurement of time taken out of the hands of the referee and lodged in those of a specialist, but the element of "guessing" is removed. The game and the clock are stopped between actions, and time begins to elapse only when the referee whistles for play to resume. There is also a more sophisticated ordering of the game. Each half is divided into two, which helps to equalize opportunity more successfully. In soccer and rugby it is very easy to waste time, but in North America time is not only precise, it is precious.

4   The penalty for time wasting is the loss of territory. Here is another limitation, the way in which space is conceived and handled. European games are most cavalier when it comes to fixing the playing area; in both soccer and rugby, maximum/minimum dimensions are given. These boundary lines serve to mark off a neutral, equal space. The only serious irruption into the emptiness of a soccer field is the penalty area around the goal, a magical exception designed to protect the goalkeeper, the one player permitted to handle the ball. Rugby is somewhat more space conscious. Although overall dimension is equally fluid, the dividing up of the field is more apparent.

5   Such thinking is foreign to the North American pattern. To begin with, the dimensions of the playing area are rigidly prescribed. The game's characteristic—making ten yards' progress in a given number of attempts—calls for marking each yard on the field. No point of the field is of more value than any other. While soccer players know that the relatively small goal is all-important (an infraction inside the magic territory guarding it results in a penalty that is an almost automatic goal), the North American player refuses to acknowledge that any point is more important than another—forward movement at any point of the field is what counts.

6   At this point the deeper significance of space and its handling begins to emerge, a significance that goes to the root of the various codes. Soccer sees its field, other than the goal area, as a neutral space within which the action is allowed to build up. The objective is the goal, and the field exists merely to allow the team to group itself, mount an attack, and move in on that goal. Rugby, while not so pure in this respect, is essentially very similar. On the other hand, for the North American player each piece of the field is, in a sense, the goal line. Whereas the soccer player scores explosively, the North American must score on the installment plan.

7   The basic divergence may be illustrated by a comparison of penalties. In European games the method of compensating for infraction is a kick or "scrum" taken at the point of infraction, the ball being handed over to the team offended against. This amounts to little more than giving this team a chance of better position. In North America an infraction usually means the loss of a certain number of yards, so that the team offended against creeps another installment nearer.

8   The North American game is much more precise, standardized, indeed efficient than the European. In short, it approaches the scientific criteria of control and replication as closely as any sport can without forfeiting that element of unpredictability that must always be there. The clinching point is the use of statistics. The American sports fan is avid for figures that will make possible "true" comparisons and facilitate that favorite pastime, the composition of "dream teams." While not totally unknown in Europe, such attitudes are exceptional. Nor is it enough to say that North American sports lend themselves to this approach whereas European ones do not; the development of North American games was governed precisely by this urge to quantify.

9   The next dimension is the way in which the participant is perceived. Until recently European games have restricted a team to the actual number allowed by the rules to be in play at any one time. Should one player have to withdraw, no substitute was allowed. This situation has been modified of late, and limited substituting is now permitted. In North America, however, the practice of substitution has had a long history. Alongside this distinction is another akin to it. The North American coach never relinquishes control of his team, and he and his rooftop spotter are constantly analyzing the game and adjusting the team strategy accordingly: the captain on the field has but limited power of shaping the game.

10   These two points taken together lead to the conclusion that in North America the player is devalued—the players are not so much playing as being played. When unsatisfactory, the player is removed. The team, in a way, overshadows the individuals who compose it. This impression is confirmed by the American practice of specialization, and here McLuhan is quite wrong in his characterization. Rather than the game being one of interchanging players able "to switch to any role during play," football is a most restricted form. For a long time the game has been played by two squads, one for offense and one for defense, and a total changeover accompanies a change in ball possession. But specialization goes further than this: even on the offense, there are players who are held to be ineli-

gible receivers, and clubs keep players on the roster whose sole function is to kick the ball. In European games the trend has been the other way. In older forms of soccer a distinction was made between the heavier backs and the lighter forwards. But the logic of the game, especially as developed by the Latins, destroyed this nascent specialization, and now all must be potential attackers, all possible defenders.

11   One must conclude that McLuhan was wrong in claiming that football was not "a game of one thing at a time, fixed positions and visibly delegated specialist jobs." Far from football's belonging to the electronic age, it belongs to a way of life now superseded. If any sport is suited to the electronic age, that sport is soccer.

12   But if football belongs to the mechanical age, the problem still remains of why it is rising and baseball declining. In fact, there is one ground on which the two sports diverge radically.

13   Baseball has about it elements that have to be described as unfair. Whereas in football each yard gained is identical, in baseball one hit is not the same as another. For example, a team may load three bases by successively having its hitters gain a base at a time, which, since the game's glory is the home run, may be looked upon as relative failures. At this point the big hitter may unleash a home run and count four for his side. Had the same hit been made at the start of an inning, only one run would have resulted. It is true that the way would be open for the bases to be loaded and for the big hitter to make another appearance; indeed this process could go on indefinitely. The point is that this possibility is not real to the spectators. Another way of illustrating this point is to contrast the episodic nature of baseball with the continuous narrative of football. In baseball, the end of the inning ends any advantage; for instance, three loaded bases count for nothing. But consider the analogous situation in football when there are two evenly matched teams unable to make first downs and obliged to kick. Eventually the superior team will approach the opponent's goal line, if only by the difference between the two punts, and in this way it is possible for any interim advantage to be transformed into a score.

14   Then again, there is the very meaning of the home run. There is something apocalyptic about such an explosion of power which, once it has connected with the ball, makes a formality of the hitter's tour of the bases. There is nothing comparable in football. The nearest is the long pass, but there is nothing so clear-cut about this—either in definition or in execution—and there is nothing in the statistics to set beside the home run. The favorite football statistics are averages, and these are decidedly nonapocalyptic.

15   The implication is that if both baseball and football are similarly attuned to a rational capitalist environment, baseball is the game of an early, football of a mature capitalism. The early capitalist period, above all in the United States, was a time when the rational, calculating approach was yet shot through with a gambling, piratical residue—the robber baron era, in fact. Baseball is a robber baron game. But when capitalism matures and moves into the stage of staid corporateness that prefers safety to spectacle, certain small gains to risky windfalls, its sports style must similarly shift.

16   Japan, still in the early, heroic stages of capitalism, has avidly taken to baseball but not to football. It is not a question of Japanese physique serving as a determinant, for rugby has long had a following in Asia. It may be predicted, then, that when their capitalism moves into a higher stage, the Japanese will move on to football.

CONSIDERATIONS

Do you agree that the players are "being played" in a football game? (paragraphs 9 and 10) Are all athletes in team sports merely pawns in an electric-age style of college and professional athletics? If this is true, is it demeaning to be a player? Could this be related to the rising trend toward antiheroes in sports—the Joe Namaths and Duane Thomases who break the rules off the field? Do you see parallel situations outside of sports—men and women who are pawns in their jobs or their roles in life?

In this article Finlay presents a highly unified argument beginning with the quotation from Marshall McLuhan (paragraph 1) and concluding in the final two paragraphs with an analogy between capitalism and the sports of football and baseball. Analyze his argument: what are its main contentions? How are transitions accomplished? (Note the use of key words, such as *time,* between paragraphs 3 and 4.) What is the effect of diction in the article?

Do you think Finlay's primary reason for expressing this view of sports was to analyze the development of the American form of capitalism? If so, has he used a good analogy? What other analogies might you use? Write your own analysis of one or more aspects of American capitalism; use analogies to illustrate your view.

VOCABULARY

(4) **irruption**   invasion
(10) **nascent**   beginning to develop
(14) **apocalyptic**   prophetic or divinely revealing

Other
Rhetorical
Features

GOOD BEGINNINGS

Where to begin. That can pose the biggest hurdle of all for the college freshman who faces writing assignments almost weekly. It's too easy, and not particularly helpful, to say that one begins, naturally, at the beginning.

First, in opening whatever you write you want to engage the interest of your reader. All your life you have been storing up experiences, so chances are you do have certain things of interest to relate. Ask yourself some questions: What is my topic about? What do I know about it? Why should someone else want to hear what I have to say? What are my options in treating this subject? What direction shall I take? Where will I lead my reader? Should I sound conversational, formal, humorous, serious? (In other words, what is the appropriate tone for the subject?) How shall I gain the immediate attention of my audience? The beginning must, first of all, introduce. Second, it should give some indication of the way in which your paper will be developed. You should get your reader's attention with your first word or sentence. You can do this either by the manner of expression—the style—or by the subject itself. If the subject is sufficiently interesting, a straightforward statement about it might work: "The Mississippi River reached the highest water mark in recorded history yesterday." A more dramatic statement would pique the curiosity of a wider audience: "Reaching levels higher than ever in recorded history, the Mississippi River inundated parts of southwest Missouri, destroying the homes and farmlands of hundreds of small farmers."

If you are treating a controversial or moot subject, you might want to open with key words only, a fragment (incomplete sentence): "Space program dumped!" Then follow with an explanatory sentence. This is rather like the short headlines in newspapers. It is a device to get your foot wedged in the door of someone's mind (to use a metaphor). Of course, if you start off with a bang you should sustain the intensity, not flounder off into some vague generalities. Or, you might begin with a question: "Why has Congress been so reluctant to renew NASA's funds for space exploration?" You may want to challenge an accepted fact, prevailing attitude, common belief: "Defense budget moneys would be better spent on space exploration than on developing new weapons systems."

Your beginning should set the tone or mood of what you intend to write. It should be consistent with what follows. It should also be appropriate to the length of the essay. It can be of any length, but a five-paragraph opening, followed by two paragraphs in the middle and a three-paragraph closing would be out of proportion.

The one essential is clarity. If the beginning is muddled, the reader will be muddled. He will have to work too hard to decipher what you are trying to say and lose whatever interest he might have. The surest way to achieve clarity is to have your destination in mind when you begin. In fact, you might start with the part of your conclusion that seems most attention getting. And there's a bonus: with your conclusion firmly in mind at the beginning of your work, you will avoid cluttering up the body of your paper with irrelevant sidetracks and tangents that do not belong in your thesis.

Put yourself in your reader's place and you may see your writing in a new way. For instance, try taking the role of a reader who dislikes your subject or is hostile to your point of view. What might capture your interest in spite of these feelings? Probably the same approach will engage your reader as well.

A good introduction, then, helps your reader with both the interest and organization of the paper. It sets the tone, it suggests the direction you will take, and it gives the reader some promise of things to come.

PRACTICE

1. Write three one-paragraph beginnings, about a hundred words each, for a critique of any campus activity. Use three different approaches to the same topic; for example, a shock statement, an attention-getting fact, and an historical reference.

2. Read several recent magazine articles, concentrating on the effectiveness of the introductory paragraphs and select the best two. In a short paragraph analyze or describe why they are effective.

The Overeducation of America: Too Many for Too Few Jobs

By stating his thesis in a fresh and interesting manner, El et captures the attention of the reader in the opening paragraph of his essay. He creates a desire in him to continue reading. Write three one-paragraph beginnings that stimulate the interest of the reader and that indicate whether the essay is to be argumentation, exposition, narration, or description. (You can do this by clearly stating your thesis.) You may want to appeal to the reader's interest in conflict by choosing controversial topics of current interest.

- Write several beginnings using the devices below as attention-getters:

  Interesting or amusing incident or anecdote

  Striking facts, statistics, instead of dull generalizations

  Shocking statement

  Allusion or historical reference

  Subtle hint of something startling to come—a "teaser"

  Statement of a serious problem and a solution to be offered in the essay

  Reference to a common emotional experience with which the reader can easily identify

  Asking a rhetorical question

- Write three beginning paragraphs in which you set the tone for the rest of the essay. For example, one might be serious or formal, one humorous or satirical, and one informal or conversational. Choose topics that lend themselves to these particular tones.

- In newspapers or magazines find two or three articles that you feel have weak beginnings. Rewrite these so that they are more effective in terms of capturing reader attention.

For examples of individual paragraphs, that have *good beginnings*, see p.15, ¶1, p.27, ¶1, p.108, ¶1-4, p.143, ¶1, p.234, ¶1-3, p.381, ¶1, p.406, ¶1-6.

CONCLUSIONS (Good Endings)

All writing must come to an end at some point, but too many college essays end with a whimper instead of a bang—a whimper that goes like this: "Well, that's all I have to say about this subject and I mean, well, I can't think of anything else to write, and I just sort of, well, I mean that's it, I quit. . . . ." An ending that is anything like this one is certain to leave nothing but a bad impression on your reader. You cannot hope to persuade, convince, or impress anyone if your conclusion is inconclusive.

A conclusion should help the reader gain insight or offer him some sense of satisfaction that the subject has been covered, the questions answered, the doubts resolved—that he got where you headed him to with your beginning.

You may even propel the reader into another situation, prompt him to read further on the subject, or give him a sense of enlightenment. Here are several types of conclusions. Which one you use depends on your style, your purpose, and your tone.

1. A restatement, summary, or quick review.

2. A prediction based on supporting historical evidence.

3. A call to action. If your prediction is negative, you may want to make a plea to change the direction of it; if it is positive, you probably would reinforce it by some call to action in order to ensure it.

4. A question or suggestion, used to point the reader in a new direction or give him an idea of what to do. ("If the new ecology center is to operate successfully, you must help. Bring your aluminum cans, all kinds of glass, and bundled newspapers to the center each Saturday from 9 to 5.")

5. An anecdote, a bit of irony, or simply a memorable comment. Whichever of these approaches you take, your conclusion should be:

*   Consistent with the tone of the whole piece

*   Proportionate to the length of the entire essay

*   Clear

*   Relevant to what has gone before, and except in special cases should not introduce new ideas

One test of a good conclusion is that it can't be moved around. Even if you write it first, you can't place it first—you can't put it in the middle of the theme. If it is truly a conclusion, it belongs only at the end of the paper.

Conclusions (Good Endings)

• In the beginning of the essay, Ellet mentions ". . . the ghost of the Dream." In his concluding paragraph he refers to this idea again but gives the reader new insight into the nature of the "ghost." The ending is also a restatement (or summary) of what has been discussed in the essay. Write a one-paragraph ending for each of the three beginnings you wrote in the exercises for *Good Beginnings*. Be sure that they agree in length and tone and that they are relevant to the beginnings.

- An ending functions to re-emphasize the thesis, to help the reader remember it and to give him the feeling that the essay is complete. Choose three more beginnings that you wrote for that section and write endings for them in which you use some device *other than* a restatement of the thesis. You can conclude with:

PRACTICE

1. Choose two conclusions from current magazine or newspaper articles. In a short paragraph, analyze the reasons for the effectiveness (or failure) of each.

2. Write three different paragraphs about the same topic using three different types of conclusions. These conclusions will necessarily be short if they are in proportion to the length of the whole piece, which in this case is a paragraph.

   An analogy that illustrates your thesis

   An anecdote or dramatic incident that relates to your topic

   A prediction

   A question to provoke further thought

   A challenge to the reader

   A solution to the problem

- In a magazine like *Harper's* or the *Atlantic Monthly*, find an example of a good ending to an essay. Write a paragraph in which you explain why the ending is effective, and how it ties in with the thesis.

- In a popular magazine find an example of a poor, weak ending, one that does not relate to the thesis, is not consistent in tone or diction to the rest of the essay, or leaves the reader with the sense that the piece has not ended at all—just "stopped." Then carefully analyze the essay and rewrite the ending so that the weaknesses are corrected.

- Go back to one of your old essays, review it, and revise it, paying particular attention to the beginning and ending. Make a note of any weaknesses you have discovered.

For examples of individual paragraphs having *good endings* or *conclusions,* see p.42, ¶36, p.63, ¶31, p.184, ¶62–63, p.217, ¶38, p.233, ¶79, p.345, ¶12–13.

The Overeducation of America

WILLIAM ELLET

1   No one would dare mention the American Dream at graduations anymore, because, like God, it's been put to rest. But the ghost of the Dream hovers over the ceremonies, whether or not the participants are aware of it. *Beg*

2   I avoided my graduation at the University of Chicago (the postal system handed me my degree), <u>but I couldn't avoid the ghost.</u> I found, much to my surprise, that the pale shade the Dream has become drifted through everything I expected in school and now in facing the long run. *Allus*

3   <u>Even with the Dream as a constant companion,</u> I should have been prepared for the confrontation with the long run, if only because my term in the university was one of many confrontations. But my classmates and I graduated thinking ourselves to be bright, knowing ourselves to be generally well-off and expecting things to remain the same. *Fig*

4   With prosperity the rule and having mostly generous parents, it was easy to have a sense of destiny. The world was not expected to fall into our laps, yet it was expected to be generous and welcome us. *Dict*

5   We were wrapped in the American Dream, the confidence in expectation and opportunity. So we had something in common, after all, with the Class of 1908, whose only significance to Chica-

go's Class of 1971 was its senior gift, a semicircular stone bench.

6   After growing to maturity entirely within the educational system, however, <u>leaving the university was like leaving home for the</u>   *Sim* <u>first time</u>—everybody does it, but the loss of horizons, the confusions of purpose and the sense that no one gives a damn were keenly felt.

7   The departure can be avoided. One Chicago student—balding, enervated and whose room was filled with a mountain of notes— had spent eight years getting a BA and making starts on several advanced degrees. He embarrassed some professors who gave the same lectures year after year by silently mouthing their words before they said them. <u>He wasn't a gadfly, but more like a ghost</u>   *Sim* <u>haunting the library corridors and reading rooms.</u>

8   For most of us, four years was quite enough. Besides, we had our own ghost, but ours impelled us to leave the university. We poured from the sanctuary of the university with degrees and expectations in hand to find the departure a shock.

9   <u>The first encounter with the long run was similar to a dose of</u>   *Angy* <u>tear gas: The eyes, nose and throat are invisibly attacked, sending</u> <u>one blindly and clumsily groping for escape.</u>

10   The Class of '71 stumbles because the ghost of the Dream is no longer a presence; now it haunts us. Mere assimilation of graduates into the work force has become a problem.

11   Affluence has created the sprawling educational complex. The   *C&E* universities are monuments to government and foundation spending; the huge number of students is a tribute to parental benevolence and ideas of success—the Dream perpetuated.

12   Alarm has grown as the demand for degree-holders has shrunk. Allan M. Cartter, chancellor of New York University, says flatly, "We have created a graduate education and research establishment in American universities that is about 30% to 50% larger than we shall effectively use in the 1970s and early 1980s. . . ."

13   The crunch has finally come for the educational establishment. Universities are retrenching, yet the number of degree-holders still outstrips demand. BAs, like our currency, have been devalued, only more drastically.

14   Graduation was a ritual of despair in light of facts like these: In eight years one-third of all eligible young people will hold degrees, but only one-fifth of the available jobs will require them.

15   Numbers being what they are in the job market, the premium is on experience, an adult monopoly which places the young at an immediate disadvantage. Unlike the Depression, the price paid is

underemployment rather than unemployment in a setting of prosperity and ostentation. We are a product of the Dream, a favored generation given all the breaks; we are victims of the Dream as youthful, human surpluses.

16   Sometimes dangers are seen only in retrospect; that seems to be the case with our education. Samuel Clemens never went to college, but he put it this way: "Soap and education are not as sudden as a massacre, but they are more deadly in the long run." | *Ante*

17   The danger of our education is the Dream, inflated by affluence and shattered by the experience of the long run. I know now this has come about out of good intentions; I was part of the Dream as a favored son given a good education; I knew of harm, but none came to me.

18   Learning has been my occupation for 17 years. I developed early, though I don't know exactly how, the most important skill of my occupation: testing well. I also read and write efficiently, although my grammar is a little shaky, and once I even knew the mysteries of calculus. | *Tran*

19   I could say the same for most of my classmates. Our occupation has enjoyed enormous popularity as the American educational system has responded to growing prosperity, the prolongation of education and the high educational demands of this society.

20   I knew these things dimly in passing through the grades of my occupation, but facing the long run from lobbies and personnel offices has shown me something more—I have had a liberal education in a conservative society which has only limited use for the skills of my occupation.

21   But I have been in a waiting room for a long time; this I was not even dimly aware of. The same factors that brought expansion in the educational system have also gradually transformed it into a large, well-appointed anteroom to society. | *Ext* *Meta*

22   There are certain comforts to the anteroom, particularly the highest one, the university: Responsibilities, at least the mundane ones of "getting by," are at a minimum outside the classroom; money for the most part is something parents and administrators worry about; and freedom can be talked about without a bemused smile.

23   We of the anteroom have formed a class that is neither adolescent nor adult. | *Tran*

24   Bitter experience has washed over the anteroom—for at Kent State, Jackson State, Berkeley and Columbia education has seen occasions as cruel as a massacre. Seeing a city burn, going outside

only during daylight, lying in bed hearing shots ring out—these were *Sarc*
aspects of education not advertised in Chicago's catalog, but the
Martin Luther King riots, which ravaged the city's south and west
sides in 1968, saw to it that a life-long suburbanite received graphic
lessons in urban warfare.

25   Sanctuaries, however benign in purpose, are maintained by   *Sync/*
power of some sort and education is no exception. It is the manifest   *Tone*
destiny of a university, fueled by the prestige of and need for education, to expand.

26   Thus, I saw apartment buildings of ghetto residents fall in my
neighborhood until mine, filled with students and employes of the
university, was the only one left standing. After the bulldozers left,
the land remained vacant for two years until I graduated.

27   The university's bulldozers, crashing away only a few feet from
my room, literally brought home the difference between an institution's saying and doing: All men merit respect, but student housing
is more valuable than ghetto housing.

28   With these lessons in mind, it's clear the siege of the anteroom
from within isn't a coincidence; it grew out of what the room is like,
the kinds of consciousness it produces and bears the marks the
Dream places on it.

29   A university, as a center of learning rather than as a manipula-
tor of land, is a place of realism and ferment. Inevitably, performance of the academic mission has an effect on students who claim
that knowledge has a moral force which dictates action. Naive as
this claim is, it has led to a lot of earnest effort—if poorly planned
and often bungled—toward changing the anteroom.

30   The pressure for action has caused teachers to look on students
as antithetical to the spirit of the university in much the same way
Aristotle did: "A young man is not a proper hearer of lectures . . .   *Þdx*
because the end aimed at is not knowledge but action."

31   Sometimes the reaction has been to throw students out of
school; more often, the reaction has taken the shape of a rhetorical
battleground, in the background of the visible campus struggle, in
which teachers have sought to convince students that discourse is
action and real change is possible only by working within other
institutions.

32   During my years in the anteroom, the most persuasive argument against action was the violent turn it almost always took; now,
it seems, the teachers' arguments have taken hold. Perhaps a new
realism contributes to this; students seem to understand better how
things stand, that administrators seek to save the anteroom from

financial ruin and that faculty members seek to save their intellectual and power prerogatives.

33   Violence always puts an end to philosophy and with us it did, of course. Yet our real weakness was that we have been citizens of no country. Utopia means "no place" and maybe we have suffered from that in the anteroom as an isolated, affluent minority demanding a suspension between adolescence and adulthood. We, like the administrators and teachers, have attempted to maintain our prerogatives while trying to break through the isolation.

34   Defeat in changing the anteroom has been accepted because the room is still cozy and it is still prestigious just to be there. Yet the defeat foreshadows a larger one that can be encountered only outside.

35   The Dream became a ghost during the early defeat; only now, however, has it begun to haunt us with the cold and deadly lessons about the intransigence of what is outside the anteroom, about the difficulty of finding even a minor role in the order of things and about how sadly prepared we were to face these facts.

CONSIDERATIONS

What are the origins of "The American Dream" and how has it been propagated through the years? In what sense does its "ghost" follow the college graduate into "the long run"? Do you think that education defined as formal classroom study is incapable of preparing its graduates for life outside those classrooms?

By what means does the author define the terms he uses—*the American Dream, the long run, the anteroom, the ghost*? Is this the type of writing you are accustomed to reading in newspaper stories? Toward what audience is this article directed?

Do you agree with Ellet that college students are neither adolescents nor adults? (paragraph 23) Might there be advantages in entering college a few years *after* high-school graduation? Develop a plan that would alter the present educational process so that (1) leaving the university would no longer be like leaving home for the first time (paragraph 6), and (2) studying would not be the student's sole occupation.

VOCABULARY

(7) **enervated**   weakened
(7) **gadfly**   a person who repeatedly and persistently annoys others
(13) **retrenching**   curtailing
(22) **bemused**   confused

(30) **antithetical**   opposing
(32) **prerogatives**   exclusive rights limited to persons of a particular category
(35) **intransigence**   uncompromising condition, inflexible

TRANSITIONS

Just as a collection of detached, isolated words does not make a sentence, so a group of disconnected, isolated thoughts and sentences does not make an essay. Both constructions require some kind of connections to their loose parts. In writing, these bridges are called *transitions*. Transitions connect words, sentences, and paragraphs; they give coherence to the writing, make it smoother and easier to read, and help prevent ambiguity. If you say, "He's very short of breath, he swims competitively," you have not only committed a comma fault, but the second part seems to be a non sequitur. (It doesn't seem to follow logically.) If you insert *but* after the comma, the sentence becomes clearer.

Sentences often need transitions between them as well as within them. Suppose you wrote: "The quarterback was benched for the season. The fans cheered the rookie." There is not a very clear connection. We need to know more—that the quarterback was replaced with a second stringer who had made a brilliant pass the game before. Again, suppose you wrote: "Young people today reject traditional religious beliefs and practices. Many of them have started going to church." You need a transition in order to connect two ideas. In this case, it could be a discussion of the fact that a lot of churches have begun to change their practice and ritual, or that the new generation is simply bringing new ideas to the old churches.

Paragraphs often need connections too. A historical reference to the Civil War may not be clearly related to a current commentary on Southeast Asia. An intermediate sentence would help by establishing the elements common to both, or explaining in some way that history often repeats itself. You might make do with just a few words: *But today . . .* or *If we compare the situation today, ...*"

If you still have trouble figuring out what a transition is, look at this list of words and phrases:

However	*but*	*and*	*or*	*moreover*	*finally*
in conclusion		*nevertheless*		*on the other hand*	
consequently	*but*	*these*			

You use them regularly; you are aware of them and know what they mean without much trouble. Now you will be conscious that they are transitions. When you come across them in your reading, try leaving them out and see what happens to the meaning. As you do this, you will become more and more adept at using them effectively in your own writing.

PRACTICE

1. Write a five-hundred word essay on some aspect of food—growing it, buying it, cooking it, eating it—and make a list of specific words you use as transitions or transitional sentences. (If you consciously put in transitions when you write or rewrite the essay, it will help in making the list.)
2. Reread one of the essays in your anthology and underline the transitions. Pay specific attention to whether there are any paragraphs you consider to be transitional.
3. In an essay of your own make marginal notes indicating those words, phrases, and paragraphs that you specifically intended to be transitional.

Disease as a Way of Life

In his essay Cassell presents specific information regarding a study of the Navajo Indians (paragraphs 3 and 4). Paragraph 5 presents additional information but with a different perspective. The two sets of ideas are linked by the transitional word *but* to reinforce the relation of ideas and create a smooth flow in meaning and structure. Make a list of the transitional words and phrases in this essay and analyze the way in which they weave it together.

- Read the following paragraph and supply the missing transitions. If you feel that the paragraph should be divided in two, provide a smooth and logical *paragraph* transition. (Justify and explain your choices by explaining the functions of each transition.)

  I was tense and excited on the first day of classes. I was also tired. I did not sleep well the night before. I was late for my first class. That made matters worse. I heard the teacher explaining that we could leave after he took role. He was tired too. He was excited and tense. It was his first teaching job. He did not sleep well the night before, either. I felt much better. I noticed the look of tension on the faces of some of the other students. I certainly was not alone.

- Write an essay about a particular craft or hobby in which you are involved. Explain what it is, how it is done, what skills and materials are needed, or what errors are to be avoided. Underline the specific words, phrases, and sentences you use as transitions.

• Write an outline for an essay on a subject of your choice. In planning your organization include a list of transitions you intend to use in order to smoothly and logically tie your ideas together. (Your objective is coherence.)

For examples of individual paragraphs using *transitions*, see p.28, ¶10, p.32, ¶38, p.109, ¶14, p.133, ¶5, p.174, ¶3, p.239, ¶38, p.334, ¶22, p.356, ¶28, p.407, ¶10.

Disease as a Way of Life

ERIC J. CASSELL

1   In all the recent talk about the "crisis" in medical care, a major *Thes*
concern—whether explicitly stated or merely implied—has been
the disproportionate burden of disease borne by America's poor.
The way in which to lift that burden, it has been generally assumed,
is to provide more health services: better financing, more doctors, a
greater application of technology. There can be no doubt that these
services are necessary, nor that some form of national health insurance over and above the present system of Medicare is a matter of
the utmost urgency. Yet in pressing for these goals we would do
well to take a hard look at some of the assumptions behind the
demand for better health services, lest in mistaking the true nature
of the problem we lead ourselves to the wrong solution.

2   As Warren Winkelstein, Jr. has recently noted, there may in
fact be good reason to dispute "the underlying belief among both
the lay public and people in the technical professions that the quantity and quality of medical services are directly related to the health
status of the population." As Winkelstein goes on to state, there is
little evidence to support the assumption that the health of a population is primarily a function of its medical services, and much to
contradict it.

3   To illustrate this contention, let us consider briefly the case of *Exemp*
the Navajo Indians, a poor and disease-ridden people that (begin-

ning in 1955) was the object of study of the Navajo-Cornell Field
Health Research Project. Working in close cooperation with the
tribal leaders, the study group brought modern medical services to a
part of the Navajo Indian reservation, providing a well-equipped
ambulatory care facility, transportation, physicians and nurses,
trained indigenous health aides, and access to hospital care. All of
this was introduced into an extremely poor, non-literate environment, among people living in extended families in windowless one-
room log-and-mud dwellings with dirt floors.

4   Both the Navajos and the study group were pleased with the
day-to-day achievements of the technology and the delivery system
that had been introduced into the reservation. Medical care—in the
classical form of clinical physicians (a complete innovation for the
Navajos when it was introduced)—was well received and utilized.
"The system was set up with full community participation, and
there was a mechanism for effective, continued community control." And by objective criteria as well, quite apart from the issue of
patient-satisfaction, the project had successes to report over the
course of its five years of operation. Tuberculosis, a common problem among the Navajos, was sharply reduced, and, by the end of the
study, so was the amount of significant ear infection among children.

5   But the really startling findings were on the negative side. Aside
from the reduction in tuberculosis and ear infections, at the end of
five years the investigators discerned *no evidence of any real change
in the pattern or prevalence of disease.* There was a possible slight
diminution in the overall death rates, despite an infant mortality
rate that persisted at three times the national average, but no reduction at all in the incidence of the diarrhea-pneumonia complex
which remained the single greatest cause of illness and death among
Navajo infants.

6   As the term "diarrhea-pneumonia complex" suggests, infants in
the Navajo environment commonly suffered or died from a combination of respiratory and intestinal complaints that are not caused
by any single bacterium or virus. Major contributing factors are
malnutrition and poor sanitation. Nor, in general, are antibiotics
helpful; the "normal" bacteria and viruses appear to get the upper
hand and keep it. The disease, in other words, is in some sense a
function of the way in which the Navajos lived and raised their
infants. Thus, in general terms, the entire disease pattern of the
tribe—unresponsive as much of it was to modern technology—
could not be changed until basic changes took place in the tribe's

Exmp/
Narr

Tran

Def

way of life. In a social setting conducive to a particular pattern of disease, medical care alone—no matter how modern, well delivered, or technically complete—cannot be expected to lift the burden of sickness.

7   Our own past as a nation is further illustrative of this point. Everyone is aware of the profound changes that have occurred over the past two generations in the patterns of disease in America. Moreover, since the disappearance of the common infectious scourges of the past has been more or less simultaneous with the growth and development of modern scientific medicine and its technical wizardry, it is commonly believed that the dramatic improvement in the health of our society was brought about by the achievements of physicians and medical science. By and large, however, this is not true.   *Bal S*

8   In the United States and other Western nations at the beginning of the 20th century the pattern of disease showed a high overall death rate (about 28 deaths per 1,000 population per year—the present rate is about 9 per 1,000 per year) with a certain monotony of cause: pneumonia and influenza, tuberculosis, typhoid fever, and the various dysenteries. Among the infants the common killer was the same diarrhea-pneumonia complex we noted among the Navajos. Now, this high rate of mortality, as well as the specific pattern of diseases, was in part traceable directly to the urban social conditions brought on by the Industrial Revolution. Mass shifts of the rural poor into the cities had resulted in poverty, crowding, unbelievable filth, and poor sanitation, and had provided fertile ground for the transmission of disease. In the United States the problem was compounded by the continuous influx of poverty-stricken immigrants.   *C&E*

9   In 1900 the annual death rate from tuberculosis in the United States was 200 per 100,000. By 1960 the rate was 5 per 100,000. Throughout these sixty years the death rate fell rapidly and steadily, so that by the 1950's, when the first effective anti-tuberculosis drugs became available, the annual rate was *already* below 20 per 100,000. Prior to the advent of the new drugs, whatever treatment was available was frequently ineffective, and was restricted primarily to those who could afford it. It seems reasonable to speculate, then, in the absence of any clear evidence to the contrary, that the improvement in the mortality rates that took place before the 1950's was due in large part to improved living conditions, including better nutrition and diminished crowding. (It is also true of the infectious   *Induc*

diseases like tuberculosis that a falling rate promotes a further diminution in the disease, simply because the fewer the individuals carrying it, the lower the chances of contracting the disease through contact.)

10   As with tuberculosis, so with typhoid. After 1905 cases of typhoid fever became steadily less common in New York City, so that by the time effective drugs became available, typhoid was already a very rare disease. In years past it was usual to attribute the decrease to typhoid immunization, but we know now that the vaccine at best is not very effective; rather, the improvement can be traced to the introduction of good sanitation, to chlorination of the water supply, and to improvements in personal hygiene.   *S Var*

11   Perhaps the most gratifying change of all was the decrease in infant mortality during the early decades of this century in New York. By far the greater part of this decrease can be attributed to the sharp reduction in the diarrhea-pneumonia complex which "occurred before there were any antimicrobial drugs at all; neither were there any vaccines for this disease complex. . . . The fall occurred during a time in which biomedical science and technology could put no specific, no decisive therapies or preventatives into the hands of our clinical physicians." Here again no single reason for the improvement can be pointed to, but it can be noted that it occurred during a period in which standards of living, education, nutrition, and sanitation all improved.   *Exemp*

12   In like manner we are today protected against many food-borne diseases more by the pattern of our society than by anything specific we do for our health. It is the economics of modern food distribution, not considerations of health, which demands that foods be packaged and protected against spoilage or contamination. The rapid bankruptcy of a soup company that had produced a few cases of botulism illustrates dramatically how much more effectively health may be protected by the mass media than by food inspectors.   *Comp*

13   Of course, our present pattern of death and disease is not merely what is left over after we have escaped the ravages of infectious diseases. Along with affluence and the good life has come a new pattern of disease: cancer, heart disease, stroke. Yet just as medical care played a minor role in reducing death rates in the past, so we should not expect that it alone will relieve us of our present burdens. In fact, after fifty years of consistent decline in the mortality rates, we witnessed in the 1960's a new upward trend, particularly among white males. The connection of a single personal habit—   *Tran*

Arg

cigarette smoking—with one disease, lung cancer, seems proved. In the case of our worst epidemic, coronary heart disease, however, the chain of causations is more complex. Diet, level of activity, cigarette-smoking, stress, as well as other factors are so interrelated here that it is fair to say that a whole pattern of life is involved—the pattern characteristic of an affluent society. It would be naive to expect that medical science by itself can "cure" us of this condition. Even if present surgical techniques were perfected, the value of a new or revised heart in the body of a patient whose life pattern remains otherwise unchanged would not be very high.

14   The general health of populations, then, is not directly dependent on medical services. Medical care did not get us out of our past troubles, and it will not get us out of our present ones. These propositions should be self-evident, yet the truth is that widespread confusion still remains on the subject. This is evidenced most strikingly by the continued use of infant mortality statistics in justification of proposed changes in the medical care structure. Although the first year of life is the most hazardous single year in the human life span until advanced old age, it is clearly more hazardous in some countries than in others. It is the apparent low showing of the United States in relation to a country like Sweden (24.8 infant deaths per 1,000 live births in the U.S. as against 14.2 in Sweden in 1963 [United Nations, 1967]) that distresses medical reformers. Mortality among black infants in America is almost twice as high as among whites; in certain New York ghettos infant mortality is three times the rate in more favored areas of the city.

15   The assumption is widespread that these differences reflect the inadequacy of the medical care provided in the United States as opposed to Sweden, or, within the United States, to the areas or groups with higher than average mortality rates. But this assumption does not stand up to close examination. The applicability here of the Navajo experiment cited above should be clear. For the Navajo Indians, the major factor determining the diarrhea-pneumonia complex and the high infant mortality was the pattern of tribal life, specifically the home environment; improved medical care did not, and could not alone, affect that pattern. (Nor, incidentally, could a program of what is generally called "health education," since health-associated learning would involve not merely the acquisition of facts but a change in world view. For example, teaching the importance of hand washing would require imparting not only some idea of germs, but also the basic belief that fate can be con-

Top S

C↯C

Exmp

trolled—even supposing soap and water were universally available.)

16   As with the Navajo Indians, so with our society at large: the immediate environment is the crucial factor. This can be seen by examining infant mortality in relation to its influential determinants, such as age of mother, educational level of mother and father, and family income—all regardless of race. In every instance the less well-educated and the poor carry the greatest burden of mortality. When a family income reaches $5,000 per year, and the education of the parents runs through high school or beyond, the infant mortality rates become markedly lower. These findings hold true for whites and blacks although black mortality rates are consistently higher than those of whites. Dr. M. Harvey Brenner of John Hopkins has recently concluded a study showing that periods of economic instability resulting in a rise in the unemployment rate have also been associated with a rise in the rate of infant mortality (New York *Times*, November 15, 1972). Further evidence of the direct bearing of social factors on infant mortality (and on other indices of health) is seen in California, where the Japanese and Chinese population consistently display better statistical indices of health than either whites or blacks, independent of income. Simply stated, disease is tied to the way of life.

Expo

This

17   Poverty, at least when it comes to questions of health, means more than being without the money to purchase adequate medical care. Medicine, and medical care, will not by themselves eradicate the diseases of the poor. The British experience under the National Health Service, where access to physicians is open to all, is illustrative: the lowest social classes still bear more than their share of illness and disability. As one observer has remarked, "The National Health Service was conceived on the basis that, with the eradication of infection and deprivation of medical services, disease would become less common. This has not happened. Experience . . . reveals that over the years, the less affluent have continued to constitute a hospital class. . . ." Another example is afforded by the experience of the American military, where the same high quality of medical care is received by all dependents irrespective of rank. A study has shown that perinatal mortality increases with the decreasing military rank of the husband (in order to exclude the effect of race, only whites were included in the study).

Tran

Exemp/
C&E

18   In order to relieve the poor of their burden of disease, then, we must work to alleviate poverty itself, which is to say the way of life of the poor. The goal of a healthy society will not be reached

simply by the infusion of massive amounts of money and other
resources into the medical-care system, even if that system should
be widely reorganized. It goes without saying that the poor, like
everyone else, should be free to avail themselves of the best medical
care this society can provide; access to the nation's medical services
is a fundamental right. But it would be naive to suppose that medical services alone will relieve the poor of the burden of sickness
which they disproportionately bear. It is the way we live that determines our health problems, and it is social change, not medical
technology, that will help solve them. Without a clear understanding of what causes the disease patterns of a society and how those
patterns are affected, even the best-intentioned health planning may
go seriously awry.

Conc/
Arg

CONSIDERATIONS

Cassell states that the general health of a nation is not directly dependent on the medical services available, but very clearly, disease is dependent in the greatest degree upon the way of life of people. After
reading his argument, do you agree with his contention? Are you convinced that most, if not all, disease can be controlled primarily through
sensible environmental controls? What examples of widespread disease now under control or completely eradicated can you think of in
addition to the ones mentioned in the article? Which has been the
major factor in control of such diseases as polio—immunization or
improved living conditions?

How does Cassell achieve clarity without talking down to lay readers?
What elements of style and structure are particularly conducive to clarity? Analyze the introductory section. (paragraphs 1–7) Through anecdote Cassell explicitly illustrates the thesis of his argument. To what
extent does the study of health conditions among the Navajo Indians
lend credence to his thesis? Does Cassell achieve his aim of clarifying a
problem in order to avoid taking the wrong approach to solutions?
(paragraph 1) Comment on paragraph 18, the concluding statement,
which restates the thesis and carefully evaluates the problem-solution
dilemma of health care for the poor.

If you agree with Cassell's basic argument (that the health problems of
our nation are determined by the way we live), do you believe that
social change and not medical technology will help solve them? What
is the responsibility of the federal government? Is it to "alleviate poverty itself . . . the way of life of the poor"? (paragraph 18) Or is the
responsibility of medical care and personal-health conditions strictly
an individual matter, not the concern of federal government?

CONNOTATION AND DENOTATION

Denotation is the literal meaning of a word, its meaning by definition. It is important in promoting clarity and accuracy in communication. Connotation is the suggested, implied, or associated meanings that most words carry.

Let's explore the difference. A word can have several literal meanings or dictionary definitions; that is, several denotative meanings. For example, *bat* may refer to a mammal, a wooden club, or the act of swinging that club. It is important that both parties are using the word in the same sense. (With the word *bat* there would not be much likelihood of confusion, but with abstract words such as *freedom, liberalism, revolution, equality,* and *honor,* differences in shades of meanings—nuances—become extremely important.)

Connotation is important because the word a writer may use in its literal sense will have certain inevitable connotations for the reader. Several images may be brought to mind by the words *questionable, alleged, radical,* and so on. So the reaction in your reader may be different from what you expected—unless you know your audience well.

Connotative language that depends heavily on slang or colloquialisms hinders communication because it tends to become vague—to mean different things to different people. There are too few concrete referents for common understanding.

Connotative language is best used in writing that seeks to persuade or stimulate the emotions of the audience. By using words with favorable or unfavorable connotations, a writer may slant his work in a desired direction. It should be pointed out, too, that many words have general connotative meanings; that is, emotional overtones or special associations that are common to the general population. The word *Nazi* is an example of this type of connotation. Most words have, in addition, personal connotations determined by the individual experiences of each person. Such words as *solitude, peace, education, power, summertime,* and *love* would elicit different emotional responses from different people.

It is your job to communicate in both your written work and spoken words precisely the connotative meaning you wish to ascribe to a given word. The reader often has to rely on the context in which a word appears and the tone of the writer in order to determine which of several meanings is intended. *Pacification* may mean different things to a tot (who wouldn't care about the word, only the pacifier) and to a Southeast Asian. It is only through context and tone that such a distinction can be made. The author's intended meaning should be readily discernible if the writing is to be effective.

PRACTICE

1. Select five pairs of words from the following list and use each in a sentence (use one word from each pair in one sentence). Be sure that your sentence reflects the difference in connotation.

    statesman—politician
    associate—crony
    fib—lie
    daring—foolhardy
    individual—oddball
    salesman—huckster
    inquisitive—prying

Friday Night in the Coliseum

Find examples of connotative language in this essay and analyze the contextual meaning, as well as the other connotations the words or phrases may hold for you. Don't forget to consider the word *coliseum*, in the title. Write a paragraph based on your analysis, and for contrast include the denotations of the same words and phrases.

Sex Is a Four-Letter Word

Analyze the sarcasm in the ending paragraph of this essay. In addition to being amusing, the statement carries an additional meaning, or connotation—particularly in view of the preceding paragraph. In a paragraph, explain the nature of the serious message being conveyed through connotation in the last two paragraphs.

*   The following list of words are categorized according to similar meanings. Consult your dictionary to discover the subtle nuances of meaning and then use each word correctly in a sentence:

    man, gentleman, dude

    defenseless, harmless, powerless

    mist, haze, fog

    happy, joyful, cheerful

    complex, intricate, involved

    toil, labor, work

• Write an essay on the use of connotation and denotation in television commercials. Be sure to provide examples and pay attention to the connotation and denotation of your own diction.

For examples of individual paragraphs using *connotation* and *denotation*, see p.35, ¶1, p.37, ¶13, p.240, ¶44, p.265, ¶6, p.344, ¶6, p.352, ¶14, p.422, ¶9.

Friday Night in the Coliseum

WILLIAM C. MARTIN

1   "When I die, I want to be cremated, and I want my ashes scattered   *Beg*
in the Coliseum on Friday night. It's in my will." Thus spoke a little
old lady who hasn't missed a Friday night wrestling match for—
well, she's not exactly sure, but "it's been a long time, son, a long
time." On Friday night, fifty times a year, more than 6500 fans
stream into the Coliseum in downtown Houston for promoter Paul
Boesch's weekly offering of Crushers, Killers, Bruisers, and Butch-   *Class*
ers, Commies, Nazis, Japs, and A-rabs, Dukes, Lords, and Barons,
Professors and Doctors, Cowboys and Indians, Spoilers and Sissies,
Farmers and Lumberjacks, Bulls and Mad Dogs, Masked Men and
Midgets, Nice Girls and Bitches, and at least one Clean-cut, Finely
Muscled Young Man who never fights dirty until provoked beyond
reason and who represents the Last, Best, Black, Brown, Red, or
White Hope for Truth, Justice, and the American Way.

2   Though scoffed at by much of the public as a kind of gladiato-   *Pdx*
rial theater in which showmanship counts for more than genuine
athletic skill, professional wrestling enjoys steadily increasing success not only in Houston but in hundreds of tank towns and major
cities all over America. This is not, of course, the first time around.
Pro wrestling has been part of the American scene for more than a
century and has enjoyed several periods of wide popularity. For
most fans over thirty, however, it began sometime around 1949,

with the arrival of television. Lou Thesz was world champion in those days, but the man who symbolized professional wrestling to most people was Gorgeous George, <u>a consummate exhibitionist</u> *Desc* <u>whose long golden curls, brocade and satin robes, and outrageously effeminate manner drew huge crowds wherever he went, all hoping</u> to see a local he-man give him the beating he so obviously deserved.

3   The Gorgeous One's success at the box office ushered in a new era of wrestler-showmen, each trying to appear more outrageous than the others. For many, villainy has provided the surest route to fame and fortune. The overwhelming majority of professional wrestling matches pit the <u>Good, the Pure, and the True against the Bad,</u> *Symb* <u>the Mean, and the Ugly,</u> and a man with a flair for provoking anger and hatred has an assured future in the sport. Since shortly after World War II, the most dependable source of high displeasure has been the Foreign Menace, usually an unreconstructed Nazi or a wily Japanese who insults the memory of our boys in uniform with actions so contemptuous one cannot fail to be proud that our side won the war.

4   Houston's most recent Nazi was Baron von Raschke, a snarling *Class /* Hun with an Iron Cross on his cape and red swastikas on his shoes, *Exemp* who acknowledged his prefight introductions with a sharply executed goose step. Raschke, however, managed to make one think of George Lincoln Rockwell more often than Hitler or Goebbels, and so never really achieved first-class menacehood. It must be disappointing to be a Nazi and not have people take you seriously.

5   Now, <u>Japs [sic], especially Big Japs,</u> are a different story. For *Tone* one thing, they all know karate and can break railroad ties with their bare hands. For another, they are sneaky. So when Toru Tanaka climbs into the ring in that red silk outfit with the dragon on the back, and bows to the crowd and smiles that unspeakably <u>wicked *Oxy* smile</u>, and then caps it off by throwing salt all over everything in a ceremony designed to win the favor of god knows how many of those pagan deities Japanese people worship, you just know that nice young man up there in the ring with him is in serious trouble.

6   Another major Foreign Menace is, of course, the Russian. Russian wrestlers are named Ivan, Boris, or Nikita, and although they *Sarc* <u>have defected from Russia in quest of a few capitalist dollars, they still retain a lot of typically Communist characteristics,</u> like boasting that Russians invented certain well-known wrestling techniques and predicting flatly that the World Champion's belt will one day hang from the Kremlin wall. Furthermore, they value nothing unless it serves their own selfish aims. After a twenty-year partnership with

Lord Charles Montague, Boris Malenko states flatly, "I owe his lordship nothing. Remember one thing about us Russians. When we have no more use for anybody or anything, we let them go. Friendship means nothing to a Russian. When we get through with the Arabs and Castro, you will see what I mean. When we want something we don't care who we step on." *Gen*

7   Wrestling fans are generally an egalitarian lot, at least among themselves, and they do not appreciate those who put on airs. So they are easily angered by another strain of crowd displeaser one might call Titled Snobs and Pointy-Headed Intellectuals. These villains, who love to call themselves "Professor" or "Doctor" or "Lord" Somebody-or-other, use the standard bag of tricks—pulling a man down by his hair, rubbing his eyes with objects secreted in trunks or shoes, stomping his face while he lies wounded and helpless—but their real specialty is treating the fans like ignorant yahoos. They walk and speak with disdain for common folk, and never miss a chance to belittle the crowd in sesquipedalian putdowns or to declare that their raucous and uncouth behavior calls for nothing less than a letter to the *Times*, to inform proper Englishmen of the deplorable state of manners in the Colonies. *Desc* *Allus*

8   A third prominent villain is the Big Mean Sonofabitch. Dick the Bruiser, Cowboy Bill Watts, Butcher Vachone, Killer Kowalski—these men do not need swastikas and monocles and big words to make you hate them. They have the bile of human meanness by the quart in every vein. If a guileless child hands a Sonofabitch a program to autograph, he will often brush it aside or tear it into pieces and throw it on the floor. It isn't that he has forgotten what it was like to be a child. As a child, he kicked crutches from under crippled newsboys and cheated on tests and smoked in the rest room. Now, at 260 pounds, he goes into the ring not just to win, but to injure and maim. Even before the match begins, he attacks his trusting opponent from behind, pounding his head into the turnbuckle, kicking him in the kidneys, stomping him in the groin, and generally seeking to put him at a disadvantage. These are bad people. None of us is really safe as long as they go unpunished. *Class/ Exemp* *Hyper* *Hyper*

9   Fortunately, these hellish legions do not hold sway unchallenged by the forces of Right. For every villain there is a hero who seeks to hold his own against what seem to be incredible odds. Heroes also fall into identifiable categories. Most of them are trim and handsome young men in their twenties or early thirties, the sort that little boys want to grow up to be, and men want to have as friends, and women want to have, also. Personable Bobby Shane *Allus*

wins hearts when he wrestles in his <u>red, white, and blue</u> muscle suit   *Symb*
with the "USA" monogram; and when <u>Tim Woods, dressed all in
white, is introduced as a graduate of Michigan State University,</u>
older folk nod approvingly. They want their sons and grandsons to
go to college, even though they didn't have a chance to go themselves, and it is reassuring to see living proof that not everybody who
goes to college is out burning draft cards and blowing up banks.

10   Though quick to capitalize on the jingoist appeal of matches   *Anly /*
involving Menacing Foreigners, few promoters will risk a match   *C&E*
that might divide the house along racial lines. So black and brown
wrestlers usually appear in the role of Hero, behind whom virtually
the entire crowd can unite. Browns—Mexicans, Mexican-Americans, and Puerto Ricans—are almost invariably handsome, lithe,
and acrobatic. They fight "scientifically" and seldom resort to
roughhouse tactics until they have endured so much that the leg-
endary Latin temper can no longer be contained. If a black chooses
to play the villain, he will soften the racial element; when Buster
Lloyd, the Harlem Hangman, came into town, he belittled the skills
of his opponents not because they were white, but because they
were Texans and therefore little challenge for a man who learned to
fight at the corner of Lenox Avenue and 125th Street. Several white
grapplers might have been able to handle Buster, but the hero selected to take his measure and send him packing back to Harlem
was Tiger Conway, a black Texan.

11   The purest of pure Americans, of course, and a people well
acquainted with villainy, are Red Indians. Most wrestling circuits
feature a Red Indian from time to time; in Houston, ex-Jets line-
backer Chief Wahoo McDaniel is the top attraction and has wres-
tled in the Coliseum more than a hundred times in the last three
years. Like Chief White Owl, Chief Suni War Cloud, and Chief
Billy Two Rivers, Wahoo enters the ring in moccasin-style boots,
warbonnet, and other Indian authentica. He can endure great pain   *Lit*
and injustice without flinching or retaliating in kind, but when enraged, or sometimes just to get the old adrenalin going, he will rip
into a furious war dance and level his opponent with a series of
karate-like Tomahawk Chops to the chest or scalp, then force him
into submission with the dreaded Choctaw Death Lock.

12   <u>Although no Nazi fights clean and few Red Indians fight dirty,</u>   *Hyper*
not all wrestlers can be characterized so unambiguously. The   *Desc*
Masked Man, for example, is sinister-looking, and usually evil, with
a name indicative of his intentions: The Destroyer, The Assassin,
The Hangman, and Spoilers One, Two, and Three. But some
masked men, like Mr. Wrestling and Mil Mascaras (who stars in

Mexican movies as a masked crime-fighting wrestler), are great fa-
vorites, and Clawman has tried to dignify mask-wearing by having
Mrs. Clawman and the Clawchildren sit at ringside in matching
masks.

13   The majority of Houston's wrestling fans appear to be working- | *Desc*
class folk. The white and Mexican-American men still wear crew
cuts and well-oiled pompadours, and many black men and boys cut
their hair close to the scalp. Family men, often with several children
in tow, wear Perma-Prest slacks and plaid sport shirts with the T- | *Symb*
shirt showing at the neck. Others, who stand around before the
matches drinking Lone Star Beer and looking for friendly ladies,
favor cowboy boots, fancy Levis, and Western shirts with the top
two or three pearl buttons already unsnapped. Occasionally, a black | *Slang*
dude in a purple jump suit and gold ruffled shirt shows up, but the
brothers in nondescript trousers and short-sleeve knits far outnum-
ber him. The women cling stubbornly to bouffant hairstyles, fre- | *Symb*
quently in shades blonder or redder or blacker than hair usually
gets, and at least 80 percent wear pants of some sort.

14   One basic reason these people come to the Coliseum is reflected in the motto displayed in Boesch's office: "Professional
Wrestling: the sport that gives you your money's worth." Approximately half the Houston cards feature at least one championship
bout or a battle for the right to meet the men's, women's, midgets',
tag-team, or Brass Knucks champion of Texas, the United States, or
the World. If fans grow jaded with championships, Boesch adds
extra wrestlers to produce two-, three-, and four-man team matches,
heavyweight-midget teams, man-woman teams, and Battles Royale,
in which ten men try to throw each other over the top rope, the
grand prize going to the last man left in the ring. . . .

15   For many regulars, Friday night at the Coliseum is the major | *Sarc*
social event of the week. All over the arena blacks, browns, and
whites visit easily across ethnic lines, in perverse defiance of stereotypes about blue-collar prejudices. A lot of people in the ringside
section know each other, by sight if not by name. Mrs. Elizabeth
Chappell, better known simply as "Mama," has been coming to the
matches for more than twenty-five years. Between bouts, she walks
around the ring, visiting with old friends and making new ones.
When she beats on a fallen villain with a huge mallet she carries in
a shopping bag, folks shout, "Attaway, Mama! Git him!" and agree
that "things don't really start to pick up till Mama gets here."
When a dapper young insurance salesman flies into a rage at a

referee's decision, the fans nudge one another and grin about how "old Freddy really gets worked up, don't he?"

16   Professional wrestling offers fans an almost unparalleled oppor- *Anly*
tunity to indulge aggressive and violent impulses. A few appreciate
the finer points of a take-down or a switch or a Fireman's Carry, but
most would walk out on the NCAA wrestling finals or a collegiate
match between Lehigh and Oklahoma. They want hitting and kicking and stomping and bleeding. Especially bleeding.

17   Virtually all bouts incite a high level of crowd noise, but the
sight of fresh blood streaming from a wrestler's forehead immediately raises the decibel level well into the danger zone. This is what *Hyper*
they came to see. If both men bleed, what follows is nothing less
than orgiastic frenzy. Mere main events and world championships
and tag-team matches eventually run together to form murky puddles in the back regions of the mind, but no one forgets the night he
saw real blood. One woman recalled such a peak experience in
tones that seemed almost religious: "One night, about six or seven
years ago, Cowboy Ellis was hit against the post and got three
gashes in his head. I grabbed him when he rolled out of the ring and
got blood on my dress all the way from the neckline to the hem. I
thought he would bleed to death in my arms. I never washed that
dress. I've still got it at the house. I keep it in a drawer all by itself."

18   The lust for blood is not simply ghoulish, but a desire to witness the stigmata, the apparently irrefutable proof that what is seen
is genuine. Wrestling fans freely acknowledge that much of the
action is faked, that many punches are pulled, that the moisture
that flies through the air after a blow is not sweat but spit, and that
men blunt the full effect of stomping opponents by allowing the
heel to hit the canvas before the ball of the foot slaps the conveniently outstretched arm. They not only acknowledge the illusion;
they jeer when it is badly performed: "Aw my goodness! He can't
even make it look good!" Still, they constantly try to convince
themselves and each other that at least part of what they are seeing
on a given night is real. When Thunderbolt Patterson throws
Bobby Shane through the ropes onto the concrete, a woman shouts
defiantly, "Was that real? Tell me that wasn't real!" And when
Johnny Valentine and Ernie Ladd are both disqualified after a
three-fall slugfest, a young man tells his buddy, "I think that was
real. You know, sometimes they do get mad. One time Killer Kowalski got so mad he tore old Yukon Eric's ear plumb off." But
when blood flows, no one seeks or needs confirmation.

19   The effects on fans of viewing such violence are disputed.

Some experiments with children and college students offer evidence | *Expo*
that observing violent behavior either produces no change or raises
the level of aggressive tendencies in the spectator. Other research,
however, indicates that wrestling fans do experience a decrease in
aggressive tendencies after viewing wrestling matches. Still, manipu-
lating hatred and aggressive tendencies is not without its risks. Every
wrestler has seen or heard about the time when some fan went
berserk and clubbed or burned or cut or shot a villain who played
his role too convincingly, and Tim Woods, it is said, has had only
nine fingers since the night a challenger from the audience grabbed
his hand, bit down extra hard, and spat the tenth out onto the mat.
Then, too, the possibility always exists that in the highly charged
atmosphere of the arena, a wrestler may lose control of himself and
cause real damage to his opponent. If he were alive today, old
Yukon Eric could tell you something about that.

20   The Portrayal of Life that unfolds in the ring is no naïve melo- | *Angy*
drama in which virtue always triumphs and cheaters never win.
Whatever else these folk know, they know that life is tough and
filled with conflict, hostility, and frustration. For every man who
presses toward the prize with pure heart and clean hands, a dozen
Foreigners and so-called Intellectuals and Sonsofbitches seek to
bring him down with treachery and brute force and outright meanness. And even if he overcomes these, there are other, basically
decent men who seek to defeat him in open competition. . . .

CONSIDERATIONS

Professional wrestling is often compared with professional roller skating, and at times with professional ice hockey. Would you agree that these are comparable sports? Perhaps the most obvious common denominator among these sports events is the type of fan who patronizes them. Does Martin's article clarify why wrestling fans are an egalitarian lot? What binds them together in their Friday-night fellowship?

In paragraph 2 Martin states that professional wrestling is "scoffed at" by much of the public. What clues in word choice, description, and carefully selected anecdotes let the reader know what Martin's attitude is toward professional wrestling? Does he, too, scoff? Is he condescending? In paragraph 18, there is a subtle transition in tone. How does Martin achieve this shift in emphasis?

In paragraph 17 Martin explains the fans' lust for blood as a demand for proof that the fight is real or genuine. Is it a logical explanation? Do you believe the violence and aggression witnessed at a professional wrestling match raises or lowers aggressive tendencies in the spectators? Explain.

VOCABULARY

(7) **sesquipedalian**   using long words

(10) **jingoist**   boastingly patriotic; favoring an aggressive, warlike foreign policy

(18) **stigmata**   bleeding from the palms and insteps, resembling Christ's wounds

Sex Is a Four-letter Word

ART HOPPE

In the Beginning Was the Word

1   It was in the third year of the reign of Alaric the Square (223–207 B.C.), King of all the Angles and Saxons, that the historic Obscenity Trials swept the land. Most typical, perhaps, was that of Miss Demmorrah Muldoon, the famed "Love Poetess." She was arrested and jailed after writing a poem which read:

> When the dew is on the buttercup,
> I yearn to xptl with you.

2   What outraged moralists, of course, was Miss Muldoon's bold use of the ancient four-letter Druid word "xptl," hitherto seen only on men's-room walls.

3   "Miss Muldoon is guilty of pandering to the decadence gnawing at our society by deliberately employing the obscene Druid word "——,'" wrote an incensed editorial writer. "After all, there is a perfectly good four-letter Anglo-Saxon word that adequately describes the act."

4   As sales of Miss Muldoon's poem passed the million mark, her trial opened.

5   "We will prove," thundered the grim-faced prosecutor, "that this poem violates contemporary community standards of morality,

appeals solely to the prurient interest and is utterly without redeeming social importance."

6   His first witnesses were the two veteran police officers who arrested Miss Muldoon. Both said blushingly that they had never been so shocked and embarrassed in their lives as upon seeing "xptl" on other than a men's-room wall. And one testified he hadn't been able to look any female in the eye since. Next came a high priest who, as an expert witness, said that no husband ever would use the word "xptl" with his wife. He added that he certainly wouldn't—granted that his church allowed him to marry, which, thank heaven, it didn't—even if he knew what it meant. Last was a famed physician known far and wide for his treatment of mental disorders. He said the very word "xptl" would drive his patients crazy. And as for himself, he said, hearing the word filled him with shame, loathing, disgust, feelings of inadequacy, a hatred of his mother with whom he still lived, and an overwhelming desire to eat peanut butter sandwiches.

7   The defense countered a learned professor of literature who pronounced the poem "an ennobling and spiritually uplifting classic that depended for its eternal verity on the single word 'xptl.'" After a two-week trial, the jury of twelve ox-cart drivers and mule-skinners took thirteen minutes to find Miss Muldoon guilty of "attempting to destroy our cherished Anglo-Saxon heritage." She was beheaded on May 24, 220 B.C.—her last defiant words being: "History will absolve me! Xptl you all!"

8   But thanks to the example made of Miss Muldoon, no Anglo-Saxon writer ever again dared employ the ancient Druid word "xptl," and it fell to disuse. Instead, much to the gratification of moralists, they stuck to common, ordinary, garden-variety words that could be clearly spelled out anywhere in the land without giving offense.

9   You know, four-letter Anglo-Saxon words like "——," "——," and "——."

CONSIDERATIONS

Why is the discussion of public morality and sexual customs such an appropriate subject for satire? What is the effect of placing this historic event some 2200 years in the past?

Hoppe reduces his subject to an absurd level by several devices, including the spelling of the offensive word, *xptl*. What other humorous rhetorical devices does he use in his satire? Is there any serious intent behind the humor?

Write a short satirical essay with the comparison between a modern situation and its earlier counterpart as your theme. Some ideas for satire might be education (then and now), the collapse of public morality, a political or military situation, fashion, or public tastes (in entertainment, religion, and so forth).

VOCABULARY

(3) **pandering**   catering to, basely
(5) **prurient**   lascivious or lustful

SENTENCE VARIETY

Good writing displays the use of a variety of sentence structures. The quickest way to bore your reader is to use the same sentence structure or pattern over and over. "This is my house. My room is upstairs. The kitchen is big and cheery." Make your writing interesting by changing the length, word order, and rhetorical pattern of your sentences. This practice should be comfortable; it should come naturally to you as you gain experience in writing.

If you know something about your language, you can make it work for you when you write. The English language is characterized primarily by the sentence, which has fundamental parts and a basic pattern. It matters that you see this basic form, and it matters how you use it and whether it functions for you the way it must do if you are to make the best use of it.

The word sentence comes from *sentire*: to think, to feel, to perceive. A sentence is, in a simplified definition, a group of words expressing one thought, but there can be much other information included. It has a subject—usually placed first in the sequence or pattern—and a predicate, which usually follows the subject. A sentence gives a sense of completion most of the time. We feel something has been said in some way that we understand. It should be your aim in writing to say what you want to say as clearly and as interestingly as possible.

A series of long sentences can be as monotonous as a string of short ones (see example in paragraph 1). Additionally, if you are too wordy, you run the risk of being obscure and bogging down your reader. Interrogative sentences can provoke interest and relieve a desert of declarative ones.

A short sentence surrounded by longer ones calls attention to itself. Such a combination can be used for emphasis, to drive home a point of special importance or interest:

> "They searched all day, in every store in town, for the one item they needed in order to complete the project. It was all in vain."

If you have too many short sentences, perhaps you can combine some of them. In the example that follows even the sequence of points has been changed:

> "I waited for almost two hours. He didn't show up. I went on home. He later said he arrived at four o'clock."

Combine them:

> "I went home after waiting two hours for him to show up. He said he finally arrived at four o'clock."

The same information has been conveyed, but how much better the combination of sentences sounds.

Or long sentences can be broken into shorter ones. Here we get four related sentences with a good transition, and the sequence stays the same:

> "It has been predicted that in the near future we will work a four-day week, and even though it will be some time before the change takes place, some people are already beginning to worry about what they will do with their leisure time."

Break up this sentence and you get:

> "It has been predicted that in the future we will work a four-day week. It will be some time before this change takes place. However, many people are already beginning to worry about it. What will they do with all that leisure time?"

A series of sentences that all start with the subject followed by the verb can also get monotonous. Alter this basic pattern; start some sentences with various modifiers—single words, phrases, or clauses—or put other relevant information between the subject and verb.

1. Single-word modifiers: "Cold, tired, hungry, he trudged toward the house."

2. Phrase modifiers: "With a wave to her family, she boarded the plane."

3. Clause modifiers: "Although he was disappointed, he managed to smile."

4. Separation of the subject from the verb: "Bart, who was an outstanding athlete, represented the school at the meet."

Sentences vary in other ways. The pattern can affect the impact or the meaning of a sentence.

1. Loose sentences, the type most often used, begin with the main idea or statement, followed by the details and modifiers. Since the main idea comes first, the rest of the sentence lacks emphasis and tends to be anticlimactic: "He walked all the way home from the stadium, which was amazing since they had had to carry him off the football field in the third quarter."

2. Periodic sentences have the main idea at the end so that the reader is engaged right up to the final punctuation. He must read all the way through to get the point. These sentences can be completed in various ways, and they make no sense until they are completed: "Since they had to carry him off

the football field in the third quarter, it was amazing that he walked all the way home from the stadium."

3. Balanced sentences have words, phrases, or clauses of equal weight and similar structure set off against each other. This is particularly effective in comparison and contrast and for emphatic statements. "He is modest but confident, quiet but engaging."

Effective writing involves more than mastering grammar. You should cultivate an interesting style. Knowing how to manipulate and vary sentences, both internally and as they appear in a paragraph, will help you create an interesting style.

PRACTICE

1. Write three versions (about a hundred words each) of a report on a sports event you saw or took part in. In each one use a different style of sentence—loose, periodic, or balanced.

2. Analyze the use of sentence variation in a piece by your favorite author. Try to demonstrate how sentence variation adds to the overall effectiveness or style of the writing.

The Rootless Americans—Signs of a Turnabout

Analyze this essay and identify the types of sentences used: loose, periodic, and balanced. Then choose one sentence from each group and rewrite it twice, using the two other forms of sentences.

• Review an old essay you have written and analyze it for sentence variety. Revise the essay to make it more interesting and effective by rewriting the sentences in a different style. To aid your analysis you might count the words in each sentence of one paragraph. If they are all of the same length (generally), try to vary them.

• Choose two essays from your text and classify the sentences according to type. Write an essay in which you contrast and compare the two essays in terms of style; in other words, sentence variety that creates interest and effectiveness.

For examples of individual paragraphs using good *sentence variety*, see p.10, ¶9, p.20, ¶20-21, p.36, ¶7-8, p.56, ¶2, p.71, ¶30, p.132, ¶3, p.234, ¶4-5, p.445, ¶12-13.

The Rootless Americans—Signs of a Turnabout

VANCE PACKARD

1   Item: A few weeks ago the U.S. Census Bureau revealed that one *Beg /*
fourth of all American jobholders have to go into a different county *Expo*
in order to get from their homes to their jobs.

2   Item: The average American moves 14 times in his lifetime,
and the rate is increasing. Altogether, about 40,000,000 Americans
change their home address at least once a year.

3   Item: With the growth of continuous operation plants, more
than a third of all jobholders in many cities work after dark. In
Akron, Ohio, the rubber center of the nation, 16% of all industrial
employes work from midnight to dawn, which means that they tend
to gear their socializing to people on the same workshift rather than
to people in their neighborhood.

4   Item: Because of the ethnic churning in inner cities, the Hyde
Park area of Chicago has undergone three complete changes of
character in its population in twenty-five years. And because of urban sprawl and the growth of spillover cities, Parma, Ohio, iş a city
of 100,000 that does not have a daily newspaper, nor a hotel, nor a
TV station, nor a bus system of its own, nor a map of the city that
you can buy. Parma borders Cleveland.

5   Item: The trend to family fragmentation is reflected in the
facts that about 60% of all marriages now end in divorce, annul-
ment or separation; 2 million young people cross state lines each

year to "go away" to college, and most do not return to settle, and hundreds of thousands of retiree "snowbirds" now go to the South to retirement "communities" in the fall and return to the North in the spring.

6   These items taken together suggest a profound and disquieting trend that is occurring in America: We are becoming a nation of strangers.   *Thes*

7   Social fragmentation is setting in on a vast scale in many parts of the nation. Millions of people are losing any sense of having any significance to places or to other people. Community life is being undermined.   *Anly / C & E*

8   This growing sense of loss of moorings has a lot to do with what ails America today. And it is a fundamental factor in American political life: The widespread disgruntlement and loss of sense of having "a say" rocketed George Wallace and George McGovern, appealing to quite different constituencies, into the political limelight.

9   The rootlessness of Americans has many facets. I became aware of some of them while trying, in some of my books, to explain some of the curious behavior I was reporting. It was a factor, for example, in status anxiety, in the necessity of corporate managers who hoped to succeed to be mobile, in the increased surveillance of our lives, and in the drop in adult scrutiny of the sexual development of young people. And I notice the curious fact that in my own neighborhood in Connecticut the longer I live there, the fewer nice neighbors I seem to know.   *Exmp*

10   At any rate, in 1968 I set out to explore this evident growing rootlessness of Americans. The exploration took me into seventeen states to examine specific types of communities. And I obtained useful information while visiting seven other states.   *Tran*

11   I visited corporate transfer towns, aerospace towns, trailer towns, areas of migratory workers, recently invaded towns, spillover cities, inner-city areas of ethnic clash, retiree towns, and so on. I talked with wives who had moved twenty times in the twenty-five years they had been married. I saw children who had changed schools every year for eight successive years.   *Exmp / Class*

12   Most conspicuous was a society in upheaval. Some people liked all the movement; others were uneasy or downright miserable. Although we do seem to be finding that people—especially in the middle and upper classes—can adjust to a rootless lifestyle, a bigger question looms. Should we permit ourselves to become a society that has learned to be rootless?   *Rhet Q*

13   Proponents of high mobility point to the broadening effect on the individual in getting to know different parts of the country. You have a chance to make new friends. You can escape frustrations. You can sometimes broaden your economic opportunities.

14   And then there are the possible advantages to the economy. From a mechanistic viewpoint, companies with many outlying plants and offices can be more efficient <u>if their people "resources"</u>   *Meta*
<u>become interchangeable cogs.</u> Also an overall economy can come closer to operating at something close to full capacity if manpower resources automatically flow to areas where developments have opened up manpower shortages. (But wouldn't better planning have put the developments where the people are rather than vice versa?)

15   However, we should face up to the impact that all the rootlessness is having upon the way we behave, as individuals and as social groupings.

16   In terms of lifestyle, for example, there seems to be a clear   *Exmp*
tendency for loosely rooted people to show less concern for the social consequences of their behavior. They do things they wouldn't ordinarily do in a traditional-style community.

17   And they have less sense that anyone cares how one acts.

18   It is in the sprawling, newly formed suburbs where there is little sense of real community that we get the most reports of extramarital, casual sex, group sex, etc. And in the anonymity of metropolitan areas the unmarrieds are most likely to experience sexual intercourse and involve themselves in unstructured cohabitation.

19   Quite probably, too, the tripling of personal backruptcies in the past decade reflects this little concern for the consequences of one's behavior.

20   Crime, too, soars when strangers are packed together in large groups as they are in urban areas. It is easier to steal from a stranger than from an acquaintance.

21   I discovered that people in a more stable town clearly tend to   *C&C*
have a greater sense of personal wellbeing. They have more 'shared concerns with other people, know more people who respect them for some reason, have more close friends they can visit. And there is a mass of evidence in medical literature that loosely rooted people are more susceptible to malaise and, in some situations, to physical or emotional disorders.

22   Another aspect of this problem that should concern parents is the possible impact of a loosely rooted lifestyle upon children. The evidence indicates that children are resilient enough so that their schoolwork is not seriously affected if they are above-average stu-

dents. The average and below-average students do have trouble.

23   In terms of emotional development there is most likely to be an adverse effect if the children are moved frequently when they are in the 3- to 4-year-old phase and when they are in the 13- to 14-year-old phase.

24   But perhaps the most serious casualty of the uprooted society is the nation's communities. Thousands are seriously impaired in their functioning by the high transience of their population.

25   Unfortunately, today's transients who are at the prime of life are likely to be among the talented people in the population—the managerial and professional types. If they move every two or three years—as millions do—they never get to know their community well enough to make a real contribution. They leave membership on the town boards to local hacks. (If they serve, they don't have *Conn* enough time to learn the problems to be effective.)

26   But now we see individuals by the millions starting to fight *Conc* back. Corporations are meeting greater resistance to free-and-loose transfer policies. Some, such as IBM, are deliberately putting the brakes on transfers.

27   And we see people in urban areas almost suddenly reaching out for community and demanding to have a say about the way their lives are run.

28   In this new groping for community we might use as guides four criteria that favor a healthy society:

—The important social groupings are small.

—All aspects of life are closely integrated. Work, for instance, is not something distinct.

—Social belonging is automatic.

—Changes occur relatively slowly, and their purpose and direction are apparent.

29   If these were followed, we would greatly improve the chance of providing man with a setting that gives him a chance to achieve some personal serenity.

CONSIDERATIONS

According to Packard, is rootlessness the most serious result of our mobile society? Do you think the support of George McGovern and George Wallace reflected feelings of alienation, as Packard implies in paragraph 8? Can you think of other types of behavior (besides unconventional sexual activities) that might support Packard's claim (in paragraph 16) that people in the new society care less about the social consequences of their behavior?

Does Packard use loaded words in order to convince or persuade the reader to accept his viewpoint? Is this an effective device in formal argument? Does it distort facts, or simply enlarge upon the surface meanings (denotations) of words and ideas? What is your emotional reaction to his use of words with pejorative connotations, such as "local hacks" in paragraph 25?

In a brief essay discuss the relative advantages and disadvantages of traditional community life in providing opportunities for personal happiness. What type of community can best meet the needs of all people?

VOCABULARY

(8) **constituencies**   the groups of voters represented by legislators
(13) **proponents**   supporters; those who favor
(21) **malaise**   an unfocused feeling of mental uneasiness or discomfort
(22) **resilient**   recovering easily from adverse change

TONE

When you talk, your meaning is helped by your inflection and your facial expression. These are clues to whether you are serious, joking, sarcastic, or whatever. But when you write, how can you compensate for inflection and facial expression? How can you determine what another person's writing "sounds like"? What is his attitude toward his subject, toward his audience? (In other words, what is the *tone* of his writing?)

Tone may be the most important element in writing, for it is tone that partly determines the style of the piece. Tone reveals the author's attitude, his intent in writing. When you read a letter from a good friend, you know that reading between the lines may be more important than reading it literally. What is implied or suggested—enthusiasm, excitement, fears, depression, humor—is conveyed not through the words alone, but in how they are said, how the author intends them. That is the tone of the letter. If you know your friend well, it is likely you will interpret his feelings accurately by reading between the lines; you will not misunderstand what he means.

The writer of any article can be compared with the letter writer. No matter what the medium—magazine, film, or speech—the writer has a certain attitude toward his subject. Straight expository prose states the facts and provides information, but few other occasions and few subjects call for absolutely literal interpretation on the part of the writer. What is my subject? Who is my audience? How do I feel about both subject and audience? These are the important factors. For example:

> "Just as you've suspected, the computers are taking over. They're figuring bank balances, printing insurance notices, totaling up utility bills, scanning your federal income tax return, and maybe even writing your paycheck."

In one paragraph the author has sized up his audience, taken them into confidence, and provided a certain amount of information in a certain way. To determine the tone of this piece (and of all writing), ask yourself some questions: What level of diction is used? Is it formal or colloquial? Does the author use highly connotative diction to arouse emotions? Or does he keep to fairly direct meaning? Does he use figurative language? Can you find particular words that reveal his attitude—simply by the way he uses them?

Some subjects, by their very nature, do not lend themselves

to frivolous treatment. We would not expect a report of war operations to be couched in light and airy terms. Nor do we expect frivolous treatment of death. However, there are exceptions to this. The author who knows his audience, and knows that they are empathetic, may use the unexpected in order to emphasize his point of view. He may also hope to shock an audience, or to relieve tension by adopting an attitude that on the surface seems incongruous with the subject under discussion.)

When you are examining an article to determine its tone, ask yourself these additional questions: How is the subject developed? Is an analytical approach taken? Or is comparison or contrast used to give special emphasis to the author's point? To what extent is one point developed and therefore emphasized? How much detail does the author go into on a particular subject? Is there a lot of sarcasm? What is the author's background? Is he trying to persuade you? Or is the writing strictly for humorous intent?

Each of the following examples has an obviously different tone. What is it each time, and what determines it?

1. "In recent years two proposals, working hand in hand, appear to offer the best means of solving the bulging problems of the poor and over-populated nations. The first is to set up comprehensive birth-control campaigns to cut back their rising populations. At the same time they must develop natural resources, intensify economic growth, and promote the social welfare of their underprivileged masses."

2. "So we're all black people, so-called Negroes, second-class citizens, exslaves. You're *nothing* but an exslave. You don't like to be told that. But what else are you? You are exslaves. You didn't come here on the *Mayflower*. You came here on a slave ship. In chains, like a horse, or a cow, or a chicken."

3. "The primate groups, to which our naked ape belongs, arose originally from primitive insectivore stock. These early mammals were small, insignificant creatures, scuttling nervously around in the safety of the forests, while the reptile overlords were dominating the animal scene. Between eighty- and fifty-million years ago, following the collapse of the great age of reptiles, these little insect-eaters began to venture out into new territories."

In the first example, the subject is being explained. The tone is analytical, unemotional. Very few connotative words are used (*bulging* does present a word picture, as does *rising populations*, but these are not explosively descriptive terms); few examples of figurative language appear. In the second example, the tone is

angry, deliberately insulting, insistent. Notice the highly connotative language, the repetition, the similes, the terse sentences. It
is an impassioned speech, designed to promote action, feelings,
emotional response. The third example is highly descriptive, narrative prose. Would the same tone be appropriate if the author were
writing in a scientific journal for his peers—other anthropologists?
There is emotional involvement on the part of the writer and a
sympathetic attitude of the writer toward his subject.

Tone, then, is determined primarily by two things: the writer's
attitude toward his subject and his attitude toward his audience.
Many, many developmental techniques establish the tone of any
piece of writing; the most obvious one being diction.

PRACTICE

1. Rewrite the three paragraphs in the examples above, changing
   the tone from the original. Analyze the effect that the tone
   of each paragraph might have on the reader.

2. Find two editorials, one for and one against some current issue.
   Analyze the differences in tone. In your discussion include such
   factors as the general tone of the newspapers and some comment on what contributes to the different "sound" of each
   one.

3. Choose a topic and write two paragraphs of approximately one
   hundred words each in which you use two extremely different
   tones. (Keep in mind the effect you expect from a reader in
   each paragraph.)

STYLE

To be perfectly honest, style is almost impossible to define. It
is a subjective matter, the individual makeup of someone's very
own special type of writing. You sense it when you read, and you
have flickers of it when you write. You can recognize a James
Thurber, a Richard Brautigan, or a Hemingway; you can write easily
recognizable parodies of their writing because their styles are so
distinctive, just as mimics perform easily recognizable parodies of

Marlene Dietrich, Mae West, Humphrey Bogart, Jimmy Stewart, Richard Nixon, the Kennedys, and others whose styles are distinctive. The important thing is to recognize your own style, know what makes it up, and try and refine and reinforce it. Generally, style is considered to be an author's characteristic mode of expression—what distinguishes his writing from someone else's—its prominent qualities. You have to examine several aspects of writing to come to any conclusion about its style.

Is the tone satiric or solemn? What level of diction is used, and is connotative language prominent? Is there good use of figurative language, and what is the effect of it? Are the sentences short and terse, are they long and involved, or is there a variation? Or does it even seem important? Style, in other words, is something about writing that is more than the sum of its parts; it is the interplay of all parts of writing—the diction, sentence structure, tone, rhythm. Good style is good harmony between all those parts; form and content are appropriately welded together.

What is style? It has something to do with the alchemy of the ingredients of writing, just as a person's life style is described as the sum of the whole person—what he wears, how he thinks, his manner of speaking, his likes and dislikes, his attitudes, and so forth.

You cannot consciously cultivate a particular style in writing that is not your own, but if you recognize the strengths and weaknesses of what is your writing, you can work toward highlighting its strengths.

PRACTICE

1. Choose a short selection by a writer whose style you admire and write a three-paragraph parody of it. (Include a copy of what you are parodying when you submit your paper.)

2. Collect ten definitions of style, and then write one of your own.

3. Select three prominent public figures, people who are presently in the news or who recently were, and examine a sample of writing by each. How do their life styles and writing styles relate? Or do they? (Richard Nixon, William F. Buckley, Ralph Nader, Joan Baez, or Gloria Steinem are some suggestions.)

Students, The Good and Bad

Describe the tone of this essay in general, as well as the individual tones of the speakers. Write a short paper based on the ideas in this essay, using a serious tone.

To Abolish Children

In a paragraph, describe the author's attitude toward his thesis as revealed by the tone of the essay.

Television: The Splitting Image

Analyze this selection to determine which rhetorical devices the author has chosen to establish her particular tone, such as figurative language, connotative diction, comparison and contrast, and so on, and how they function to establish the tone.

- Write three or four paragraphs on the same topic using a different tone in each.

- Read two opposing points of view on the same issue and write an essay in which you contrast the tones and explain how they create certain attitudes and effects. (You might read two newspapers with different political persuasions as a source of material.)

- Write a report on the tone shifts used by TV news commentators when they read various types of stories.

- Contrast and compare the style of Buchwald (*Students, The Good and Bad*) and Shapiro (*To Abolish Children*) in an essay. In analyzing the differences in style, consider diction, tone, figurative language, and sentence variety.

- Write an essay on the style of one of your favorite authors. Provide examples from a few of his works in order to establish a consistent pattern which runs through the work and which constitutes a basic style.

- Choose a simple topic and write about it in three different styles, imitating writers you admire—or perhaps dislike. In the case of the latter, you may want to write a parody.

For examples of individual paragraphs showing the use of *tone*, see p.25, ¶14, p.30, ¶20–22, p.65, ¶1, p.102, ¶6, p.213, ¶27, p.333, ¶17, p.344, ¶8–10, p.421, ¶7.

Students, the Good and Bad

ART BUCHWALD

1   It is generally agreed that the student unrest is world-wide these days. It doesn't matter if the students live in a permissive society or a totalitarian one—they're still raising Cain. And for that reason, those of us watching from the sidelines are divided as to whether the unrest is a good thing or a bad thing.

At the University Club the other day I was having a brandy and cigar with some very nice chaps when the question of student demonstrations came up.

"I see where they still haven't solved the problem at Columbia," Liverwhistle said.

"It's appalling, absolutely appalling," Cartwright sputtered.

5   "The students should all be booted out on their ears. You can't have a university if you're going to have children running around locking up the faculty." *Hyper*

Conrad said, "Did you see what's going on in Paris? The French students have tied up the city." *C & C*

"AH, YES," said Cartwright. "One can't help admiring the French students' gumption. They've certainly put De Gaulle in his place."

"You have to respect their attitude," Liverwhistle said. "At least the students can see through De Gaulle, if the rest of the French people can't."

"I don't think things have cooled off at Stanford," Scarsdale commented. "They're still holding the administration building."

10   "If you ask me," said Cartwright, "it's a Communist plot. These things don't just happen. There's nothing the Commies wouldn't do to shut down the schools in this country. The only answer is force. It will make those radicals sing another tune."

"Did you read where the students of Czechoslovakia not only demonstrated, but caused the downfall of the Soviet-backed regime?"

"God bless them," said Conrad. "If we're ever going to see the *Tone* end of tyranny behind the Iron Curtain, it's going to be the students who accomplish it."

"I understand the same thing could happen in Poland," Liverwhistle said, "and perhaps even East Germany. They're a new breed, those students, and a credit to the human race."

"You know, of course," said Scarsdale, "that the administration completely collapsed at Northwestern and gave in to every demand of the students there."

15   Cartwright said, "My blood boiled when I read the story. Those damn kids don't know up from down and they're telling us how to run the country. I say we have to act now and act firmly. We ought to cut off all funds to any student who demonstrates or strikes against a university administration."

"The students in Franco's Spain have been agitating for a year now. No one knows how many are in jail," Conrad said.

"The poor kids," Liverwhistle said. "They're only trying to make a better world, and they're thrown in jail for it. I think we should get up a petition and send it to the Spanish ambassador."

"I see they're having another sit-in at Berkeley," Liverwhistle commented.

"They're always having a sit-in at Berkeley," Scarsdale said.

20   "I'll tell you what's wrong with the kids today. They've got too *C&E* much money. They don't even appreciate what we've gone through to give them an education. All they talk about is freedom. What kind of freedom do they want?"

"It's the faculty," said Conrad. "They're the ones who egg the students on. Instead of jailing the students, they ought to lock up the faculty. Then we'd stop all this anarchy on campuses."

Cartwright, who was flipping through a newspaper, said, "It says here that the students in Communist China are thinking about having another Red Guard revolution."

"Great," said Liverwhistle. "Old Mao won't be able to take another one of those."

Cartwright agreed. <u>"I must say one thing for the students</u> *Irny* <u>abroad. They sure have a lot of class."</u>

CONSIDERATIONS

Why do the middle-aged club members of Buchwald's dialog view the demonstrations by American college students as harmful and those of European and Asian students as beneficial? French students in particular have changed the course of history through their rebellions. Do you think we will be able to make the same observation about American students and American history beginning with the 1960s, or are the American students' goals too egocentric to effect national policy changes?

Why is satire a good vehicle to use in presenting an ironic situation? Is Buchwald noncommittal and completely objective, or does he express his own opinions (for instance, in his choice of character names, or in his final sentence)?

Write a satire in dialog form about another controversial topic, such as marijuana laws, military action, or the welfare system. Or write about student rebellions from the point of view of a foreigner—such as a French student, a Spanish businessman, or a Russian politician.

To Abolish Children

KARL SHAPIRO

1   Betrayal is an act of vengeance, obviously. But in an age of betrayal, when men of authority traduce their office and violate the trust placed in their hands, betrayal becomes the official morality. "Official morality" shortly becomes "public immorality"; whereupon the fabric of a society rots before one's eyes. In the years since the end of the Second World War, announced by the drop of the first Ultimate Weapon, the world has been stunned, horrified, and ultimately cajoled and won over to the official morality of America and its corollary of public immorality and anarchy. Hardly a leader, whether President, general, public-relations man, professor, publisher, or poet, can be held to be honorable in his intentions. Everywhere lies the hidden premise and the calculated betrayal, the secret and chauvinistic lie.

2   To what end? Who is the betrayer, and why? Who are the betrayed? In a pyramidal society, a hierarchy, one would know the answers. But in a jungle there are no answers, only cries of victory or death. In the modern American jungle there are no answers.

3   Must America give birth to fascism? Or can it survive its pristine Constitution? Both issues seem doubtful. Can the economic motive live with the mass monster it has created? Can the poor white who has sacrificed his brain to television, or the poor Negro who loots a TV set from the store, ever again cross the line from

somnambulism to wakeful joy? Can only the modern artist discover beauty in the twentieth century?

4   The entire world has become aware of the pervasiveness of American violence. The Americans were the last to discover it. This is as it should be. A betrayed husband is the last to know his situation. America is shocked at itself; someone has handed it a mirror. Instead of the young and handsome heir of all the ages, with his bathing-beauty consort, winners of Olympic Games, we see the soft and rotten killer (almost Hemingway style) with his call-girl W.A.S.P. girl friend, wearing a tiny crucifix between her scientifically measured bosoms. Wars are staged televised on the battlefield; all sports are openly and avowedly big business; all books sell according to the amount of money deposited for advertising; countries are bought and sold in the stock market like cattle. Not that any of this is particularly new. What is new is that it is all now *public* knowledge. And what is awesome is that nobody cares. Everyone wants a share of the rot, the *faisandage*. Ours is a gamy culture from top to bottom. Books about the gaminess are best sellers.

5   The goal of any writer or professor nowadays is to defend his—there is an old-fashioned word—honor. Can a writer write what he wants and in his manner? Can a teacher teach what he was hired to teach, in his own manner? Or must he give way to some form of blackmail from above or below, some Big Brother, who reinterprets his role for him. But we have heard enough of this structural mechanism from the time of Aldous Huxley, Orwell, McLuhan, and so forth.

6   At the bottom of the spectrum of betrayal are the "Movements," the pseudo-revolutionary insurrections without goals. The purest of these aim at simple theft and sabotage, such as occur during and after hurricanes. The more complicated are identified with civil rights and sex, freedom of drugs and pills of various forms, the right to unlimited travel vouchers and hospitalization. These are the heirs to the kingdom of Wall Street—the latest generation of betrayers and destroyers. This is the generation that uses the word Love as a synonym for Hate, that practices infantilism on a scale which has never been seen.

7   In between are the always-duped bourgeoisie, playing both ends against the middle. The bourgeois pays his children off to stay away, horrified at his mistake of educating these freewheeling organisms equipped with electric guitars.

8   Possibly because the economic structure has reached the satu-

ration point, the old order of social development is defunct. The pattern roughly used to be: immigrant (or settler), bourgeois, professional man, and artist (or patron). The child enacts the pattern in reverse: the young man or woman aspires to be artist *first*, deploring professionalism and education itself, condemning the standards of safety of the bourgeois (while exploiting the material wealth of the bourgeois exchequer), and eventually achieving the role of pseudo-immigrant or "native." The Beats and Hippies are products of the American aesthetic which has always preached disaffiliation and single combat with the forces of nature and of society. All American dissident movements tend to fall apart as soon as they are organized. Each artist and pseudo-artist is his own Huckleberry Finn, a moral expatriate. All of our best artists have been recluses of one kind or another, Melville, Faulkner, Hemingway, Cummings. The American artist who does not shun the Center is suspect. The dissident, however, misunderstands the commitment of the artist and thinks of this commitment only in terms of rebellion. The failure of the masses of dissidents to evolve a politic is inherent in the national aesthetic of individualism. And because the dissidents offer no organized threat to the existing order, the existing order continues to consolidate its gains and to ignore the threat of blackmail. The dissidents simply supply additional dry rot to the cultural fabric. The burning and looting of slums signify the abysmal failure of imagination of the would-be revolutionaries, who in fact have no goals. Their only goals are pillage and revenge. The intellectual infantilism of the American radical makes him a figure of fun or of affection (or disaffection, as the case may be). The most one can say of an Allen Ginsberg or a Timothy Leary or a LeRoi Jones is that they are sincere. Children are always sincere.

9   Dissidence spread to the professoriat with the installation of artists and writers on the campuses of the nation. (I am one of the writer-professors who encouraged the moral-intellectual dropout philosophy for about a decade.) It was easy and sometimes necessary to equate the mass university with other forms of the bureaucratic organism, but the vagueness of the issues involved and the failure to clarify them simply added up to an abstract dissent. That a university can be a democracy is patently absurd. The prattle about Free Speech at Berkeley which thrilled the sophomores of all ages served simply to debase whatever issues were at hand. Professors such as myself had already fought this issue in the courts, and won. The campus rioters were betraying these gains and taking a little private revenge on the side.

10   Vietnam itself is a falsified issue in the dissident "revolutions." The war is one of the most evil adventures in our history and its evil effects on the American character are incalculable, but the dissent is largely hypocritical. The "Underground" did not raise its voice against the Russian suppression of Hungary; it pursues a hands-off policy vis-à-vis Castro, even to the endorsement of antique Marxist slogans; it does not agitate for the overthrow of the last big brother of the Axis, Francisco Franco. On the contrary, the dissidents are to be found disporting themselves as frequently in Spain as in other exotic places, pursuing their careers and brushing up on the guitar. If it is laudable to avoid a draft, it is despicable to moralize about it.

11   The importation of mysticism and pseudo-mysticism into the West was an early stratagem of withdrawal from the known modes of communication. Mysticism is simultaneously an insult and a threat to communal behavior. Mystical evidence is by definition hearsay and inhibits communication. The conveniences of Zen and the Sutras to the dissidents (who were rarely if ever "believers") were that they opened the door to a counter-culture, one in which consciousness was superseded by unconsciousness, and provisioned their minds with a counter-literature. The literature of the Orient has never been and cannot be naturalized in the West, but the stratagem of the haiku, for instance, is supposed to put the quietus on Western poetry.

12   But neither poetry nor any of the other arts are essential to the existence and furtherance of the "Movement," as its members refer to it with typical mystification. The Beat poets were the only dissidents who maintained even diplomatic relations with poetry, but their poetry was openly propaganda for the Movement. The plans of the primitive dissident platform were simple and narcissistic: pot, homosexuality, and doom-prophecy, a tame and almost Baptist program. The poetry lacked ambition to rise above these themes.

13   Because poetry was meaningless as a vehicle or an aesthetic to the Movement, the early Beat poetry took to the drum and trumpet (nineteenth-century symbols of slave revolt). The mixture of jazz and verse laid the groundwork for the dissident aesthetic: volume of noise, mass hypnotism, pure size, all canceled out the possibility of dialogue or even thought. Nor did hatred of the electronic world preclude the utmost exploitation of the amplifier. Herewith began the invasion of parks.

14   The deliberate and mischievous inversion of modes (anything "adult" was proscribed) opened a Pandora's box for the child mentality which would have driven Lewis Carroll to suicide. The wave

of male and female hysterics with guitars and brotherhood lyrics turned into a mass industry, on the one hand, and, on the other, a generation of *révoltés* without goals. The dissident music is verbal—both the music and the language descend to levels of callousness and insensitivity heretofore unknown—but the contents are those of the infant banging its fists on the high chair. It is an amazing phenomenon that this art, pitched directly to the level of the five- or six-year-old, should also be the level of the college student. (Dissidence appears to taper off thereafter.) Dissident sartorial fashion also abolishes distinctions between the sexes; the not very subtle transvestism of the dissident costume situates the Movement in the years prior to puberty. The burlesque Edwardianism of The Beatles expresses a nostalgia for the age of aristocracy and unlimited wealth.

15   Throughout human history the fine arts have provided the nexus between intuitional insight and civilized hindsight. That is what the arts have been for. But at times when intuition usurps the more wakeful states of mind, the arts plunge into the playpen and the cry of "immediacy" fills the air. Immediacy (as in D. H. Lawrence's "immediate present" or the Zen Now!) cripples hindsight and deliberation and prevents criteria from coming into existence. The failure of the Beat community to create poetry or any of the other arts is the most significant fact about the Movement. The hidden aesthetic premise of the Movement is that art is evil and must be hamstrung. Only states of unconsciousness are valid: drug-states, violence in bed and on the street, secret languages, political nihilism. These are the *lingua franca* of the Movement.

16   The drug agitprop of the Movement is widely misinterpreted. The Movement does not want drugs to be legalized for their own use; it wants to convert others to drugs. The drug propaganda is entirely evangelistic: take acid and you will be saved is the same message as Jesus Saves. The counter-violence of the police and the drug authorities is not so much opposed by the drug propagandists as it is courted. Legalization of the drugs would remove the thrill; without the official opposition and the melodrama of rebellion, LSD would be about as attractive as ice cream. But the uses of hallucinogenic materials also provide the necessary escape from creativity, from the action of writing a poem or painting a picture. If you have been to the artificial paradise, why write about it? There all the poems and paintings and music are ready-made. There everyone is a Michelangelo, a Mozart, and a Shakespeare. The Movement maintains its puritanical aversion to alcohol ("Scotch is for

fathers"), for alcohol confers only a temporary non-activity upon the psyche. Hallucinogens show you the Promised Land.

17   As students of medieval and Oriental mysticism know, only about one in a hundred thousand mystics has ever recorded his or her "trip" in even mildly impressive prose or poetry. The jottings of drug takers are even less engaging. The taker of drugs may be trying to force the gates of the imagination, as perhaps was the case with Coleridge, but the mass movement for freedom of unconsciousness is clearly an aesthetic draft-dodge. The aesthetic arrogance of the drug user in any case lacks the substantiation of visible works. Pothead, show me your book!

18   The nihilistic mind is a runaway horse. The movement blots out literature without ever having cracked a book. Or rather, it burns all literature to the ground. The Movement cultivates cultural brain-washing; even advanced university students pretend to be ignorant of what they know. The fear of cultural infection and the demand for "immediacy" immunize their minds to any responses except to the latest fad or artifact. Their speech and writing degenerate into code (at the moment it is the underworld argot of the slum Negro, a genuine proletarian dialect for him which is, however, awkward and inapplicable to well-wishers and fellow travelers). The Movement's adulation of the Negro slum-dweller or hero-victim leads it with characteristic naïveté to adopt his sub-language as a generalized medium of communication. The very mystery of this language gives it credence: the terminology and metaphors of jazz, sex, drugs, double-speak, and revenge supply the necessary circuits of sympathy to the adolescent of the upper worlds. You dig?

19   The jazz put-on is a major form of cultural blackmail by the Movement. Anyone not "with" the jazz is a marked man. The hagiography of jazz is as immense as the Vatican Library. It is all phony, a conglomeration of the Music Corporation of America and the masses of delayed and permanent adolescents. Jazz is only a minor facet of modern folk music. What is beatified about jazz is that it is Negro. The Negro, as the most obvious victim of society since the latest massacre of the Jews, is thought to be universalizing about the human condition in jazz. Nothing could be further from reality. Negro jazz is—Negro jazz: charming, entertaining, hot, cool, abstract, evangelistic, white, black, blue, but never revolutionary. Negro jazz is masochistic, and that is precisely its failure and its appeal to the adolescent. What it lacks in content it makes up for in sentimentality, sexuality, and volume.

20   The blotting out of language in jazz lyrics, the accommodation by skillful musical improvisers to cranked-out dollar-making stanzas, many of them a half a century old, attests to the deliberate destruction of language as a medium. The nostalgia of the horn takes over; there is a vague reminiscence of language, unbelievably debased to begin with, whether it came from Tin Pan Alley or from Hollywood. The insistence on jazz, as taken over by the Movement, is the insistence on hysteria as a Way of Life. As such it appeals to the American joy in violence.

21   The Movement nominates Bob Dylan as a great poet. The whining puerilities of this phenomenon are not to be taken lightly in the stock market or in the hearts of millions of children bursting with vitamins and cash. Is he the Leader?

22   The open release of violence is always a surprise to intellectuals. Rebellion without goals is the most fascinating spectacle of all. The Media intone with relentless stupidity: Why? Why? Congresses mourn. Whole cities are put to the torch while children dance and scream as at a jazz festival or an Ice Capade. Yet violence is inculcated by the elders and is exactly predictable. Violence is the answer to the question, Why?

23   It is quite natural and expectable in psycho-politics that Negro looters should espouse white genocide and Nazi anti-Semitism. It is quite natural that W.A.S.P. children in posh suburbs should play Nazi, instead of Cowboy and Indian. In a child society the only authentic emotion is hate. In Hippie language Hate is spelled Love; any four-letter word will suffice.

24   America is the child society *par excellence*, and possibly the only one ever politically arrived at. It is the society of all rights and no obligations, the society of deliberate wreckage and waste, the only society that ever raised gangsterism to the status of myth, and murder to the status of tragedy or politics. The American adulation of the child mentality leads to an industrialized hedonism, on the one hand, and a chauvinistic psychology of greed, on the other. In advertising, anyone over the age of twenty-one or twenty-five is portrayed as an idiot who has got behind in the science and commerce of rejuvenation. The "adult" is appealed to by an almost invisible Big Brother (Mad-Ave or the Executive in the White House) because the "adult" has made the mistake of legal and contractual obligation. Therefore he is an idiot. The costuming of the so-called radical population is a form of jeering: the beard is not only a red flag with certain flickering political messages; it is also the ultimate taunt at the man in the suit. Arson, looting, and murder are also

gentle reminders to the fathers that the tumbrels are rolling. (In many of my creative-writing classes the students sit in judgment on their parents and make specific judgments about which of the elders will be allowed to live. When they are confronted with the fact that the elders and the state are paying their way through education, the students snort and sneer at the stupidity of authorities.)

25   Humanities departments, notoriously the most deprived segment of the American university system, have been powerless to halt the invasion of the child psychosis in higher education. The effeminate backstairs aggressiveness of the Humanities gives way to the Creative Writing Gestalt. "Creative Writing" is to the Humanities as strychnine is to the horse. Any symptom of guilt discerned by the undergraduate on the part of its elders is parlayed into immediate sabotage—a sabotage which stops short of the curtailment of personal benefits, however. The gangsterism of the American youth mind makes it as easy a prey to the Marine recruiter as it does to the Creative Writing instructor. The goals are not education but theft, generally theft of scholarships and undeserved preferment. As American literature heroizes the outlaw, so the outlaw student gains advantage over his more serious companions; the style of contempt, the "cool," determines to a large extent the amount of loot acquired and the length of absolution from the institutions which threaten his freedom of operation.

26   The cultivation of Youth with a capital Y has kept the growth of the American mind off balance since perhaps the early nineteenth century. The trashy frontier mythology, hand-to-hand combat, Horatio Alger, Alger Hiss, spy psychology, advertising, Hell's Angels, Beats, Hippies, Beatles, dropouts, assassins, amnesiac mass murders, pseudo-mystics lately from Kyoto or Benares, C.I.A., Black Muslims and Black Nazis, these are all part and parcel of the American dream of Youth. The dream was dreamed by the fathers, now on the proscribed list.

27   As Negro anti-Semitism is Christian (the only political training the Negro was ever given was the flaming cross), so anti-adultism is American flag-waving in reverse. For this state of affairs there would seem to be no remedy. And indeed there is not. Should one suggest a program to slow down or stop the strangulation of American life by children, it might read:

> 1. Cut off all sources of economic supply to Youth except what they earn by physical or observable mental labor.
> 2. Deny all higher education except on absolute proof of ability. No student should be admitted to a college or university unless he or she has earned a scholarship or has otherwise demonstrated unusual ability.

Public universities should be more stringent in this respect then private, rich universities (the private school is unsupervisable).
3. Deny free travel privileges to children. For instance, raise the age minimum of drivers' licenses to thirty or forty. Deny foreign travel except to those who have been granted the privilege from their school.
4. Set aside a large land area for all dissidents to reside in, with ingress but no egress. As children think the world is their personal property, give them their acre of personal property. Keep them there.
5. Discourage the cowardice and intimidation of parents and "authorities" by reeducating them to the nature of the Yahoo. Excourage construction of housing, especially suburban housing, to delimit or exclude the child, and to suit the needs and requirements of adults.
6. Abolish the child. Deliberate the intelligent society in which the infant is loved and cared for and controlled until he is ready to be shipped to a place of education, should he be worthy. Consider two types of human beings: the infant and the adult. Destroy all concepts of the adolescent.

28   Whereupon his "literature" will wither away, his "music," his drugs, his revolutions and murders, his terrorism of everything he lacks the understanding and knowledge to comprehend.

29   The power shift lies in this direction. Man is an aesthetic animal. His greatest works are slashed to ribbons by "Youth" and will continue to be until Grown Man relinquishes his image of the advertised profile of Youth. As long as Grown Man apes Youth, he will remain the victim of his seed.

30   The American adult must battle "Youth" to the death. "Youth" is a figment of the American imagination which is destroying America itself.

CONSIDERATIONS

Shapiro accuses America of cultivating inexperienced, uninformed, unenlightened, misdirected childishness in its government, social institutions, political beliefs, personal methods of communication and interaction, as well as in its economic, aesthetic, and educational philosophies. Do you feel his thesis is justifiable? Does Shapiro offer reasonable, unemotional evidence to support his allegations, or has he presented only one side, coloring that position with his own prejudices and frustrations? Can you cite counterexamples to refute his claims? Is there a positive side to the adolescence of either individuals or a nation?

Cite examples of symbolism, metaphor, and simile that give this article poetic qualities. The diction of this selection determines its tone; how would you describe that tone?

If you disagree with Shapiro's assessment of the general state of affairs in America, refute his positions in a theme. Select those specific aspects with which you disagree and present your counterarguments. For example, that jazz is not a form of "cultural blackmail," that there are goals to the rebellions going on in today's countercultures, or that mysticism will result in estimable art creations. Present evidence, not just opinion, to support your position.

VOCABULARY

- (1) **traduce**   violate; betray
- (1) **cajoled**   deceived with false promises or soothing words; sweet-talked
- (3) **pristine**   pure; original; unspoiled
- (4) **consort**   spouse
- (4) **faisandage**   corruption; decomposition
- (4) **gamy**   slightly tainted; spoiled (as meat)
- (10) **disporting**   amusing themselves
- (11) **quietus**   extinction or repression of activity
- (14) **proscribed**   forbidden
- (14) **sartorial**   pertaining to clothing or tailoring
- (15) **lingua franca**   a language widely used by members of a large and widespread group
- (16) **agitprop**   agitation and propaganda
- (19) **hagiography**   a biography of saints or venerated persons
- (21) **puerilities**   childish acts
- (23) **espouse**   adopt; take as one's own
- (24) **hedonism**   a doctrine or philosophy of life that considers pleasure the chief goal in life
- (24) **tumbrels**   carts for carrying condemned persons to the guillotine
- (27) **Yahoo**   manlike brutes in Jonathan Swift's *Gulliver's Travels;* hence, a coarse, uncouth person

Television: The Splitting Image

MARYA MANNES

1   A bride who looks scarcely fourteen whispers, "Oh, Mom, I'm so *happy!*" while a doting family adjust her gown and veil and a male voice croons softly, "A woman is a harder thing to be than a man. She has more feelings to feel." The mitigation of these excesses, it appears, is a feminine deodorant called Secret, which allows our bride to approach the altar with security as well as emotion.

2   Eddie Albert, a successful actor turned pitchman, bestows his attention on a lady with two suitcases, which prompt him to ask her whether she has been on a journey. "No," she says, or words to that effect, as she opens the suitcases. "My two boys bring back their soiled clothes every weekend from college for me to wash." And she goes into the familiar litany of grease, chocolate, mud, coffee, and fruit-juice stains, which presumably record the life of the average American male from two to fifty. Mr. Albert compliments her on this happy device to bring her boys home every week and hands her a box of Biz, because "Biz *is* better."

3   Two women with stony faces meet cart to cart in a supermarket as one takes a jar of peanut butter off a shelf. When the other asks her in a voice of nitric acid why she takes that brand, the first snaps, "Because I'm choosy for my family!" The two then break into delighted smiles as Number Two makes Number One taste Jiffy for "mothers who are choosy."

4   If you have not come across these dramatic interludes, it is because you are not home during the day and do not watch daytime television. It also means that your intestinal tract is spared from severe assaults, your credibility unstrained. Or, for that matter, you may look at commercials like these every day and manage either to ignore them or find nothing—given the fact of advertising—wrong with them. In that case, you are either so brainwashed or so innocent that you remain unaware of what this daily infusion may have done and is doing to an entire people as the long-accepted adjunct of free enterprise and support of "free" television.

5   "Given the fact" and "long-accepted" are the key words here. Only socialists, communists, idealists (or the BBC) fail to realize that a mass television system cannot exist without the support of sponsors, that the massive cost of maintaining it as a free service cannot be met without the massive income from selling products. You have only to read of the unending struggle to provide financial support for public, noncommercial television for further evidence.

6   Besides, aren't commercials in the public interest? Don't they help you choose what to buy? Don't they provide needed breaks from programing? Aren't many of them brilliantly done, and some of them funny? And now, with the new sexual freedom, all those gorgeous chicks with their shining hair and gleaming smiles? And if you didn't have commercials taking up a good part of each hour, how on earth would you find enough program material to fill the endless space/time void?

7   Tick off the yesses and what have you left? You have, I venture to submit, these intangible but possibly high costs: the diminution of human worth, the infusion and hardening of social attitudes no longer valid or desirable, pervasive discontent, and psychic fragmentation.

8   Should anyone wonder why deception is not an included detriment, I suggest that our public is so conditioned to promotion as a way of life, whether in art or politics or products, that elements of exaggeration or distortion are taken for granted. Nobody really believes that a certain shampoo will get a certain swain, or that an unclogged sinus can make a man a swinger. People are merely prepared to hope it will.

9   But the diminution of human worth is much more subtle and just as pervasive. In the guise of what they consider comedy, the producers of television commercials have created a loathsome gallery of men and women patterned, presumably, on Mr. and Mrs. America. Women liberationists have a major target in the commercial image of woman flashed hourly and daily to the vast majority.

There are, indeed, only four kinds of females in this relentless sales procession: the gorgeous teen-age swinger with bouncing locks; the young mother teaching her baby girl the right soap for skin care; the middle-aged housewife with a voice like a power saw; and the old lady with dentures and irregularity. All these women, to be sure, exist. But between the swinging sex object and the constipated granny there are millions of females never shown in commercials. These are—married or single—intelligent, sensitive women who bring charm to their homes, who work at jobs as well as lend grace to their marriage, who support themselves, who have talents or hobbies or commitments, or who are skilled at their professions.

10   To my knowledge, as a frequent if reluctant observer, I know of only one woman on a commercial who has a job; a comic plumber pushing Comet. Funny, heh? Think of a dame with a plunger.

11   With this one representative of our labor force, which is well over thirty million women, we are left with nothing but the full-time housewife in all her whining glory: obsessed with whiter wash, moister cakes, shinier floors, cleaner children, softer diapers, and greaseless fried chicken. In the rare instances when these ladies are not in the kitchen, at the washing machine, or waiting on hubby, they are buying beauty shops (fantasy, see?) to take home so that their hair will have more body. Or out at the supermarket being choosy.

12   If they were attractive in their obsessions, they might be bearable. But they are not. They are pushy, loud-mouthed, stupid, and—of all things now—bereft of sexuality. Presumably, the argument in the tenets of advertising is that once a woman marries she changes overnight from plaything to floor-waxer.

13   To be fair, men make an equivalent transition in commercials. The swinging male with the mod hair and the beautiful chick turns inevitably into the paunchy slob who chokes on his wife's cake. You will notice, however, that the voice urging the viewer to buy the product is nearly always male: gentle, wise, helpful, seductive. And the visible presence telling the housewife how to get shinier floors and whiter wash and lovelier hair is almost invariably a man: the Svengali in modern dress, the Trilby (if only she were!), his willing object.

14   Woman, in short, is consumer first and human being fourth. A wife and mother who stays home all day buys a lot more than a woman who lives alone or who—married or single—has a job. The young girl hell-bent on marriage is the next most susceptible consumer. It is entirely understandable, then, that the potential buyers

of detergents, foods, polishes, toothpastes, pills, and housewares are the housewives, and that the sex object spends most of *her* money on cosmetics, hair lotions, soaps, mouthwashes, and soft drinks.

15   Here we come, of course, to the youngest class of consumers, the swinging teen-agers so beloved by advertisers keen on telling them (and us) that they've "got a lot to live, and Pepsi's got a lot to give." This affords a chance to show a squirming, leaping, jiggling group of beautiful kids having a very loud high on rock and—of all things—soda pop. One of commercial TV's most dubious achievements, in fact, is the reinforcement of the self-adulation characteristic of the young as a group.

16   As for the aging female citizen, the less shown of her the better. She is useful for ailments, but since she buys very little of anything, not having a husband or any children to feed or house to keep, nor—of course—sex appeal to burnish, society and commercials have little place for her. The same is true, to be sure, of older men, who are handy for Bosses with Bad Breath or Doctors with Remedies. Yet, on the whole, men hold up better than women at any age—in life or on television. Lines on their faces are marks of distinction, while on women they are signatures of decay.

17   There is no question, in any case, that television commercials (and many of the entertainment programs, notably the soap serials that are part of the selling package) reinforce, like an insistent drill, the assumption that a woman's only valid function is that of wife, mother, and servant of men: the inevitable sequel to her earlier function as sex object and swinger.

18   At a time when more and more women are at long last learning to reject these assumptions as archaic and demeaning, and to grow into individual human beings with a wide option of lives to live, the sellers of the nation are bent upon reinforcing the ancient pattern. They know only too well that by beaming their message to the Consumer Queen they can justify her existence as the housebound Mrs. America: dumber than dumb, whiter than white.

19   The conditioning starts very early: with the girl child who wants the skin Ivory soap has reputedly given her mother, with the nine-year-old who brings back a cake of Camay instead of the male deodorant her father wanted. (When she confesses that she bought it so she could be "feminine," her father hugs her, and, with the voice of a child-molester, whispers, "My little girl is growing up on me, huh.") And then, before long, comes the teen-aged bride who "has feelings to feel."

20   It is the little boys who dream of wings, in an airplane commercial; who grow up (with fewer cavities) into the doers. Their little

sisters turn into *Cosmopolitan* girls, who in turn become housewives furious that their neighbors' wash is cleaner than theirs.

21   There is good reason to suspect that this manic obsession with cleanliness, fostered, quite naturally, by the giant soap and detergent interests, may bear some responsibility for the cultivated sloppiness of so many of the young in their clothing as well as in their chosen hideouts. The compulsive housewife who spends more time washing and vacuuming and polishing her possessions than communicating to, or stimulating her children creates a kind of sterility that the young would instinctively reject. The impeccably tidy home, the impeccably tidy lawn are—in a very real sense—unnatural and confining.

22   Yet the commercials confront us with broods of happy children, some of whom—believe it or not—notice the new fresh smell their clean, white sweatshirts exhale thanks to Mom's new "softener."

23   Some major advertisers, for that matter, can even cast a benign eye on the population explosion. In another Biz commercial, the genial Eddie Albert surveys with surprise a long row of dirty clothes heaped before him by a young matron. She answers his natural query by telling him gaily they are the products of her brood of eleven "with one more to come!" she adds as the twelfth turns up. "That's great!" says Mr. Albert, curdling the soul of Planned Parenthood and the future of this planet.

24   Who are, one cannot help but ask, the writers who manage to combine the sales of products with the selling-out of human dreams and dignity? Who people this cosmos of commercials with dolts and fools and shrews and narcissists? Who know so much about quirks and mannerisms and ailments and so little about life? So much about presumed wants and so little about crying needs?

25   Can women advertisers so demean their own sex? Or are there no women in positions of decision high enough to see that their real selves stand up?

26   Do they not know, these extremely clever creators of commercials, what they could do for their audience even while they exploit and entertain them? How they could raise the levels of manners and attitudes while they sell their wares? Or do they really share the worm's-eye view of mass communication that sees, and addresses, only the lowest common denominator?

27   It can be argued that commercials are taken too seriously, that their function is merely to amuse, engage, and sell, and that they do this brilliantly. If that were all to this wheedling of millions, well and good. But it is not. There are two more fallouts from this

chronic sales explosion that cannot be measured but that at least can be expected. One has to do with the continual celebration of youth at the expense of maturity. In commercials only the young have access to beauty, sex, and joy in life. What do older women feel, day after day, when love is the exclusive possession of a teen-age girl with a bobbing mantle of hair? What older man would not covet her in restless impotence?

28   The constant reminder of what is inaccessible must inevitably produce a subterranean but real discontent, just as the continual sight of things and places beyond reach has eaten deeply into the ghetto soul. If we are constantly presented with what we are not or cannot have, the dislocation deepens, contentment vanishes, and frustration reigns. Even for the substantially secure, there is always a better thing, a better way, to buy. That none of these things makes a better life may be consciously acknowledged, but still the desire lodges in the spirit, nagging and pulling.

29   This kind of fragmentation works in potent ways above and beyond the mere fact of program interruption, which is much of the time more of a blessing than a curse, especially in those rare in-stances when the commercial is deft and funny: the soft and subtle sell. Its overall curse, due to the large number of commercials in each hour, is that it reduces the attention span of a people already so conditioned to constant change and distraction that they cannot tolerate continuity in print or on the air.

30   Specifically, commercial interruption is most damaging during that 10 percent of programing (a charitable estimate) most impor-tant to the mind and spirit of a people: news and public affairs, and drama.

31   To many (and among these are network news producers), com-mercials have no place or business during the vital process of in-forming the public. There is something obscene about a newscaster pausing to introduce a deodorant or shampoo commercial between an airplane crash and a body count. It is more than an interruption; it tends to reduce news to a form of running entertainment, to smudge the edges of reality by treating death or disaster or diplo-macy on the same level as household appliances or a new gasoline.

32   The answer to this would presumably be to lump the commer-cials before and after the news or public affairs broadcasts—an an-swer unpalatable, needless to say, to the sponsors who support them.

33   The same is doubly true of that most unprofitable sector of

television, the original play. Essential to any creative composition, whether drama, music, or dance, are mood and continuity, both inseparable from form and meaning. They are shattered by the periodic intrusion of commercials, which have become intolerable to the serious artists who have deserted commercial television in droves because the system allows them no real freedom or autonomy. The selling comes first, the creation must accommodate itself. It is the rare and admirable sponsor who restricts or fashions his commercials so as to provide a minimum of intrusion or damaging inappropriateness.

34   If all these assumptions and imponderables are true, as many suspect, what is the answer or alleviation?

35   One is in the course of difficult emergence: the establishment of a public television system sufficiently funded so that it can give a maximum number of people an alternate diet of pleasure, enlightenment, and stimulation free from commercial fragmentation. So far, for lack of funds to buy talent and equipment, this effort has been in terms of public attention a distinctly minor operation.

36   Even if public television should, hopefully, greatly increase its scope and impact, it cannot in the nature of things and through long public conditioning equal the impact and reach the size of audience now tuned to commercial television.

37   Enormous amounts of time, money, and talent go into commercials. Technically they are often brilliant and innovative, the product not only of the new skills and devices but of imaginative minds. A few of them are both funny and endearing. Who, for instance, will forget the miserable young man with the appalling cold, or the kids taught to use—as an initiation into manhood—a fork instead of a spoon with a certain spaghetti? Among the enlightened sponsors, moreover, are some who manage to combine an image of their corporation and their products with accuracy and restraint.

38   What has to happen to mass medium advertisers as a whole, and especially on TV, is a totally new approach to their function not only as sellers but as social influencers. They have the same obligation as the broadcast medium itself: not only to entertain but to reflect, not only to reflect but to enlarge public consciousness and human stature.

39   This may be a tall order, but it is a vital one at a time when Americans have ceased to know who they are and where they are going, and when all the multiple forces acting upon them are daily

diminishing their sense of their own value and purpose in life, when social upheaval and social fragmentation have destroyed old patterns, and when survival depends on new ones.

40   If we continue to see ourselves as the advertisers see us, we have no place to go. Nor, I might add, has commercial broadcasting itself.

CONSIDERATIONS

Do you agree with the author's charge (in paragraph 7) that television advertising has resulted in the diminution of human worth, encouragement of undesirable social attitudes, and the fostering of distressing emotional and mental conditions? Think of examples to support each charge; can you also find examples to refute these statements? Do advertisers have a public responsibility equal to that of the broadcast medium itself? (paragraph 38) Do you think most people really see themselves as advertisers see them?

Cite outstanding examples of sarcasm in the article (for example, in paragraph 4, "dramatic interludes"). Does the sarcasm detract from the objectivity of the writer, or does it aptly emphasize her arguments? What is the function of the use of slang, as in paragraph 13: *swinging male, mod hair, beautiful chick*?

Write a satirical piece about one or more related aspects of television advertising. Or present your own critique of TV ads: which ones are especially repugnant; which are most appealing to you; how you are affected and influenced by television advertising. Express your opinions on the questions raised in paragraphs 24, 25, and 26.

VOCABULARY

(1) **mitigation**   the act of lessening the severity of pain or suffering
(2) **litany**   a ceremonial form of prayer that consists of a series of invocations and responses
(7) **diminution**   the act of reducing or lessening
(16) **burnish**   to polish or brighten
(18) **archaic**   outdated, antiquated
(18) **demeaning**   debasing, degrading
(29) **deft**   skillful, clever
(32) **unpalatable**   not pleasing or acceptable
(33) **autonomy**   independence, freedom

DICTION

Words simply do not have a one-to-one relationship with the world. That is, a word like *bat* means more than one thing. And words like *love* and *far-out* have no exact and specific referents at all. If you increase your respect for the simple fact that words mean different things to different people and that words used under one circumstance will not work under another, you are on your way to solving the problem of diction.

Once you have decided what you want to say, the next step is to figure out how to say it effectively. Diction—the words you decide to use—is your most important tool. The problem, of course, is to choose the right words, the best words.

Although English may be broken down into two main categories, Standard and Nonstandard, there are many levels of diction:

1. *Formal English* is used for such occasions as scholarly papers, sermons, public speeches, professional journals, and the like. It is highly polished language. An invitation to a formal wedding, or a quotation from a university commencement address are further examples of formal English.

2. *Informal English* is expected of the better educated. Less dignified than formal, it is still more polished and more careful than language used in free conversation, and it is the level for virtually all of the writing you will do in college. (The text of this book is, in most part, written in informal English.) News analyses and editorial writing in popular magazines such as *Time* and *Newsweek* would also be considered informal English.

3. *Colloquial language* is a type of informal English. It is conversational. It is not incorrect but simply spontaneous, with current words, contractions, and other labels of good but free conversation.

   "We sure hope all of you who are concerned with affirmative action programs will make it in to the workshop on Saturday morning. Don't forget to call the information office for details."

4. *Slang* is faddish language used for a while by some group or other. Expressions such as "he kept his cool" first mean something to a limited audience, may be adopted by the general public for a while, but more often usually disappear as they go out of style.

"All sound freaks—make it to the football field Friday p.m.—5 bells—rock concert for flood victims—free tea (no grass)—a mellow gig—you can dig it."

5. *Jargon* is used—and generally understood—by a particular group such as doctors, journalists, lawyers, or social scientists, to communicate with each other. It is "shoptalk." To the layman, it may be pretentious, vague, or downright incomprehensible.

"An informal Basic Transactional Analysis Group is being assembled to interface over tea in the Quad Wednesday at four. Facilitators and participants from the Psych Department will find it meaningful."

6. *Nonstandard English* is generally used by the uneducated, the illiterate, or the careless. It is characterized by grammatical errors, poor spelling or pronunciation, and irregular usage.

"Dear Ethel,
Them psycologists are all alike. Ain't no kid gonna be worth a lick if he been coddled to all his years. A good beatin is all that youngster of yors needs. That'll straiten him around for shure.
lov, Annabelle"

How do you improve your diction? Simply by reading a lot. You remember styles and the particular nature of the language used by a writer you like. You copy or imitate; that is, you store away enough of an author's words so that when you want to create the same effect, you can call on your vocabulary storehouse. But there are pitfalls. Watch out for these:

1. Vague expressions and words that are hard if not impossible to define. Language should be concrete enough for the reader to get the point.

2. Clichés and trite language. Tired, overused phrases are indicative of a lazy mind; the reader gets the idea that someone who writes in trite language probably has only trite, tired thoughts to express. If a phrase is self-completing ("sharp as a _____," "happy as a _____," "work your fingers to the _____," "bigger than _____"), avoid it. It will not give your reader a sense of urgency about what you have to say.

3. Obsolete, archaic words or expressions. Sometimes these can be used to flavor your writing or speech, but generally you should be up-to-date in your diction if your ideas are to strike a responsive chord in your audience. Archaic words may reflect thinking that is sadly out of date.

4. Improprieties or illiteracies. The former are words used inappropriately or incorrectly. Don't go to the opposite extreme, however, and substitute a euphemism every time a straightforward word might offend someone. We Americans tend to go overboard in that direction—sanitary engineers have replaced garbage men, and no one ever dies; they just pass away.

5. Affectation or overly ornate language. Expression can be simple and direct but still be fresh and original. A reader may respond well to polished writing but probably not to flowery, overdone language.

6. Irrelevant jargon. Trade talk may be acceptable to those acquainted with it but it can puzzle or confuse the layman. The quickest way to turn off a reader is to use language that can be understood only by an "in" group.

7. Slang. Like jargon or dialect, slang may limit your audience. Also, it is often in poor taste. It becomes easily outdated, and then it is considered simply corny.

8. Wordiness. The simplest way of saying something is not *always* the best way, but you should avoid using unnecessary words or phrases. Choose your words carefully, making every one of them count.

If your purpose is to arouse the emotions of the audience, you may use highly connotative language. If you want to amuse, you can use affected or obsolete language or pun unmercifully. You can satirize by using formal diction or emotional terms to describe trivia or ridiculous subjects. In these intentional cases, the use of what at other times might be unsuitable diction is done to produce a certain effect.

PRACTICE

1. Write two paragraphs on a substantial topic using formal diction (avoid stilted language). Write two other paragraphs about the same subject using much less formal diction. Summarize the differences in effect.

2. Find examples of what you feel are appropriate and inappropriate diction. Use them to illustrate an essay on the same subject. For example, you might discuss college students calling policemen *pigs*, or policemen calling commune residents *hippies*.

Message to the Grass Roots

In this essay Malcolm X uses a diction that is highly charged emotionally. Write a short essay stating why you think this diction is/is not appropriate to his thesis. If you think a different diction would be more effective, give examples of your suggestions.

Meditation XVII

John Donne's diction is formal and fervently religious, which is appropriate to the subject and tone of his work. Take the ideas in *Meditation* and rewrite them in modern diction that is also appropriate to the subject and intent of the work.

- Write a personal narrative using colloquial language. It should be informal and conversational—even humorous if you wish.

- In your reading find examples of diction that you feel is in some way inappropriate. In an essay suggest a more appropriate diction and provide examples. Use comparison and contrast to prove the superiority of your suggestions.

For examples of individual paragraphs using *diction*, see p.18, ¶12, p.135, ¶7, p.176, ¶13, p.183, ¶54, p.216, ¶35, p.235, ¶6–8, p.342, ¶1, p.353, ¶17, p.442, ¶2.

Message to the Grass Roots

MALCOLM X

1   We want to have just an off-the-cuff chat between you and me, us. | S Var
We want to talk right down to earth in a language that everybody
here can easily understand. We all agree tonight, all of the speakers
have agreed, that America has a very serious problem. Not only
does America have a very serious problem, but our people have a
very serious problem. America's problem is us. We're her problem.
The only reason she has a problem is she doesn't want us here. And
every time you look at yourself, be you black, brown, red or yellow,
a so-called Negro, you represent a person who poses such a serious
problem for America because you're not wanted. Once you face
this as a fact, then you can start plotting a course that will make you
appear intelligent, instead of unintelligent.

2   What you and I need to do is learn to forget our differences. | Dict
When we come together, we don't come together as Baptists or
Methodists. You don't catch hell because you're a Baptist, and you
don't catch hell because you're a Methodist. You don't catch hell
because you're a Methodist or Baptist, you don't catch hell because
you're a Democrat or a Republican, you don't catch hell because
you're a Mason or an Elk, and you sure don't catch hell because
you're an American; because if you were an American, you wouldn't
catch hell. You catch hell because you're a black man. You catch
hell, all of us catch hell, for the same reason.

3   So we're all black people, so-called Negroes, second-class citizens, ex-slaves. You're nothing but an ex-slave. You don't like to be told that. But what else are you? You are ex-slaves. You didn't come here on the "Mayflower." You came here on a slave ship. In chains, like a horse, or a cow, or a chicken. And you were brought here by the people who came here on the "Mayflower," you were brought here by the so-called Pilgrims, or Founding Fathers. They were the ones who brought you here. *Conn*

Sim

4   We have a common enemy. We have this in common: We have a common oppressor, a common exploiter, and a common discriminator. But once we all realize that we have a common enemy, then we unite—on the basis of what we have in common. And what we have foremost in common is that enemy—the white man. He's an enemy to all of us. I know some of you all think that some of them aren't enemies. Time will tell. *Rep*

Emph

5   In Bandung back in, I think, 1954, was the first unity meeting in centuries of black people. And once you study what happened at the Bandung conference, and the results of the Bandung conference, it actually serves as a model for the same procedure you and I can use to get our problems solved. At Bandung all the nations came together, the dark nations from Africa and Asia. Some of them were Buddhists, some of them were Muslims, some of them were Christians, some were Confucianists, some were atheists. Despite their religious differences, they came together. Some were communists, some were socialists, some were capitalists—despite their economic and political differences, they came together. All of them were black, brown, red or yellow. *Class*

6   The number-one thing that was not allowed to attend the Bandung conference was the white man. He couldn't come. Once they excluded the white man, they found that they could get together. Once they kept him out, everybody else fell right in and fell in line. This is the thing that you and I have to understand. And these people who came together didn't have nuclear weapons, they didn't have jet planes, they didn't have all of the heavy armaments that the white man has. But they had unity.

7   They were able to submerge their little petty differences and agree on one thing: That there one African came from Kenya and was being colonized by the Englishman, and another African came from the Congo and was being colonized by the Belgian, and another African came from Guinea and was being colonized by the French, and another came from Angola and was being colonized by the Portuguese. When they came to the Bandung conference, they *Rep*

Emph

looked at the Portuguese, and at the Frenchman, and at the English, and at the Dutchman, and learned or realized the one thing that all of them had in common—they were all from Europe, they were all Europeans, blond, blue-eyed and white skins. They began to recognize who their enemy was. The same man that was colonizing our people in Kenya was colonizing our people in the Congo. The same one in the Congo was colonizing our people in South Africa, and in Southern Rhodesia, and in Burma, and in India, and in Afghanistan, and in Pakistan. They realized all over the world where the dark man was being oppressed, he was being oppressed by the white man; where the dark man was being exploited, he was being exploited by the white man. So they got together on this basis—that they had a common enemy.

Bal S

8   And when you and I here in Detroit and in Michigan and in America who have been awakened today look around us, we too realize here in America we all have a common enemy, whether he's in Georgia or Michigan, whether he's in California or New York. He's the same man—blue eyes and blond hair and pale skin—the same man. So what we have to do is what they did. They agreed to stop quarreling among themselves. Any little spat that they had, they'd settle it among themselves, go into a huddle—don't let the enemy know that you've got a disagreement.

Symb

9   Instead of airing our differences in public, we have to realize we're all the same family. And when you have a family squabble, you don't get out on the sidewalk. If you do, everybody calls you uncouth, unrefined, uncivilized, savage. If you don't make it at home, you settle it at home; you get in the closet, argue it out behind closed doors, and then when you come out on the street, you pose a common front, a united front. And this is what we need to do in the community, and in the city, and in the state. We need to stop airing our differences in front of the white man, put the white man out of our meetings, and then sit down and talk shop with each other. That's what we've got to do.

Angy

10   I would like to make a few comments concerning the difference between the black revolution and the Negro revolution. Are they both the same? And if they're not, what is the difference? What is the difference between a black revolution and a Negro revolution? First, what is a revolution? Sometimes I'm inclined to believe that many of our people are using this word "revolution" loosely, without taking careful consideration of what this word actually means, and what its historic characteristics are. When you study the historic nature of revolutions, the motive of a revolution, the

objective of a revolution, the result of a revolution, and the methods used in a revolution, you may change words. You may devise another program, you may change your goal and you may change your mind. *Exmp*

11   Look at the American Revolution in 1776. That revolution was for what? For land. Why did they want land? Independence. How was it carried out? Bloodshed. Number one, it was based on land, the basis of independence. And the only way they could get it was bloodshed. The French Revolution—what was it based on? The landless against the landlord. What was it for? Land. How did they get it? Bloodshed. Was no love lost, was no compromise, was no negotiation. I'm telling you—you don't know what a revolution is. Because when you find out what it is, you'll get back in the alley, you'll get out of the way.

12   The Russian Revolution—what was it based on? Land; the landless against the landlord. How did they bring it about? Bloodshed. You haven't got a revolution that doesn't involve bloodshed. And you're afraid to bleed. I said, you're afraid to bleed.

13   As long as the white man sent you to Korea, you bled. He sent *Paral* you to Germany, you bled. He sent you to the South Pacific to fight the Japanese, you bled. You bleed for white people, but when it comes to seeing your own churches being bombed and little black girls murdered, you haven't got any blood. You bleed when the *Bal S/* white man says bleed; you bite when the white man says bite; and *Paral* you bark when the white man says bark. I hate to say this about us, but it's true. How are you going to be nonviolent in Mississippi, as *Rhet Q* violent as you were in Korea? How can you justify being nonviolent in Mississippi and Alabama, when your churches are being bombed, and your little girls are being murdered, and at the same time you are going to get violent with Hitler, and Tojo, and somebody else you don't even know?

14   If violence is wrong in America, violence is wrong abroad. If it *Top S* is wrong to be violent defending black women and black children and black babies and black men, then it is wrong for America to draft us and make us violent abroad in defense of her. And if it is right for America to draft us, and teach us how to be violent in defense of her, then it is right for you and me to do whatever is necessary to defend our own people right here in this country.

15   The Chinese Revolution—they wanted land. They threw the British out, along with the Uncle Tom Chinese. Yes, they did. They *Allus* set a good example. When I was in prison, I read an article—don't be shocked when I say that I was in prison. You're still in prison. *Meta*

That's what America means: prison. When I was in prison, I read an | *Anec*
article in *Life* magazine showing a little Chinese girl, nine years old;
her father was on his hands and knees and she was pulling the
trigger because he was an Uncle Tom Chinaman. When they had
the revolution over there, they took a whole generation of Uncle
Toms and just wiped them out. And within ten years that little girl
became a full-grown woman. No more Toms in China. And today
it's one of the toughest, roughest, most feared countries on this
earth—by the white man. Because there are no Uncle Toms over
there.

16   Of all our studies, history is best qualified to reward our re- | *Anly*
search. And when you see that you've got problems, all you have to
do is examine the historic method used all over the world by others
who have problems similar to yours. Once you see how they got
theirs straight, then you know how you can get yours straight.
There's been a revolution, a black revolution, going on in Africa. In
Kenya, the Mau Mau were revolutionary; they were the ones who
brought the word "Uhuru" to the fore. The Mau Mau, they were
revolutionary, they believed in scorched earth, they knocked everything aside that got in their way, and their revolution also was based
on land, a desire for land. In Algeria, the northern part of Africa, a
revolution took place. The Algerians were revolutionists, they
wanted land. France offered to let them be integrated into France.
They told France to hell with France, they wanted some land, not
some France. And they engaged in a bloody battle.

17   So I cite these various revolutions, brothers and sisters, to show
you that you don't have a peaceful revolution. You don't have a
turn-the-other-cheek revolution. There's no such thing as a nonvio- | *Allus*
lent revolution. The only kind of revolution that is nonviolent is the
Negro revolution. The only revolution in which the goal is loving | *Sarc /*
your enemy is the Negro revolution. It's the only revolution in | *Tone*
which the goal is a desegregated lunch counter, a desegregated theater, a desegregated park, and a desegregated public toilet; you can
sit down next to white folks—on the toilet. That's no revolution.
Revolution is based on land. Land is the basis of all independence.
Land is the basis of freedom, justice, and equality.

18   The white man knows what a revolution is. He knows that the
black revolution is world-wide in scope and in nature. The black
revolution is sweeping Asia, is sweeping Africa, is rearing its head in | *Meta*
Latin America. The Cuban Revolution—that's a revolution. They
overturned the system. Revolution is in Asia, revolution is in Africa,
and the white man is screaming because he sees revolution in Latin

America. How do you think he'll react to you when you learn what a real revolution is? You don't know what a revolution is. If you did, you wouldn't use that word.

19 Revolution is bloody, revolution is hostile, revolution knows no compromise, revolution overturns and destroys everything that gets in its way. And you, sitting around here like a knot on the wall, saying, "I'm going to love these folks no matter how much they hate me." No, you need a revolution. Whoever heard of a revolution where they lock arms, as Rev. Cleage was pointing out beautifully, singing "We Shall Overcome"? You don't do that in a revolution. You don't do any singing, you're too busy swinging. It's based on land. A revolutionary wants land so he can set up his own nation, an independent nation. These Negroes aren't asking for any nation—they're trying to crawl back on the plantation.

Rep Emph

Sarc

20 When you want a nation, that's called nationalism. When the white man became involved in a revolution in this country against England, what was it for? He wanted this land so he could set up another white nation. That's white nationalism. The American Revolution was white nationalism. The French Revolution was white nationalism. The Russian Revolution too—yes, it was—white nationalism. You don't think so? Why do you think Khrushchev and Mao can't get their heads together? White nationalism. All the revolutions that are going on in Asia and Africa today are based on what?—black nationalism. A revolutionary is a black nationalist. He wants a nation. I was reading some beautiful words by Rev. Cleage, pointing out why he couldn't get together with someone else in the city because all of them were afraid of being identified with black nationalism. If you're afraid of black nationalism, you're afraid of revolution. And if you love revolution, you love black nationalism.

Def / Exemp

21 To understand this, you have to go back to what the young brother here referred to as the house Negro and the field Negro back during slavery. There were two kinds of slaves, the house Negro and the field Negro. The house Negroes—they lived in the house with master, they dressed pretty good, they ate good because they ate his food—what he left. They lived in the attic or the basement, but still they lived near the master; and they loved the master more than the master loved himself. They would give their life to save the master's house—quicker than the master would. If the master said, "We got a good house here," the house Negro would say, "Yeah, we got a good house here." Whenever the master said "we," he said "we." That's how you can tell a house Negro.

Desc

22 If the master's house caught on fire, the house Negro would fight harder to put the blaze out than the master would. If the

master got sick, the house Negro would say, "What's the matter, | Tone
boss, *we* sick?" *We* sick! He identified himself with his master, more
than his master identified with himself. And if you came to the
house Negro and said, "Let's run away, let's escape, let's separate,"
the house Negro would look at you and say, "Man, you crazy.
What you mean, separate? Where is there a better house than this?
Where can I wear better clothes than this? Where can I eat better
food than this?" That was that house Negro. In those days he was
called a "house nigger." And that's what we call them today, because we've still got some house niggers running around here.

23   This modern house Negro loves his master. He wants to live
near him. He'll pay three times as much as the house is worth just
to live near his master, and then brag about "I'm the only Negro
out here." "I'm the only one on my job." "I'm the only one in this
school." You're nothing but a house Negro. And if someone comes
to you right now and says, "Let's separate," you say the same thing
that the house Negro said on the plantation. "What you mean,
separate? From America, this good white man? Where you going to
get a better job than you get here?" I mean, this is what you say. "I
ain't left nothing in Africa," that's what you say. Why, you left your
mind in Africa.

24   On that same plantation, there was the field Negro. The field | Desc
Negroes—those were the masses. There were always more Negroes
in the field than there were Negroes in the house. The Negro in the
field caught hell. He ate leftovers. In the house they ate high up on
the hog. The Negro in the field didn't get anything but what was
left of the insides of the hog. They call it "chitt'lings" nowadays. In | Comp/
those days they called them what they were—guts. That's what you | Symb
were—gut-eaters. And some of you are still gut-eaters.

25   The field Negro was beaten from morning to night; he lived in
a shack, in a hut; he wore old, castoff clothes. He hated his master.
I say he hated his master. He was intelligent. That house Negro
loved his master, but that field Negro—remember, they were in the
majority, and they hated the master. When the house caught on
fire, he didn't try to put it out; that field Negro prayed for a wind,
for a breeze. When the master got sick, the field Negro prayed that
he'd die. If someone came to the field Negro and said, "Let's separate, let's run," he didn't say "Where we going?" He'd say, "Any
place is better than here." You've got field Negroes in America | Angry
today. I'm a field Negro. The masses are the field Negroes. When
they see this man's house on fire, you don't hear the little Negroes
talking about "*our* government is in trouble." They say, "*The* government is in trouble." Imagine a Negro: "*Our* government"! I even

heard one say "*our* astronauts." They won't even let him near the plant—and "*our* astronauts"! "*Our* Navy"—that's a Negro that is out of his mind, a Negro that is out of his mind.

26   Just as the slavemaster of that day used Tom, the house Negro, to keep the field Negroes in check, the same old slavemaster today has Negroes who are nothing but modern Uncle Toms, twentieth-century Uncle Toms, to keep you and me in check, to keep us under control, keep us passive and peaceful and nonviolent. That's Tom making you nonviolent. It's like when you go to the dentist, and the man's going to take your tooth. You're going to fight him when he starts pulling. So he squirts some stuff in your jaw called novocaine, to make you think they're not doing anything to you. So you sit there and because you've got all of that novocaine in your jaw, you suffer—peacefully. Blood running all down your jaw, and you don't know what's happening. Because someone has taught you to suffer—peacefully. *Angy*

27   The white man does the same thing to you in the street, when he wants to put knots on your head and take advantage of you and not have to be afraid of your fighting back. To keep you from fighting back, he gets these old religious Uncle Toms to teach you and me, just like novocaine, to suffer peacefully. Don't stop suffer-ing—just suffer peacefully. As Rev. Cleage pointed out, they say you should let your blood flow in the streets. This is a shame. You know he's a Christian preacher. If it's a shame to him, you know what it is to me.

28   There is nothing in our book, the Koran, that teaches us to suffer peacefully. Our religion teaches us to be intelligent. Be peace-ful, be courteous, obey the law, respect everyone; but if someone puts his hand on you, send him to the cemetery. That's a good religion. In fact, that's that old-time religion. That's the one that Ma and Pa used to talk about: an eye for an eye, and a tooth for a tooth, and a head for a head, and a life for a life. That's a good religion. And nobody resents that kind of religion being taught but a wolf, who intends to make you his meal. *Def*   *Allus*

29   This is the way it is with the white man in America. He's a wolf—and you're sheep. Any time a shepherd, a pastor, teaches you and me not to run from the white man and, at the same time, teaches us not to fight the white man, he's a traitor to you and me. Don't lay down a life all by itself. No, preserve your life, it's the best thing you've got. And if you've got to give it up, let it be even-steven. *Meta*

30   The slavemaster took Tom and dressed him well, fed him well and even gave him a little education—a *little* education; gave him a

long coat and a top hat and made all the other slaves look up to
him. Then he used Tom to control them. <u>The same strategy that</u>   *Comp*
<u>was used in those days is used today, by the same white man.</u> He
takes a Negro, a so-called Negro, and makes him prominent, builds
him up, publicizes him, makes him a celebrity. And then he becomes a spokesman for Negroes—and a Negro leader.

31   I would like to mention just one other thing quickly, and that
is the method that the white man uses, how the white man uses the
"big guns," or Negro leaders, against the Negro revolution. They   *Meta*
are not a part of the Negro revolution. They are used against the
Negro revolution.

32   When Martin Luther King failed to desegregate Albany, Geor-   *Narr/*
gia, the civil-rights struggle in America reached its low point. King   *Anly*
became bankrupt almost, as a leader. The Southern Christian Leadership Conference was in financial trouble; and it was in trouble,
period, with the people when they failed to desegregate Albany,
Georgia. Other Negro civil-rights leaders of so-called national stature became fallen idols. As they became fallen idols, began to lose
their prestige and influence, local Negro leaders began to stir up the
masses. In Cambridge, Maryland, Gloria Richardson; in Danville,
Virginia, and other parts of the country, local leaders began to stir
up our people at the grass-roots level. This was never done by these
Negroes of national stature. They control you, but they have never
incited you or excited you. They control you, they contain you,
they have kept you on the plantation.

33   As soon as King failed in Birmingham, Negroes took to the
streets. King went out to California to a big rally and raised I don't
know how many thousands of dollars. He came to Detroit and had
a march and raised some more thousands of dollars. And recall,
right after that Roy Wilkins attacked King. He accused King and
CORE [Congress Of Racial Equality] of starting trouble everywhere and then making the NAACP [National Association for the
Advancement of Colored People] get them out of jail and spend a
lot of money; they accused King and CORE of raising all the
money and not paying it back. This happened; I've got it in documented evidence in the newspaper. Roy started attacking King, and
King started attacking Roy, and Farmer started attacking both of
them. And as these Negroes of national stature began to attack
each other, they began to lose their control of the Negro masses.

34   The Negroes were out there in the streets. They were talking   *Dict*
about how they were going to march on Washington. Right at that
time Birmingham had exploded, and the Negroes in Birmingham—
remember, they also exploded. They began to stab the crackers in

the back and bust them up 'side their head—yes, they did. That's | **Dict/**
when Kennedy sent in the troops, down in Birmingham. After that, | **Tone**
Kennedy got on the television and said "this is a moral issue."
That's when he said he was going to put out a civil-rights bill. And
when he mentioned civil-rights bill and the Southern <u>crackers</u> | **Slang**
started talking about how they were going to boycott or filibuster it,
then the Negroes started talking—about what? That they were going to march on Washington, march on the Senate, march on the
White House, march on the Congress, and tie it up, bring it to a
halt, not let the government proceed. They even said they were
going out to the airport and lay down on the runway and not let any
airplanes land. I'm telling you what they said. That was revolution.
That was revolution. That was the black revolution.

35   It was the grass roots out there in the street. It scared the white
man to death, scared the white power structure in Washington,
D.C., to death; I was there. When they found out that this black
steamroller was going to come down on the capital, they called in
Wilkins, they called in Randolph, they called in these national Negro leaders that you respect and told them, "Call it off." Kennedy
said, "Look, you all are letting this thing go too far." And <u>Old Tom</u> | **Symb**
said, "<u>Boss,</u> I can't stop it, because I didn't start it." I'm telling you
what they said. They said, "I'm not even in it, much less at the head
of it." They said, "These Negroes are doing things on their own.
They're running ahead of us." <u>And that old shrewd fox,</u> he said, "If | **Meta**
you all aren't in it, I'll put you in it. I'll put you at the head of it. I'll
endorse it. I'll welcome it. I'll help it. I'll join it."

36   A matter of hours went by. They had a meeting at the Carlyle | **Narr**
Hotel in New York City. The Carlyle Hotel is owned by the Kennedy family; that's the hotel Kennedy spent the night at, two nights
ago; it belongs to his family. A philanthropic society headed by a
white man named Stephen Currier called all the top civil-rights
leaders together at the Carlyle Hotel. And he told them, "By you
all fighting each other, you are destroying the civil-rights movement.
And since you're fighting over money from white liberals, let us set
up what is known as the Council for United Civil Rights Leadership. Let's form this council, and all the civil-rights organizations
will belong to it, and we'll use it for fund-raising purposes." Let me
show you how tricky the white man is. As soon as they got it
formed, they elected Whitney Young as its chairman, and who do
you think became the co-chairman? Stephen Currier, the white
man, a millionaire. Powell was talking about it down at Cobo Hall
today. This is what he was talking about. Powell knows it happened.
Randolph knows it happened. Wilkins knows it happened. King

knows it happened. Every one of that Big Six—they know it hap-pened.

37   Once they formed it, with the white man over it, he promised them and gave them $800,000 to split up among the Big Six; and told them that after the march was over, they'd give them $700,000 more. A million and a half dollars—split up between leaders that you have been following, going to jail for, crying crocodile tears for. And they're nothing but Frank James and Jesse James and the what-do-you-call-'em brothers.   *Meta*

38   As soon as they got the setup organized, the white man made available to them top public-relations experts; opened the news me-dia across the country at their disposal, which then began to project these Big Six as the leaders of the march. Originally they weren't even in the march. You were talking this march talk on Hastings Street, you were talking march talk on Lenox Avenue, and on Fill-more Street, and on Central Avenue, and 32nd Street and 63rd Street. That's where the march talk was being talked. But the white man put the Big Six at the head of it; made them the march. They   *Symb* became the march. They took it over. And the first move they made after they took it over, they invited Walter Reuther, a white man; they invited a priest, a rabbi, and an old white preacher, yes, an old white preacher. The same white element that put Kennedy into power—labor, the Catholics, the Jews, and liberal Protestants; the same clique that put Kennedy in power, joined the march on Wash-ington.

39   It's just like when you've got some coffee that's too black,   *Angy* which means it's too strong. What do you do? You integrate it with cream, you make it weak. But if you pour too much cream in it, you won't even know you ever had coffee. It used to be hot, it becomes cool. It used to be strong, it becomes weak. It used to wake you up, now it puts you to sleep. This is what they did with the march on Washington. They joined it. They didn't integrate it, they infil-trated it. They joined it, became a part of it, took it over. And as they took it over, it lost its militancy. It ceased to be angry, it ceased to be hot, it ceased to be uncompromising. Why, it even ceased to be a march. It became a picnic, a circus. Nothing but a circus, with clowns and all. You had one right here in Detroit—I saw it on television—with clowns leading it, white clowns and black clowns. I know you don't like what I'm saying, but I'm going to tell you anyway. Because I can prove what I'm saying. If you think I'm telling you wrong, you bring me Martin Luther King and A. Philip Randolph and James Farmer and those other three, and see if they'll deny it over a microphone.

40   No, it was a sellout. It was a takeover. When James Baldwin *Tone /*
came in from Paris, they wouldn't let him talk, because they *Dict*
couldn't make him go by the script. Burt Lancaster read the speech
that Baldwin was supposed to make: they wouldn't let Baldwin get
up there, because they know Baldwin is liable to say anything. They
controlled it so tight, they told those Negroes what time to hit
town, how to come, where to stop, what signs to carry, what song to
sing, what speech they could make, and what speech they couldn't
make; and then told them to get out of town by sundown. And
every one of those Toms was out of town by sundown. Now I know
you don't like my saying this. But I can back it up. It was a circus,
a performance that beat anything Hollywood could ever do, the
performance of the year. Reuther <u>and those other three devils</u> *Conn*
should get an Academy Award for <u>the best actors</u> because they
acted like they really loved Negroes and fooled a whole lot of Negroes. <u>And the six Negro leaders should get an award too, for the</u> *Sarc*
<u>best supporting cast.</u>

CONSIDERATIONS

What is the basis of unity among black people, according to Malcolm
X? What or who is the common enemy? Why does Malcolm say that
the Negro Revolution is not a true revolution? Why do you think he
makes fun of the concept? What is Malcolm X's attitude toward violence? Why, according to the author, must white blood be shed? Do
you agree?

Malcolm repeatedly reminds his audience that they won't like what
he's telling them. What are his reasons for reiterating this? What is the
relation between speaker and audience in this selection? How is that
relationship continuously reinforced? Why does Malcolm goad his audience in paragraph 12? What is the purpose, generally, of emotionally
charged, inflammatory speech like this?

Although it seems to be running behind the issues of ecology at the
moment, race relations may be the number-one priority in America in
the 1970s. Do you think the fervor of the 1960s will reoccur in the last
quarter of this century? Is racism first and foremost a white problem?
How can open warfare among the races be avoided?

VOCABULARY

(16) **Uhuru**   freedom (Swahili)
(20) **nationalism**   devotion to the interests of one's own group or
                        nation

Meditation XVII

JOHN DONNE

Nunc lento sonitu dicunt, morieris.
Now this bell tolling softly for another, says to me, Thou must die.

1   Perchance he for whom this bell tolls may be so ill as that he knows not it tolls for him; and perchance I may think myself so much better than I am, as that they who are about me and see my state may have caused it to toll for me, and I know not that. The church is catholic, universal, so are all her actions; all that she does belongs to all. When she baptizes a child, that action concerns me; for that child is thereby connected to that body which is my head too,[1] and ingrafted into that body whereof I am a member. And when she buries a man, that action concerns me: all mankind is of one author and is one volume; when one man dies, one chapter is not torn out of the book, but translated[2] into a better language; and every chapter must be so translated. God employs several translators; some pieces are translated by age, some by sickness, some by war, some by justice; but God's hand is in every translation, and his hand shall bind up all our scattered leaves again for that library where every book shall lie open to one another. As therefore the bell that rings to a sermon calls not upon the preacher only, but upon the congregation to come, so this bell calls us all; but how much more me, who am brought so near the door by this sickness. There was a

---

[1] I.e., the Christian church is the head of all men, as well as a body composed of its members.
[2] Literally, "carried across"; hence, on the spiritual level, exalted from one sphere to another.

contention as far as a suit[3] (in which piety and dignity, religion and estimation,[4] were mingled) which of the religious orders should ring to prayers first in the morning; and it was determined that they should ring first that rose earliest. If we understand aright the dignity of this bell that tolls for our evening prayer, we would be glad to make it ours by rising early, in that application, that it might be ours as well as his whose indeed it is. The bell doth toll for him that thinks it doth; and though it intermit again, yet from that minute that that occasion wrought upon him, he is united to God. Who casts not up his eye to the sun when it rises? but who takes off his eye from a comet when that breaks out? Who bends not his ear to any bell which upon any occasion rings? but who can remove it from that bell which is passing a piece of himself out of this world? No man is an island, entire of itself; every man is a piece of the continent, a part of the main.[5] If a clod be washed away by the sea, Europe is the less, as well as if a promontory were, as well as if a manor of thy friend's or of thine own were. Any man's death diminishes me because I am involved in mankind, and therefore never send to know for whom the bell tolls; it tolls for thee. Neither can we call this a begging of misery or a borrowing of misery, as though we were not miserable enough of ourselves but must fetch in more from the next house, in taking upon us the misery of our neighbors. Truly it were an excusable covetousness if we did; for affliction is a treasure, and scarce any man hath enough of it. No man hath affliction enough that is not matured and ripened by it and made fit for God by that affliction. If a man carry treasure in bullion, or in a wedge of gold, and have none coined into current money, his treasure will not defray him as he travels. Tribulation is treasure in the nature of it, but it is not current money in the use of it, except we get nearer and nearer our home, heaven, by it. Another man may be sick too, and sick to death, and this affliction may lie in his bowels as gold in a mine and be of no use to him; but this bell that tells me of his affliction digs out and applies that gold to me, if by this consideration of another's danger I take mine own into contemplation and so secure myself by making my recourse to my God, who is our only security.

---

[3] Controversy which went as far as a lawsuit.
[4] Self-esteem.
[5] Mainland.

GLOSSARY OF RHETORICAL TERMS

Abstract Words words that refer to feelings, generalities or ideas (love, fear, philosophy, patriotism) rather than to things or objects. Because they allude to referents that cannot be easily visualized, abstract words are often less forceful than concrete words.

Allusion a hint or *indirect* reference to a person, object, or action.

Analogy a comparison of two things or situations that are not exactly alike but still resemble each other in certain ways. Analogy is often used for argument or explanation.

Analysis the technique of dividing a topic into basic parts or divisions, showing their relationship and function.

Argumentation traditionally, one of the four basic kinds of discourse. (The others are *Description, Exposition,* and *Narration.*) The purpose of argumentation is to convince the reader of the truth or relevance of the author's position, to persuade him to adopt that point of view, or take the action recommended. The means used should be objective evidence and logic.

Balanced Sentence a balanced sentence is one in which similar or opposing thoughts are arranged in parallel structure. See *Parallelism.*

Beginning an effective beginning introduces the subject to be discussed and catches the reader's interest. Some ways to begin: with a statement of fact, a question, an anecdote, or a short, startling statement.

Cause and Effect a common method of development that examines events and their causes.

Chronological Order a method of development commonly used in narrative writing in which events are presented in the order they happen in time.

Classification a grouping of persons, objects, or ideas into categories on the basis of similarities or common qualities.

Cliché an overworked or trite expression or phrase.

Coherence a paragraph or an essay has coherence when its various parts (sentences or paragraphs, respectively) fit together to form an integrated whole. See *Unity*.

Comparison and Contrast a method of paragraph and theme development in which the similarities and differences between two or more objects or ideas are pointed out.

Conclusion effective conclusions bring into focus the main point. The paragraph making the last important point, or the climactic point, may be a thoroughly adequate conclusion. Avoid stopping in the middle of things, rambling, and repetition.

Concrete Words words that refer to things or objects and thus bring exactness and suggestiveness to writing.

Connotation and Denotation the denotation of a word is its literal dictionary meaning; its connotation is the meaning it conveys because of the context in which it is used or the particular associations it has for the reader.

Contrast See *Comparison and Contrast*.

Deduction a method of reasoning in which the conclusion follows necessarily from the premises presented. The pattern of development proceeds from the general to the specific. See also *Induction*.

Definition in logic, placing a term in a general class and then showing how it differs from others within that class. In rhetoric, definition is a method of development in which the meaning of a term is shown by various techniques: description, example, synonyms, origin, history, or comparison and contrast.

Denotation See *Connotation and Denotation.*

Description traditionally, one of the four basic kinds of discourse. (The others are *Argumentation, Exposition,* and *Narration.*) Description conveys a sensory impression of a person, object, feeling, or event.

Diction in rhetoric, diction refers to choice of words in speaking or writing. The skillful writer chooses words that are clear, effective, and appropriate.

Ending your themes should not merely stop; they should end with an effective conclusion. Some ways to end your essay: summarize your major ideas, conclude with a restatement of your thesis, draw a logical conclusion from the facts you have presented.

Equivocation a fallacy in which the same term is used with different meanings. In writing, equivocation occurs when abstract words like *democracy* or *freedom* are used in one way at the beginning of a paper and in another way later on.

Euphemism an indirect reference or softening expression that refers to unpleasant or embarrassing things. Examples: "passed on" for "died," "expecting" for "pregnant."

Exemplification the use of examples to explain or clarify a subject. Examples may be used either as evidence to support the author's thesis or as illustrations in a deductive pattern.

Exposition traditionally, one of the four basic kinds of discourse. (See also *Argumentation, Description,* and *Narration.*) The purpose of exposition is to inform, illustrate, or explain. Most textbooks depend heavily on exposition, especially in mathematics.

Figurative Language the broad category for language that goes beyond the literal meaning of the words or phrases. (See also *Hyperbole, Litotes, Metaphor, Metonymy, Oxymoron, Personification,* and *Simile.*)

Generalization   a general statement, idea, or principle based on specific instances. Writers often use generalizations to introduce the topic or thesis.

Hyperbole   the use of extravagant exaggeration for emphasis or intensification (a figure of speech): "He must have been thirty feet tall!"

Idiom   an expression in a language that either does not conform to conventional rules of grammar or has a meaning that cannot be derived from the literal meaning of the words involved. Common expressions such as to "strike a bargain" and "catch a cold" are idioms. (As idioms wear, they often turn into clichés.)

Illustration   a method of developing a generalization through the use of examples that illustrate the subject or thesis.

Imagery   language that conveys sensory impressions. In writing, images tell us about the feelings, sounds, smells, tastes, and sights of life.

Induction   a method of reasoning in which a conclusion is reached by observing a number of specific examples. The pattern of development proceeds from the specific to the general. See also *Deduction*.

Irony   the expression of a meaning that is different from, and sometimes the exact opposite of, the literal meaning of the words themselves; an incongruity. In other words, irony says one thing but means another. (Compare *Paradox*.)

Litotes, or Understatement   a figure of speech that affirms an idea by denying its opposite. For example: "This is no small change you have suggested."

Loose Sentence   a sentence with the main element or idea at the beginning and subordinate elements following.

Metaphor   strictly speaking, a figure of speech that implies a likeness between two otherwise unlike objects; for example: "Tommy wolfed down his dinner" or "He was a tornado." (Compare *Simile*.)

Metonymy and Synecdoche   metonymy is the use of one name for something closely related to it, as when we say "The White

House (actually, a representative of the executive branch of the government) announced the appointment of a new Secretary of the Interior this morning." Synecdoche is the use of the part to signify the whole, or vice versa. ("He asked for the girl's hand in marriage.") Some authorities make a distinction between these two figures of speech; others use metonymy to cover both.

Mood   the dominant emotional state or feeling of a literary work.

Narration   the recounting of action over a period of time. Narration is one of the four basic kinds of discourse. (The others are *Argumentation, Description,* and *Exposition.*)

Non Sequitur   an instance in which the conclusion drawn does not follow from the evidence or claims already made.

Onomatopoeia   words whose names are derived from the sounds they describe: for example, "the boom of the cannon," "the buzzing of the bees."

Oxymoron   a paradoxical combination of seemingly contradictory words in one figure of speech. For example: "friendly enemy," "eloquent silence," "mournful optimist."

Paradox   a statement that seems to contradict itself. As a rhetorical device, paradox can be used to attract attention or to create emphasis.

Parallelism   the arrangement of syntactically similar words, phrases, or clauses in equal or parallel structures.

Parody   a literary work that closely imitates the style of another work or author for purposes of humor or ridicule.

Periodic Sentence   a sentence in which main elements and ideas are placed at the end rather than the beginning.

Personification   a figure of speech in which human feelings or characteristics are ascribed to nonhuman creatures, objects, or abstract ideas: "the courageous tree," "the sighing of the sand."

Plagiarism   stealing someone's ideas and passing them off as one's own, particularly in term papers and other documented research.

Précis   A formal summary or abridgement that retains the order, language, and style of the original work.

Premise   a specific proposition in logical writing. In certain kinds of logical organization, the premise precedes the conclusion.

Proposition   in scholarly writing, it refers to the kind of statement that is being affirmed or denied in an argument.

Pun   a play on the meaning or sounds of words. For instance, "He learned to drive by accidents," "Working with oil colors can be a paint in the neck."

Rhetoric   the study of the principles of composition. Included in the study of rhetoric: usage, coherence, unity, logic, and persuasion.

Rhetorical Question   a question to which no answer is expected or required. This device is used by writers to dramatize a situation or to make a comment.

Rhythm   the notion that the way a sentence "sounds" is important in writing. Such matters as alliteration and kinds of sentences add to rhythm.

Satire   any use of derisive wit to attack human follies or vices by making them appear ridiculous or contemptible.

Semantics   the study of language, especially the relationship of signs and symbols. Also the study of the way sentences work and the effect they have on the reader.

Sentence Variety   variation in the length and structure of sentences. There are certain pitfalls to overcome: a series of short, choppy sentences; rambling, directionless long ones; a series of sentences beginning only with the subject, rather than an occasional modifier; a series of periodic sentences with main ideas buried and a resultant lack of emphasis.

Simile   a figure of speech in which two essentially unlike things are explicitly compared; usually introduced by *like, as,* or *than.* (Compare *Metaphor.*)

Slang   the nonstandard vocabulary of a given culture, subculture, or group, often characterized by raciness and spontaneity. Some slang words are colorful or specific and eventually become respectable; others are trite, flat, or vague in meaning.

Style   the distinctive characteristics or qualities of a writer's work.

Support   in argumentative writing, evidence furnished to prove the author's thesis. Support often consists of observation, personal experience, validated facts, or reliable authority.

Symbolism   a device in which one thing is used to represent another because of association, resemblance, or convention. The moon, for example, is often used as a symbol for romance or distance.

Synecdoche   See *Metonymy*.

Syntax   the arrangement of words into phrases and sentences. This term is generally used in commenting on the structure of a literary work.

Thesis   the central topic or idea in a composition; the sentence containing such a statement.

Tone   the author's attitude toward his topic or his audience as reflected in his writing. Tone can vary from neutral or objective to pompous, sentimental, arrogant, cynical, ironic, or sarcastic. It is determined by diction as well as by selection and arrangement of facts.

Transition   way in which an author moves from one topic—or aspect of a topic—to another. Transition is usually accomplished by recognizable linguistic devices such as repetition of words and phrases, restatement of sentences, indirect references or words like *thus, therefore, in conclusion,* or *to summarize* and so on. In a great deal of contemporary writing, mechanical devices such as stars, subheads, or a series of centered periods (called bullets) are used to show transitions.

Understatement   See *Litotes*.

Unity   the development of one subject or theme at a time. A paragraph or composition that has unity contains only those sentences and ideas that develop its central or guiding purpose. (See also *Coherence*.)

INDEX

Edited by   James C. Budd
Designed by   Michael Rogondino
Sponsoring Editor   Gerald Richardson

The text copy for *Models for Writing* is set in Electra and Zenith; display type is Vega and Vega Medium. Both were set by Computer Typesetting.